Wei-Shi Zheng   Zhenan Sun   Yunhong Wang
Xilin Chen   Pong C. Yuen   Jianhuang Lai (Eds.)

Biometric Recognition

7th Chinese Conference, CCBR 2012
Guangzhou, China, December 4-5, 2012
Proceedings

 Springer

Volume Editors

Wei-Shi Zheng
Jianhuang Lai
Sun Yat-Sen University, Guangzhou, 510275, China
E-mail: wszheng@ieee.org; stsljh@mail.sysu.edu.cn

Zhenan Sun
Chinese Academy of Sciences, Beijing, 100190, China
E-mail: znsun@nlpr.ia.ac.cn

Yunhong Wang
Beihang University, Beijing, 100191, China
E-mail: yhwang@buaa.edu.cn

Xilin Chen
Chinese Academy of Sciences, Beijing, 100190, China
E-mail: xlchen@ict.ac.cn

Pong C. Yuen
Hong Kong Baptist University, Kowloon Tong, Kowloon, Hong Kong, China
E-mail: pcyuen@comp.hkbu.edu.hk

ISSN 0302-9743
e-ISSN 1611-3349
ISBN 978-3-642-35135-8
e-ISBN 978-3-642-35136-5
DOI 10.1007/978-3-642-35136-5
Springer Heidelberg Dordrecht London New York

Library of Congress Control Number: 2012952153

CR Subject Classification (1998): I.4, I.5, I.2.10, F.2.2, I.3.5, K.6.5

LNCS Sublibrary: SL 6 – Image Processing, Computer Vision, Pattern Recognition, and Graphics

Typesetting: Camera-ready by author, data conversion by Scientific Publishing Services, Chennai, India

Printed on acid-free paper

Springer is part of Springer Science+Business Media (www.springer.com)

Preface

Biometrics is now an important application in China, from academia to industry and from business to government. It has been applied in access control, secure bank transactions, national ID cards, welfare distribution, etc. However, existing current biometric systems still need a lot of improvement in terms of usability, accuracy, robustness, scalability, and security to make them satisfactory in real-world applications. Research and development of innovative biometric sensors and techniques are highly motivated and required.

Biometric recognition has attracted a large number of researchers in China. Chinese researchers are focussing on advancing the biometrics development in the world, and their works have been presented at top conferences, such as ICCV and CVPR, and appeared in top journals, such as TPAMI. All this research has made the field of biometric recognition move forward significantly, supported by a number of research funding projects through the Natural Science Foundation of China, National Basic Research Program of China, and the National Hi-Tech Research and Development Program of China, etc. Outside of academia, there are more than 200 biometrics-related companies in China and the annual growth of the Chinese biometrics market is over 30%. Large-scale biometrics systems have been deployed in government, banking, telecommunication, education, and public infrastructure.

The Chinese Conference on Biometric Recognition (CCBR) has been successfully held in Beijing, Hangzhou, Xi'an, and Guangzhou for six times since 2000. The 7th Chinese Conference on Biometric Recognition (CCBR 2012) was held in Guangzhou, also known as Canton, on 4–5 December 2012. This volume of conference proceedings contains 46 papers selected from among 80 submissions, and all papers have been carefully reviewed by three to four reviewers on average. The papers address the problems in face, iris, hand biometrics, speaker, handwriting, gait, soft biometrics, security, and other related topics, and contribute new ideas to the research and development of reliable and practical solutions for biometric authentication.

We would like to express our gratitude to all the contributors, reviewers, and program committee and organizing committee members, who made this conference successful. We also wish to acknowledge the support of the Chinese Association for Artificial Intelligence, Springer-Verlag, the Chinese Academy of

Sciences' Institute of Automation, and Sun Yat-sen University for sponsoring this conference. Special thanks are due to Jianfang Hu, Jun-Yong Zhu, Chunchao Guo, Binbin Den, Haiying Tian, and Jiansheng Wu for their hard work in organizing the conference.

October 2012

Wei-Shi Zheng
Zhenan Sun
Yunhong Wang
Xilin Chen
Pong C. Yuen
Jianhuang Lai

Organization

Advisors

Tieniu Tan	CASIA, China
Anil K. Jain	Michigan State University, USA
Jing-yu Yang	Nanjing University of Science & Technology, China

General Chairs

JianHuang Lai	Sun Yat-sen University, China
Xilin Chen	ICT, CAS, China
Pong C. Yuen	Hong Kong Baptist University, China

Program Chairs

Yunhong Wang	Beijing University of Aeronautics and Astronautics, China
Zhenan Sun	CASIA, China
Wei-Shi Zheng	Sun Yat-sen University, China

Program Committee Members

Jaihie Kim	Yonsei University, Republic of Korea
Suthep Madarasmi	KMUT, Thailand
Karthik Nandakumar	I2R, Singapore
Koichiro Niinuma	Fujitsu Labs, Japan
Chengjun Liu	New Jersey Institute of Technology, USA
Gang Hua	IBM Watson Research Center, China
Qiang Ji	Rensselaer Polytechnic Institute, USA
Wen-Yi Zhao	Sarnoff Corporation, USA
Xiaoqing Ding	Tsinghua University, China
Yilong Yin	Shandong University, China
Yuchun Fang	Shaihai University, China
Kuanquang Wang	Harbin Institute of Technology, China
Chaoyang Lu	Xi'an University of Electronic Science and Technology, China
Qiuqi Ruan	Beijing Jiaotong University, China
Xihong Wu	Beijing University, China
Changshui Zhang	Tsinghua University, China
Zhaoxiang Zhang	Beijing University of Aeronautics and Astronautics, China
Shiguang Shan	ICT, CAS, China

Stan Z. Li   CASIA, China
Wenxin Li   Beijing University, China
Jie Yang   Shanghai Jiao Tong University, China
Jian Yang   Nanjing University of Science & Technology,
                               China

Yingchun Yang   Zhejiang University, China
Xin Yang   CASIA, China
Zengfu Wang   IIM, CAS, China
Guangda Su   Tsinghua University, China
Jie Zhou   Tsinghua University, China
Ran He   CASIA, China
Jufu Feng   Beijing University, China
Dewen Hu   National University of Defense Technology,
                               China
Xudong Jiang   Nanyang Technological University, Singapore
Shiqi Yu   Shenzhen University, China
Xiangwei Kong   Dalian University of Technology, China
Jianjiang Feng   Tsinghua University, China
Zhicun Mu   University of Science and Technology Beijing,
                               China
GuoCan Feng   Sun Yat-sen University, China
Huicheng Zheng   Sun Yat-sen University, China
Haifeng Hu   Sun Yat-sen University, China
Wensheng Chen   Shenzhen University, China
Lifang Wu   North China University of Technology, China
Xiaohua Xie   SIAT, CAS, China
Bin Fang   Chongqin University, China
Weiqi Yuan   Shenyang University of Technology, China
Jinfeng Yang   Civil Aviation University of China, China

Organizing Committee Chair

Huicheng Zheng   Sun Yat-sen University, China

Organizing Committee Members

Junyong Zhu   Sun Yat-sen University, China
Na Liu   Sun Yat-sen University, China
Jianfang Hu   Sun Yat-sen University, China
Yan Liang   Sun Yat-sen University, China
Jiansheng Wu   Sun Yat-sen University, China
Chunchao Guo   Sun Yat-sen University, China
Haiying Tian   Sun Yat-sen University, China
Binbin Pan   Sun Yat-sen University, China

Table of Contents

Section I: Face

Section II: Hand

Section III: Iris

Section VIII: Other Biometrics

Section IX: Security

Section X: Learning for Biometrics

Patch-Based Bag of Features
for Face Recognition in Videos

Chao Wang, Yunhong Wang, and Zhaoxiang Zhang

School of Computer Science and Engineering, Beihang University, China
chaowang@cse.buaa.edu.cn, {yhwang,zxzhang}@buaa.edu.cn

Abstract. Video-based face recognition is a fundamental topic in image processing and video representation, and presents various challenges and opportunities. In this paper, we introduce an efficient patch-based bag of features (PBoF) method to video-based face recognition that plenty exploits the spatiotemporal information in videos, and does not make any assumptions about the pose, expressions or illumination of face. First, descriptors are used for feature extraction from patches, then with the quantization of a codebook, each descriptor is converted into code. Next, codes from each region are pooled together into a histogram. Finally, representation of the image is generated by concatenating the histograms from all regions, which is employed to do the categorization. In our experiments, 100% recognition rate is achieved on the Honda/UCSD database, which outperforms the state of the arts. And from the theoretical and experimental results, it can be derived that, when choosing a single descriptor and no prior knowledge about the data set and object is available, the dense SIFT with ScSPM is recommended. Experimental results demonstrate the effectiveness and flexibility of our proposed method.

Keywords: Face recognition, video-based face recognition, bag of feature, sparse coding.

1 Introduction

In recent years, face recognition is always an active topic in the field of biometrics. Compared to traditional face recognition in still images, video-based face recognition has great advantages. First, videos contain more abundant information than a single image. Thus, more robust and stable recognition can be achieved by fusing information of multi frames. Second, temporal information becomes available to be exploited in videos to improve the accuracy of face recognition. Finally, multi-poses of face in videos make it possible to employ spatial information to refine the performance of face recognition. Thus, researchers have developed interest in video-based face recognition, in which both the enrolment and recognition sets are facial videos. However, video-based face recognition is also a very challenging problem, which suffers from low quality facial images, illumination changes, pose variations and so on.

Early video-based face recognition algorithms were frame-based, employed the input face video as still face images to identify or recognitionIn these systems,

W.-S. Zheng et al. (Eds.): CCBR 2012, LNCS 7701, pp. 1–8, 2012.
© Springer-Verlag Berlin Heidelberg 2012

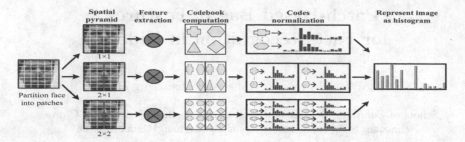

Fig. 1. Extraction pipeline of patch-based bag of features

the facial feature extraction and classification are applied independently to each frame, then the similarity scores are integrated using post-mapping information fusion techniques, like the majority voting or averaging criterion.

In recent years, many video-based face recognition algorithms use the complete detected face to extract global features [1,2,3,4]. Whereas, these global features are sensitive to registration errors, occlusions and pose variations. Bag of features (BoF), which represents an image as an orderless collection of local features, have recently demonstrated impressive levels of solving the problem of recognizing the semantic category of an image [5,6]. But bag of features has not achieved much attention in video-based face recognition because of the worry about global data missing due to the dividing images in to pathes or local features. However, BoF is important as they can fully exploit the spatiotemporal information in videos, and it tends to be robust to pose, illumination and expression changes of a face.

This paper proposes a patch-based bag of features (PBoF) algorithm for face recognition in videos, which does not make any assumptions about the pose, expressions or illumination of face regions. First, face images are divided into $m \times n$ patches, and descriptors are extracted from each patch. Then, each descriptor is converted into code with the quantization of a codebook. So, the utilization ratio of spatiotemporal information is raised and little global data is missing with the contribution of every descriptor to the construction of the codebook in a muti-level way. Finally, the final representation of the image for classification generated by concatenated the histograms from all regions.

The rest of paper is organized as follows. Section 2 describes our PBoF algorithm.Section 3 and 4 describe the experimental results and conclusions.

2   Patch-Based Bag of Features

In this paper, we proposes a PBoF algorithm to extract facial features for face recognition in videos. As shown in Fig. 1 , first, face images are divided into $m \times n$ patches. The patches are spaced by $p \times p$ pixels on a regular grid. Next, during the feature extraction, descriptors are extracted from each patches. Then, a codebook is applied to quantize every descriptor, and each descriptor is converted

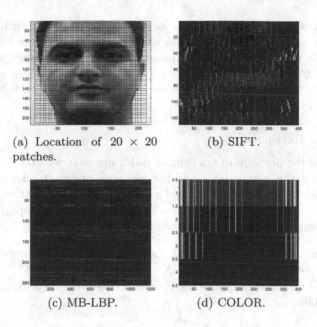

(a) Location of 20 × 20 patches.

(b) SIFT.

(c) MB-LBP.

(d) COLOR.

Fig. 2. Gray face image example and feature maps

into code. Finally, the histograms from all sub-regions are concatenated together to generate the final representation of the image for classification.

2.1 Descriptors

Dense SIFT, dense MB-LBP and dense COLOR are employed in this paper for extracting features and comparing their performance. The proposed algorithm is generic and not tied up to specific features, while a set of dense features is obtained from every patch of each face image. So advantages of the algorithm are that it does not impose any restrictions on the localization of features, and features can be extracted from any part of the face image and do not need to be registered.

SIFT (dense). The SIFT (Scale-invariant feature transform) descriptor was proposed by Lowe [7]. SIFT describes the local shape of a region using edge orientation histograms, obtained by considering pixels around a radius of the key location, blurring and resampling of local image orientation planes and robust to local affine distortion.

MB-LBP (dense). The MB-LBP (Multi-Block LBP) [8,9] encodes rectangular regions' intensities by local binary pattern operator, and the resulting binary patterns can describe diverse local structures of images. In our algorithm, we extract Histograms of Multi-Block LBP on a regular dense grid and computed on image I after color projection.

COLOR (dense). There are many color descriptors based on histograms, the gray color histogram is a combination of three 1D histograms based on the channels of the gray color space. In this paper, we choose dense gray color to compute histograms of color projection on a regular dense grid.

Fig. 2 shows the location of patches on a gray face image, and feature maps of three descriptors described above.

2.2   Feature Extraction

By overcoming the problem of traditional BoF approach, which discards the information about the spatial layout of the features, one particular extension of the BoF model, called spatial pyramid matching (SPM) [5] , has made a remarkable success on image classification. With the employed of spatial pyramid, additional features are extracted for specific parts of the image.

Spatial Pyramid Matching (SPM). Let X be a set of appearance descriptors in a D-dimensional feature space, i.e. $X = [x_1; \ldots, x_M]^T \in \mathbb{R}^{M \times D}$. The vector quantization (VQ) method applies the K-means clustering algorithm to solve the following problem:

$$\min_C \sum_{i=1}^{N} \min_{k=1}^{K} \| x_i - b_k \|^2 \tag{1}$$

where $B = [b_1, \ldots, b_K]^T$ are the K cluster centers to be found, called codebook, and $\| \cdot \|$ denotes the l^2 norm of vectors. The optimization problem can be re-formulated into a matrix factorization problem with cluster membership indicators $C = [c_1, c_2, \ldots, c_N]$, which is the set of codes for X. SPM [5] uses VQ coding which solves the following constrained least square fitting problem:

$$\arg\min_C \sum_{i=1}^{N} \| x_i - Bc_i \|^2 \tag{2}$$

$$s.t. \| c_i \|_{l^0} = 1, \| c_i \|_{l^1} = 1, c_i \succeq 0, \forall i$$

The cardinality constraint $\| c_i \|_{l_0} = 1$ indicate that there will be only one non-zero element in each code c_i, corresponding to the quantization id of x_i. The non-negative, l^1 constraint $\| c_i \|_{l^1} = 1, c_i \succeq 0$ means that the weight for x is 1.

Sparse Codes Spatial Pyramid Matching (ScSPM). In (ScSPM) [10], to ameliorate the quantization loss of VQ, the restrictive cardinality constraint $\| c_i \|_{l_0} = 1$ in Eq. (2) can be relaxed by using a sparsity regularization term. The sparsity regularization term is selected to be the l^1 norm of c_i, and coding each local descriptor x_i thus becomes a standard sparse coding (SC) problem:

$$\arg\min_C \sum_{i=1}^{N} \| x_i - Bc_i \|^2 + \lambda \| c_i \|_{l^1} \tag{3}$$

$$s.t. \| b_k \| \le 1, \forall k = 1, 2, \ldots, K$$

where a unit l^2 norm constraint on b_k is applied to avoid trivial solutions.

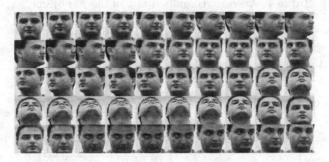

Fig. 3. Sample faces in the Honda/UCSD database

Our purposed method calculate image representation by SPM, each subregion in SPM can provide holistic spatial information of different facial components, and additional features are extracted for specific parts of the image. So that the PBoF features have strong distinctive power to do the recognition without any assumptions about the pose, expressions or illumination of face regions.

3 Experiments

In experiments, we use the first dataset of Honda/UCSD Video Database [2,11] to test our purposed approach. The database includes 20 individuals moving their heads in different combinations of 2-D and 3-D rotation, expression and speed. The resolution of each video sequence is 640×480. Face is detected in the video frame using the algorithm of Viola and Jones [12] . Then, CAMSHIFT [13] is employed for face tracking and the face region is clipped from each frame. And face images are cropped to 222×214 pixels without histogram equalization, affine transformation or registration. Fig. 3 shows sample faces of one person in the Honda/UCSD database, and we can see the face region changes in size when the pose changes and does not perfectly enclose the face. However, the proposed method is robust to these problems and does not depend on the cropping window. Because even in a complicated situation of a train frame, every descriptor extracted from each patch will have contributions to the construction of the codebook, so no frame will be wasted. Thus, a face frame for test can always find appropriate codes to represent itself under any conditions of the cropping window.

In classification, large-scale linear SVM (LinearSVM) [14] and non-linear kernel SVM (KernelSVM) [15,16] are used to train the classifier, respectively. In the training phase, the cost parameter is set to 0.07, and the weight for the cost parameter of per class is set to $\frac{nneg}{npos}$, where $nneg$ is the number of negative instances in the train set and $npos$ is the number of positive instances. At the testing stage, input face image sequence are converted to histograms of codewords using the trained codebook, and concatenated to a whole one. Classification results can be obtained using the trained models by the classifiers.

Table 1. Average recognition rate of the 20 objects

Classifier	Pyramid	Descriptor	Recognition rate(%)
LinerLINEAR	SPM	SIFT	88.2
		MB-LBP	82.2
		Color	91.7
	ScSPM	SIFT	100
		MB-LBP	98.85
		Color	96.35
KernelSVM	SPM	SIFT	80.5
		MB-LBP	76.2
		Color	85.8
	ScSPM	SIFT	100
		MB-LBP	98.85
		Color	95.2

In this experiment, we investigate three dense descriptors and compare their performance with LinerSVM and KernelSVM training algorithm. First, we partition a face image into 20×20 patches, the patches are spaced by 16×16 pixels, and calculate dense features on every sampling grid. Next, the spatial pyramid is 3 levels pyramid with $21 = (1 + 4 + 16)$ non-overlapping sub-windows. For each level, we count the features that fall in each sub-window, weight each spatial histogram due to [5], and the codebook size is $K = 1024$ to generate histograms. Finally, classification is done with LinerSVM and KernelSVM algorithm, respectively, while using the one-versus-all rule: a classifier is learned to separate each person from the rest, and each frame in test video is assigned the label of the classifier with the highest response.

Tab. 1 shows the average recognition rate of 20 objects, the dense SIFT descriptor with ScSPM achieved a recognition rate of 100%, using LinerSVM and KernelSVM for classification, respectively. We can find that, in terms of recognition accuracy, SPM based on sparse coding always significantly outperforms the linear SPM. The average precision of recognition increases about 11 percent when sparse coding is employed. And the ScSPM is more efficient for SIFT and MB-LBP, while relative to the SIFT descriptor, an increase of 12 percent and 20 percent is observed.

From the ROC curves in Fig. 4, the performance of SIFT and MB-LBP with LinerSVM are better than those of KernelSVM. Comparing the AUC performance of SIFT, MB-LBP and COLOR, we can see that the COLOR descriptor show little influence on classifier. The AUC of dense SIFT with ScSPM is always 1, we conclude reasons of the effectiveness of the method is that, dense SIFT features are calculated patch by patch, and SIFT features do not lack invariance, which means that the subtle and refined discriminative features are extracted from every local patch. And discriminative features of a certain facial region will be mapped to the corresponding visual words of the corresponding sub-window cumulatively, which is significant for face recognition.

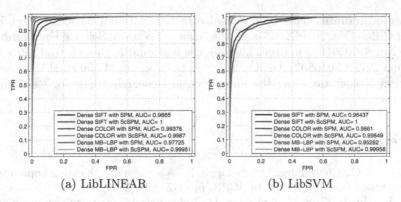

(a) LibLINEAR   (b) LibSVM

Fig. 4. ROC curves

In the last experiment, we compared our method against four methods including Aggarwal et al. [1], Lee et al. [2], Hadid et al. [3] and Ajmal Mian [4] on the Honda/UCSD database. As shown in Tab. 2, it can be said that our purposed method achieves the best performance compared with the previous works.

Table 2. Comparison against video-base face recognition approaches in the literature

	Approaches	Recognition rate(%)
Aggarwal et al. [1]	Video level matching using ARAM	90
Lee et al. [2]	Matching frames using appearance manifolds	92.1
Hadid et al. [3]	LBP feature boosting	96
Ajmal Mian [4]	Local feature clutering	99.5
Proposed method	Matching frames using Patch-based BoF	100

4   Conclusions

In this paper, we extend the bag of features and SPM methods to patch-based bag of features for video-based face recognition, the features can capture more spatiotemporal information about face image sequences than traditional approaches, and the proposed method can robustly give distinctive face recognition performance under various conditions. Our method also performed on the Honda/UCSD database and 100% recognition rate is achieved.

Acknowledgement. This work is funded by the National Basic Research Program of China (No. 2010CB327902), the National Natural Science Foundation of China (No. 61005016, No. 61061130560), the National High-tech R&D Program of China (2011AA010502), the Open Projects Program of National Laboratory of Pattern Recognition, and the Fundamental Research Funds for the Central Universities.

References

1. Aggarwal, G., Chowdhury, A., Chellappa, R.: A system identification approach for video-based face recognition. In: ICPR, pp. 175–178 (2004)
2. Lee, K., Ho, J., Yang, M., Kriegman, D.: Video-based face recognition using probabilistic appearance manifolds. In: CVPR, pp. 313–320
3. Hadid, A., Pietikäinen, M.: Combining appearance and motion for face and gender recognition from videos. PR 42(11), 2818–2827 (2009)
4. Mian, A.: Online learning from local features for video-based face recognition. PR 44(5), 1068–1075 (2011)
5. Lazebnik, S., Schmid, C., Ponce, J.: Beyond bags of features: Spatial pyramid matching for recognizing natural scene categories. In: CVPR, pp. 2169–2178 (2006)
6. Van De Sande, K., Gevers, T., Snoek, C.: Evaluating color descriptors for object and scene recognition. IEEE Trans. PAMI 32, 1582–1596 (2009)
7. Lowe, D.: Distinctive image features from scale-invariant keypoints. IJCV 60(2), 91–110 (2004)
8. Zhang, L., Chu, R., Xiang, S., Liao, S., Li, S.: Face detection based on multi-block lbp representation. Advances in Biometrics, 11–18 (2007)
9. Ahonen, T., Matas, J., He, C., Pietikäinen, M.: Rotation invariant image description with local binary pattern histogram fourier features. Image Analysis, 61–70 (2009)
10. Yang, J., Yu, K., Gong, Y., Huang, T.: Linear spatial pyramid matching using sparse coding for image classification. In: CVPR, pp. 1794–1801 (2009)
11. Lee, K., Ho, J., Yang, M., Kriegman, D.: Visual tracking and recognition using probabilistic appearance manifolds. CVIU 99, 303–331 (2005)
12. Viola, P., Jones, M.: Rapid object detection using a boosted cascade of simple features. In: CVPR, Intel, Microprocessor Research Labs, p. 511 (2001)
13. Carnegie, R.C.: Mean-shift blob tracking through scale space. In: CVPR, pp. 234–240 (2003)
14. Hsieh, C., Chang, K., Lin, C., Keerthi, S., Sundararajan, S.: A dual coordinate descent method for large-scale linear svm. In: ICML, pp. 408–415 (2008)
15. Chang, C., Lin, C.: Libsvm: a library for support vector machines (2001)
16. Vedaldi, A., Zisserman, A.: Efficient additive kernels via explicit feature maps. In: CVPR, pp. 3539–3546 (2010)

Fusion of Local Features for Face Recognition
by Multiple Least Square Solutions

Yuting Tao and Jian Yang

Nanjing University of Science & Technology
Nanjing China 210094
tao.yuting@yahoo.com.cn,
csjianyang@gmail.com

Abstract. In terms of supervised face recognition, linear discriminant analysis (LDA) has been viewed as one of the most popular approaches during the past years. In this paper, taking advantage of the equivalence between LDA and the least square problem, we propose a new fusion method for face classification, based on the combination of least square solutions for local mean and local texture into multiple optimization problems. Extensive experiments on AR_Gray and Yale face database indicate the competitive performance of the proposed method, compared to the traditional LDA.

Keywords: linear discriminant analysis, least square, fusion method.

1   Introduction

In terms of classification, LDA is the state-of-the-art approach and has been popular for many years [3]. The classical version is raised by Fisher in 1936 for the first time, aiming at seeking some directions for projection, onto which the within-class scatter should be minimized while the between-class scatter should be maximized [4]. It is often called Fisher criterion, or FLDA. From the viewpoint of optimization, FLDA in the binary class case is proven to be equivalent to least square problem [2]. Later, the author in [1] did further research, and built up the relation between multi-class FLDA and least-square problem via an orthogonal transformation, in the premise of some certain constructed class labels. Since any orthogonal transformation keeps all pairwise Euclidean distances, theoretically the classification result achieved by the least square solution is identical to that by FLDA if the distance metric takes 2-norm.

Generally speaking, the traditional LDA is solely conducted based on the variance of all the pixels' grey values involved in face recognition. In addition to pixels' grey values, another kind of image's feature is local texture, of which the very famous one is local binary patterns (LBP). It operates the convolution for coding each pixel's adjacent information [5, 6].

Since face images themselves are of too many pixels (i.e. high dimension) compared to the number of available samples, the problems of singularity and huge computational complexity are often encountered. In our proposed fusion method, we divide each image into 4 x 4 patches, and extract the average of the 16 pixels' grey

W.-S. Zheng et al. (Eds.): CCBR 2012, LNCS 7701, pp. 9–16, 2012.

values and local texture information in each patch. In this way, such two kinds of local features can be taken advantage of, to construct local mean and local texture matrices, respectively. Moreover, these two matrices' sizes are reduced by 16 times compared to the original image, thus the computational work can be much more simplified.

Benefiting from the equivalent performance between FLDA and least square solution, our proposed fusion method splits local mean matrix and local texture matrix into solving separable least square solutions firstly, and combines them into multiple optimization problems secondly. We discover that our proposed method outperforms traditional FLDA that solely performs based on one feature, in terms of recognition accuracy. Additionally, it is statistically stable since its classification accuracies take up very small standard deviation, if the whole samples are randomly split into training and testing sets for many times' running.

The remaining part of this paper is arranged as follows: Section.2 provides the relation between LDA and least-square solution; we show the details of our proposed fusion method in Section.3; experiments and analysis are demonstrated in Section.4; the final conclusion is made in Section.5.

2   The Relation between LDA and Least Square Solution

In this section, we show the relation between FLDA and least-square solution in two different situations, i.e. binary-class and multi-class cases.

For FLDA, the objective function is :

$$G^{LDA} = arg \, \max_G \{trace(G^T S_b G \cdot (G^T S_t G)^+)\} \qquad (1)$$

2.1   Binary-Class Case

In Eq.(1), the corresponding FLDA solution is [1, 2]:

$$G^{LDA} = S_t^+(c_1 - c_2) \qquad (2)$$

where S_t^+ is the pseudo inverse of S_t, c_1 and c_2 are the centroids of Class 1 and Class 2 respectively.

Suppose the total sample number is $n = n_1 + n_2$, where n_1 and n_2 are the number of samples in Class 1 and Class 2 respectively. And the training set $X = [x_1, x_2, \dots, x_n]$, $x_i \in R^p$, and the class labels $y_i \in \{-1, \, 1\}$.

After X and y are centralized, i.e. $\sum_{i=1}^n x_i = 0$, $\sum_{i=1}^n y_i = 0$, then $\tilde{y}_i \in \{-n/n_2, n/n_1\}$ and the corresponding least square objective function is:

$$L(w) = ||\tilde{y} - \tilde{X}^T \cdot w||^2 \qquad (3)$$

Eq.(3) is the quadratic objective function w.r.t w, and the least square solution is [7]:

$$w_{opt} = (\tilde{X}\tilde{X}^T)^+ \tilde{X}\tilde{y} \qquad (4)$$

Since $\tilde{X}\tilde{X}^T = nS_t$ and $\tilde{X}\tilde{y} = \frac{2n_1 n_2}{n}(c_1 - c_2)$, it follows that :

$$w_{opt} = \frac{2n_1 n_2}{n^2} S_t^+(c_1 - c_2) = \frac{2n_1 n_2}{n^2} G^{LDA}.$$

2.2   Multi-class Case

The total number of orthogonal discriminant vectors in Eq.(1) is k-1, if the number of classes is $k>2$, i.e.

$$G^{LDA} = [g_1, \ g_2, \cdots g_{k-1}]. \tag{5}$$

Quite similar to Eqs.(3,4), the least square solution for each $L(w_j), (j = 1, \ldots k)$ is:

$$w_{opt\_j} = (\tilde{X}\tilde{X}^T)^+ \tilde{X}\tilde{y}_j.$$

The whole optimal solution set for the k classes is:

$$W_{opt} = (\tilde{X}\tilde{X}^T)^+ \tilde{X}\tilde{Y} \tag{6}$$

where $W_{opt} = [\ w_{opt_1, \ldots,}\ w_{opt\_k}]$

Due to the symmetry of the scatter matrix, we can decompose $S_b = H_b H_b^T$, where

$$H_b = \frac{1}{\sqrt{n}}[\sqrt{n_1}(c_1 - c), \ldots, \sqrt{n_k}(c_k - c)] \tag{7}$$

where c is the centroid of all the data.

If the class label matrix is constructed as follows [1]:

$$Y(i,j) = \begin{cases} \sqrt{\dfrac{n}{n_j}} - \sqrt{\dfrac{n_j}{n}} & if \ x_i \in Class \ j \\[2ex] -\sqrt{\dfrac{n_j}{n}} & otherwise \end{cases} \tag{8}$$

where $Y = [y_1, y_2, \ldots, y_k]$, $Y \in R^{n \times k}$. Then the optimal solution set in Eq.(6) becomes as below:

$$W_{opt} = (\tilde{X}\tilde{X}^T)^+ \tilde{X}\tilde{Y} = (nS_t)^+ nH_b = S_t^+ H_b \tag{9}$$

Here Y is centered in terms of each column, i.e. $\tilde{Y} = Y$

If rank(S_t)=rank(S_w)+rank(S_b), it satisfies that:

$$W_{opt} = [G^{LDA}, \ 0]Q^T \tag{10}$$

where $0 \in R^{p \times 1}$ is one column of all zeros, and Q is an orthogonal matrix generated by a special decomposition of $S_t^+ H_b$. Generally speaking, human face images are of high dimension and small sample hence meet the condition in Eq.(10). For more details, please refer to [1].

3   The Details of Our Fusion Method

Our proposed fusion method extracts the mean grey value and local texture from every 4×4 patch for all the images. Suppose every image contains p pixels, i.e. $p = row \times column.$ Before processing, the condition that $mod \ (row, \ 4)=0$ and $mod \ (column, \ 4)=0$ must be ensured. Otherwise the image has to be resized to meet this demand. Fig.1 shows how to divide the face image into patches.

3.1   Local Mean Matrix Construction

The local mean matrix $X_{mean} \in R^{\frac{P}{16} \times n}$, of which $X(u,v)_{mean}$ stores the average grey value of the 16 pixels in the u-th patch of the v-th image. Every mean image is of the size $\frac{row}{4} \times \frac{column}{4}$. If the condensed mean image is amplified up to the original size, as in Fig.1, it keeps the general profile very well although looks blurred after amplification.

Fig. 1. Original face image(left), the division of 4 x 4 patches of image (middle), the amplified mean image (right)

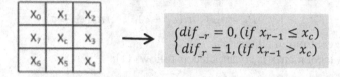

Fig. 2. The exact operation of LBP

3.2   Local Texture Matrix Construction

Local binary pattern (LBP) is an effective yet very simple local texture descriptor [5, 6]. Imposing $Dif = [dif_{-1}, ..., dif_{-8}]$, then according to Fig.2, after starting from the left top x_0 then doing a clockwise circle to x_7, the 8-bit binary code Dif is converted into the decimal number within the range of 0~255.

Motivated by LBP, in our method local texture is extracted in each 4 x 4 patch for all the images. We take $X(u, v)_{mean}$ as the central value of the u-th patch in the v-th image, which is quite similar to x_c in Fig.2, and visit the 16 pixels in any uniquely predefined order. Since $2^{16} = 65536$, the range of code is 0~65535. For the convenience of representation and computation, the decimal number converted from the 16-bit binary code is imposed within (0,1), i.e.

$$X(u, v)_{tex} = \frac{1}{65536} \times Dif_{dec}$$

where Dif_{dec} is the decimal transform from the binary code. Here, the local texture matrix $X_{tex} \in R^{\frac{P}{16} \times n}$.

3.3   Our Proposed Fusion Method

Split LDA into Multiple Least Square Problems. If the training samples' class labels are defined as Eq.(8), the whole LDA is equivalent to splitting into k (number of classes) separable quadratic objective functions. After merging the k least square solutions together, as Eq.(6), W_{opt} can preserve the pairwise Euclidean distance (x_a, x_b) in the LDA transformed space, i.e. $\sum_{j=1}^{k} ||w_{opt_j}^T x_a - w_{opt_j}^T x_b||^2 = ||W_{opt}^T x_a - W_{opt}^T x_b||^2 = ||G^{LDA^T} x_a - G^{LDA^T} x_b||^2$. And in this case, $W_{opt} = \text{argmin} \sum_{j=1}^{k} L(w_j)$.

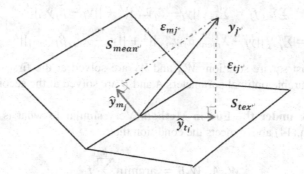

Fig. 3. Illustration of the class label y_j orthogonal projected onto the spaces of S_{mean} and S_{tex} respectively

Fusion of These Two Kinds of Features. As illustrated in Fig.3, S_{mean} and S_{tex} are the spaces spanned by the centralized X_{mean} and X_{tex} respectively. From the geometrical interpretation of the least square, orthogonal projection of y_j i.e. the j-th column of Y in Eq.(6) onto the centralized X_{mean} and X_{tex} are:

$$\hat{y}_{mj} = \tilde{X}_{mean}^T w_{m\_j} = \tilde{X}_{mean}^T (\tilde{X}_{mean}\tilde{X}_{mean}^T)^+ \tilde{X}_{mean} y_j$$

$$\hat{y}_{tj} = \tilde{X}_{tex}^T w_{t\_j} = \tilde{X}_{tex}^T (\tilde{X}_{tex}\tilde{X}_{tex}^T)^+ \tilde{X}_{tex} y_j$$

$W_m = [w_{m\_1} ..., w_{m\_k}]$ and $W_t = [w_{t\_1} ..., w_{t\_k}]$ are the sets of least square solutions for all of the corresponding y_j $(j=1,...,k)$ orthogonally project onto the centralized X_{mean} and X_{tex} respectively.

The fusion objective function for y_j $(j=1,...,k)$ is:

$$f_j = min_{\alpha_j,\beta_j} \ ||y_j - \alpha_j.\hat{y}_{mj}||^2 + ||y_j - \beta_j.\hat{y}_{tj}||^2$$
$$s.t. \ \alpha_j + \beta_j = 1 \qquad (11)$$

Since $y_j = \hat{y}_{mj} + \varepsilon_{mj} = \hat{y}_{tj} + \varepsilon_{tj}, \hat{y}_{mj}^T \perp \varepsilon_{mj}$ and $\hat{y}_{tj}^T \perp \varepsilon_{tj}$, if we define $d_{mj} = \hat{y}_{mj}^T\hat{y}_{mj}$ and $d_{tj} = \hat{y}_{tj}^T\hat{y}_{tj}$, then Eq.(11) can be converted into the following form by adding a Lagrange multiplier λ:

$$f_j = min_{\alpha_j,\beta_j} \ (\alpha_j^2 - 2\alpha_j)d_{mj} + (\beta_j^2 - 2\beta_j)d_{tj} + \lambda(\alpha_j + \beta_j - 1) \quad (12)$$

Since Eq.(12) is a convex function w.r.t α_j and β_j [7], we can set the first derivative of α_j and β_j to zeros, and get the optimal solution $\tilde{\alpha}_j$ and $\tilde{\beta}_j$:

$$\begin{cases} (2\alpha_j - 2)d_{mj} + \lambda = 0 \\ (2\beta_j - 2)d_{tj} + \lambda = 0 \\ \alpha_j + \beta_j = 1 \end{cases} \rightarrow \begin{cases} \tilde{\alpha}_j = \dfrac{d_{mj}}{d_{mj}+d_{tj}} \\ \tilde{\beta}_j = \dfrac{d_{tj}}{d_{mj}+d_{tj}} \end{cases} \quad (13)$$

If $A = diag(\tilde{\alpha}_1 ... \tilde{\alpha}_k)$ and $B = diag(\tilde{\beta}_1 ... \tilde{\beta}_k)$ are two sets of the optimal solutions solved as in Eq.(13), then our fusion method in essence is to pursue the summation of the k optimal problems defined in Eq.(11), i.e.:

$$\sum_{j=1}^{k} f_j = \sum_{j=1}^{k} ||y_j - \tilde{\alpha}_j \hat{y}_{m_j}||^2 + ||y_j - \tilde{\beta}_j \hat{y}_{t_j}||^2 \tag{14}$$

$$= \sum_{j=1}^{k} ||y_j - \tilde{X}_{mean}^T \tilde{\alpha}_j w_{m_{-j}}||^2 + ||y_j - \tilde{X}_{tex}^T \tilde{\beta}_j w_{m_{-j}}||^2$$

In one word, least square solutions W_m and W_t are solved at the first step, then the two sets of k separable optimal parameters A and B are solved at the second step.

Distance Metric under the Fusion Method. Very similar to what is described in Section 3.3.1, Eq.(14) above meets the condition that:

$$W_m A, \ W_t B = \operatorname{argmin} \sum_{j=1}^{k} f_j$$

For an arbitrary pair of image samples $(x_a, \ x_b), x_a, \ x_b \in R^p$, their corresponding local mean features $x_{am}, x_{bm} \in R^{\frac{p}{16}}$, local texture features $x_{at}, x_{bt} \in R^{\frac{p}{16}}$.

The square of the fused distance D_{fuse} of $(x_a, \ x_b)$ is:

$$D_{fuse}^2 = ||(W_m A)^T x_{am} - (W_m A)^T x_{bm}||^2 + ||(W_t B)^T x_{at} - (W_t B)^T x_{bt}||^2 \tag{15}$$

4   Experiments and Analysis

We compare our proposed fusion method with the traditional LDA performed on the original data, X_{mean} and X_{tex} respectively. The whole classification work adopts Euclidean distance by the nearest neighbor (1-NN) classifier.

4.1   Experiments on the Yale Database

The Yale face dataset (http://cvc.yale.edu/projects/yalefaces/yalefaces.html) contains 11 grayscale images for each of the 15 individuals. These eleven images per person were collected from each individual with varying facial expressions and configurations All the images are 100×80 pixels. 6 images per person are randomly selected for training and the rest are used for testing.

We average the realizations over 30 random splits. In Fig.4, it is obvious that our proposed fusion method outperforms the 3 other ones, and demonstrates relatively less fluctuation.

4.2   Experiments on the AR_Gray Database

The AR face database [8, 9] contains over 4000 grayface images of 126 people. The images of each subject have different facial expressions, and we reacquired under lighting conditions and with and without occlusions. Each subject provided 26 face images. We note that 12 face images of each subject are occluded with sunglasses or a scarf. The face images of 120 subjects were taken in two sessions. We used only the images of these120 subjects in our experiment. We manually cropped the face portion of every image and then normalized them to50×40 pixels [10]. We used only the 14 non-occluded face images of each subject to test different solution schemes. The first and eighth images were used as training samples and the remaining images were used as testing samples.

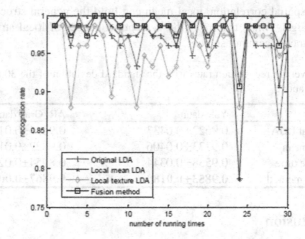

Fig. 4. The recognition rates performed on Yale face database if the samples are randomly split for 30 times

For the performance in this paper, we resize each image from 50×40 pixel into 48×44 as the pre-process. 7 images per person are randomly selected for training and the rest are used for testing. We average the realizations over 30 random splits. Fig.5 provides the recognition rates and their fluctuation by 30 random splits of AR_Gray database.

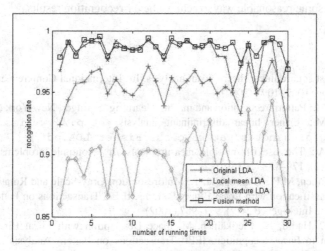

Fig. 5. The recognition rates performed on AR_Gray database if the samples are randomly split for 30 times

4.3   Statistical Analysis

Based on the recognition performances of 30 random splits as shown in Fig.4 and Fig.5, the statistical result is given in Table.1. Bold figures show the best achievements. Fusion method gets the best average accuracy and the smallest deviation on both Yale face database and AR_Gray face database.

Due to the spatial correlation, local mean can hold the general structure of images, as shown in Fig.1. Since texture is the very good keeper of local structure, both of their performances seem not so poor.

Table 1. The average recognition rates with the standard deviation of the 30 random splits on the 2 databases above

	Yale data	AR_Gray data
Original LDA	0.9622 ± 0.0433	0.9546 ± 0.0130
Local mean	0.9773 ± 0.0406	0.9822 ± 0.0119
Local texture	0.9538 ± 0.0344	0.8954 ± 0.0233
Fusion method	**0.9853 ± 0.0180**	**0.9867 ± 0.0063**

5   Conclusion

In the field of face recognition, the problem of high dimension while small sample size is generally encountered. In addition, local texture is very useful information for images, which keeps local structure very well. Our proposed fusion method divides the image evenly into patches, to large extent relives the computational burden. Unlike traditional FLDA that only focuses on one feature, i.e. grey value, our fusion method also takes advantage of local texture information as well, then combines these two features into an optimization way. Our further research will focus on how to combine more kinds of information in some reasonable way to achieve better recognition results.

References

1. Ye, J.: Least square linear discriminant analysis. In: International Conference on Machine Learning, pp. 1087–1094 (2007)
2. Bishop, C.M.: Pattern recognition and machine learning. Springer, New York (2006)
3. Welling, M.: Fisher linear discriminant analysis, http://www.ics.uci.edu/~welling/classnotes/papers_class/Fisher-LDA.pdf
4. Fisher, R.A.: The use of multiple measurements in taxonomic problems. Annals of Eugenics 7(2), 179–188 (1936)
5. Ojala, T., Èinen, M.P., MaÈenpaÈa, T.: Multiresolution Gray-Scale and Rotation Invariant Texture Classification with Local Binary Patterns. IEEE Transactions on Pattern Analysis and Machine Intelligence 24(7), 971–987 (2002)
6. Ahonen, T., Hadid, A., Pietikäinen, M.: Face Description with Local Binary Patterns: Application to Face Recognition. IEEE Transactions on Pattern Analysis and Machine Intelligence 28(12), 2037–2041 (2006)
7. Boyd, S., Vandenberghe, L.: Convex optimization. Cambridge University Press (2004)
8. Martinez, A.M., Benavente, R.: The AR face database. CVC Technical Report, no. 24 (June 1998)
9. Martinez, A.M., Benavente, R.: The AR Face Database (2003), http://rvll.ecn.purdue.edu/_aleix/aleix_face_DB.html
10. Yang, J., Zhang, D., Frangi, A.F., Yang, J.Y.: Two dimensional PCA: a new approach to appearance-based face representation and recognition. IEEE Trans. Pattern Anal. Machine Intell. 24(1), 131–137 (2004)

Complete Gradient Face: A Novel Illumination Invariant Descriptor

Jun-Yong Zhu[1], Wei-Shi Zheng[2], and Jian-Huang Lai[2]

[1] School of Mathematics and Computational Science, Sun Yat-sen University, China
[2] School of Information Science and Technology, Sun Yat-Sen University, China
mc04zhjy@mail2.sysu.edu.cn, sunnyweishi@gmail.com,
stsljh@mail.sysu.edu.cn

Abstract. In the past decade, illumination problem has been the bottleneck of developing robust face recognition systems. Extracting illumination invariant features, especially the gradient based descriptor [13], is an effective tool to solve this issue. In this paper, we propose a novel gradient based descriptor, namely Complete Gradient Face (CGF), to compensate the limitations in [13] and contribute in three folds: (1) we incorporate homogeneous filtering to alleviate the illumination effect and enhance facial information based on the Lambertian assumption; (2) we demonstrate the gradient magnitude in logarithm domain is insensitive to lighting change; (3) we propose a histogram based feature descriptor to integrate both magnitude and orientation information. Experiments on CMU-PIE and Extended YaleB are conducted to verify the effectiveness of our proposed method.

Keywords: Face recognition, illumination problem, gradient, homomorphic filtering.

1 Introduction

Illumination problem, as a difficult issue in the face recognition, has become a barrier in the development of many face related applications, such as video surveillance, face detection, cooperative user applications, etc. The well known face recognition vendor test FRVT 2006 [1] has also revealed that large variation in illumination would probably affect the performance of face recognition algorithms. How to tackle this problem becomes an urgent task.

Recently, a variety of work has been proposed to address this issue. The approaches for solving this problem can be generally divided into three categories [2]: preprocessing and normalization techniques [3, 7], face modeling based approaches [4, 6] and invariant feature extraction [8, 10–14]. With the help of image processing techniques, preprocessing and normalization methods like histogram equalization (HE) [7] attempt to normalize face images in an efficient way, such that the normalized images appear to be consistent under different lighting conditions. However, it is hard to obtain notable improvement in recognition though the visual effects appeared acceptable.

W.-S. Zheng et al. (Eds.): CCBR 2012, LNCS 7701, pp. 17–24, 2012.
© Springer-Verlag Berlin Heidelberg 2012

To further investigate the cause of illumination problem, modeling based approaches turn to explore the mechanism of face imaging. Belhumeur et al. [4] found that the set of face images with fixed pose but under varying illumination is indeed a convex cone, namely illumination cone. Assuming the surface of face is Lambertian, [5] proves that images of the same face under varying lighting conditions span a low dimensional linear subspace. What's more, face image with arbitrary illumination can be generated via spherical harmonic model which is used to represent this face subspace. These methods describe the illumination variation quite well. Nevertheless, it needs a great deal of training samples for the learning procedure, which on the other hand restricts their implementations in real applications.

Compared to the above two categories, invariant feature based methods are more effective and do not demand any learning process. Classical methods such as Local Binary Pattern (LBP) [8] and Gabor [9] are commonly regarded robust to slight illumination change, but the performance drops when the lighting condition becomes severe. Self Quotient Image (SQI) [10] reduces the effect of illumination by dividing itself with the blurred version. Following this way, Logarithmic Total Variation (LTV) [11] incorporates TV model to preserve the edge information and obtain a more elaborate reflectance component. Xie et al. [2] further improved the reflectance component by using Logarithmic Non-subsampled Contourlet Transform and obtain significant improvement although it is a bit time consuming. In contrast, some methods are simple but powerful. Tan and Triggs suggested applying a pipeline of image preprocessing (PP) to reduce the effect of illumination and achieve great improvement. Inspired by the Weber's Law, Wang in [14] took the radio between local difference and the center degree as a kind of illumination invariant component. Zhang et al. showed that the gradient orientation, denoted as Gradient Face [13], can be calculated efficiently and proved insensitive to the illumination change. However, there are still some limitations: (i) the gradient orientations of all pixels are involved to describe a face image, which takes some face unrelated information into account and will probably degenerate the recognition performance; (ii) some important information in gradient domain like the gradient magnitude is not used since it does not satisfy the illumination invariant property. Nevertheless, the magnitudes of gradient for a face contain much valuable information because the pixels with large degrees are always belonging to edges or contours, which are commonly regarded as discriminative elements; (iii) the matching between two gradient faces is based on the pixel-wise comparison. As a result, it requires strict alignment across face images, which is unrealistic for most applications.In this paper, we inherit the high efficiency property of Gradient Face and achieve the following improvements:

1. On the basis of the Lambertian assumption, we incorporate homogeneous filtering to alleviate the illumination effect and enhance facial information.
2. We complement the gradient based illumination invariant feature by simultaneously using gradient magnitude and orientation in the logarithm domain.
3. We propose a histogram based feature description CGF to integrate both magnitude and orientation information, which is reliable to miss-alignment.

2   Homomorphic Filtering

According to the Lambertian reflectance function, the intensity of a 2D surface I can be described as $I(x, y) = R(x, y)L(x, y)$, where $I(x, y)$ is the intensity value at pixel (x, y), L represents the illumination component which is assumed changing smoothly, while R is determined by both albedo and surface normal, which is regarded as illumination insensitive component. Meanwhile, R and L are named as reflectance component and illumination component respectively.

Homomorphic filtering [15] is a classical tool used in image processing, attempting to normalize the brightness across an image and increase contrast. As indicated in the Lambertian model, the reflectance component and illumination component combine multiplicatively. They can be made additive after logarithm transformation, so that these multiplicative components can be separated linearly in the logarithm domain. Consider that illumination variations being regarded as low-frequency components, it is possible to eliminate its effect by taking filtering in the log-spectral domain:

$$H(u,v)\mathscr{F}(\tilde{I}(u,v)) = H(u,v)\mathscr{F}(\tilde{R}(u,v)) + H(u,v)\mathscr{F}(\tilde{L}(u,v)) \qquad (1)$$

where $\tilde{I}(u,v) = \ln(I(x,y))$, $\tilde{R}(u,v) = \ln(R(x,y))$ and $\tilde{L}(u,v) = \ln(L(x,y))$, $\mathscr{F}(\cdot)$ denotes the Fourier Transform (FT), $H(u,v)$ is the filtering function.

Note that the high-frequency components are assumed to represent mostly the reflectance, whereas the illumination effect is mainly assumed lying in the low-frequency domain. Therefore, high-boost filtering can be applied here to suppress low frequency illumination effect and amplify high frequency facial characteristics. Specifically, we adopt a kind of high-boost filter as follow:

$$H(u,v) = (\gamma_H - \gamma_L)(1 - e^{-\frac{(u-u_0)^2 + (v-v_0)^2}{\sigma^2}}) + \gamma_L \qquad (2)$$

where (u_0, v_0) represents the center location, γ_H, γ_L and σ are parameters to control the filter. After the filtering processing, we can obtain the enhanced images in the spatial domain via Inverse Fourier Transform (IFT). That is,

$$\hat{I}(x,y) = \mathscr{F}^{-1}(H(u,v)\mathscr{F}(\tilde{I}(u,v))) \qquad (3)$$

Note that, different from general homomorphic filtering that takes exponential transform on $\hat{I}(x,y)$ at a further step, we are going to extract the illumination invariant feature on $\hat{I}(x,y)$ directly.

3   Complete Gradient Face

As mentioned in Section 1, the gradient magnitude which is abandoned in Gradient Face contains much valuable information though it does not satisfy the illumination invariant requirement. Indeed, this problem can be solved by transferring the derivation into the logarithm domain since the multiplicative combination in original domain will turn into additive form. Thus, different from Gradient Face

---

Algorithm 1. Generating Histogram for CGF

Input: *CGF-M*, *CGF-O*, k (number of bins in histogram encoding each block)
Output: H (histogram of a face image)
1: Quantify *CGF-O* in k bins $\{b_1, \cdots, b_k\}$ to increase the fault-tolerant capability;
2: Divide *CGF-M* and *CGF-O* into small blocks evenly, and denote M^i and O^i as the *ith* block in *CGF-M* and *CGF-O* separately;
3: For each M^i, calculate the weighted normalized gradient magnitude as $\tilde{M}^i(p,q) = \frac{M^i(p,q)W(p,q)}{\sum_{(p',q')\in N(p,q)} M^i(p',q')W(p',q')}$, where W denotes the gaussian weight matrix.
4: After that, we can generate the histogram for each block, $H^i(t) = sum\{M^i(j)|O^i(j) == b_t\}$, for $t = 1, \cdots, k$, and then concatenate them in to a long vector $H = [H^i]$ to represent a face image.

---

that only retains gradient orientations as the illumination invariant features, we are able to incorporate both gradient magnitude and orientation in the logarithm domain to generate our illumination invariant features. The illumination invariant of our proposed features are based on the following theorem.

Theorem 1. *For any face image $I(x,y)$ captured under arbitrary lighting condition, let $\tilde{I}(x,y) = ln(I(x,y))$, its gradient magnitude and the gradient orientation, i.e. $\sqrt{(\partial_x\tilde{I}(x,y))^2 + (\partial_y\tilde{I}(x,y))^2}$ and $arctan(\partial_y\tilde{I}(x,y)/\partial_x\tilde{I}(x,y))$ are both illumination invariant components, where $\partial_x\tilde{I}$ and $\partial_y\tilde{I}$ denote the partial derivatives.*

Proof. Assume $I(x,y) = R(x,y)L(x,y)$, then $\tilde{I}(x,y) = \tilde{R}(x,y) + \tilde{L}(x,y)$, where $\tilde{R}(x,y) = ln(R(x,y))$ and $\tilde{L}(x,y) = ln(L(x,y))$. Since $L(x,y)$ changes smoothly, we can obtain the conclusion that $\partial_x L(x,y) = 0$ and $\partial_y L(x,y) = 0$ as [13], that is, we have $\partial_x\tilde{L}(x,y) = 0$ and $\partial_y\tilde{L}(x,y) = 0$ as well. As a result,

$$\partial_x\tilde{I}(x,y) = \partial_x R(x,y)/R(x,y) \quad and \quad \partial_y\tilde{I}(x,y) = \partial_y R(x,y)/R(x,y) \quad (4)$$

Thus, it is easy to check that $\sqrt{(\partial_x\tilde{I}(x,y))^2 + (\partial_y\tilde{I}(x,y))^2}$ is independent of $L(x,y)$, so as to $arctan(\partial_y\tilde{I}(x,y)/\partial_x\tilde{I}(x,y))$. #

Until now, we have proposed a pair of illumination invariant components by full use of the gradient information in logarithm domain, that is, the gradient magnitude and orientation, denoted as *CGF-M* and *CGF-O*. However, it is not reliable to directly conduct pixel-wise matchings on these two components among different face images. Hence, in the following part, we are going to integrate *CGF-M* and *CGF-O* into a unified histogram based feature representation.

The whole procedure is listed in Algorithm 1. Note that, in Step 3, we impose gaussian weights to M^i to alleviate the boundary effect. And then, we calculate the normalized magnitudes by dividing the local sum around pixels in M^i. It is worth mentioning that there are shadows in face images since the Lambertian assumption does not strictly hold here. As a result, the pixels with large values in M^i may belong to the shadows when the light condition becomes severe and taking the local normalized procedure is able to restrain this effect.

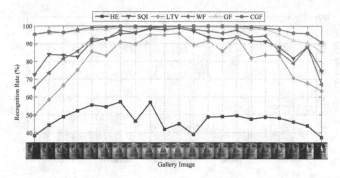

Fig. 1. Recognition rates with different galleries on CMU-PIE

4 Experiments

4.1 Experimental Setting

In this section, we conducted a series of experiments on two public databases including CMU-PIE [16] and Extended YaleB [4] to validate the effectiveness of our proposed illumination invariant descriptor. In the experiments, 1428 frontal face images from 68 individuals under 21 different illumination conditions were selected. For Extended YaleB, face images from 38 individuals were captured under 64 different lighting conditions on 9 poses, and we only used $64 \times 38 = 2432$ frontal face images here. All images were simply aligned according to the eyes coordinates and resized to 128×128.

We compared our CGF to several state-of-the-art algorithms, including HE [7], SQI [10], LTV [11], Weber Face [14] and Gradient Face [13]. Note that, we adopted Euclidean distance as similarity measurement and used nearest neighborhood classifier for classification. All methods were implemented with parameters set as the authors recommended. For our CFG, the parameters of homomorphic filtering were empirically fixed as $\gamma_H = 2.0$, $\gamma_L = 0.5$ and $\sigma = c * L$, where L is the width of image, c denotes a constant to control the radius of high-pass filter which was set $c = 0.1$ during all experiments. What's more, without specifical declaration, the block size was set as 4×4, unsigned gradient orientation was adopted and 5 bins were used in quantization.

4.2 Results for CMU-PIE and Extended YaleB

In this part, we focused on the adaptability of each descriptor in various lighting conditions. A series of experiments were designed to compare CGF with several state-of-the-art algorithms and validate the effectiveness of our proposed method.

Results for CMU-PIE: Only one image per individual was chosen as gallery and the other formed the probes. We varied the gallery images to ensure all illumination conditions were covered. The final results were shown in Fig. 1. As we can see, all methods degenerate as the light source diverged from the frontal direction. All six methods excepted HE achieve the best performances when

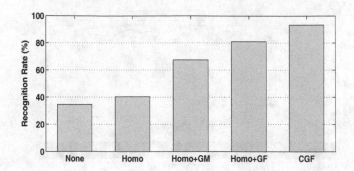

Fig. 2. Performances of different components in CGF

using the frontal lighting image as gallery. That is, 98.82% for SQI, 95.81% for LTV, 99.71% for WF, 99.93% for GF and 100% for CGF. What's more, some approaches such as SQI, LTV and WF turn out less effective when the illumination condition became severe, while both GF and CGF perform well even under the most extremely situation. Also, our proposed CGF outperforms all other methods almost in each lighting condition and achieves the best average recognition rate at 98.19%.

Results for Extended YaleB: Different from the CMU-PIE database, the face images in Extended YaleB database were captured in even more complex environments. To better investigate the effectiveness of our proposed illumination invariant descriptor, we conducted experiments following the two protocols and report performances on set 1 to 5 separately: *(i) the frontal lighting image per subject was chosen as gallery set and the rest for probe set; (ii) three images under arbitrary lighting conditions were randomly chosen to form the gallery set and the rest formed the probe set.*

It is worth mentioning that, the angles between frontal face directions and orientations of light source increase from set 1 to set 5. That is, generally, it is more challenging to handle the face recognition task as set index increases, which is consistent to the results in Table 1 and Table 2. Note that, results of *All* in Table 1 were calculated by taking all other images per subject excepting the gallery one as probe. As shown in Table 1, it is interesting to find that HE obtains the highest accuracy 97.81% in Set 1 using single frontal illuminated images as gallery. It makes sense because the illumination effect is limited in Set 1 and the HE performed well in this scenario. Meanwhile, our proposed CGF outperforms all methods by following both protocol I and protocol II excepted the case in Set 1 as tabulated in Table 1. To further investigate this problem, we conducted another experiment using three randomly chosen images instead of the one with frontal illumination to consist the gallery set in protocol II. As can be found in Table 2, both average recognition rates and corresponding standard deviations of 20 random trials were reported. We found that our proposed CGF achieved consistent highest performance in this case.

Table 1. Results of Extended YaleB Following Protocol I (in accuracy (%))

	Set1	Set2	Set3	Set4	Set5	All
HE [7]	**97.81**	92.76	36.18	10.90	13.43	41.25
SQI [10]	88.60	**100.00**	85.75	87.97	81.02	87.82
LTV [11]	87.28	99.78	66.67	45.49	44.32	63.86
WF [14]	79.39	99.78	75.88	77.07	74.38	80.56
GF [13]	94.74	**100.00**	83.33	75.94	74.65	83.51
CGF	94.74	**100.00**	**92.54**	**96.43**	**86.70**	**93.30**

Table 2. Results of Extended YaleB Following Protocol II (in accuracy (%))

	Set1	Set2	Set3	Set4	Set5
HE [7]	66.61±31.37	60.26±21.49	53.34±10.98	45.37±12.72	54.29±14.78
SQI [10]	81.05±19.49	80.14±19.81	85.80±12.17	88.51±5.52	94.51±1.82
LTV [11]	79.85±22.92	78.47±22.89	70.31±16.43	56.57±8.62	73.34±8.16
WF [14]	90.38±8.17	86.68±13.13	90.01±8.65	88.58±3.82	93.61±3.21
GF [13]	94.32±7.73	91.40±10.78	91.21±7.68	89.86±4.34	96.13±5.82
CGF	**98.88±1.25**	**97.96±2.55**	**99.49±0.78**	**97.59±1.67**	**96.39±2.22**

4.3   Contribution of Each Component in CGF

Since CGF consists of three parts including homomorphic filtering, local normalized gradient magnitude and gradient orientation (denoted as *Homo*, *GM* and *GF* respectively), we would like to explore the improvement for each components. Thus, in this section, we conducted experiments on Extended YaleB database by using the frontal illuminated image as gallery and the others consist the probe ones regardless which set they belonged to. The results were shown in Fig. 2 and it validates our previous analysis that (i) the homomorphic filtering was able to restrain the illumination effect in some respect; (ii) gradient magnitude and gradient orientation in logarithm were both insensitive to the illumination change; (iii) our proposed CGF formulates the above two components in an effective way and achieves great success in tolerating lighting changes.

5   Conclusions

In this paper, a novel illumination invariant descriptor CGF has been proposed to compensate the limitations of Gradient Face. On the basis of illumination invariant property analysis, we integrate both gradient magnitude and orientation in the logarithm domain followed by homomorphic filtering and propose a histogram based feature representation. Experimental results verify the effectiveness of our proposed CGF in tackling with illumination problem.

Acknowledgments. This research is supported by the National Natural Science of Foundation of China (Nos.61102111, 61173084), Specialized Re-search Fund for the Doctoral Program of Higher Education (No.20110171120051), and the 985 Project at Sun Yat-sen University under Grant No.35000-3281305.

References

1. Phillips, P., Scruggs, W., OToole, A., Flynn, P., Bowyer, K., Schott, C., Sharpe, M.: FRVT 2006 and ICE 2006 Large-Scale Results. In: NISTIR (2007)
2. Xie, X., Lai, J.H., Zheng, W.: Extraction of Illumination Invariant Facial Features from a Single Image Using Nonsubsampled Contourlet Transform. Pattern Recognition 43(12), 4177–4189 (2010)
3. Shan, S., Gao, W., Cao, B., Zhao, D.: Illumination normalization for robust face recognition against varying lighting conditions. In: Proceedings of International Workshop Analysis and Modeling of Faces and Gestures (2003)
4. Georghiades, A., Belhumeur, P., Kriegman, D.: From few to many: illumination cone models for face recognition under variable lighting and pose. IEEE Trans. on PAMI 23, 643–660 (2001)
5. Basri, R., Jacobs, D.: Lambertian reflectance and linear subspaces. IEEE Trans. on PAMI 25(2), 218–233 (2003)
6. Shim, H., Luo, J., Chen, T.: A subspace model-based approach to face relighting under unknown lighting and poses. IEEE Trans. on IP 17, 1331–1341 (2008)
7. Pizer, S.M., Amburn, E.P.: Adaptive histogram equalization and its variations. Comput. Vis. Graph. Image Process. 39(3), 355–368 (1987)
8. Ahonen, T., Hadid, A., Pietikainen, M.: Face description with local binary patterns: application to face recognition. IEEE Trans. on PAMI 28, 2037–2041 (2006)
9. Zhang, W., Shan, S., Gao, W., Chen, X., Zhang, H.: Local Gabor binary pattern histogram sequence(LGBPHS): an novel non-statistical model for face representation and recognition. In: Proceeding of IEEE Conference on ICCV (2005)
10. Wang, H., Li, S.Z., Wang, Y.: Generalized quotient image. In: Proceeding of IEEE Conference on CVPR (2004)
11. Chen, T., Yin, W., Zhou, X., Comaniciu, D., Huang, T.S.: Total variation models for variable lighting face recognition. IEEE Trans. on PAMI 28, 1519–1524 (2006)
12. Tan, X., Triggs, B.: Enhanced local texture feature sets for face recognition under difficult lighting conditions. IEEE Trans. on IP 19(6), 1635–1650 (2010)
13. Zhang, T., Tang, Y., Fang, B., Shang, Z., Liu, X.: Face recognition under varying illumination using gradient faces. IEEE Trans. on IP 18(11), 2599–2606 (2009)
14. Wang, B., Li, W., Yang, W., Liao, Q.: Illumination Normalization Based on Weber's Law With Application to Face Recognition. IEEE Trans. on SP Letters 18(8), 462–465 (2011)
15. Gonzalez, R.C., Woods, R.E.: Digtial Image Processing, 2nd edn. Prentice-Hall (2002)
16. Sim, T., Baker, S., Bsat, M.: The cmu pose, illumination, and expression database. IEEE Trans. on PAMI 25(12), 1615–1618 (2003)

A Face Authentication Scheme Based on Affine-SIFT (ASIFT) and Structural Similarity (SSIM)

Lifang Wu[1], Peng Zhou[1], Shuqin Liu[1], Xiuzhen Zhang[2], and Emanuele Trucco[3]

[1] School of Electronic Information and Control Engineering, Beijing University of Technology, Beijing, China, 100124
[2] School of CS&IT, RMIT University, GPO Box 2476, Melbourne, VIC 3001, Australia
[3] School of Computing, University of Dundee, Dundee DD1 4HN, The United Kingdom
lfwu@bjut.edu.cn, {king_zhoupeng,liushuqin}@emails.bjut.edu.cn,
xiuzhen.Zhang@rmit.edu.au, manueltrucco@computing.dundee.ac.uk

Abstract. In this paper, we propose a novel face authentication approach based on affine scale invariant feature transform (ASIFT) and structural similarity (SSIM). The ASIFT descriptor defines key points which are used to match the gallery and probe face images. The matched pairs of key points are filtered based on the location of points in the gallery face image. Then the similarity between sub-images at a preserved pair of matched points is measured by Structural Similarity (SSIM). A mean SSIM (MSSIM) at all pairs of points is computed for authentication. The proposed approach is tested on FERET, CMU-PIE and AR databases with only one image for enrollment. Comparative results on the AR database show that our approach outperforms state-of-the-art approaches.

Keywords: Face Authentication, Affine-SIFT, Structural Similarity.

1 Introduction

Among existing biometric modalities, 2D face authentication and identification remains a great challenge [1]. Some state-of-the-art approach had good results but they required a lot of images in the enrollment phase. In a real application with a large database one can not easily acquire many images because it would cost too much in terms of resources, including storage and human subjects. In this paper, we study the problem of face recognition using a single face image per person in the enrollment stage.

Face recognition algorithms can be generally divided into global feature based and local feature based approaches. The former includes PCA, Fisherface, and ICA. The latter generally uses the local gabor features at some feature points. The feature points generally include eye corner, nose tip, and mouth corners. These features (eye center, eye corners, etc) are semantic features. It is difficult to locate these semantic feature points because there is a gap between semantic features and low-level features. In comparison, locating the key points based on low-level features is easier and more reliable.

Scale-invariant feature transform (or SIFT) is an algorithm in computer vision to detect and describe local features in images. Key locations are defined as maxima and

W.-S. Zheng et al. (Eds.): CCBR 2012, LNCS 7701, pp. 25–32, 2012.
© Springer-Verlag Berlin Heidelberg 2012

minima of the result of difference of Gaussians function applied in scale-space to a series of smoothed and resampled images [2]. We can see that SIFT is detected based on the difference of pixel value. There is a stable connection between the feature point and the pixel value. This kind of points extraction is more reliable. Some related approaches have been proposed [3-5,7,8]. Bicego [3] firstly used SIFT points for face authentication. They designed three matching strategies, the minimum pair distance, the matching eyes and mouth and matching on a regular grid. The experimental results on the BANCA database showed that the SIFT based approach is promising. Furthermore, Kisku [4] proposed Graph Matching Technique to improve the overall system performance. Rosenberger and Brun [5] also proposed a graph representation of SIFT points for face authentication. They modeled the authentication problem as a graph matching process. They obtained EER (Equal Error Rate) of 12% on the AR benchmark [6] containing the face of 126 individuals with different alterations with only one image for enrollment. Hemery et al. [7] further studied how the color space influenced the performance of Rosenberger's approach. They got 10 matching scores in 10 color spaces. All scores were normalized and fused for authentication. The EER was 4.4% in the same experiment. Liao [8] constructed a large gallery dictionary of multi key-point descriptors (MKD) by pooling all the SIFT descriptors. For a probe face image, the SIFT descriptors were extracted. Its identity is determined by the multi-task sparse representation based classification algorithm.

In all the above approaches, only the spatial relationship of the SIFT key points is used for face authentication. They did not take into account the appearance similarity between a pair of matched SIFT points, which we think represents image similarity visually, and is also related to visual perception. How could we measure such similarity? Structural Similarity (SSIM) [9] is a full reference image quality assessment approach, and is thought to be an image quality metric consistent with human perception. In this paper the SSIM is used to measure the similarity between two images.

In our face authentication approach to measuring the similarity between gallery and probe face images, ASIFT descriptors are used to define key points. These points are located in the gallery and probe face images and matched using ASIFT descriptors. The matched pairs of key points are filtered based on the location of points in the gallery face image. Then the similarity between the sub-images at a preserved pair of key points is measured by Structural Similarity (SSIM). A mean SSIM (MSSIM) measure at all the pairs of points is computed for authentication. Experimental results on FERET, CMU-PIE and AR face databases show that our approach has good performance for face images with expression variation, constrained pose variation or occlusion using only one frontal face image for enrollment. Comparative results on AR database show that our approach outperforms state-of-the-art approaches.

2   Framework of the Proposed Approach

The framework of the proposed approach is shown in Fig. 1. First, the ASIFT points are extracted by Yu and Morel's approach [10] for both the gallery and probe face images. These points are represented and matched in pairs using the ASIFT descriptors. Generally, there are more matching pairs of SIFT points. These points are usually clustered and local regions of these points overlap very much. Computing similarity for all these points is computationally costly. Therefore we filter out some matching pairs. Matched pairs of key points are filtered by the location of the SIFT points in the gallery face image. The MSSIM is then computed from all the preserved pairs to measure the similarity between two face images. If the MSSIM is greater than a preset threshold, the authentication is successful, the preset threshold is got by experiment.

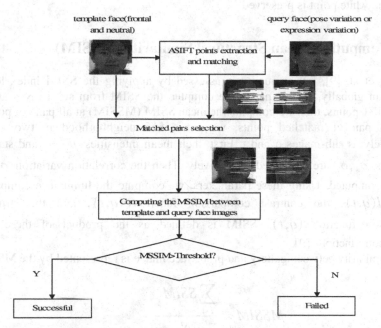

Fig. 1. The framework of the proposed approach

3   Matched Pairs Selection

We usually get thousands of ASIFT points in a face image. Most of them are concentrated in the eye, mouth and nose regions. Some points are close to each other so that the neighborhoods of these points are usually overlap. In order to reduce the computation, we select some matched pairs for authentication.

Fig. 2. A face image divided with patch of 8×8   **Fig. 3.** Illustration of key points filtering

We divide the gallery face image into small patches of size of $h \times w$. In our approach h and w are both 8 pixels, a face image of 80×80 is divided into 10*10 patches, as shown in Fig. 2.

If there is not any ASIFT point in a patch, the patch is considered invalid. If there is more than one matched ASIFT points in a patch, only one point will be preserved, and the others should be removed. In order to avoid overlapping, and therefore redundant sub-images at a key point, the ASIFT point closest to the center of the patch is preserved, and others are discarded. In Fig. 3, there are 7 key points in the patch. The white point is preserved.

4   Computing Mean Structural Similarity (MSSIM)

In Wang et al. [9], image quality is assessed by applying the SSIM index locally rather than globally. In this paper, we compute the SSIM from sub-images at each pair of SIFT points, then we compute the mean SSIM (MSSIM) at all pairs of points.

For a pair of matched points, we get a 5x5 neighborhood in two images respectively as sub-mages q and t. First, their mean intensities μ_q, μ_t and standard variations σ_q, σ_t are computed respectively. Then the correlation variation σ_{qt} of q and t is computed. Using these parameters, we compute the luminance comparison function $l(q,t)$, the contrast comparison function $c(q,t)$, and the structural comparison function $s(q,t)$. SSIM is defined as the product of these three comparison functions [9].

The similarity between gallery and probe face image is represented by the MSSIM:

$$MSSIM = \frac{\sum_{i=1}^{N} SSIM_i}{N} \tag{1}$$

Where $SSIM_i$ is the SSIM of the ith pair of patches, and N is the number of the valid patches in the gallery face image.

5   Experiments

We test our approach on three face databases: the FERET [11], CMU-PIE [12] and AR [6] face databases. These databases include face images with illumination, pose and expression variations. Some databases include face images with occlusion.

In face authentication, pose variation is usually limited because the users are expected to be imaged in pre-defined poses. In a real application, with a large database one cannot easily acquire as many images because it would cost too much in terms of resources, including storage and human subjects. It is reported in literature only one image is captured [5] for enrollment. In our experiments, the frontal face image is selected for enrollment. The probe set includes face images with expression variation, limited pose variation and occlusion.

The FERET face database includes several databases (fa,fb,ba-bk). In our experiments, the ba database is selected as a gallery set, which includes frontal face images of 200 individuals. The face images of the corresponding individuals in other five databases (bd, bg, be, bf and bj) are selected as a probe set. Example face images of an individual are shown in Fig. 4.

ba   bd   be   bf   bg   bj

Fig. 4. The example face images from FERET

The CMU-PIE face database includes 68 individuals. Each individual has face images with pose, illumination or expression variations. For each subject, we select 7 face images with expression and pose variations. Figure 6 shows the face images of the same individual. N_W_27 is chosen as a gallery set, the others as a probe set.

N_W_27   N_W_05   N_W_29   N_W_07   N_W_09   B_W_27   S_W_27

Fig. 5. Example face images from CMU-PIE

We compare our approach with state-of-the-art approaches by testing on the AR face database using 126 subjects. The same samples as in [5] and [7] are chosen in our experiments. Fig. 6 shows face images of the same individual. The first sample is the gallery set, and others are the probe set.

01   04   05   08   11

Fig. 6. Example face images from AR database

5.1   Performance of Face Authentication

We compare our approach with ASIFT+LBP approach. In ASIFT+LBP approach, the averaging LBP distance of all the matched SIFT points between the probe face image and each gallery face image is computed. If the distance is smaller than the assigned threshold, the probe face image is thought the subject same as the corresponding gallery image.

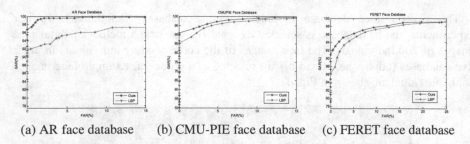

(a) AR face database   (b) CMU-PIE face database   (c) FERET face database

Fig. 7. ROC curves on three face databases

The ROC (Receiver operating characteristic) curves on the three face databases are shown in Fig. 7. From Fig. 7, we can see that our approach get over 90% GAR (Genuine Acceptance Rate) with these three databases when FAR (False Acceptance Rate) is 0. It is about 5.0% higher than ASIFT+LBP. In general, the ROC curve of SIFT+LBP is under our approach, it shows that our approach is better than ASIFT+LBP. It further shows that the SSIM could represent the visual similarity of local region than LBP.

Table 1. Comparison of Equal Error Rate (EER)

Approaches	EER (%)
Rosenberger's [5]	12.0
Hemery's [7]	4.4
ASIFT+LBP	4.2
Our's	1.6

We further compare our approach with Hemery's [7] and Rosenberger's approach [5] on the AR face database. Table 1 shows the compared EER.

Table 1 indicates that Hemery's approach is better than Rosenberger's, because they fused the similarity in 10 color spaces. Our approach outperforms both of them, although we use only the gray component. ASIFT+LBP get EER of 4.2%. It is also bigger than our approach.

5.2   How Does the Matching Pairs Selection Influence the Performance?

In order to test how the matching pair filtering algorithm influence the performance of face recognition. We test the algorithm with all matching pairs, matching pairs selected using our algorithm and the matching pairs selected randomly. The results are shown in Fig. 8.

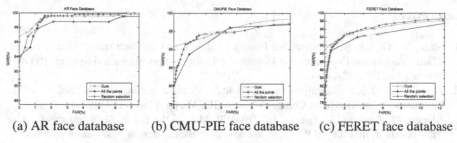

(a) AR face database   (b) CMU-PIE face database   (c) FERET face database

Fig. 8. ROC under different way of point selection

We also test the average running time under three ways of point selection. In order to compare these approaches conveniently, all the running times are divided by that of our selection way. The compared results are shown in Table 2.

Table 2. Normalized average running time under different points selection

Point selection	FERET	CMUPIE	AR
All matching pairs	1.17	1.16	2.35
Randomly selection	1.07	1.05	1.1
Our's	1.0	1.0	1.0

From Fig. 8 and Table 2, we can see that the performance using all the match pairs is the generally worst than other two ways. We think the feature of SIFT point on the face contour influences the performance. The performance of random selection is unstable. The proposed way has the stable performance and requires the least running time.

6   Conclusion

A novel face authentication approach based on Affine-SIFT and SSIM (ASIFT-SSIM) is proposed. We extract the ASIFT points and match these points in the gallery and probe face images by ASIFT descriptors. The matched pairs of key points are filtered based on the location of points in the gallery face image. A mean SSIM (MSSIM) measure is computed from the preserved pairs of points for authentication. Experimental results show that our approach is robust to expression variation, pose variation (within rotation angle up to 25 degree) and occlusion. Comparative results on the AR face database show that our approach outperforms state-of-the-art approaches when each person is imaged with only one frontal training sample.

Acknowledgments. This paper is partially supported by the Beijing municipal Nature Science Foundation under Grant No 4091004 and Beijing Municipal Talent Training Program under Grant No 2009D005015000010.

References

1. Struc, V., Gajsek, R., Pavesic, N.: Principal gabor filters for face recognition. In: IEEE Third International Conference on Biometrics: Theory, Applications and Systems (BTAS), Washington, DC, USA (2009)
2. Lowe, D,G.: Object recognition from local scale-invariant features. In: Proceedings of the International Conference on Computer Vision (ICCV), pp. 1150–1157 (1999)
3. Bicego, M., Lagorio, A., Grosso, E., Tistarelli, M.: On the use of SIFT features for face authentication. In: Proc. of IEEE Int. Workshop on Biometrics, in Association with CVPR, p. 35 (2006)
4. Kisku, D., Rattani, A., Grosso, E., Tistarelli, M.: Face identification by SIFT-based complete graph topology. In: IEEE Workshop on Automatic Identification Advanced Technologies, pp. 63–68 (2007)
5. Rosenberger, C., Brun, L.: Similarity-based matching for face authentication. In: International Conference on Pattern Recognition, ICPR (2008)
6. Martinez, A., Benavente, R.: The AR face database. CVC Tech. Report 24 (1998)
7. Hemery, B., Schwartzmann, J.J., Rosenberger, C.: Study on Color Spaces for Single Image Enrollment Face Authentication. In: International Conference on Pattern Recognition (ICPR), pp. 1249–1252 (2010)
8. Liao, S., Jain, A.: Partial Face Recognition: An Alignment Free Approach. In: Proc. 2011 IEEE International Joint Conference on Biometrics, pp. 1–8 (2011)
9. Wang, Z., Bovik, A.C., Sheikh, H.R., Simoncelli, E.P.: Image quality assessment: From error visibility to structural similarity. IEEE Transaction on Image Processing, 600–612 (2004)
10. Yu, G., Morel, J.-M.: A fully affine invariant image comparison method. In: ICASSP, pp. 1597–1600 (2009)
11. Phillips, P., Wechsler, H., Huang, J., Rauss, P.: The feret database and evaluation procedure for face recognition algorithms. Journal of Image and Vision Computing 16(5), 295–306 (1998)
12. Sim, T., Baker, S.: The CMU Pose, Illumination Expression Database. IEEE PAMI 25(12) (2003)

A Study on the Effective Approach
to Illumination-Invariant Face Recognition
Based on a Single Image

Jiapei Zhang[1,2] and Xiaohua Xie[1,2,*]

[1] Shenzhen Institutes of Advanced Technology, Chinese Academy of Sciences, 518055, China
[2] Shenzhen Key Laboratory for Visual Computing and Analytics, Shenzhen, 518055, China
{jp.zhang,xiaohua.xie}@siat.ac.cn,
sysuxiexh@gmail.com

Abstract. In this paper, the methods for single image-based face recognition under varying lighting are reviewed. Meanwhile, some representative methods as well as their combinations are evaluated by experiments, and the underlying principle of the experimental results is investigated. According to our investigation, it is almost impossible to attain a satisfied face recognition result by using only one facial descriptor/representation especially under drastically varying illuminations. However, the "two-step" framework, including an illumination preprocessing and an illumination-insensitive facial features extraction, could be an effective approach to addressing this problem. We further study what are the appropriate illumination preprocessing and feature extraction for this framework.

Keywords: face recognition, illumination normalization, feature extraction.

1 Introduction

As a technology which possesses a promising and extensive applicative future, face recognition enjoys a close concern by many researchers in past decades. As we know, the variations in illumination, pose, and expression are the most important factors that restrict the development and spread of face recognition [2]. Researches also indicated that variation of face images caused by the varying illuminations had exceeded the variation caused by the change in face identity [1].

Many practical systems implement the face recognition in the form of "one-to-one" match, i.e., one gallery image and one probe image per subject. Under such a constraint, the supervised learning such as Fisherfaces and the subspace representation such as Eigenface become invalid. Therefore, the single image based face recognition is more challenging than that based on "one-to-set" or "set-to-set" match. In this paper, we focus on investigating the face recognition issue based on a single image under varying illumination.

---

* Corresponding author.

W.-S. Zheng et al. (Eds.): CCBR 2012, LNCS 7701, pp. 33–41, 2012.

We not only perform the experiment to assess the effects of representative techniques, but also derive a series of combinational methods based on the existing algorithms and evaluate their performances. The experimental results demonstrate that it is almost impossible to attain a satisfied face recognition result by employing only one kind of facial descriptor/representation especially under drastically varying illuminations. However, by combining an illumination preprocessing and an illumination-insensitive facial descriptor, the "two-step" framework could result in an effective performance for face recognition. We further study what are the appropriate illumination preprocessing and feature extraction, respectively, for this framework. The detailed analysis is presented in Section 4. Note that we don't want to conduct an experimental comparison on state-of-the-art methods, but to study "why" and "how" the two-step framework works well for the mentioned issue in this paper.

2   Review of Related Work

Numerous illumination-insensitive face recognition methods have been proposed in the past decades. In 2007, Xuan et al. had presented an extensive survey of the passive techniques [32]. In this section, we briefly introduce the representative and the up-to-date techniques to address the problem of illumination variation in face recognition based on single image. Existing methods to solve such a problem fall into two categories: (a) extracting illumination insensitive representation, and (b) restoring a frontal-illuminated face image [4].

(a)   Extracting Illumination Insensitive Representation

Approaches to extract illumination invariant/insensitive facial representation have almost gone through a development along with the image processing theories. Early researches employed simple descriptors such as logarithmic transformation, edge map, and image gradient to reduce the impact of illumination variation. These methods are built on primitive image processing theories and they are easy to implement, but are also with a relatively limited performance. However, the recently proposed Gradientface method [5] developed from the image gradient presents a very good performance. As the time-frequency analysis develops, many approaches attempt to extract illumination-invariant facial features in the frequency domain. Representative works include the wavelet transform based method [6, 10], the Gabor feature based method [7], the DCT based method [8], the DFT based method (Spectroface) [9], Wiener filter based method [37], and the maximum filter based method [36]. Since the high frequency component of a face image is proved to be insensitive to illumination variation, it is mostly extracted as facial feature by the above-mentioned methods. The concept of "illumination cone" [11] tells us that the images of the same convex Lambertian object under different lighting conditions lie in a low-dimension linear subspace. Thus subspace-based methods emerge in large number, such as the quotient image (QI) [12] and Spherical Harmonic presentation [13]. Other kind of dominant methods are based on Land's Retinex theory [14], including the Self-Quotient Image (SQI) [29], the Logarithmic Total Variation (LTV) model [26], logarithmic Wavelet [31], and the Non-Subsampled Contourlet Transform based method

(LNSCT) [30]. Moreover, the WeberFace [27], the Local Binary Pattern (LBP) [33], and the Local Ternary Patterns (LTP) [28] are all effectual descriptors robust to illumination changing.

(b)   Restoring the Frontal-Illuminated Face Image

Methods to restore the frontal-illuminated face image support improving recognition performance as well as generating the face image with a good visual appearance. In an early stage, simple gray-scale adjustment such as Gamma correction, histogram equalization, and histogram match are often used. Later researchers take the light properties estimated specially from the target face image into account to normalize the illumination. Such methods include morphing face [16], shape from shading (SFS) [17], linear lighting model-based illumination compensation [18], difference image based shadow compensation [19], and illumination compensation by truncating low frequency coefficients of DCT in the logarithm domain [20]. The illumination subspace theory also supports some novel relighting methods, e.g., quotient image (QI) relighting method [21], spherical harmonic basis morphable model [22], bilinear illumination model [23], Harmonic relighting [24], and pixel-dependent relighting model [25].

There are still some other related approaches beyond the above two categories. For example, researchers recently propose lighting insensitive metrics/measures to compare images [15, 38]. Xie et al. [4] propose to recapture the useful face information from the large-scale face features (low-frequency component), which is always discarded by many other methods.

3   Evaluation Scheme

3.1   Referred Methods

We conduct the experiment to evaluate the representative approaches to addressing the illumination problem in face recognition based on a single image. The referred technologies include the LTV method [26], the WeberFace [27], the GradientFace [5],

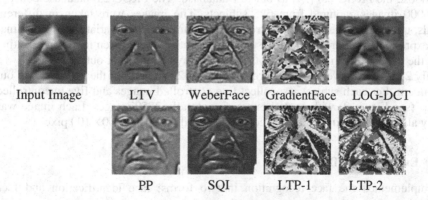

Input Image   LTV   WeberFace   GradientFace   LOG-DCT

PP   SQI   LTP-1   LTP-2

Fig. 1. The examples of illumination preprocessing by using different methods. The upper left is the original input image. Others are the processed results by different methods.

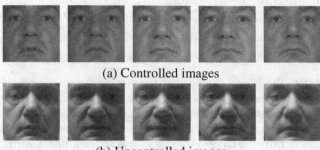

(a) Controlled images

(b) Uncontrolled images

Fig. 2. Samples of face images from the FRGC 2.0 database. These images were captured under (a) the controlled environment, and (b) the uncontrolled environment, respectively.

the logarithmic DCT (LOG-DCT) algorithm [20], SQI method [29], LTP [28], and the illumination Pre-Processing chain (PP) [28]. The PP chain is an illumination normalization method, which contains the Gamma correction, the Difference of Gaussain (DoG) filtering, and the contrast equalization. Fig. 1 illustrates the results produced by the above mentioned methods. Here LTP-1 and LTP-2 are two LBPs used in LTP algorithm.

Like the experiments in [28], in our experiment we employ the LTV, WeberFace, GradientFace, LOG-DCT, and the SQI as preprocessing, even though these methods have been used as feature extraction in their source literatures. By adopting LTP to further extract the features, we thus derive new approaches: LTV+LTP, Weber-Face+LTP, GradientFace+LTP, LOG-DCT+LTP, PP+LTP, and SQI+LTP.

The above-mentioned primitive and the derived algorithms were all involved in our evaluation.

3.2   Face Database

We choose the FRGC 2.0 [34] as our test database. The FRGC 2.0 database consists of 50,000 images captured from 625 subjects. The images were taken in different periods, under controlled and uncontrolled environments, with variations in illumination, expression, and ornaments. The controlled images were taken in a studio setting while the uncontrolled images were taken in hallways, atriums, or outside.

Only 275 subjects were selected from the total 625 subjects of the FRGC 2.0 in our experiment. For each subject, we collect five controlled images and five uncontrolled images (see Figure 2) with neutral expression, totally 2750 images. Each image was simply aligned according to the eye coordinates and resized to 100×100 pixels.

3.3   Experimental Details

We implemented the face recognition in two forms: face identification and face verification.

- Face identification

For each subject, one controlled (uncontrolled) image was used as the reference image, and rest four controlled (uncontrolled) images were used as the query images. The Nearest Neighbor (NN) classifier was used, where the normalized correlation was selected as the similarity metric (for LTP, *Chi2* distance was used). The rank-one recognition rate is used to measure the performance of face identification

- Face Verification

In the verification case, one controlled (uncontrolled) image of each subject was registered as the reference image and the rest controlled (uncontrolled) images were used as the probe ones. Accordingly, for each subject, there were 4 client samples and $1096(= 4 \times 274)$ imposter samples. The ROC curve [3] and Equal Error Rate (EER) is used to measure the performance of face verification, where the ROC curves show the false accept rate (FAR) versus face verification rate (FVR).

4   Results and Discussion

We present the recognition rates and the EERs in Table 1 and illustrate the ROC curves in Figures 3. The higher value of recognition rate, the lower value of EER and the upper curve of ROC of a method displays, the better performance that method reveals.

The experimental results show that, GradientFace algorithm reaches the optimum performance for controlled images, no matter in face identification or in face verification. This result may be not surprised because GradientFace has essentially done the feature extraction besides illumination normalization. However, the performance will be degraded if we further extract LTP on GradientFaces.

Table 1. Face recognition rates and EERs of different methods

Methods	Recognition rates		EERs	
	Controlled images	Uncontrolled images	Controlled images	Uncontrolled images
LTV	60.6364	36.0000	0.1609	0.2336
WeberFace	64.7273	38.0909	0.1655	0.2200
Gradient	**92.3636**	56.7273	0.0555	0.2127
LOG-DCT	68.4545	45.4545	0.1245	0.2427
PP	68.4545	44.3636	0.1427	0.1873
SQI	60.5455	38.0909	0.1745	0.2218
LTP	88.0909	53.1818	0.0709	0.2245
LTV+LTP	58.5455	21.3636	0.1973	0.3309
WeberFace+LTP	77.7273	50.2727	0.1382	0.1991
GradientFace+LTP	87.2727	**87.2727**	**0.0645**	0.1945
LOG-DCT+LTP	69.1818	38.2727	0.1736	0.2500
PP+LTP	89.4545	65.1818	**0.0645**	**0.1509**
SQI+LTP	58.5455	24.5455	0.2082	0.3091

The operators like SQI, LTV, WeberFace, and LOG-DCT actually extract the small-scale features (high-frequency component or middle-frequency component) of the face images as the illumination insensitive representation. Such a preprocessing discard the low-frequency component of the images, which will necessarily leads to the lack of recognition information [4]. High-frequency component of images mainly record the linear features (e.g., the contour of eyes and mouths), so even a tiny variation of pose and expression will affect the alignment between features, which further affects the recognition performance. On the other hand, low-frequency component of images mainly represent the illumination. Since illumination is slow-varying, the low-frequency component maintains certain robustness for the alignment between features. Therefore, though SQI, LTV, WeberFace, and LOG-DCT perform well for face recognition in Yale B [11] and CMU-PIE [35] face databases[1] according to the experimental reports from their source literatures, the performance on the FRGC 2.0 is largely degraded.

As a local feature operator, LTB/LTP describes the gray gradient between a certain pixel and its neighbor pixels. However, distinctive from ordinary gradient operators, LBP/LTP is also a statistical operator because it adopts binary encoding and histogram measure. So, LBP/LTP has the trait of translation invariant and rotation invariant. Those traits guarantee certain the robustness of LTP to illumination, posture and expression. However, under the illumination with sharp variations, even the local gray gradients are still chanced, thus it is hard to extract stable features relying only on LBP/LTP. For this reason, the LTP doesn't obtain a good recognition on uncontrolled images, and an illumination preprocessing is necessary.

LTV, WeberFace, LOG-DCT, and SQI are all effective to eliminate the illumination, unfortunately, also discard too much low-frequency component. Therefore, the LTP following these preprocessing cannot capture enough facial features, leading to weaker performances comparing to using LTP on the original images. Nevertheless, PP achieves outstanding performance in spite that it's only composed of some simple gray rectification algorithms. For the subset of controlled images, PP+LTP's performance is quite close to GradientFace. More than that, for the subset of uncontrolled images in which the illumination varies sharply, PP+LTP's performance even exceed GradientFace.

In conclusion, under the condition of varying illumination with subtle changes of posture and expression, the **"two-step"** framework (appropriate preprocessing for illumination + feature extraction) could be the most effective method for face recognition. In the first preprocessing step, it is best not to completely remove illumination effects by discarding too much low-frequency components of the face images. In the second step, the used feature descriptor must be robust to the sober variations in illumination, posture and expression.

---

[1] In CMU-PIE and Yale B face databases, the images from the same identity on a same pose but under different lighting conditions were captured among a period shorter than 3 seconds, which leads to a strictly alignment (without posture or expression change) for the face images of the same person.

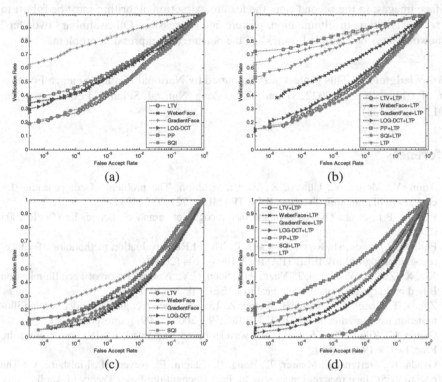

Fig. 3. ROC curves: (a) preprocessing methods on controlled images; (b) preprocessing plus feature extraction methods on controlled images; (c) preprocessing methods on uncontrolled images; and (d) preprocessing plus feature extraction methods on uncontrolled images.

5 Conclusion

The approaches to addressing the illumination variation problem in the single image-based face recognition have been reviewed in this paper. Some representative technologies and the cooperation between them have been investigated in depth. Among existing methods, the extraction of small-scale features (high-frequency components) of face images is a good approach to get an illumination-insensitive representation. One drawback of such an approach is that using only the high-frequency component causes a stricter requirement for face alignment. Furthermore, discarding the low-frequency components may make some useful identity information lost. Another situation is that the existing facial descriptors (e.g., LBP and Gabor) are robust to subtle variations in lighting, pose, and expression, but are still seriously affected by large variations in these factors.

According to our investigation, the "two-step" framework, including an appropriate illumination preprocessing and a facial feature extraction, is suggested for capturing the effect face representation in face recognition under varying illumination. In the first step, it is best to reserve a balanced amount of low-frequency components of the face images. In the second step, the feature extraction algorithm must be robust to the sober variations in illumination, posture and expression. Other similar "two-step" frameworks may be suitable for tackling the posture and expression problem.

Acknowledgments. This project was supported by National Natural Science Foundation of China (No. 61202223) and Guangdong Natural Science Foundation (No. S2011040000433).

References

1. Adini, Y., Moses, Y., Ullman, S.: Face recognition: The problem of compensating for changes in illumination direction. IEEE TPAMI 19, 721–732 (1997)
2. Phillips, P.J., et al.: Overview of the face recognition grand challenge. In: CVPR 2005 (2005)
3. Phillips, P., Moon, H., Rizvi, S., Rauss, P.: The FERET evaluation methodology for face-recognition algorithms. IEEE TPAMI 22, 1090–1104 (2000)
4. Xie, X., Zheng, W.-S., Lai, J., Yuen, P.C., Suen, C.Y.: Normalization of Face Illumination Based on Large-and Small-Scale Features. IEEE TIP 20 (2011)
5. Zhang, T., Tang, Y.Y., Fang, B., Shang, Z., Liu, X.: Face recognition under varying illumination using gradientfaces. IEEE TIP 18, 2599–2606 (2009) (correspondence)
6. Garcia, C., Zikos, G., Tziritas, G.: A wavelet-based framework for face recognition. In: Proc. ECCV 1998 (1998)
7. Okada, K., Steffens, J., Maurer, T., Hong, H., Elagin, E., Neven, H., Malsburg, C.: The bochum/USC face recognition system. In: Face Recogntion: From Theory to Applications, pp. 186–205. Springer, Berlin (1998)
8. Hafed, Z., Levine, M.: Face recognition using the discrete cosine transform. Int. J. Comput. Vis. 43, 167–188 (2001)
9. Lai, J., Yuen, P.C., Feng, G.: Face recognition using holistic Fourier invariant features. Pattern Recognition 34, 95–109 (2001)
10. Liu, C.-C., Dai, D.-Q.: Face recognition using dual-tree complex wavelet features. IEEE TIP 18, 2593–2599 (2009)
11. Georghiades, A., Belhumeur, P., Kriegman, D.: From few to many: Illumination cone models for recognition under variable lighting and pose. IEEE TPAMI 23, 643–660 (2001)
12. Shashua, A., Riklin-Raviv, T.: The quotient image: Class-based re-rendering and recognition with varying illuminations. IEEE TPAMI 23, 129–139 (2001)
13. Basri, R., Jacobs, D.: Lambertian reflectance and linear subspaces. IEEE TPAMI 25, 218–233 (2003)
14. Land, E.H., McCann, J.J.: Lightness and retinex theory. J. Opt. Soc. Amer. 61, 1–11 (1971)
15. Jorstad, A., Jacobs, D., Trouvé, A.: A Deformation and Lighting Insensitive Metric for Face Recognition Based on Dense Correspondences. In: CVPR 2011 (2011)
16. Blanz, V., Vetter, T.: Face recognition based on fitting a 3D morphable model. IEEE TPAMI 25, 1063–1074 (2003)
17. Zhao, W., Chellappa, R.: Symmetric shape-from-shading using self-ratio image. In: Proc. ICCV 2001 (2001)
18. Xie, X., Lam, K.: Face recognition under varying illumination based on a 2D face shape model. Pattern Recognition 38, 221–230 (2005)

19. Choi, S., Kim, C., Choi, C.-H.: Shadow compensation in 2D images for face recognition. Pattern Recognition 40, 2118–2125 (2007)
20. Chen, W., Er, M., Wu, S.: Illumination compensation and normalization for robust face recognition using discrete cosine transform in logarithm domain. IEEE Trans. Syst., Man, Cybern. B. Cybern. 36, 458–466 (2006)
21. Shashua, A., Riklin-Raviv, T.: The quotient image: Class-based re-rendering and recognition with varying illuminations. IEEE TPAMI 23, 129–139 (2001)
22. Zhang, L., Wang, S., Samaras, D.: Face synthesis and recognition under arbitrary unknown lighting using a spherical harmonic basis morphable model. In: CVPR 2005 (2005)
23. Lee, J., Moghaddam, B., Pfister, H., Machiraju, R.: A bilinear illumination model for robust face recognition. In: ICCV 2005 (2005)
24. Qing, L., Shan, S., Gao, W., Du Face, B.: recognition under generic illumination based on harmonic relighting. Int. J. Pattern Recognit. Artif. Intell. 19, 513–531 (2005)
25. Shim, H., Luo, J., Chen, T.: A subspace model-based approach to face relighting under unknown lighting and poses. IEEE TIP 17, 1331–1341 (2008)
26. Chen, T., Yin, W., Zhou, X., Comaniciu, D., Huang, T.S.: Total variation models for variable lighting face recognition. IEEE TPAMI 28, 1519–1524 (2006)
27. Wang, B., Li, W., Yang, W., Liao, Q.: Illumination Normalization Based on Weber's Law with Application to Face Recognition. IEEE Signal Processing Letter 18, 462–465 (2011)
28. Tan, X., Triggs, B.: Enhanced local texture feature sets for face recognition under difficult lighting conditions. IEEE TIP 19, 1635–1650 (2010)
29. Wang, H., Li, S.Z., Wang, Y., Zhang, J.: Self quotient image for face recognition. In: Image Processing, ICIP 2004 (2004)
30. Xie, X., Lai, J., Zheng, W.-S.: Extraction of Illumination Invariant Facial Features from a Single Image Using Nonsubsampled Contourlet Transform. Pattern Recognition 43, 4177–4189 (2010)
31. Zhang, T., Fang, B., Yuan, Y., Tang, Y., Shang, Z., Li, D., Lang, F.: Multiscale facial structure representation for face recognition under varying illumination. Pattern Recognition 42, 251–258 (2009)
32. Xuan, Z., Kittler, J., Messer, K.: Illumination Invariant Face Recognition: A Survey. In: IEEE International Conference on Biometrics: Theory, Applications, and Systems (2007)
33. Ahonen, T., Hadid, A., Pietikainen, M.: Face description with local binary patterns: Application to face recognition. IEEE TPAMI 28(12) (2006)
34. Phillips, P.J., et al.: Overview of the face recognition grand challenge. In: CVPR 2005 (2005)
35. Sim, T., Baker, S., Bsat, M.: The CMU Pose, Illumination, and Expression (PIE) Database. In: Proc. Conf. Automatic Face and Gesture Recognition, Washington (2002)
36. Amirhosein, N., Esam, A.-R., Majid, A.: Illumination invariant feature extraction and mutual-information-based local matching for face recognition under illumination variation and occlusion. Pattern Recognition 44, 2576–2587 (2011)
37. Chen, L.-H., Yang, Y.-H., Chen, C.-S., Cheng, M.-Y.: Illumination Invariant Feature Extraction Based on Natural Images Statistics – Taking Face Images as An Example. In: CVPR 2011 (2011)
38. Schroff, F., Treibitz, T., Kriegman, D.J., Belongie, S.: Pose, illumination and expression invariant pairwise face-similarity measure via Doppelgänger list comparison. In: ICCV 2011 (2011)

Weighted Group Sparse Representation
Based on Robust Regression for Face Recognition

Xin Tang[1] and Guocan Feng[1,*]

School of Mathematics and Computational Science,
Sun Yat-sen University, 510275, Guangzhou, China
tangxint@gmail.com,
mcsfgc@mail.sysu.edu.cn

Abstract. Recently, sparse representations have attracted a lot of attention. In this paper, we present a novel group sparse representation based on robust regression approach (GSRR) by modeling the sparse coding as group sparse constrained robust regression problem. Unlike traditional group sparse representation, we propose a weighted group sparse penalty which integrates similarity between the test sample and distinct classes and data locality. An efficient iteratively reweighted sparse coding algorithm is proposed to solve the GSRR model. The proposed classification algorithm has been evaluated on three publicly available face databases under varying illuminations and poses. The experimental results demonstrate that the performance of our algorithm is better than that of the state of the art methods.

Keywords: Group sparsity, face recognition, robust regression, sparse representation.

1 Introduction

Face recognition is a very active research field in biometrics in recent twenty years. Although current face recognition algorithms are proved effective under controlled conditions, constructing robust face recognition techniques to handle occlusion, pose, illumination, and expression variations is still an open and challenging problem.

The sparse representation based method [9], which aims to recovering the sparse linear representation of any test sample with respect to a set of training samples, has been successfully employed for various vision applications such as face recognition [10] [15] [5] [3] [1], general image classification [15] [8]. Wright *et al* [10] proposed the sparse representation classification (SRC) scheme, which achieves impressive face recognition performance. The ℓ_1 norm based approach leads to sparse models, but it does not take into account any prior information about the structure of training samples. When the training samples and the test samples are organized as groups, group sparse representation based methods [15] [14] [11] [1] impose the $\ell_{2,1}$ mixed-norm penalty on the reconstruction coefficients.

---

*Corresponding author.

W.-S. Zheng et al. (Eds.): CCBR 2012, LNCS 7701, pp. 42–49, 2012.

In SRC, the representation fidelity is measured by ℓ_2-norm of coding residual. Such a sparse coding model actually assumes that the coding residual follows Gaussian distribution, which may not be accurate enough to describe the coding error in practice. Yang proposed a robust sparse coding model (RSC) [13] and an effectively reweighted sparse coding for RSC. The RSC seeks for the maximum likelihood estimation solution of the sparse coding problem, and it is much more robust to outliers (e.g., occlusions, corruptions, etc). He *et al* presented a sparse correntropy framework for computing robust sparse representation of face images for recognition [5]. In [6], Naseem *et al* developed a linear model representing a probe image as a linear combination of class-specific galleries and proposed an efficient linear regression based classification (LRC) for face recognition. The recent work locality-constrained linear coding (LLC)[8] has shown that the image classification performance can be improved by enforcing the sparsity and locality.

In this work, we propose a novel weighted group sparse representation based on robust regression theory. As we known, the prior information is important for classification. Inspired by [11],our method explicitly incorporate reconstruction error of the test sample approximated by the linear combination of class-specific training samples, group sparsity and data locality into robust regression problem. In our framework, our goal is to find a representation of a test sample that uses the training samples which not only close to the test sample but also have high similarity between the test sample and the classes of them. The representation of the test sample is sparsity at class level. Compared with group sparsity methods, such as [1] [15], our group sparsity method combines data locality and class locality. Furthermore, experiments confirm that our method is robust to pose and illumination variations.

2 Related Works

Suppose that we have c classes of subjects, and let $X = [X_1, X_2, \ldots, X_c] \in R^{m \times n}$ be the set of original training samples, where $X_i = [x_{i1}, x_{i2}, \ldots, x_{in_i}] \in R^{m \times n_i}$ is the sub-set of the training samples from class i. Here n_i is the number of training samples in class i, and $\sum_{i=1}^{c} n_i = n$ is the total number of training samples. Given a test sample $y \in R^m$.

2.1 Sparse Coding for Image Representation

Wright *et al.* [10] proposed the sparse representation based classification (SRC) method for robust face recognition. The SRC minimizes the image reconstruction error with a ℓ_1-norm regularizer, i.e.

$$\min_{\beta} ||y - X\beta||^2 + \lambda||\beta||_1. \tag{1}$$

Wang *et al.* [8] proposed a locality-constrained linear coding algorithm. Unlike the sparse coding, LLC enforces locality instead of sparsity. Specifically, the LLC code uses the following criteria:

$$\min_{\beta} ||y - X\beta||^2 + \lambda||d \odot \beta||_2^2 \quad s.t. \quad 1^T\beta = 1. \tag{2}$$

where $\odot$ denotes element-wise multiplication and d measures the similarity between the query sample and all the reference samples.

3   Group Sparse Representation Based on Robust Regression

3.1   The Problem of Robust Estimation

Consider a linear model

$$y = X\beta + e. \tag{3}$$

In classical statistics the error term e is taken as a zero-mean Gaussian noise. A traditional method to optimize the regression is the least squares problem

$$\arg\min_{\beta} \sum_{j=1}^{m} r_j^2, \tag{4}$$

where $r = y - X\beta$, r_j is the jth component of the residual vector r. Linear least squares estimates can be behave badly when the error distribution is not normal. In this situation, robust methods are to be preferred.

The most common method of robust regression is M-estimation. M-estimators have shown superiority due to their generality and high breakdown point. Primarily M-estimators are based on minimizing a function of residuals

$$\arg\min_{\beta} \sum_{j=1}^{m} \rho(r_j), \tag{5}$$

where $\rho(r)$ is a symmetric function with a unique minimum at zero. In this paper, we consider the bisquare function, i.e.,

$$\rho(r) = \begin{cases} \frac{k^2}{6}\{1 - [1 - (\frac{e}{k})^2]^3\} & \text{for } |e| \le k \\ \frac{k^2}{6} & \text{for } |e| > k \end{cases} \tag{6}$$

k is a positive tuning threshold. Such threshold k adaptively controls the objective function's behavior to differently penalize small and large residuals. Fig. 1 shows bisquare function and weight function. From Fig. 1, we known that the weights for the bisquare function decline as soon as e departs from 0, and are 0 for $|e| > k$. Solving the robust estimation problem is equivalent to a weighted least-squares problem [4].

3.2   GSRR Algorithm

Although SRC in (1) produces a sparse coefficient vector β, it might reconstruct a test sample by training samples from distinct subjects. Recently, the group sparse representation based method has been widely adopted in computer vision [15] [11]. Group sparse representation methods impose the $\ell_{2,1}$ mixed-norm penalty on the reconstruction coefficients such that only a limited number of groups in the training set would

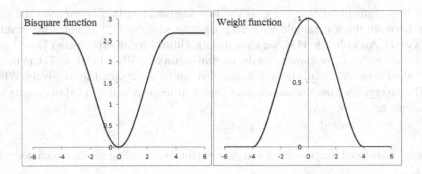

Fig. 1. Bisquare function and weight function

be chosen. To further promote group selection we consider the following weighted $\ell_{2,1}$ regularization

$$\min_{\beta} \sum_{j=1}^{m} \rho(y_j - X^j \beta) + \lambda \sum_{i=1}^{c} ||d_i \odot \beta_i||_2, \qquad (7)$$

where $\rho(\cdot)$ is bisquare function in (6), which is robust to outliers. $X = [X^1; X^2; \cdots ; X^m]$ is training set and each row vector X^j represents the jth row of X. $\beta = [\beta_1; \beta_2; \cdots ; \beta_c] = [\beta_{11}, \beta_{12}, ..., \beta_{cn_c}]^T \in R^{n \times 1}$, $\beta_i = [\beta_{i1}, \beta_{i2}, \cdots , \beta_{in_i}]^T \in R^{n_i \times 1}$ is the coefficient vector of X_i. In equation (7), $d_i = [d_{i1}, d_{i2}, ..., d_{in_i}]^T$ is the similarity vector between the training samples of the i-th class and the test sample y. The definition of $\{d_{ik}\}_{k=1}^{n_i}$ is

$$d_{ik} = exp(\frac{r_i - r_{min}}{\sigma_1}) exp(\frac{||y - x_{ik}||}{\sigma_2}), \qquad (8)$$

where σ_1 and σ_2 are the bandwidth parameters and $r_i = ||y - X_i \beta_i^*||$, $\beta_i^* = \arg\min_{\beta_i} ||y - X_i \beta_i||_2^2$. Clearly, r_i measures the distance between the test sample y and the training samples of the ith class. r_{min} denotes the minimum reconstruction error of $\{r_i\}_{i=1}^{c}$.

Integrating group sparsity, locality constraints and linear reconstruction error of test sample approximated by class-specific training samples, our GSRR representation preserves the similarity between the test input and its neighboring training data and the similarity with distinct subjects.

3.3   Optimization for GSRR and the Classification Rule

We can note that the second term in (7) is a weighted $\ell_{2,1}$ norm regularization. As shown in Appendix A, the minimization problem in (7) is equivalent to the following problem:

$$\min_{\beta} \sum_{j=1}^{m} \rho(y_j - X^j D^{-1} \beta) + \lambda \sum_{i=1}^{c} ||\beta_i||_2, \qquad (9)$$

where $D = diag([d_1; d_2; ...; d_c]) \in R^{n \times n}$ is a diagonal matrix. D represents the similarity between the test sample with each training sample. D^{-1} denotes the inverse matrix of D. According to [13], we have the algorithm 1 to solve problem (7).

From algorithm 1, we known that the minimization of GSRR model in (7) can be accomplished iteratively, while in each iteration W and β are updated alternatively. When GSRR converges, we use the same classification strategy as in RSC [13] to classify the test sample y:

$$identity(y) = \arg \min_{i \in \{1,...,c\}} ||W^{\frac{1}{2}}(y - X_i \beta_i)||_2,$$

where W is the final weight matrix and β_i is the final sub-coding vector associated with class i.

W represents the reliability of each dimension of the test sample. From weight function in Figure 1, we known that if the reconstruction error exceeds the threshold k, the outlier will be assigned small weight and thus less affects the solution of (7). Meanwhile, if some training sample is similar to the test sample, the coefficient of this training sample will be large.

Algorithm 1: GSRR Algorithm

- **Input:**   Training set $X = [X_1, X_2, ..., X_c]$; parameters $\sigma_1, \sigma_2, \lambda$; test sample y.
- **Output:** W, β.
    1. Compute similarity matrix D.
    2. Initialize $\beta = \beta^0$.
    3. Start from $t = 1$:
        1) Compute residual $r^t = y - X\beta^t$.
        2) Estimate weight as, (refer [5])

        $$W_t(r_j^t)^* = \begin{cases} [1 - (\frac{r_j^t}{k})^2]^2, & |r_j^t| \le k \\ 0, & |r_j^t| > k \end{cases}, \quad j = 1, 2, ..., m$$

        where $k = 4.685\bar{\sigma}$, $\bar{\sigma} = MAR/0.6745$, $MAR = median(r^t)$.
        3) Weighted regularized robust coding:

        $$\beta^t = \text{argmin}_\beta \left\| W_t^{-\frac{1}{2}}(y - XD^{-1}\beta) \right\|_2^2 + \lambda \sum_{i=1}^{c} ||\beta_i||_2$$

        4) Go back to step 1 untill the condition of convergence is met, or the maximal number of iteration is reached.
    4. Compute $\beta = D^{-1}\beta^t$, $W = W_t$.

---

* Fig. 1 shows the weight function $W_t(r)$ (right figure).

4   Experiments

In the proposed GSRR, there are three parameters, i.e., $\lambda, \sigma_1, \sigma_2$. We empirically set the parameter $\lambda = 0.001$, set the bandwidth parameter $\sigma_1 = \{1/2^7, 1/2^6, ..., 2\}, \sigma_2 = \{1/2^7, 1/2^6, ..., 2\}$.

1) ORL Database: The ORL database [7] contains 10 different images of 40 distinct subjects. The face images were taken at varying the lighting, facial expressions. We randomly select $l(l=3, 4, 5, 6$ and 7) samples of each individual for training, and the remaining ones are used for testing. In the experiments, each face image is projected onto a 100-dimensional vector using PCA. Fig. 2(a) shows the recognition rates of LRC, SRC, RSC, LLC, GSRR under the number of training samples from 3 to 7. RSC outperforms SRC and LRC due to reweighted each dimension of the test sample. GSRR regards locality constraints and linear reconstruction error of test sample approximated by class-specific training samples as prior information and incorporates them. We consider the label of each training sample and can see that GSRR achieves better results than the other methods in all situations.

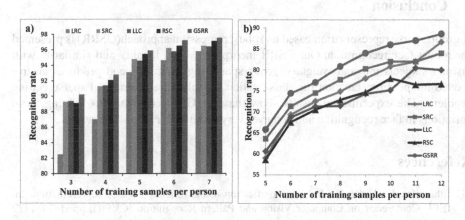

Fig. 2. Recognition rates on databases. a) ORL, b) GT.

2) Extended Yale B database: Extended Yale B database [2] consists of 2,414 frontal face images of 38 subjects under various lighting conditions. The database was divided in five subsets [6]. All experiments are conducted with images down-sampled to 20×20. Table 1 lists the detailed recognition rates of LRC, LLC, SRC, RSC and GSRR under the different lighting conditions. All algorithms showed excellent performance for moderate light variations, i.e., subsets 2 and 3. The performance of all algorithms, however, has experienced a sharp fall in recognition rate for severe light variations, i.e., subsets 4 and 5. LRC approach has shown better tolerance for considerable illumination variations compared to SRC, LLC and RSC. Certainly, GSRR shows the best result.

Table 1. Classification accuracy on Extended Yale B database

Approach	Subset2	Subset3	Subset4	Subset5
LRC	100	100	82.32	34.45
SRC	100	100	69.01	23.95
LLC	100	99.56	57.41	18.35
RSC	100	100	71.48	23.25
GSRR	100	100	82.32	55.46

3) Georgia Tech Database: The Georgia Tech database* consists of 50 subjects with 15 images per subject. It characterizes several variations such as pose, expression, cluttered background, and illumination. Images were resized to 15×15. The first $l(l = 5, 6, ..., 12)$ images of each subject were used for training, while the remaining served as testing samples. Fig. 2(b) shows the results of all algorithms under different number of training samples. the performance of RSC is not good. However, LRC reveals a number of interesting outcomes. That means the knowledge of the structure of the training sample is important. Obviously, GSRR outperforms other methods.

5   Conclusion

A group sparse representation based on robust regression approach(GSRR) is presented for robust face recognition. Our GSRR incorporates data locality and similarity with distinct subjects into our weighted group sparse regularization and produces an improved image representation for classification by solving a reweigthed sparse coding problem. The experimental results show that our GSRR is robust to lighting, pose variations in face recognition and achieves very promising recognition results.

References

1. Elhamifar, E., Vidal, R.: Robust classification using structured sparse representation. In: IEEE Conference on Computer Vision and Pattern Recognition (CVPR), pp. 1873–1879 (2011)
2. Georghiades, A., Belhumeur, P., Kriegman, D.: From few to many: Illumination cone models for face recognition under variable lighting and pose. IEEE Transactions on Pattern Analysis and Machine Intelligence 23(6), 643–660 (2001)
3. He, R., Hu, B., Zheng, W., Guo, Y.: Two-stage sparse representation for robust recognition on large-scale database. In: Twenty-Fourth AAAI Conference on Artificial Intelligence (2010)
4. Rousseeuw, P., Leroy, A., Wiley, J.: Robust regression and outlier detection, vol. 3. Wiley Online Library (1987)
5. He, R., Zheng, W., Hu, B.: Maximum correntropy criterion for robust face recognition. IEEE Transactions on Pattern Analysis and Machine Intelligence 33(8), 1561–1576 (2011)
6. Naseem, I., Togneri, R., Bennamoun, M.: Linear regression for face recognition. IEEE Transactions on Pattern Analysis and Machine Intelligence 32(11), 2106–2112 (2010)
7. Samaria, F., Harter, A.: Parameterisation of a stochastic model for human face identification. In: Proceedings of the Second IEEE Workshop on Applications of Computer Vision, pp. 138–142 (1994)
8. Wang, J., Yang, J., Yu, K., Lv, F., Huang, T., Gong, Y.: Locality-constrained linear coding for image classification. In: IEEE Conference on Computer Vision and Pattern Recognition (CVPR), pp. 3360–3367 (2010)
9. Wright, J., Ma, Y., Mairal, J., Sapiro, G., Huang, T., Yan, S.: Sparse representation for computer vision and pattern recognition. Proceedings of the IEEE 98(6), 1031–1044 (2010)
10. Wright, J., Yang, A., Ganesh, A., Sastry, S., Ma, Y.: Robust face recognition via sparse representation. IEEE Transactions on Pattern Analysis and Machine Intelligence 31(2), 210–227 (2009)

---

*http://www.anefian.com/research/face_reco.htm.

11. Xu, D., Huang, Y., Zeng, Z., Xu, X.: Human gait recognition using patch distribution feature and locality-constrained group sparse representation. IEEE Transactions on Image Processing 21(1), 316–326 (2012)
12. Yang, J., Yu, K., Gong, Y., Huang, T.: Linear spatial pyramid matching using sparse coding for image classification. In: IEEE Conference on Computer Vision and Pattern Recognition (CVPR), pp. 1794–1801 (2009)
13. Yang, M., Zhang, L., Yang, J., Zhang, D.: Robust sparse coding for face recognition. In: IEEE Conference on Computer Vision and Pattern Recognition (CVPR), pp. 625–632 (2011)
14. Yuan, M., Lin, Y.: Model selection and estimation in regression with grouped variables. Journal of the Royal Statistical Society: Series B (Statistical Methodology) 68(1), 49–67 (2006)
15. Yuan, X., Yan, S.: Visual classification with multi-task joint sparse representation. In: IEEE Conference on Computer Vision and Pattern Recognition (CVPR), pp. 3493–3500 (2010)

A Appendix: $\ell_{2,1}$-Norm and Weight $\ell_{2,1}$-Norm

In this appendix, we will prove the equivalence between the two minimization problems (7) and (9).

Let us denote

$$f(\beta) = \sum_{j=1}^{m} \rho(y_j - X^j\beta) + \lambda\|D\beta\|_{2,1}, \qquad (10)$$

which is equivalent to problem (7) and

$$g(\beta) = \sum_{j=1}^{m} \rho(y_j - X^j D^{-1}\beta) + \lambda\|\beta\|_{2,1}. \qquad (11)$$

Obviously, we have $f(\beta) = g(D\beta)$. We define

$$\beta^* = \arg\min_{\beta} f(\beta),$$

$$\beta_0^* = \arg\min_{\beta} g(\beta).$$

Then

$$\beta^* = D^{-1}\beta_0^*.$$

3D Face Pose Estimation Based on Multi-template AAM

Chunsheng Liu, Faliang Chang, and Zhenxue Chen

School of Control Science and Engineering, Shandong University, Ji'nan, China
Liuchunsense@163.com, {flchang,chenzhenxue}@sdu.edu.cn

Abstract. Based on analysis of the pro-existing face pose estimation methods, a new 3D face pose estimation method based on Active Appearance Model(AAM) and T-Structure is proposed. Firstly, a set of multi-view face detection model is established by boosting algorithm to detect multi-view faces. Then, a set of AAM models can be obtained after training different poses faces, and the objective face is matched with the set of AAM models to choose the optimum model to accurate position the key face feature points. Finally, the T structure is built with the two eyes and the mouth, which is used to estimate the face pose. The experiments show that the method can adapt to large rotation angles, and can reach a high accuracy of 3D face pose estimation.

Keywords: Active Appearance Model, face pose estimation, characteristic points location, T-Structure, face detection.

1 Introduction

Face Pose Estimation is an important research direction in the field of pattern recognition and artificial intelligence, which has been widely used in human-computer interaction, virtual reality, and driver fatigue detection systems, and so on. However, due to the 2D features of the image, the face of non-rigid and individual differences factors, to accurately estimate face 3D pose is still challenging.

Over the past decade, many scholars have made contributions to Face Pose Estimation. Takahiro Ishawa etc. [1] restore the face of the 3D model by estimating the 2D AAM model that in the video sequence, and use the 3D model to estimate the face pose. Lis etc. [2] train the multi-pose face subspaces using ICA(Independent Component Analysis) in Face Pose Estimation. Mazumdar etc. [3] establish T-Model for Face Pose Estimation by the centers of two eyebrows and mouth of a face. Li etc. [4] get a sparse 3D shape model from the video, and to constitute a hypersurface with each person's series of 3D shape and texture parameters in the geometric space. Romdhani etc. [5] get the dense three-dimensional data using laser scanner to train the deformation models, and then get the synthesis image to detect 3D pose. Hu etc. [6] use ASM positioning method to establish multi-view model to estimate face 3D poses. Wang etc. [7] achieve a good attitude estimate of Face Pose Estimation with multi-camera arrays.

The analysis of the face pose estimation methods above shows that, in the face pose estimation process, the precise positioning of the facial feature points is critical, and

W.-S. Zheng et al. (Eds.): CCBR 2012, LNCS 7701, pp. 50–57, 2012.

also affects the face pose estimation accuracy. To overcome the shortcomings brought from low accuracy methods, we put forward a novel face pose estimation method based on multi-template AAM [8] and T-structure. Before applying this pose estimation method, the Multi-view face detection method based on boosting is applied to detect multi-view faces. Then, a multi-template AAM set is trained to precisely locate of the feature points. Lastly, the 3D posture estimation of the human face is achieved by calculating T-structure parameters. The experiments results in FERET database [9] prove the effectiveness of the proposed method.

2   Multi-View Face Detection

Multi-view face detection (MVFD) is used to detect upright faces in images that with ±90-degree rotation-out-of-plane (ROP) pose changes and rotation invariant means to detect faces with 360-degree rotation-in-plane (RIP) pose changes. The introduction of boosted cascade face detector by Viola and Jones [10] stimulated great interest in the development of more general systems[11-14]. One of these most effective systems is Huang etc.' MVFD(multi-view face detection) detector [15], which adopt a varietal Boosting algorithm called Vector Boosting and a new cascade to construct a high-performance rotation invariant multi-view face detector, which can achieves a speed of about 10 fps and the rotation invariant MVFD runs at a speed of about 3~4 fps on common video sequences of QVGA size (320×240) .

Multi-view face detection is necessary in 3D pose face estimation, and Viola's face detector is aimed to detect frontal face only, which is invalid to detect multi-view face. So in this paper, Huang's MVFD is used to detect multi-view faces. After detection, the 3D face pose estimation method can be used in the detected faces.

3   3D Face Pose Estimation

The proposed pose estimation process framework can be divided into three parts: (a) Multi-view template AAM training part; (b) face detection and localization part: the MVFD algorithm described in chapter 2 is used to detect multi-view face; (c) AAM template matching and 3D pose estimation: the AAM templates are used for the precise positioning of the key feature points, and then the T-structure of the facial features is established to estimate 3D pose of the face.

3.1   Introduction to AAM

The AAM (Active Appearance Model) [9] is defined by the combination of shape model and texture model. The shape model is the 2D triangulated mesh and in particular the vertex locations of the mesh. Mathematically, the shape s of an AAM as the 2D coordinates of n vertices that make up the mesh: $x = (x_1, y_1, x_2, y_2, \cdots, x_n, y_n)^T$.

Texture model of the AAM is defined within the base mesh, and use the set of pixels inside the base mesh to allow linear shape variation. The model is as shown in equation (1).

$$x = \bar{x} + Q_s c$$
$$G = \bar{g} + Q_g c \tag{1}$$

Where, $\bar{x}$ is the mean shape vector, $\bar{g}$ is the mean texture vector, Q_s and Q_g are variables of the change of shape and texture, and c is the control parameter.

The shape model vector X includes three parameters: scale s, rotation parameter θ, and translation parameter (t_x, t_y). Among these parameters, scale and rotation parameters can be presented as (s_x, s_y): $s_x = s \cdot \cos\theta - 1$, $s_y = s \cdot \sin\theta$. Then, the whole model parameters can be use a vector presentation $t : t = (s_x, s_y, t_x, t_y)^T$. The change of shape can be presented as $S_{t+\delta t}(x)$:

$$S_{t+\delta t}(x) \approx S_t(S_{\delta t}(x)) \tag{2}$$

The texture vector G have two parameters: the scale to control illumination and the translation: $g_{im} = T_{ii}(g) = (u_1 + l)g_{im} + u_2 l$, where u is the texture parameter vector, and the change of the texture can be presented as $T_{u+\delta u}(g)$:

$$T_{u+\delta u}(g) \approx T_u(T_{\delta u}(g)) \tag{3}$$

Fitting a AAM is usually formulated as minimizing the sum of squares difference between the shape model instance and the texture model instance.

$$E(X, X_{gt}) = \frac{1}{n}\sum_{i=1}^{n}\sqrt{(x_i - x_{gt,i})^2 + (y_i - y_{gt,i})^2} \tag{4}$$

Where, $X = (x, y)$ is the fitting result coordinates, $X_{gt} = (x_{gt}, y_{gt})$ is the manual pointing coordinates.

3.2   3D Pose Face Template Training Method

The selection of feature points aims to be able to match the characteristics of the face, and to avoid irrelevant information. In this paper, eyebrows, eyes, nose, mouth, face outline are selected, and provide 68 feature points: a total of 6 feature points in each eyebrow, 5 feature points of each eye, 12 feature points in nose; 19 feature points in mouth; 15 feature points describe the facial contour. The 31th point and the 36th point in the center of the left and right eye, and the 66th point in the center of the mouth are used for 3D pose calculation, and the other feature points are mainly used to assist in positioning the feature points. All points are marked as Figure 1 (a) shown. The triangle split can effectively express facial features as shown in Figure 1 (b).

(a) Manual positioning   (b) Triangle distribution

Fig. 1. Manual positioning and triangle distribution

This paper uses multi-template AAM to position multi-view face feature points, and the training procedure is as follows :

Step 1 : Select and build face sample library for training, the angle ϕ that these different faces changes in the horizontal and vertical meet: $-60° \leq \theta \leq 60°$.

Step 2: Face images in face sample library are divided into nine different attitudes: front, left, right, up, down, left, lower left, upper right, lower right, and the training sample is divided into nine different training sample databases.

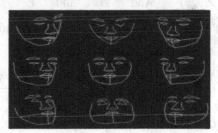

Fig. 2. Multi-view AAM temples

Step3 : Face images in training face sample library have been size normalized, and manual feature points pointed, as in Figure 1 (a) shown.

Step4: The training samples of nine attitudes are trained to get the corresponding attitude of a series of AAM template. When the training is completed, different attitude AAM template set are got, parts of the template are shown in Figure 2.

3.3   Pose Estimation

Face pose detection, also known as face attitude parameter estimates, is mainly approximately calculating the deflection of the face corresponding to the three axes, as shown in Figure 3 (a). In this paper, a T-shaped structure using eyes and mouth is established based on the method in paper[3], as shown in Figure 3 (b).

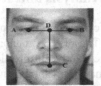

(a) Face Rotation   (b)T-structure

Fig. 3. 3D face pose

Points A and B is respectively the center of left and right eye, corresponds to the 31th point and 36th point in AAM template in Figure 1 (a); C is the center of mouth, corresponding to the 66th in AAM template in Figure 1 (a), D is the prescriptive center of rotation in the calculation of the point man face model.

In this experiment, assume that point A, B, C in the z-axis direction have the same depth $z = Z_{ABC}$, the rotation of point A can be expressed as:

$$\begin{bmatrix} A_x''' \\ A_y''' \\ A_z''' \end{bmatrix} = R_\alpha R_\beta R_\gamma \begin{bmatrix} X_{AD} \\ 0 \\ Z_{ABC} \end{bmatrix} \tag{5}$$

Where, $R = R_\alpha R_\beta R_\gamma$ is the attitude rotation matrix, α is the rotation angle around the x-axis, β is the rotation angle around the y-axis, γ is around the z-axis rotation angle, $A = (X_{AD}, 0, Z_{ABC})^T$ .And B''' and C''' can be obtained by $B = (X_{BD}, 0, Z_{ABC})^T$ and $C = (0, Y_{CD}, Z_{ABC})^T$ .Three rotation angle can be obtained by calculating α, β and γ is:

$$\alpha = \arccos \frac{A_x C_y''' \cos \beta - C_y A_y''' \cos \gamma}{A_x C_y \cos \gamma \sin \beta} \tag{6}$$

$$\beta = \arccos(A''' / A_x \cos \gamma) \tag{7}$$

$$\gamma = \arcsin \frac{C_x'''}{C_y} \tag{8}$$

The A_y''' and C_y''' in (3) is calculated as follows:

$$A_y''' = (A_x \cos \beta \sin \gamma) \cos \alpha - (A_x \sin \beta) \sin \alpha \tag{9}$$

$$C_y''' = (C_y \cos \gamma) \cos \alpha \tag{10}$$

By calculating formula (6) (7) (8) can get the rotation angle of the 3D human face posture. α, β and γ are the representative face rotation angle around the x-axis y-axis and z-axis respectively.

4   Experiments Analysis and Results

In order to verify the effectiveness of the proposed algorithm, the FERET database is used in this experiment. The FERET database contains 14051 face images with views ranging from frontal to left and right profiles, which can effectively judge the performance of the pose estimation methods. In this database, nine different view angles denoted as β ($\beta = 0°, \pm15°, \pm25°, \pm40°, \pm60°$) are chosen in this experiment, and different view faces are used to judge the accuracy of the proposed algorithm.

Experimental results are mainly reflected in two aspects: First, to test the location effects of the multi-view AAM template set; Second, to test the 3D attitude estimation error of the proposed method. The traditional AAM template is used as a comparison. The comparison of the key features location effects in multi-view face is tested, and the accuracy of the distribution of feature points is shown in Figure 4.

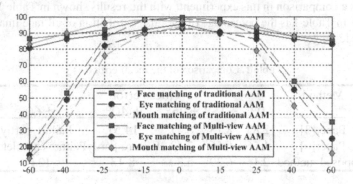

Fig. 4. Matching accuracy of the face features

It can be seen that the traditional AAM template in large angle views fail radically, while our multi-view AAM templates still have very good positioning accuracy.

After key points positioning, the T structure is used to calculate the estimated view of the input face, with the result form as (α, β, γ). Parts of the detected faces are shown in Figure 5.

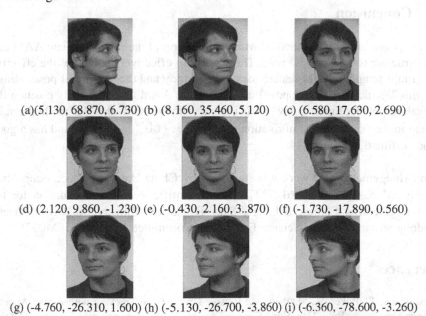

(a)(5.130, 68.870, 6.730) (b) (8.160, 35.460, 5.120)   (c) (6.580, 17.630, 2.690)

(d) (2.120, 9.860, -1.230) (e) (-0.430, 2.160, 3..870)   (f) (-1.730, -17.890, 0.560)

(g) (-4.760, -26.310, 1.600) (h) (-5.130, -26.700, -3.860) (i) (-6.360, -78.600, -3.260)

Fig. 5. Part of estimation results

In 3D view estimation experiments, the β angle around the Y axis is used to evaluate the accuracy of the method. Suppose that the face angles provided by FERET face database have zero error. And if the difference between calculated angles and provided angles is within the range from $-10°$ to $+10°$, the estimation is judged as correct. The method just use T structure [3] and the method of ASM feature location [6] are used as a comparison in this experiment, with the results shown in Table 1. And the mean error in Table 1 is the percentage of the false estimation of all face images in the certain angle range.

Table 1. Comparison of the mean error (%)

Method	Mean error(%)				
	$0°$	$\pm15°$	$\pm25°$	$\pm40°$	$\pm60°$
Paper[3]	2.83	8.13	8.47	14.51	Failure partly
Paper[6]	1.56	6.56	7.53	Failure partly	Failure completely
Proposed method	2.16	6.39	5.30	8.13	12.68

According to results in Table 1, the proposed method can adapt to large angle views, and can achieve 3D pose estimation with low error. When the rotation angle β is $\pm40°$, the methods of [3] and [6] begin to fail partly, and when the angle β is $\pm60°$, these methods fail completely, while the proposed method still has relatively high estimation accuracy.

5   Conclusion

This paper presents a novel method with combination of the multi-template AAM and the T-structure to estimate 3D pose. This algorithm effectively combines the effective of the multi-template AAM feature location accuracy and the validity of pose estimation with T-structure. The proposed multi-template AAM can effectively position the key feature points of multi-view faces. The experiments show that this method can be adapted to the posture angle of rotation range from $-60°$ to $+60°$, and has a good attitude estimation accuracy.

Acknowledgement. This work was supported by China Natural Science Foundation Committee(No. 60975025, 61273277), the Scientific Research Foundation for the Returned Overseas Chinese Scholars, State Education Ministry(No.20101174) and Shandong province Natural Science Foundation Committee(No.ZR2011FM032).

References

1. Ishikawa, T., Baker, S., Matthews, I.: Passive Driver Gaze Tracking with Active Appearance Models. In: Proc. 11th World Congress on Intelligent Transportation Systems (October 2004)

2. Li, S., Lu, X., Hou, X.: Learning multi-view face subspaces and facial pose estimation usingindependent component analysis. IEEE Trans. on Image Process 14(6), 705–712 (2005)
3. Yilmaz, A., Shah, M.A.: Automatic Feature Detection and Pose Recovery for Faces. In: The 5th Asian Conference on Computer Vision (2002)
4. Li, Y., Gong, S., Liddell, H.: Recognising trajectories of facial identities using kernel discriminant analysis. Image and Vision Computing 21(13-14), 1077–1086 (2008)
5. Romdhani, S., Blanz, V., Vetter, T.: Face Identification by Fitting a 3D Morphable Model Using Linear Shape and Texture Error Functions. In: Heyden, A., Sparr, G., Nielsen, M., Johansen, P. (eds.) ECCV 2002, Part IV. LNCS, vol. 2353, pp. 3–19. Springer, Heidelberg (2002)
6. Hu, B., Qiu, L.: 3D Face Pose Estimation Based on Multi-points Model. Journal of Image and Graphics 7(13), 1353–1358 (2008)
7. Lei, W., Chao, H., Jie, W.: Multi-camera face gesture recognition. Journal of Computer Applications 30(12), 3307–3310 (2010)
8. Phillips, P.J., Moon, H., Rizvi, S.A., Rauss, P.J.: The FERET Evaluation Methodology for Face Recognition Algorithms. IEEE Trans. on Pattern Analysis and Machine Intelligence 22, 1090–1104 (2000)
9. Edwards, G.J., Lanitis, A., Taylor, C.J., Cootes, T.F.: Statistical Models of Face Images—Improving Specificity. Image Vision Computing 16(3), 203–211 (1998)
10. Viola, P., Jones, M.: Rapid object detection using a boosted cascade of simple features. In: IEEE Conf. on Computer Vision and Pattern Recognition, pp. 511–518 (2001)
11. Mita, T., Kaneko, T., Hori, O.: Joint Haar-Like Features for Face Detection. In: Proc. 10th IEEE Int'l Conf. Computer Vision (2005)
12. Lienhart, R., Maydt, J.: An Extended Set of Haar-Like Features for Rapid Object Detection. In: Proc. IEEE Int'l Conf. Image Processing (2002)
13. Baluja, S., Sahami, M., Rowley, H.A.: Efficient Face Orientation Discrimination. In: Proc. IEEE Int'l Conf. Image Processing (2004)
14. Wang, P., Ji, Q.: Learning Discriminant Features for Multi-View Face and Eye Detection. In: Proc. IEEE Conf. Computer Vision and Pattern Recognition (2005)
15. Huang, C., Ai, H.: High-Performance Rotation Invariant Multiview Face Detection. IEEE Trans. on Pattern Analysis and Machine Intelligence 29(4), 671–686 (2007)

3D Aided Face Recognition across Pose Variations

Wuming Zhang[1,2], Di Huang[2], Yunhong Wang[2], and Liming Chen[1]

[1] MI Department, LIRIS, CNRS 5205, Ecole Centrale de Lyon, 69134, Lyon, France
[2] IRIP, School of Computer Science and Engineering, Beihang Univ., 100191, Beijing, China
wuming.zhang@hotmail.com, dhuang@buaa.edu.cn

Abstract. Recently, 3D aided face recognition, concentrating on improving performance of 2D techniques via 3D data, has received increasing attention due to its wide application potential in real condition. In this paper, we present a novel 3D aided face recognition method that can deal with the probe images in different viewpoints. It first estimates the face pose based on the Random Regression Forest, and then rotates the 3D face models in the gallery set to that of the probe pose to generate specific gallery sample for matching, which largely reduces the influence of head pose variations. Experiments are carried out on a subset of the FRGC v1.0 database, and the achieved performance clearly highlights the effectiveness of the proposed method.

Keywords: Face recognition, pose estimation, random regression forests, LBP.

1 Introduction

Due to its scientific challenges and application potential, machine-based face recognition has always been an active topic in the field of computer vision and pattern recognition [1]. Compared with other biometrics, e.g. fingerprint and iris, recognition based on the face is more in accord with the nature of human; moreover, it can be achieved without physical contact which endues it with an extra important advantage.

In the past several decades, 2D image based face recognition has rapidly developed and a great number of milestone techniques have been proposed and studied, such as PCA [2], LDA [3], ICA [4], FDA [5], EBGM [6], LBP [7], SIFT [8], etc. However, despite the great progress made in this domain, 2D face images do not remain reliable when affected by changes of lighting, pose and expression. Recently, 3D face recognition has emerged as a major solution to deal with the unsolved issues in 2D domain, i.e. lighting and pose variations [9, 10]. Unfortunately, 3D face recognition approaches are currently limited by their high acquisition, registration and computation cost.

More recently, 3D aided face recognition has attracted increasing interests, since it is expected to limit the use of 3D data where it really helps to improve the face recognition accuracy [11], i.e. aiming to handle the problem of illumination and pose in 2D area. For example, based on a generic 3D face model, re-lighting or de-lighting techniques [12] are adopted to reduce the influences caused by lighting variations. While, in this study, we address the problem of pose changes. In order to deal with such an issue, a few attempts have been made. Blanz and Vetter [13] build a statistical model using a set of training data (also named as 3D morphable model) and densely fit it to a

W.-S. Zheng et al. (Eds.): CCBR 2012, LNCS 7701, pp. 58–66, 2012.
© Springer-Verlag Berlin Heidelberg 2012

given facial image for matching, but it generally requires a long convergence process. Toderici et al. [14] first locate some pre-defined key landmarks (eye corners and nose tip etc.) on face images in different poses, and then roughly align them to a frontal 3D model for the recognition step. Nevertheless, to achieve accurate localization in multi-view facial images involves in another tough topic.

In this paper, we propose a novel method for 3D aided face recognition, aiming to improve the tolerance of 2D face recognition against pose variations. It first estimates the face pose status based on Random Regression Forest, and then rotates the 3D face models in the gallery set to the one of the probe pose achieved previously to generate specific gallery samples for the matching step. In contrast to the existing methods that only process probe data for matching, the proposed approach operates on the enrolled data, and thanks to the Random Regression Forest algorithm, pose variations of probe faces are estimated and largely reduced before matching. Experiments are carried out on a subset of the FRGC v1.0 database, and performance clearly highlights the effectiveness of the proposed method.

The rest part of the paper is organized as follows: an overview of the proposed approach is presented in Section 2. Section 3 describes the process of pose estimation in detail, and Section 4 introduces LBP based face recognition. Experimental results are shown and analyzed in Section 5, and Section 6 concludes the paper.

2   Framework Overview and Data Preparation

An entire framework is shown by two flowcharts (in Fig. 1 and Fig. 3), demonstrating the training stage and the test stage respectively.

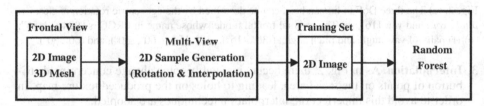

Fig. 1. Framework of training stage

At the training stage, a collection of textured frontal 3D face models, each of which consists of one 3D mesh and its texture counterpart, is required. We select some models from the FRGC v1.0 dataset, and based on our previous work [15], the nose tip of each face can be localized automatically. For the lack of 2D facial images in arbitrary viewpoint, we have to generate samples for training as follows:

1. **Loading.** First of all, we read a face model in the FRGC v1.0 dataset, including its 3D coordinates in real space and its texture information. In addition, we record the position of its nose tip calculated previously.
2. **Rotation**. The rotation of human head runs according to three degrees-of-freedom (DoF), and it can thus be described by three angles, i.e. *yaw*, *pitch* and *roll*, namely egocentric rotation angles [16] as shown in Fig. 2. We then rotate the face model to another viewpoint according to these three angles using rotation matrix defined as:

$$R_x(\theta_x) = \begin{bmatrix} 1 & 0 & 0 \\ 0 & cos\theta_x & -sin\theta_x \\ 0 & sin\theta_x & cos\theta_x \end{bmatrix} = exp \begin{bmatrix} 0 & 0 & 0 \\ 0 & 0 & \theta_x \\ 0 & -\theta_x & 0 \end{bmatrix} \tag{1}$$

$$R_y(\theta_y) = \begin{bmatrix} cos\theta_y & 0 & sin\theta_y \\ 0 & 1 & 0 \\ -sin\theta_y & 0 & cos\theta_y \end{bmatrix} = exp \begin{bmatrix} 0 & 0 & -\theta_y \\ 0 & 0 & 0 \\ \theta_y & 0 & 0 \end{bmatrix} \tag{2}$$

$$R_z(\theta_z) = \begin{bmatrix} cos\theta_z & -sin\theta_z & 0 \\ sin\theta_z & cos\theta_z & 0 \\ 0 & 0 & 1 \end{bmatrix} = exp \begin{bmatrix} 0 & \theta_z & 0 \\ -\theta_z & 0 & 0 \\ 0 & 0 & 0 \end{bmatrix} \tag{3}$$

where θ_x is pitch angle; θ_y is yaw angle; θ_z is roll angle. In our system, we generate diverse angles, with yaw angle from -90° to +90° and pitch angle from -45° to +45°, aiming to cover all possible poses. Some examples are shown in Fig. 3.

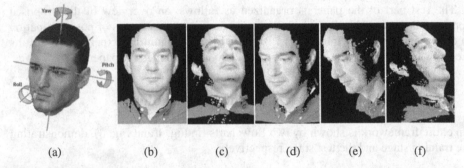

   (a)   (b)   (c)   (d)   (e)   (f)

Fig. 2. (a) The three DoF of human head can be described by the egocentric rotation angles, i.e. *pitch*, *roll*, and *yaw* [16]; (b) The original frontal model whose name in FRGC is "02463d456"; (c)-(f) pairs of yaw angle and pitch angle: (-30°, -15°), (30°, 15°), (-60°, -30°), and (60°, 30°).

3. **Interpolation.** As in Fig. 2, there occurs inevitably some change concerning distribution of points on the facial area, leading to holes on the produced texture map. In order to avoid this imperfection, interpolation techniques are adopted.
4. **Cropping.** For the purpose of reducing calculation burden, we simply crop the face area according to the nose tip position.

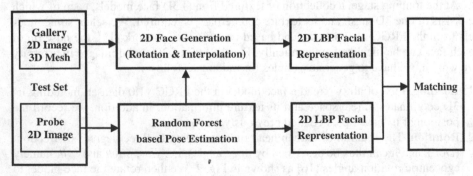

Fig. 3. Framework of test stage

We hence obtain the 2D images with different views to make up of the training set. With the help of random regression forests, we are able to generate a set of regression trees which should be regarded as a classifier for pose estimation.

At the test stage, each probe facial image will be traversed through the random forest pre-trained to estimate the pose status. As its pose is determined, all 3D face models in the gallery set are rotated to generate a facial image under this pose. The identification operates between the original probe face image and the new produced gallery one by comparing their similarity in the LBP feature space.

3   Pose Estimation

3.1   Problem Statement

Head pose variations can incur serious change in the appearance of human faces, and thus introduce a quite difficult problem in the domain of 2D face recognition. Without a proper solution to handle pose changes, even the most sophisticated face recognition systems probably fail. In the framework of the proposed 3D aided face recognition, to a 2D probe facial image, we estimate its pose status. Compared with 3D model based methods, pose estimation based on 2D facial images is a much greater challenge since 3D data are continuously distributed and offer distinctive geometry features.

In literature, there exist several studies on 2D image based pose estimation, which can be roughly categorized into four streams. **Geometry based methods** [17] [18] use the pre-detected facial feature points, such as inner and outer corners of eyes and nose tip, to calculate head pose directly on the basis of the prior knowledge of their relative configuration. Its advantages are their simplicity and rapidness, only a few geometric cues are required and no training process is used; however, their performance highly relies on the feature point detection accuracy. **Model based methods** [19] [20] seek a non-rigid face model which conforms to the facial structure so that it can be fit by the face image, and then head pose estimation can be achieved. These models cost rather low computation and are invariant to head localization error, yet they depend largely on the facial features and they are robust neither to illumination variation nor to far-field head pose estimation. **Manifold embedding methods** [21] [22] hunt for optimal low-dimensional manifolds which can describe the intrinsic pose variations in order to embed the new images into these manifolds and thus estimate their pose. These methods successfully reduce the dimensionality and the computation cost, but it remains a problem separating pose variations from appearance variations, such as identity, scale and illumination. **Learning based methods** [23] [24] aim to map the input image to discrete or continuous head poses by using machine learning tools, for instance, SVM and Neural Networks. It has attracted increasing attention over the last few years for its powerful classification capacity and robustness to appearance variation. The disadvantage of these methods lies in the problem of overfitting, which means the performance is vulnerable to noise in the training data. A proposed remedy to this problem is the application of random regression forests [25] which avoid the influence of noise data by introducing a set of decision trees. It has proved to achieve outstanding performance in 3D head pose estimation [26] [27]. In this paper we further investigate its effectiveness on 2D pose estimation.

3.2   Random Forest

Derived from classification and regression trees, random regression forests have successfully optimized the problem of overfitting by introducing a series of trees at
random while keeping the powerful capacity in handling large datasets.

In our work, all training images with different poses are divided into patches. Each
patch is annotated with a vector $\theta = \{\theta_x, \theta_y, \theta_{yaw}, \theta_{pitch}\}$, here θ_x and θ_y represent
an offset vector pointing from the center of the patch to nose tip, and $\theta_{yaw}, \theta_{pitch}$
record respectively the yaw and pitch angle of image which the patch belongs to.

At the beginning of the training step, a number of patches are randomly selected as
input data for each tree, and at each split node there will be a set of binary tests defined with similar style:

$$|R_1|^{-1} \sum_{q \in R_1} RGB^c(q) - |R_2|^{-1} \sum_{q \in R_2} RGB^c(q) > \tau \tag{4}$$

where R_1 and R_2 are two rectangles randomly selected inside the patch, c is one out
of the three channels R, G or B, $RGB^c(q)$ represents the texture value of pixel q in
channel c, finally τ is a random threshold.

Secondly, it is essential to determine an appropriate test for each node which could
maximize the distinctiveness of the actual node. Here, we adopt the concept of information gain defined as the difference between the differential entropy of these patches
at the parent node and one of patches at the children nodes as value of distinctiveness:

$$IG = H(S) - (\omega_L H(S_L) + \omega_R H(S_R)) \tag{5}$$

where H is the abbreviation of differential entropy, S, S_L, S_R represent the set of patches at the parent node, at the left child node and at the right child node respectively, ω_L
and ω_R are weight for each child node defined as the ratio between number of patches
at the child node and the one at the parent node.

Finally, besides the split nodes, there exist also the nodes which store the result of
training, namely leaf nodes. A node should be regarded as a leaf node if at least one of
the two conditions is achieved: number of patches arriving at this node is smaller than
pre-defined threshold; or the tree has attained its maximum depth. Once a leaf node is
created, it will be annotated with mean and covariance of patches reaching it.

In this way, we are capable to obtain a collection of trees randomly generated, for
each tree a test at every split node is recorded and so are mean and covariance at every leaf node, these values will serve to our test process.

3.3   Pose Estimation

Given an unseen 2D image of a face, patches with the same scale of those in the training set are extracted and sent to each tree well trained.

For each patch, it could generate the same number of leaves as the number of trees
used, all the leaves will be gathered and the ones with a covariance larger than threshold will be firstly abandoned because they are much less informative.

The rest of leaves have the honor to be called a "vote" for our last test; they will be
clustered to discard the noise and select the most centralized area on the vector plan.

Finally, we sum up all the leaves remaining active and calculate their mean vector
which indicates the final estimation of test image's pose. Fig. 4 shows some results.

Fig. 4. Some results of pose estimation (x axis in green; y axis in red; z axis in blue)

4   LBP Based Multi-view Face Recognition

As one of the most distinguished texture descriptors, the LBP operator [28] has been widely used in numerous applications. It has turned out to be a highly discriminative operator and its core advantages, i.e. its invariance to monotonic illumination changes and computational efficiency, make it reasonable for undertaking the responsibility of representing faces. This powerful operator labels each pixel of an image by thresholding its 3x3-neighbourhood with the center value and considering the result as a binary number. Then the histogram of the labels can be used as a texture descriptor.

Afterwards, in order to fit in textures with different sizes, the LBP operator was extended to the neighborhoods of different sizes [29]. Using circular neighborhoods and the bilinear interpolation technique, the pixel values allow any radius and number of pixels within the neighborhood. We use the notation *(P, R)* for neighborhoods which means *P* sampling points on a circle of radius of *R*.

Furthermore, it has been shown that among 2^P possible binary patterns there exist certain patterns which contain more information than the others, and we thus come up with another extension: uniform patterns. This concept proposed by Ojala et al. represents the patterns that contain at most two bitwise transitions from 0 to 1 or vice versa when the binary string is considered circular.

After pose estimation, we rotate each 3D face model in the gallery set and generate its texture map I_g in the pose of the probe I_p for face matching. The LBP face image is separated firstly in *m* regions from each of which we extract a histogram, and we then combine them to construct final histograms encoding both the local texture and spatial information. At last, the Chi square distance is exploited to decide the similarity between the final vectors H_g and H_p of gallery and probe face.

5   Experimental Results

The dataset for technique evaluation is based on FRGC v1.0. 50 3D face models from different individuals are randomly selected for training. While another 100 out of the rest subjects, each of which possesses more than two face models, are used for testing. For the 100 subjects used in the test step, their first models make up of the gallery set and their second models are regarded as probes. For the 50 training samples as well as the 100 probes, we rotate them with an interval 15° between -90° and 90° in yaw angle (totally 13 poses) and between -45° and 45° in pitch angle (totally 7 poses), leading to a considerable capacity of 150×13×7 = 14k 2D facial images of various poses.

In our experiments on pose estimation, there are three main parameters that influence estimation performance: i.e. number of trees, threshold of angle error and threshold of nose error. It should be noted that the pose estimation accuracy in this study indicates ratio between the number of samples that are correctly estimated and the total number with respect to a pre-defined threshold angle error or nose error as [26]. The result of pose estimation is depicted in Fig.4.

From Figure 4 (a), we can infer that following the increase of number of trees, both nose error and angle error become smaller which highlights the superiority of random regression forests compared with the standard decision tree. Considering that increase the number of trees produces much more calculation amount, we have set tree number at 10 to achieve a compromise between accuracy and computation cost.

According to the results shown in Figure 4(b) and 4(c), we can achieve remarkable estimation performance even if the thresholds of angle and nose error are limited in a very narrow range. As we increase the threshold, our performance is improved.

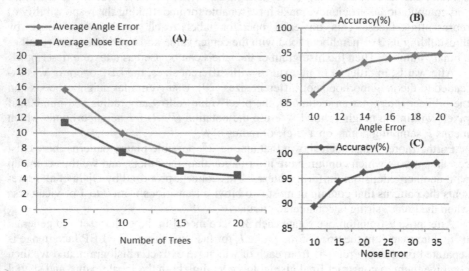

Fig. 5. (a) average error of angle and nose with respect to number of trees; (b) estimation accuracy with respect to angle error threshold; (c) estimation accuracy with respect to the nose error threshold in *mm*.

In face recognition, we rotate the 3D face models in the gallery set to the estimated pose of the probe to generate 2D face images for matching. We calculate recognition performance based on different thresholds of nose error and angle error, and the result is displayed in Table. Considering that the profiles do not contain enough information for identification, we discard the faces -90° and 90° in yaw angle, composing a probe set of 7,700 facial images.

From Table 1, we can see that although slightly influenced by the accuracy of head pose estimation, we are still able to achieve very high recognition rates (around 90%). It is worthy of noting that the LBP descriptor used in this experiment is a quite basic one (its radius is set at 1 and the number of neighbors is set at 8), the effectiveness of the propsoed is hence emphasized.

Table 1. Recognition rates using LBP and influence of pose estimation accuracy

Nose Error Threshold	Angle Error Threshold	Pose Estimation Accuracy	Rank-one Recognition Rate
10	10	0.8660	0.8441
15	12	0.9082	0.8688
20	14	0.9297	0.8958
25	16	0.9383	0.8992
30	18	0.9441	0.9000
35	20	0.9483	0.9014

6   Conclusions

This paper presents a novel 3D aided face recognition method which owns the capacity to handle the 2D probes in different viewpoints. It first estimates the pose status by introducing the approach of Random Regression Forest, and then rotates the 3D face models in the gallery set to that of the probe pose to generate specific gallery samples for the final LBP based matching. The proposed method largely reduces the influence caused by pose variations. Experiments are carried out on a subset randomly extracted from the FRGC v1.0 database, and the achieved performance in both pose estimation and face recognition clearly highlights the effectiveness of the proposed method.

Acknowledgment. This work was funded in part by the National Basic Research Program of China under grant No. 2010CB327902; the National Natural Science Foundation of China (NSFC, grant No. 61273263, No. 61202237, No. 61061130560); the French research agency, Agence Nationale de Recherche (ANR), under grant ANR 2010 INTB 0301 01; the joint project by the LIA 2MCSI lab between the group of Ecoles Centrales and Beihang University; and the Fundamental Research Funds for the Central Universities.

References

1. Zhao, W., Chellappa, R., Rosenfeld, A., Phillips, P.J.: Face recognition: a literature survey. ACM Computing Surveys 35, 399–458 (2003)
2. Turk, M., Pentland, A.: Eigenfaces for recognition. J. Cognitive Neuroscience 3(1), 71–86 (1991)
3. Yu, H., Yang, J.: A direct LDA algorithm for high-dimensional data-with application to face recognition. PR 34(10), 2067–2070 (2000)
4. Comon, P.: Independent component analysis, a new concept? Signal Processing 36(3), 287–314 (1994)
5. Huang, J., Yuen, P., Chen, W., Lai, J.: Choosing parameters of kernel subspace LDA for recognition of face images under pose and illumination variations. IEEE TSMC-B 37(4), 847–862 (2007)
6. Wiskott, L.H., Fellous, J.M., Kuiger, N., von der Malsburg, C.: Face recognition by elastic bunch graph matching. IEEE TPAMI 19, 775–779 (1997)

7. Ahonen, T., Hadid, A., Pietikäinen, M.: Face Recognition with Local Binary Patterns. In: Pajdla, T., Matas, J(G.) (eds.) ECCV 2004. LNCS, vol. 3021, pp. 469–481. Springer, Heidelberg (2004)

8. Lowe, D.G.: Distinctive image features from scale-invariant keypoints. IJCV 60(2), 91–110 (2004)

9. Bowyer, K.W., Chang, K., Flynn, P.J.: A survey of approaches and challenges in 3d and multi-modal 3d + 2d face recognition. CVIU 101, 1–15 (2006)

10. Scheenstra, A., Ruifrok, A., Veltkamp, R.C.: A Survey of 3D Face Recognition Methods. In: Kanade, T., Jain, A., Ratha, N.K. (eds.) AVBPA 2005. LNCS, vol. 3546, pp. 891–899. Springer, Heidelberg (2005)

11. Huang, D., Ardabilian, M., Wang, Y., Chen, L.: Oriented gradient maps based automatic asymmetric 3D-2D face recognition. In: ICB (2012)

12. Zhang, L., Wang, S., Samaras, D.: Face synthesis and recognition under arbitrary unknown lighting using a spherical harmonic basis morphable model. In: CVPR (2005)

13. Blanz, V., Vetter, T.: Face recognition based on fitting a 3D morphable model. IEEE TPAMI 25(9), 1063–1074 (2003)

14. Toderici, G., Zafeiriou, S., Tzimiropoulos, G., Petrou, M., Theoharis, T., Kakadiaris, I.A.: Bidirectional relighting for 3D-aided 2D face recognition. In: CVPR (2010)

15. Szeptycki, P., Ardabilian, M., Chen, L.: A coarse-to-fine curvature analysis-based rotation invariant 3d face landmarking. In: BTAS (2009)

16. Murphy-Chutorian, E., Trivedi, M.: Head pose estimation in computer vision: a survey. IEEE TPAMI, 442–449 (2008)

17. Beymer, D.: Face recognition under varying pose. In: Proc. CVPR (1994)

18. Liang, X., Tong, W.: Face pose estimation using near-infrared images. In: CSNT (2012)

19. Krüger, K.N., Pötzsch, M., van der Malsburg, C.: Determination of face position and pose with a learned representation based on labeled graphs. IVC 15(8), 665–673 (1997)

20. Cootes, T.F., Edwards, G., Taylor, C.J.: Active Appearance Models. IEEE TPAMI (2001)

21. Wu, J., Trivedi, M.: A two-stage head pose estimation framework and evaluation. PR 41(3), 1138–1158 (2008)

22. Liu, X., Lu, H., Zhang, D.: Head Pose Estimation Based on Manifold Embedding and Distance Metric Learning. In: Zha, H., Taniguchi, R.-i., Maybank, S. (eds.) ACCV 2009, Part I. LNCS, vol. 5994, pp. 61–70. Springer, Heidelberg (2010)

23. Murphy-Chutorian, E., Doshi, A., Trivedi, M.M.: Head pose estimation for driver assistance systems: A robust algorithm and experimental evaluation. In: Proc. IEEE Int. Transp. Syst. Conf., pp. 709–714 (2007)

24. Osadchy, M., Cun, Y.L., Miller, M.L.: Synergistic face detection and pose estimation with energy-based models. JMLR 8, 1197–1215 (2007)

25. Breiman, L., Friedman, J., Olshen, R., Stone, C.: Classification and regression trees. Wadsworth and Brooks, Monterey (1984)

26. Fanelli, G., Gall, J., Van Gool, L.: Real time head pose estimation with random regression forests. In: CVPR (2011)

27. Tang, Y., Sun, Z., Tan, T.: Real-Time Head Pose Estimation Using Random Regression Forests. In: Sun, Z., Lai, J., Chen, X., Tan, T. (eds.) CCBR 2011. LNCS, vol. 7098, pp. 66–73. Springer, Heidelberg (2011)

28. Ojala, T., Pietikäinen, M., Maenpaa, T.: Multi-resolution gray-scale and rotation invariant texture classification with local binary patterns. IEEE TPAMI 24(7), 971–987 (2002)

29. Huang, D., Ardabilian, M., Wang, Y., Chen, L.: Asymmetric 3D/2D face recognition based on LBP facial representation and canonical correlation analysis. In: ICIP (2009)

Comparing Studies of Learning Methods
for Human Face Gender Recognition

Yanbin Jiao[1], Jucheng Yang[2], Zhijun Fang[1], Shanjuan Xie[3], and Dongsun Park[3]

[1] School of Information Technology, Jiangxi University of Finance and Economics,
Nanchang, China
jiaoyanbincool@gmail.com, zjfang @jxufe.edu.cn
[2] College of Computer Science and Information Engineering, Tianjin University of Science
and Technology, Tianjin, China
yangjucheng@hotmail.com
[3] Division of Electronics and Information Engineering, Chonbuk National University, Korea

Abstract. Recently, some machine learning algorithms such as Back Propagation (BP) neural network, Support Vector Machine (SVM) and other algorithms are proposed and proven to be useful for human face gender recognition. However, they have lots of shortcomings, such as, requiring setting a large number of training parameters, difficultly choosing the appropriate parameters, and much time consuming for training. In this paper, we proposes a new learning method to use Extreme Learning Machine (ELM) for face gender recognition and compare it with other two main state-of-the-art learning methods for face gender recognition by using BP, SVM respectively. Experimental results on public databases show that ELM plays the best performances for human face gender recognition with higher recognition rate and faster speed. Compared with SVM, the learning speed of ELM is obvious reduced. And compared with BP neural network, it has faster speed, higher precision, and better generalization ability.

Keywords: Face Gender recognition, BP, SVM, ELM.

1 Introduction

Human face gender recognition is a two-class classification problem by automatically identify and analysis human face gender attributes through the face image information. Now, it owns wide application prospects. For example, in the intelligent robot, intelligent computers and other electronic products need automatically recognize a user's gender to provide appropriate user interfaces and services. So it can make all kinds of electronic products more personalized, user-friendly by face gender recognition [1]. It is very easy for a human being to identify the human gender. But it is a challenging task for computers or machines to do it.

Recently, numerous researchers has dedicated on human face gender recognition with machine learning algorithm or other approaches. Golomb et.al [2] proposed to train two neural networks to identify the 30×30 face images of human gender. Brunelli and Poggio [3] used a HyperBF network with sixteen geometric features for

W.-S. Zheng et al. (Eds.): CCBR 2012, LNCS 7701, pp. 67–74, 2012.

gender classification. Tamura et.al. [4] trained a three-layer BP network, on the 8×8 low-resolution face images and achieved 93% of the classification results. BP algorithm based on feed-forward neural network need to set a large number of neural network training parameters. In addition, it hard to choose the right parameters and have the demerits such as very easy to local optimal solution, not convergence, long training time. Moghaddam et.al [5] use the SVM based on RBF classifier to classify the gender of "thumbnail" images of face. They found a better significant effect classification of SVM than other classification methods according to the systematic comparison with traditional neural network methods and linear classification method. Wilhelm et. al [6] combined principal component analysis (PCA) with independent component analysis (ICA) for feature selection and used a nearest neighbor classifier and RBF network to identify. Wang and Liu [7] proposed a feature extraction algorithm based on two-dimensional Gabor Wavelet transform and then use SVM for classification with classification accuracy of 93%. Xia and Sun [8] proposed a method based on local Gabor binary mapping pattern and SVM which achieved a good result. However, SVM has powerful classification and regression abilities. But it needs to artificially set the kernel function, error control parameters, penalty factor and other parameters. Because of parameters are difficult to determine, so it need a long time to adjust the parameters.

Recently, based on the Single-hidden Layer Feed-forward Neural Network (SLFN) [9] [15], Huang proposed a new learning algorithm [10] [11] [12] [13] named ELM. It can apply to classification and regression problems with simple process and fast speed. By setting the appropriate hidden layer nodes, ELM random assigns the input weights and hidden layer bias, and the output layer weights are obtained by the least-squares method. The whole process completed only once and no iteration. Huang et al [14] applied ELM to the face recognition. Yang et al [19] applied ensemble ELM to the face recognition. They had found ELM and SVM have similar prediction accuracy.

In order to explore which learning method is better for face gender recognition, in this paper, we propose to use three state-of-the-art learning methods BP, SVM and ELM to identify the face gender and compare their performances. Experimental results on public databases show that ELM has the best performance for face gender recognition. ELM has obvious advantages in learning speed compared with SVM. And with BP neural network, ELM has faster speed, higher precision, and better generalization ability. So the ELM-based face gender recognition is more suitable for real-time processing.

The organization of the rest of paper is as below. Sections 2 introduce the brief theory of ELM. In Section 3, the proposed method is explained in details. In Section 4, the experimental results are analyzed. At the last, conclusions are drawn in Section 5.

2   Extreme Learning Machine Theory

Huang put forward the ELM algorithm based on SLFN algorithm. For N samples $\{X_i, T_i\}$, $X_i = [x_{i1}, x_{i2}, ..., x_{in}]^T \in R^m$, $T_i = [t_{i1}, t_{i2}, ..., t_{im}]^T \in R^m$, a hidden layer has $\tilde{N}$ units, excitation function $f(x)$ in the ELM:

$$\sum_{i=1}^{\tilde{N}} \beta_i f_i(X_j) = \sum_{i=1}^{\tilde{N}} \beta_i f(a_i \bullet X_j + b_i) = t_j, j = 1, 2, ..., N \tag{1}$$

The above equation can be defined as follows:

$$H\beta = T \tag{2}$$

$$H(a_1,...,a_{\tilde{N}},b_1,...,b_{\tilde{N}},X_1,...,X_N)$$

$$= \begin{bmatrix} f(a_1 \bullet X_1 + b_1) & \cdots & f(a_{\tilde{N}} \bullet X_1 + b_{\tilde{N}}) \\ & \cdots & \\ f(a_1 \bullet X_N + b_1) & \cdots & f(a_{\tilde{N}} \bullet X_N + b_{\tilde{N}}) \end{bmatrix}_{N \times \tilde{N}} \tag{3}$$

$$\beta = \begin{bmatrix} \beta_1^T \\ \cdots \\ \beta_N^T \end{bmatrix}_{\tilde{N} \times m} \quad T = \begin{bmatrix} t_1^T \\ \cdots \\ t_N^T \end{bmatrix}_{N \times m} \tag{4}$$

ε_j is defined to express the error between expectation value and practical value:

$$\sum_{i=1}^{\tilde{N}} \beta_i f(a_i \bullet X_j + b_i) - Y_j = \varepsilon_j, j = 1, 2, ..., N \tag{5}$$

$E(W)$ is defined to express the error square between expectation value and Practical value, the answer for the problem is searching for the optimal weight $W = (a, b, \beta)$, which makes $E(W)$ be smallest:

$$\underset{W=(a,b,\beta)}{\arg\min} E(W) = \underset{W=(a,b,\beta)}{\arg\min} \| \varepsilon \|^2 \tag{6}$$

Due to the super learning ability of the standard SLFN, the actual output can be nearly equal to the ideal output as the formula said:

$$\sum_{j=1}^{\tilde{N}} \| t_j - y_j \| = 0 \tag{7}$$

So the formula 2 can be expressed as follows:

$$H\beta = Y \tag{8}$$

Huang has certificated in [16] Input connection weights a_i and hidden nodes deviation b_i can be chosen randomly before the training begin, and are fixed in the training process. So the main job is searching for the output weight between hidden layer and output layer, and it can be achieved by solute the linear equations through by the least square method:

$$\| H(a_1,...,a_{\tilde{N}},b_1,...,b_{\tilde{N}},X_1,...,X)\beta - Y \| =$$
$$\underset{\beta}{\min} \| H(a_1,...,a_{\tilde{N}},b_1,...,b_{\tilde{N}},X_1,...,X)\beta - Y \| \tag{9}$$

The answer is:

$$\beta = H^+ Y \tag{10}$$

H^+ is the Moore-Penrose of generalized inverse of the output layer matrix H. the characteristics of β: Through this solution can get minimum training error, the minimum paradigm of the weight vector and best generalization performance, the least-square solution of paradigm is the only. So the solution for the final question is changed to solute the output connection weight. If the optimal solution of the output connection weight has been figured out, we can get the minimum error between actual output values and ideal targets value and get the classification of the training sets.

3   Proposed Method

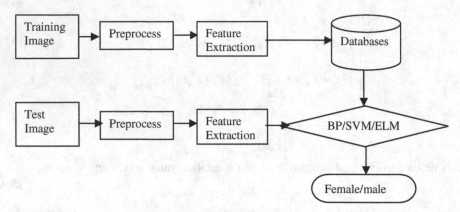

Fig. 1. Block diagram of the learning method-based human face gender recognition

The diagram of the learning method -based human face gender recognition system is shown as in Figure 1. As shown in Figure 1, there are three main steps for human face gender recognition. The first step is image preprocessing, it normalizes the images into the same size and light compensation. The second step is feature extraction, to find an effective representation of the face images. Instead of using complex feature extraction methods, Enginface [18] is an effective way to represent the face image. Similar, we use the whole face image as the input, and using PCA to get the Enginface as the input feature. The last step is to apply our learning method to classify the input into female and male. For example, the entire process of ELM-based face gender recognition is as follows:

(1) First, the appropriate training strategy based on the selected training set, we randomly selected from a face database as part of the training set $TrainSet = \{x_i + y_i\}, i = 1, ..., N$, where N is the total training samples, and the remaining samples as the test set;

(2) Image pre-processing for training set, through the face image positioning, calibration and standardization, we can get on the face scale, lighting and the location which is not sensitive to the frontal face image;

(3) Image feature extraction of the training set by Enginface method to extract the optimal recognition feature vector.

(4) Set the input weight parameters a_i and $b_i, i = 1, ..., \tilde{N}$ randomly.

(5) Select appropriate activation function g(x) and obtain the Hidden layer matrix H.

(6) Output weight value β: $\beta = H^+Y$.

(7) Get the optimal parameter values W= (a, b, β), the model of training has been trained, the training process is complete.

(8) ELM test phase. Testing the model parameters obtained from the training model, and then we can obtain the actual output through the test image by the formula

$$t_j = \sum_{i=1}^{L} \beta_i f(a_i \bullet X_j + b_i),$$ L is number of hidden layer nodes, in order to determine male or female.

From the steps, we can draw that comparing with BP neural networks and SVM, weight adjustment does not need much iteration. Therefore, training speed of ELM has improved significantly.

4   Experiments and Analysis

4.1   Gender Public Database

To test the performance of the proposed method in the face gender recognition, we do some experiments over three public face database. These databases includes: Stanford university database[17], ORL database, and FERET database, Among them, the Stanford university database consists of 200 men and 200 women images by the school of hospital in Stanford university. The ORL database is collected from 40 persons; each one has 10 images with different illuminations, and expressions like smile, eye closing etc. It includes forty (4×10) female images. Different from the previous two databases, FERET database has large variation on illumination, background, light face images, and we choose 126 persons for our experiments. Half of those images are female and half is male.

4.2   Experiments Results

We did three experiments using BP, SVM and ELM algorithms on three different public human face gender databases. In the first experiments on Stanford university database, we randomly selected 160 male and 160 female images as a training set; the remaining images are as test set. Training set was to select the optimal parameters for SVM, BP, ELM and test set was used to test the training time and recognition accuracy. We chose the pixel of image as the features, the size of the input image is 200×200, after PCA, we kept the most 95% features, and the reduced dimension of the features was 157. For ORL database, we randomly select 80 individuals' images, namely, 40 male and female images. We selected 30 male and 30 female images as the training set, and the rest of the images as the test set. After PCA the reduced dimension of the features is 47. For FERET database, we select out 882 individual face images with 441 male and 441 female, among them, 340 images are taken for training. And after PCA, the reduced dimension of the features is 154.

Because the features may have large differences in value, in order to avoid large values of features to submerge the contributions of the small value of features, all samples are normalized between -1 and 1 before sending to the learning algorithms as input.

We used SVM, BP and ELM for testing on the public on Stanford university database with the selected optimal parameters, recording training time in the training process of the three algorithms. Ultimately, we calculated the average training time and the average test time through 20 experiments. The cost times of the experiments are shown in table1. From the table, we can see that SVM and BP training times are relative longer than the ELM training time. While for testing time, SVM and BP cost a little longer time to the ELM, basically in the same curve. The average time costing of SVM, BP and ELM is as shown in Table 1. From the table, the average total time of ELM, SVM, BP are 1.0031, 42.424, 36.397 seconds respectively. Therefore, the method of ELM has the highest speed.

Table 1. Time cost (seconds) of BP, SVM, ELM based on the Stanford university database

	Average training time	Average testing time	Average total time
BP	36.005	0.392	36.397
SVM	42.36	0. 064	42.424
ELM	0.9421	0.061	1.0031

We calculate the recognition accuracies of BP, SVM and ELM algorithms on the Stanford University database are shown in Table 2. From the table, we can see the recognition accuracies of the three methods about male are higher than the female. The total accuracy of BP is lowest, which is 87.5%. And the accuracy of SVM and ELM respectively is 93.13% and 93.75%. The ELM has the similar accuracy of SVM.

Table 2. Recognition accuracies of BP, SVM and ELM based on the Stanford database

	SVM	BP	ELM
Female	91.25%	85.00%	92.50%
Male	95.00%	90.00%	95.00%
Total	93.13%	87.50%	93.75%

We compare the three kind of algorithm from the training time and identification the two aspects. The whole performance result of the comparison as shown in Figure2.The ELM is significantly higher than the other two algorithms.

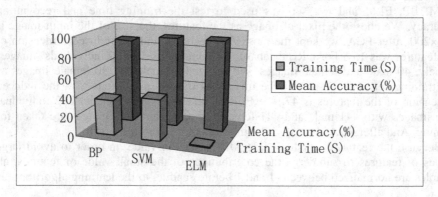

Fig. 2. The whole performance of BP, SVM and ELM based on the Stanford database

In order to comparing with different learning algorithms, we conducted the experiments on the three public databases in Figure 3.

Figure 3 shows the comparison recognition rate of several algorithms. From the table, we can get that the accuracy of ELM is higher than that of the BP algorithm and that of SVM in the database of Standford. The accuracy is 93.75%. And the SVM and ELM has the same accuracy that is 90% in the ORL database. The accuracy of the ELM and the SVM in FERET respectively is 90.10% and 87.98%. From the whole, the accuracy of SVM and ELM is similar.

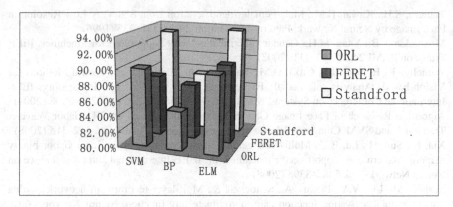

Fig. 3. Three algorithms for the recognition results of different databases

Overall, the performances of ELM overweigh SVM and BP in face gender recognition.

5   Conclusions

Face gender recognition is a very challenging problem in the human-computer interaction and some intelligence environment. In this paper, we propose to use three learning methods for face gender recognition. Also, we compare their performances over three public databases. From the experimental results, we can see that, compared with traditional learning algorithm, such as SVM, and BP, ELM has faster speed, better generalization performances. In the further work, the discriminate features for the human face gender recognition will be further promoted.

Acknowledgements. This work was supported in part by the National Natural Science Foundation of China under Grant 61063035, the China Postdoctoral Science Foundation under the grant No.2012M510977, and the advanced project of Jiangxi Provincial Postdoctoral Science Foundation, and was also supported by the Ministry of Education, Science Technology (MEST) and National Research Foundation of Korea (NRF) through the Human Resource Training Project for Regional Innovation.

References

1. Chen, D.-Y., Lin, K.-Y.: Robust Gender Recognition for Real-time Surveillance system. In: 2010 IEEE International Conference on Digital Object Identifier, ICME, pp. 191–196 (2010)
2. Golomb, B.A., Lawrence, D.T., Sejnowski, T.J.: SEXNET: A Neural Network Identifies Sex from Human Face. In: Advances in Neural information Processing Systems, pp. 572–577 (1991)
3. Brunelli, R., Poggio, T.: HyperBF Networks for Gender Classification. In: DARPA Image Understanding Workshop, vol. 3 (1992)

4. Tamura, S.H., Kawai, H.M.: Male/Female Identific-ation from 8*8 Very Low Resolution Face Image by Neural Network. Pattern Recognition 29(2), 331–335 (1996)
5. Moghaddam, B., Yang, M.H.: Gender Classification with Support Vector Machines. IEEE Trans. on PAMI 24(5), 707–711 (2002)
6. Wilhelm, T., Bohme, H.J., GroB, H.M., Backhaus, A.: Statistical and Neural Methods for Vision-based Analysis of Facial Expressions and Gender. In: Proceedings-IEEE International Conference on Systems, Man and Cybernetics, vol. 3, pp. 2203–2208 (2004)
7. Algorithm Research of Face Image Gender Classification Based on 2-D Gabor Wavelet Transform and SVM. Computer Science and Computational Technology, 312–315 (2008)
8. Xia, B., Sun, H., Lu, B.L.: Multi-view gender classification based on local Gabor binary mapping pattern and support vector machines. In: IEEE International Joint Conference on Neural Networks, pp. 3388–3395 (2008)
9. Leshno, M., Lin, V.Y., Pinkus, A., Schochen, S.: Multilayer feedforward networks with a nonpolynomial activation function can approximate any function. Neural Networks 6(6), 861–867 (1993)
10. Huang, G.B., Zhu, Q.Y., Siew, C.K.: Extreme Learning Machine: Theory and Applications. Neurocomputing 70, 489–501 (2006)
11. Huang, G.B., Chen, L.: Convex Incremental Extreme Learning Machine. Neurocomputing 70, 3056–3062 (2007)
12. Huang, G.B., Chen, L.: Enhanced Random Search Based Incremental Extreme Learning Machine. Neurocomputing 71, 3460–3468 (2008)
13. Huang, G.B., Zhu, Q.Y., Siew, C.K.: Extreme Learning Machine: Theory and Applications. Neurocomputing 70, 489–501 (2006)
14. Zong, W., Huang, G.-B.: Face recognition based on extreme learning machine. Neurocomputing 74, 2541–2551 (2010)
15. Deng, W.-Y., Zheng, Q.-H., Chen, L.: Research on Extreme Learning of Neural Networks. Chinese Journal of Computers 33(2) (2011)
16. Huang, G.B.: Learning capability and storage capacity of two hidden-layer feed-forward networks. IEEE Transactions on Neural Networks 14(2), 274–281 (2003)
17. http://scien.stanford.edu/pages/labsite/2000/ee368/projects2 000/project15/dataset.html
18. Turk, M.A.: Face recognition using eigenfaces. In: IEEE Computer Society Conference on Computer Vision and Pattern Recognition, pp. 586–591 (1991)
19. Yang, J., Jiao, Y., Xie, S., Fang, Z., Yoon, S., Park, D.: Image Latent Semantic Analysis based Face Recognition with Ensemble Extreme Learning Machine. World Wide Web Journal (accepted, 2012)

Fusion of mSSIM and SVM for Reduced-Reference Facial Image Quality Assessment

Pengjun Ji, Yuchun Fang, Zhonghua Zhou, and Jiazhen Zhu

School of Computer Engineering and Science, Shanghai University,
200072 Shanghai, China
ycfang@shu.edu.cn

Abstract. Image Quality Assessment (IQA) is a critical part in face recognition system for helping to pick out the better quality images to assure high accuracy. In this paper, we propose a simple but efficient facial IQA algorithm based on Bayesian fusion of modified Structural Similarity (mSSIM) index and Support Vector Machine (SVM) as a reduced-reference method for facial IQA. The fusion scheme largely improves the facial IQA and consequently promotes the precision of face recognition when comparing to mSSIM or SVM alone. Experimental validation shows that the proposed algorithm works well in multiple feature spaces on many face databases.

Keywords: Image quality assessment, face recognition, biometrics, fusion.

1 Introduction

With the exploding increase in the number of installed video surveillance cameras and the deployment of face recognition software, the demand for high performance face recognition system is obvious, which also impels facial IQA to play a more important role. While factors such as illumination, pose variation, blur and focus change may drastically deteriorate recognition precision [1], thus it is necessary to take these factors into account to automatically evaluate quality of facial images.

For general IQA, there are several most popular full-reference schemes such as the Mean Squared Error (MSE) [2], Peak Signal-to-Noise-Ratio (PSNR) [3], the SSIM index [4] and Tone Rendering Distortion Index (TRDI) [5], but they all need reference images which are hard to obtain in practical application. Thus, no-reference and reduced-reference IQA arouse special attention. Natural Scene Statistics (NSS) model was applied by Sheikh et al. to blindly measure the quality of images [6]. Li et al. deployed a general regression neural network to assess quality of distorted images [7]. Li and Wang extracted a set of distortion detection features from a divisive normalization representation of the image [8].

For concrete application such as biometrics, IQA is designed to specially take the recognition performance into consideration. El-Abed et al. utilized a multi-class SVM-based method combining image quality and pattern-based quality to predict biometric sample quality [9]. Breitenbach and Chawdhry [10] assessed the impact of

W.-S. Zheng et al. (Eds.): CCBR 2012, LNCS 7701, pp. 75–82, 2012.
© Springer-Verlag Berlin Heidelberg 2012

image quality on multimodal biometric recognition performance, including iris and face. Jain et al. [11] proposed a likelihood ratio-based fusion scheme that takes the quality of multi-biometric samples of iris and fingerprint into consideration.

In this paper, we propose a Bayesian fusion model to specially handle the quality degradation of facial image based on our previous work of facial image quality ranking with mSSIM and SVM [12]. Experimental results show that the fusion algorithm works well in several popular feature spaces on different benchmark databases.

This paper is organized as follows. In Section 2, we introduce the Bayesian fusion model of mSSIM and SVM. Section 3 analyzes the experimental results and the conclusions are drawn in Section 4.

2   Bayesian Fusion for Facial IQA

For biometric images such as face, pose variation and lighting condition are two main factors affecting the quality of image. It is hard for the general no-reference and re-duced-reference methods to handle both problems. In our previous work [12], we proposed a Reduced-Reference Automatic Ranking (RRAR) method for facial IQA, which utilizes the mSSIM and SVM to handle the two problems respectively. In this paper, we use Bayesian decision rule to fuse the two modules.

2.1   mSSIM and SVM

Due to its relatively low computational complexity and coherence with human visual system, SSIM is adopted as the full-reference metric to solve the problem of "illumination unevenness" in facial IQA. It is proposed based on the hypothesis that human vision system is highly adaptive to structure [13]. Frontal facial image is a good example with strong structural appearance. However, usually there is no so-called "original image" as reference in face recognition system. By constructing the automatically updated average face as reference, we modify the normal SSIM into a reduced-reference IQA method. The mSSIM is simple yet robust [12].

In order to solve the problem of pose variation, we train a binary SVM classifier in the Uniform Local Binary Pattern (ULBP) feature space to discriminate the frontal and non-frontal facial images, and eliminate facial images with "out-of-plane" rotation [14]. The ULBP is not precise enough in personal identification but proves good enough in discriminating frontal and non-frontal face in our experiments with much lower feature dimension.

2.2   Bayesian Fusion Model

Depending only on the mSSIM, the influence of pose variation is ignored. While just considering the SVM classifier, the illumination condition is left behind. It is necessary to find a way to combine their merits. We adopt the Bayesian decision rule as a simple parametric fusion model, which aims at finding a classification surface in two-dimensional space constructed by the outputs of mSSIM and SVM.

Denote the sample as $x = (c_x, r_x)$ where c_x, r_x separately denotes the outputs of mSSIM and SVM classifiers. Let $p(F \mid x), p(\overline{F} \mid x)$ be the posterior probability of good quality and poor quality images.

According to Bayesian formula,

$$p(F \mid x) = \frac{p(x \mid F)p(F)}{p(x \mid F)p(F) + p(x \mid \overline{F})p(\overline{F})} \tag{1}$$

$$p(\overline{F} \mid x) = \frac{p(x \mid \overline{F})p(\overline{F})}{p(x \mid F)p(F) + p(x \mid \overline{F})p(\overline{F})} \tag{2}$$

Thus we get the Bayesian decision rules with negative log likelihood ratio format as,

$$-\ln p(x \mid F) + \ln p(x \mid \overline{F}) \begin{array}{c} > \\ < \end{array} \frac{\ln p(F)}{\ln p(\overline{F})} = Threshold \qquad x \in \left\{ \begin{array}{c} F \\ \overline{F} \end{array} \right. \tag{3}$$

Because of the complexity of facial images, it is acceptable to assume that the outputs of SSIM and SVM are independent, thus

$$p(x \mid F) = p(c_x, r_x \mid F) = p(c_x \mid F)\, p(r_x \mid F) \tag{4}$$

$$p(x \mid \overline{F}) = p(c_x, r_x \mid \overline{F}) = p(c_x \mid \overline{F})\, p(r_x \mid \overline{F}) \tag{5}$$

The final decision rule is,

$$-[\ln p(c_x \mid F) + \ln p(r_x \mid F)] + [\ln p(c_x \mid \overline{F}) + \ln p(r_x \mid \overline{F})]$$

$$\begin{array}{c} > \\ < \end{array} \ln \frac{p(F)}{p(\overline{F})} = Threshold, x \in \left\{ \begin{array}{c} F \\ \overline{F} \end{array} \right. \tag{6}$$

2.3   Fitting of Probability Density Function

To estimate the four posterior probabilities mentioned above, Maximum Likelihood Estimate (MLE) is utilized to fit several distributions, including Normal distribution, Beta distribution, Gamma distribution, Weibull distribution and the non-parametric Parzen Window respectively, then select the most suitable distribution with statistical Kolmogorov-Smirnov test.

Table 1 shows the statistical results for each distribution where the confidence coefficient is 0.05. It can be observed that $p(c_x \mid F), p(c_x \mid \overline{F}), p(r_x \mid F)$ and $p(r_x \mid \overline{F})$ separately fit the Parzen Window distribution, the Parzen Window distribution, the Gamma distribution and the Beta distribution. The fitting results on our self-collected database are shown in Figure 1 (a) and (b), where the dotted line denotes histogram of samples, while solid line is the curve of probability density function. As can be observed, the estimation is very close to the real distribution of samples.

Table 1. Kolmogorov-smirnov test results

	Nomal	Beta	Gamma	Weibull	Parzen	critical value
$p(c_r \mid F)$	0.1383	0.0952	0.1325	0.4632	**0.0496**	0.0837
$p(c_r \mid \overline{F})$	0.0473	0.1373	0.0864	0.0415	**0.0247**	0.0289
$p(r_x \mid F)$	0.0636	0.1453	**0.0620**	0.6118	0.0932	0.0657
$p(r_x \mid \overline{F})$	0.0435	**0.0271**	0.0382	0.0329	0.0577	0.0315

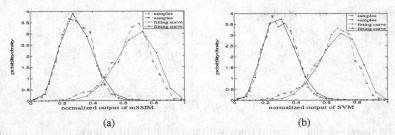

Fig. 1. Fitting results of probability density function on self-collected database: (a) mSSIM ($p(c_x \mid F)$ and $p(c_x \mid \bar{F})$ fit with the Parzen Window distribution); (b) SVM ($p(r_x \mid F)$ and $p(r_x \mid \bar{F})$ separately fits the Gamma and the Beta distribution)

3   Experimental Results and Analysis

Normally, IQA measures quality based on reference images. In the case of face recognition, the IQA serves to improve the recognition accuracy. Hence, we use the accuracy of face recognition to evaluate the effect of the IQA method. To validate the results of IQA, we perform face recognition tests in several popular feature spaces on several face databases.

3.1   Face Databases and Feature Spaces

The experiments are performed on four face databases listed in Table 2. D1 is collected in our lab without lighting constraint. D2, D3 and D4 are subsets randomly selected respectively from expression database of CAS-PEAL [15], FERET [16] and FRGC. D2 contains expression variations. D3 contains lighting, aging, pose, expression and decoration variations. D4 contains images collected in uncontrolled environments with complex lighting variations.

Table 2. Face databases

	Origin	#Subjects	#Images per Subject	Complexity
D1	Self-collected	50	10	Uncontrolled
D2	CAS-PEAL	100	5	Controlled
D3	FERET	256	4	Controlled
D4	FRGC	459	6	Uncontrolled

For each database, we classify facial images of each subject as better and poorer quality subsets in the following way: the facial images of each subject are sorted in descending order according their quality scores obtained from the fusion model, the better half are regarded as the Better Quality Set (BQS), while the other half are denoted as the Poorer Quality Set (PQS). The union of BQS and PQS is the set of all images (ALLS). On BQS, PQS and ALLS of all 4 databases, we respectively extract the ULBP, Principal Component Analysis (PCA) feature and Linear Discriminant

Analysis (LDA) features to evaluate the proposed facial IQA method with the Nearest Neighbor classifier.

3.2   Effectiveness of the Proposed IQA Method

To verify the effect of the proposed IQA model, we perform face verification experiments and adopt the Equal Error Rate (EER) point of False Rejection Rate (FRR) and False Acceptance Rate (FAR) to measure accuracy as in Table 3.

Table 3. ERRs of the BQS, ALLS and PQS in 3 feature space on 4 face databases

Set	Method	D1	D2	D3	D4
	BQS	**0.0949**	**0.0650**	**0.1500**	**0.3428**
PCA	ALLS	0.1435	0.0654	0.2056	0.3435
	PQS	0.1453	0.0908	0.2241	0.3698
	BQS	**0.0573**	0.0412	**0.1590**	**0.2800**
LDA	ALLS	0.0643	**0.0407**	0.2047	0.2928
	PQS	0.0692	0.0516	0.2252	0.3241
	BQS	**0.0974**	**0.0820**	**0.0860**	**0.0746**
ULBP	ALLS	0.1294	0.1364	0.1318	0.1272
	PQS	0.1594	0.1596	0.1581	0.1356

It can be observed that for PCA, LDA and ULBP, the BQSs selected with the Fusion model are all of prominently better performance compared with PQS for the 4 face databases. On D2, the accuracy of BQS in LDA feature space is slightly worse than that in ALLS. This is because that the LDA feature works well on the relatively good quality image dataset D2. However, in all the other cases, the accuracy on BQS outperforms that on ALLS. Such results demonstrate that our IQA model adapts to different kinds of features and works well on different databases.

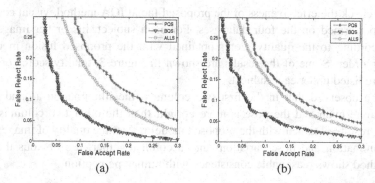

Fig. 2. Comparison among BQS, PQS and ALLS in ULBP feature space on (a) D2 and (b)D4

We also compare the performance with the Receive Operating Characteristic (ROC) Curve of FRR with respect to FAR. An example with the ULBP feature is shown in Figure 2(a) for D2 with relatively high quality images from CAS-PEAL and Figure 2(b) for D4 with images obtained in uncontrolled environment from FRGC. The promotion of accuracy with the proposed model is about the same for both image sets.

3.3   Comparison of the Fusion Algorithm with the Other Methods

In the four experimental databases, we also compare the performance of the proposed IQA method with the non-fusion IQA methods through face verification test in the ULBP feature space. The EERs of FAR and FRR are shown in Table 4.

Table 4. ERRs of three algorithms on ALLS

Method	D1	D2	D3	D4
SVM	0.1789	0.1707	0.2339	0.2645
mSSIM	0.1520	**0.1359**	0.1817	0.1966
Proposed method	**0.1294**	0.1364	**0.1318**	**0.1272**

It can be observed that the fusion algorithm performs much better than both mSSIM and SVM in all the other cases except for the results on D2. In D2, the pose variation is so small that SVM does not contribute much for the fusion algorithm. Hence, the fusion algorithm has very close performance with that of mSSIM. From Table 4, it can also be observed that mSSIM outperforms SVM due to its flexibility to structural information in IQA.

3.4   Examples of Quality Ranking

To further check the effectiveness of the proposed facial IQA method, visual comparisons are performed on the four databases. For each subject, his or her images are ranked according to the quality scores obtained with the proposed fusion model in descending order. Some of the results are shown in Figure 3, quality scores of three methods are listed under each subject.

It can be observed that in the first two columns, the illumination around facial region is more even and the pose is more upright than the other two columns. The facial IQA results obtained with the proposed model reflect the quality of image when taking illumination and pose variations into account together. It's obvious that our fusion method shows reasonable consistency with human perception.

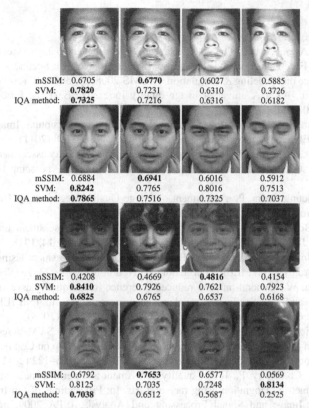

	mSSIM:	0.6705	**0.6770**	0.6027	0.5885
	SVM:	**0.7820**	0.7231	0.6310	0.3726
	IQA method:	**0.7325**	0.7216	0.6316	0.6182

	mSSIM:	0.6884	**0.6941**	0.6016	0.5912
	SVM:	**0.8242**	0.7765	0.8016	0.7513
	IQA method:	**0.7865**	0.7516	0.7325	0.7037

	mSSIM:	0.4208	0.4669	**0.4816**	0.4154
	SVM:	**0.8410**	0.7926	0.7621	0.7923
	IQA method:	**0.6825**	0.6765	0.6537	0.6168

	mSSIM:	0.6792	**0.7653**	0.6577	0.0569
	SVM:	0.8125	0.7035	0.7248	**0.8134**
	IQA method:	**0.7038**	0.6512	0.5687	0.2525

Fig. 3. Examples of quality ranking results of the fusion model in descending order from left to right, each row one subject from one database (Row 1: Pose changes from upright to slanting; Row 2: expression changes from slight to severe; Row 3: combined changes of expression and lighting; Row 4: illumination becomes more uneven)

4   Conclusion

In this paper, we propose a fusion facial IQA algorithm based on the Bayesian rule, it fuses mSSIM and SVM to rank the quality of facial images with a simple decision function. The proposed model can prominently improve the precision of face recognition compared to mSSIM or SVM alone. Experimental results show that the proposed algorithm works well in multiple feature spaces on multiple face databases. The ranking results of facial image quality are coherent with the human visual system considering illumination and pose variations.

Acknowledgments. The work is funded by the National Natural Science Foundation of China (No.61170155) and the Shanghai Leading Academic Discipline Project (No.J50103).

References

1. Zamani, A.N., Awang, M.K., Omar, N., Nazeer, S.A.: Image Quality Assessments and Restoration for Face Detection and Recognition System Images. In: Second Asia International Conference on Modeling & Simulation, AICMS 2008, pp. 505–510 (2009)
2. Zhou, W., Bovik, A.C.: A universal image quality index. IEEE Signal Processing Letters 9, 81–84 (2002)
3. Zhou, W., Qiang, L.: Information Content Weighting for Perceptual Image Quality Assessment. IEEE Transactions on Image Processing 20, 1185–1198 (2011)
4. Zhou, W., Bovik, A.C., Sheikh, H.R., Simoncelli, E.P.: Image quality assessment: from error visibility to structural similarity. IEEE Transactions on Image Processing 13, 600–612 (2004)
5. Jang-Kun, S., Seung Beom, P.: Assessment of Image Quality Degraded by Tone Rendering Distortion. Journal of Display Technology 7, 365–372 (2011)
6. Sheikh, H.R., Bovik, A.C., Cormack, L.: No-reference quality assessment using natural scene statistics: JPEG2000. IEEE Transactions on Image Processing 14, 1918–1927 (2005)
7. Chaofeng, L., Bovik, A.C., Xiaojun, W.: Blind Image Quality Assessment Using a General Regression Neural Network. IEEE Transactions on Neural Networks 22, 793–799 (2011)
8. Qiang, L., Zhou, W.: General-purpose reduced-reference image quality assessment based on perceptually and statistically motivated image representation. In: 15th IEEE International Conference on Image Processing, ICIP 2008, pp. 1192–1195 (2008)
9. El-Abed, M., Giot, R., Hemery, B., Charrier, C., Rosenberger, C.: A SVM-based model for the evaluation of biometric sample quality. In: 2011 IEEE Workshop on Computational Intelligence in Biometrics and Identity Management (CIBIM), pp. 115–122 (2011)
10. Breitenbach, L., Chawdhry, P.: Image quality assessment and performance evaluation for multimodal biometric recognition using face and iris. In: Proceedings of 6th International Symposium on Image and Signal Processing and Analysis, ISPA 2009, pp. 550–555 (2009)
11. Nandakumar, K., Yi, C., Jain, A.K., Dass, S.C.: Quality-based Score Level Fusion in Multibiometric Systems. In: 18th International Conference on Pattern Recognition, ICPR 2006, pp. 473–476 (2006)
12. Jiazhen, Z., Yuchun, F., Pengjun, J., Abdl, M.E., Wang, D.: RRAR: A novel reduced-reference IQA algorithm for facial images. In: 2011 18th IEEE International Conference on Image Processing (ICIP), pp. 3313–3316 (2011)
13. Zhou, W., Guixing, W., Sheikh, H.R., Simoncelli, E.P., En-Hui, Y., Bovik, A.C.: Quality-aware images. IEEE Transactions on Image Processing 15, 1680–1689 (2006)
14. Ojala, T., Pietikainen, M., Maenpaa, T.: Multiresolution gray-scale and rotation invariant texture classification with local binary patterns. IEEE Transactions on Pattern Analysis and Machine Intelligence 24, 971–987 (2002)
15. Wen, G., Bo, C., Shiguang, S., Xilin, C., Delong, Z., Xiaohua, Z., Debin, Z.: The CAS-PEAL Large-Scale Chinese Face Database and Baseline Evaluations. IEEE Transactions on Systems, Man and Cybernetics, Part A: Systems and Humans 38, 149–161 (2008)
16. Phillips, P.J., Hyeonjoon, M., Rauss, P., Rizvi, S.A.: The FERET evaluation methodology for face-recognition algorithms. In: 1997 IEEE Computer Society Conference on Computer Vision and Pattern Recognition. Proceedings, pp. 137–143 (1997)

A Survey of Face Hallucination

Yan Liang[1], Jian-Huang Lai[1], Wei-Shi Zheng[1], and Zemin Cai[2]

[1] Sun Yat-sen University, China
sysuly@gmail.com, stsljh@mail.sysu.edu.cn, wszheng@ieee.org
[2] Department of Electronic Engineering, College of Engineering, Shantou University, China
zmcai@stu.edu.cn

Abstract. Due to the numerous important applications of face images, such as long-distance video surveillance and identity verification, face hallucination has been an active research topic in the last decade. This paper makes a survey of approaches to high quality face hallucination by looking at theoretical backgrounds and practical results. The strengths and weaknesses of these approaches are identified to form a base for a new sparsity-based method for super-resolving mis-aligned face images.

Keywords: Face hallucination, face prior, mis-alignment, sparsity.

1   Introduction

Super-resolution is a technique of inferring a missing high-resolution (HR) image from the low-resolution (LR) input. Super-resolution of face images, also called face hallucination, has been an independent branch in super-resolution research field since the pioneering work by Baker and Kanade [1][3] and has been extensively and actively studied in recent years. This is mainly due to the numerous important applications of faces, such as long-distance video surveillance and identity verification. Psychological researchers have revealed that the fine-scale information of faces is indispensable for face recognition by human [2], which strongly supports the importance of face hallucination. Although the input for processing LR images can consist of one or more images or frames, this paper focuses on single frame super-resolution in view of many applications that only have one single input image, such as the super-resolution of "thumbnails" in the web pages. Single frame super-resolution is also known as image scaling, zooming and enlargement.

The face hallucination methods developed in the past few years differ from each other. They can be categorized in two approaches, namely global and local, corresponding to the global similarity and the local similarity of faces respectively. The global similarity means that if considering each face image as a data point, face images are close to each other and span a small subspace in the high dimensional image space. Some classical face space model, such as Principal Component Analysis (PCA) [4], Locality Preserving Projections (LPP) [5], and Non-negative Matrix Factorization (NMF) [6] has been used to super-resolve faces. In contrast, the basic idea of local approaches is based on local similarity of images at the same face position.

W.-S. Zheng et al. (Eds.): CCBR 2012, LNCS 7701, pp. 83–93, 2012.
© Springer-Verlag Berlin Heidelberg 2012

In this paper, we aim to describe and compare the existing face hallucination techniques and algorithms by looking at theoretical backgrounds and practical results. Strengths and weaknesses of each algorithm are summarized to form a base for proposing our new method, which is especially effective to hallucinate the mis-aligned face images.

2   Review of the Existing Methods

The existing state-of-the-art face hallucination methods are all based on specific face prior. As introduced in Section 1, one prior is global similarity of facial appearances. [8]-[10] used PCA as global model constraint. Ayan et al. [11] used a Kernel Principal Component Analysis (KPCA)-based prior model. Zhuang et al. [12] proposed the locality preserving hallucination method by LPP. Yang et al. [13] used NMF to linearly represent global face, and combine reconstruction constraint and coefficient regularization to estimate the HR face image.

Another prior that is explicitly directed at producing local facial details is the local similarity of facial appearances. Baker and Kanade [1] first proposed a local face hallucination method, which constructs high frequency components of a HR face image by finding the nearest "Parent Structure" at each pixel position through a training set. A variant of this method using steerable filter pyramid is presented in [14]. Ma et al. [15] hallucinated the face image patch by linearly combining the same position image patches of each training image. Zou and Yuen [16] proposed a linear regression approach to learn the relationship between the HR image patch and the LR image patch for face hallucination.

Since global approaches are good for hallucinating common characteristics of a human face, but usually lose specific local characteristics of this face, the hybrid of the global and local approaches are then proposed to take the advantages of both approaches. The hybrid methods such as [10] and [12] usually are designed in two steps: (i) hallucinate a smooth global face image by global approaches, and (ii) compensate the residue with the HR ground truth by local approaches. Yang et al. [13] zoomed the face image to a medium resolution by global methods, and then employed local methods to recover details.

Next, we will elaborate some representative methods [1][8][10][15][17] serving as links between past and future to take a closer look at the essence of face hallucination.

2.1   Pyramid-Based [1]

In this method, face hallucination is posed as finding the maximum a posteriori (MAP) HR image h given the LR input l. The Bayes law for this estimation problem is:

$$P(h\mid l) = \frac{P(l\mid h)P(h)}{P(l)} \tag{1}$$

Since $P(l)$ is a constant, the MAP estimation is written as:

$$\arg\max_h P(h\mid l) = \arg\min_h(-\ln P(l\mid h) - \ln P(h)) \tag{2}$$

The first term $-\ln P(l\mid h)$ is normally set to be a quadratic function of the error in the reconstruction constraint:

$$-\ln P(l \mid h) = \frac{1}{2\sigma_\eta^2} \sum_{m,n} (l(m,n) - \frac{1}{s^2} \sum_{i=0}^{s-1} \sum_{j=0}^{s-1} h(s*m+i, s*n+j))^2 \tag{3}$$

where s is the magnification factor. For formulating the second term $-\ln P(h)$, a multiscale facial feature called the Parent Structure is defined. Given an image I, its Gaussian pyramid $G_0(I), \cdots, G_N(I)$, Laplacian pyramid $L_0(I), \cdots, L_N(I)$, the horizontal $H_0(I), \cdots, H_N(I)$ and vertical $V_0(I), \cdots, V_N(I)$ first derivatives of the Gaussian pyramid, and the horizontal $H_0^2(I), \cdots, H_N^2(I)$ and vertical $V_0^2(I), \cdots, V_N^2(I)$ second derivatives of the Gaussian pyramid are formed. Finally, a pyramid of features

$$F_j(I) = (L_j(I), H_j(I), V_j(I), H_j^2(I), V_j^2(I)), j = 0, \cdots, N \tag{4}$$

is formed. The Parent Structure vector of a pixel (m,n) in the lth level is defined as:

$$PS_l(I)(m,n) = (F_l(I)(m,n), F_{l+1}(I)(\lfloor \frac{m}{2} \rfloor, \lfloor \frac{n}{2} \rfloor), \cdots, F_N(I)(\lfloor \frac{m}{2^{N-1}} \rfloor, \lfloor \frac{n}{2^{N-1}} \rfloor)) \tag{5}$$

For each pixel (m,n) in the HR image to be predicted, a closest matching pixel in the training images is found by comparing the LR input's Parent Structure vector against all of the training Parent Structure vectors at the same level. By imposing the constraint that the first derivatives of h at this point should equal the derivatives of the closest matching pixel, we have:

$$-\ln P(h) = \frac{1}{2\sigma_\nabla^2} \sum_{m,n} (H_0(h)(m,n) - H_0(I_{match})(m,n))^2$$

$$+ \frac{1}{2\sigma_\nabla^2} \sum_{m,n} (V_0(h)(m,n) - V_0(I_{match})(m,n))^2 \tag{6}$$

Ignoring the concrete details, this pyramid-based method has two characters. Firstly, it presents a MAP super-resolution framework to fuse reconstruction constraint and HR image prior together. Actually, the MAP framework has been proposed since 1994 [18], and is adopted over and over again in the emerging new methods. Secondly, the HR image prior is achieved with the help of a set of training HR-LR image feature pairs. The predicted HR feature can be enforced to be equal to the training HR feature with the nearest neighbor LR feature matching.

2.2 Eigentransformation [8]

Different from most of the face hallucination methods based on probabilistic models, this method views face hallucination as a transformation between different image styles. This method use PCA to represents LR input face image as a linear combination of the LR training images:

$$l = \sum_{i=1}^{M} c_i l_i + m_l \tag{7}$$

where $l_i, i = 1, \cdots, M$ are the LR training images, m_l is the LR mean face and the $c_i, i = 1, \cdots, M$ are the combination coefficients. The HR image is rendered by replacing the LR training images with HR ones h_i, while retaining the same combination coefficients:

$$h = \sum_{i=1}^{M} c_i h_i + m_h \qquad (8)$$

This method has two advantages. Firstly, h meets the reconstruction constraint $Ah = l$, where A is a linear operation denoting the smoothing and down-sampling process. Operating A at both sides of (8), we have:

$$Ah = A(\sum_{i=1}^{M} c_i h_i + m_h) = \sum_{i=1}^{M} c_i Ah_i + Am_h = \sum_{i=1}^{M} c_i l_i + m_i = l \qquad (9)$$

Secondly, (8) shows that the result lies in a linear subspace spanned by the HR face images, so it should be face-like. These two advantages are both significant to a high quality hallucination, however, they are not sufficient to reconstruct local details. A pure global approach usually loses specific local characteristics of face, and the hybrid of the global and local approach is effective for this problem as introduced in the next section.

2.3   Two-Step Approach [10]

The two-step approach described in [10] is based on a global parametric model and a local nonparametric model. The theoretical derivation is still from MAP criterion, which requires solving:

$$h^* = \arg \max_{h} p(l \mid h) p(h) \qquad (10)$$

After separating the HR face image as the sum of a global face image h^g and a local feature image h^l, (10) is rewritten as

$$h^* = \arg \max_{h^g, h^l} p(l \mid h^g) p(h^g) p(h^l \mid h^g) \qquad (11)$$

The optimization strategy is naturally divided into two steps. At the first step, a global face h^{g*} is found by maximizing $p(l \mid h^g) p(h^g)$. By PCA, h^g is represented as

$$h^g = BX + \mu \qquad (12)$$

where B is the eigenvector matrix, μ is the mean face, and X is the combination coefficients. Thus, maximizing $p(l \mid h^g) p(h^g)$ is equivalent to maximizing $p(l \mid X) p(X)$. $p(l \mid X)$ is formulated to be a quadratic function of the error in the reconstruction constraint which is in the same way as (3). $p(X)$ is approximated as a Gaussian distribution:

$$p(X) = \frac{1}{Z} \exp(-\frac{1}{2} X^T \Lambda^{-1} X) \qquad (13)$$

where Λ is the diagonal matrix of eigenvalues and Z is a constant. At the second stage the optimal local feature image h^{l*} is computed by maximizing $p(h^l \mid h^{g*})$ using belief propagation [19]. Finally, $h^* = h^{g*} + h^{l*}$.

The two-step approach can be seen as a coarse-to-fine hallucination and can be summed up to be a unified framework: firstly hallucinate a coarse global face image by global approaches, and then compensate the residue between the original HR image and the reconstructed global face image by local approaches. The two-step approaches are usually superior to a pure global approach.

2.4   Position-Patch-Based Method [15]

The Neighbor Embedding (NE) [20] is a classical generic image super-resolution method. The basic idea of NE is to divide each image into overlapped square patches and perform super-resolution patch by patch. For a given LR image patch, it can be reconstructed by a linear combination of k-nearest neighboring LR training image patches. Then, we can synthesize the corresponding HR image patch by replacing the LR training image patches with the corresponding HR training image patches, while maintaining the same combination coefficients. Finally, the whole HR image is obtained by integrating these HR image patches by averaging the overlapped parts.

The position-patch method in [15] is an improvement of NE for face images. The authors find an easy way to hallucinate the HR image patch using the same position image patches of each training image instead of the nearest neighboring patch. Although the algorithm improvement is small, the local similarity of face image is fully utilized and the hallucination results are impressive. This inspires that the incorporation of face prior with generic image super-resolution methods may achieve unexpected success.

2.5   From Local Pixel Structure to Global Image Super-Resolution [17]

As mentioned before, the local similarity of face images is a very powerful prior for a high quality super-resolution. To maximize the local similarity, it should require: 1, accurate image alignment, 2, similar face samples. Hu et al. [17] proposed an effective preprocessing to meet these requirements. In their method, the first step is to search the database for K example faces that are the most similar to the input, and then warps the K example images to the input using optical flow. The second step uses the warped HR version of the K example faces to learn the local pixel structures for the target HR face. Step 3 estimates the target HR face by enforcing it to have the learned local pixel structures in addition to the reconstruction constraint.

In our experiment, we find this method is robust to the alignment error in a very small range. When the landmark alignment error is larger than 2 pixels on a 32 ×24 sized LR face image, the results are not acceptable.

2.6   Sparsity-Based Method

The face prior is not stable in practical application due to the variation of pose, expression, illumination and unaccurate alignment [7]. The mis-alignment of face images can directly interfere with the face similarity prior. In this section, we solve this problem based on two schemes:

1. We use a discriminative global model to represent different face alignment forms with proper basis elements.

2. We weaken the utilizing of local similarity prior, but use clustering analysis to collect similar image patches from all facial positions.

3. We combine the global and local schemes in an iterative manner to handle the mis-alignment problem to tuning the result from coarse to fine step by step.

Following this thinking, given the estimated value $x^{(n)} \in R^{n\times 1}$ of the HR face image in the nth iteration, we solve the following optimization problem:

$$\alpha^{(n+1)} = \arg\min_{\alpha} \frac{1}{2} \| x^{(n)} - H\alpha \|_2^2 + \lambda \| \alpha \|_0 \qquad (14)$$

where $H = [h_i, \cdots, h_m] \in R^{n\times m}$ is a dictionary covering all possible alignment forms. $\alpha \in R^{m\times 1}$ is the combination coefficient vector and λ is a Lagrange multiplier. Based on the discriminative nature of sparse representation discussed in [21] for face recognition, the basis elements with the same alignment form as $x^{(n)}$ are preferentially selected for reconstructing $x^{(n)}$. Inspired by the local detail compensation step of the two-step approach [10], given the LR input y, we super-resolve the LR residue $y - AH\alpha^{(n+1)}$ by a local operator SR, and compensate the result to $H\alpha^{(n+1)}$ to have:

$$x^{(n+1)} = SR(y - AH\alpha^{(n+1)}) + H\alpha^{(n+1)} \qquad (15)$$

We solve this problem by an alignment-independent similarity preserving process onto the HR/LR image patches. In the training phase, we jointly learn the HR and LR visual vocabularies [22]. Clustering analysis gives us pairs of HR and LR visual words and different linear regressions from LR to HR patches are learned on these visual words respectively. In the testing phase, we estimate the optimum visual word the LR input patch belongs to, and then the super-resolution is achieved by linear regression on that HR/LR visual word.

3   Experiments

3.1   Databases and Experimental Settings

The experiment was conducted on the CAS-PEAL-R1 face database [23], which consists of 99594 images of 1040 individuals. The Normal subset of CAS-PEAL-R1, in which the face images are under normal conditions, i.e., frontal pose, even illumination, and neutral expression, was used. The Normal subset contains 1040 images for one image per person. In this database, the coordinates of two eyes centers are provided which can be used for ground-truth alignment. Using two eye centers as landmarks, each original HR face image is cropped with the size 128×96. We collected three kinds of image sets for training. The image Set 1 contains 500 face images of frontal views and cropped with accurate localization of landmarks. The image Set 2 contains 5000 face images of frontal views with ±1 to 2 pixels landmarks localization error. The third image set contains 300 residue faces by randomly subtracting between two face images in image Set 1 and Set 2 within 1-pixel difference of localization for each landmark.

We show experiments by comparing the state-of-the-art methods, including [1], [8], [10] [12], [13], [15], [17], and the sparsity-based method. Set 1 and Set 2 form the training set for all methods. Set 3 is used for the clustering and the linear regression learning of the sparsity-based method. For existing hybrid two-step methods [10], [12], [13], 400 images in Set 1 and 4000 images in Set 2 are used for the global face model training, and the rest 1100 images for local model training. For the sparsity-based

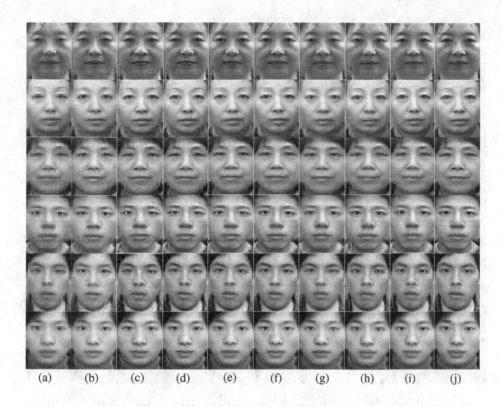

(a)   (b)   (c)   (d)   (e)   (f)   (g)   (h)   (i)   (j)

Fig. 1. The visualized comparison results of Experiment 1. (a) Input LR face image. (b) Baker and Kanade [1]. (c) Wang and Tang [8]. (d) Liu et al. [10]. (e) Zhuang et al. [12]. (f) Ma et al. [15]. (g) Hu et al. [17]. (h) Yang et al. [13]. (i) The sparsity-based method. (j) Ground truth HR face image.

method, all of 5500 HR images are used for dictionary learning, and the number of basis elements is set to be 3000. We randomly generate 100,000 HR and LR patch pairs from Set 3 for local model training. The number of visual words is set to be 1000.

In all experiments, the magnification factor is 4, that is, super-resolve 32×24 to 128×96. For subjective evaluation, we demonstrate the visual results. For quantitative evaluation, we measure the mean square error (MSE) per pixel between the original HR images and their hallucinated images. Besides, under the assumption that human visual perception is highly adapted for extracting structural information from a scene, we compared another evaluation measure, the structural similarity (SSIM) index [24]. If the original HR image and the result are the same, it equals the maximum value 1.

3.2   Face Hallucination with Well Alignment

In this section, we present the experimental results on near frontal-view face images with well alignment. We select 40 face images for testing. The experimental results are shown in Figs. 1, 3 and 4. With well-aligned face images, the quality of these results

(a)   (b)   (c)   (d)   (e)   (f)   (g)   (h)   (i)   (j)

Fig. 2. The visualized comparison results of Experiment 2. (a) Input LR face image. (b) Baker and Kanade [1]. (c) Wang and Tang [8]. (d) Liu et al. [10]. (e) Zhuang et al. [12]. (f) Ma et al. [15]. (g) Hu et al. [17]. (h) Yang et al. [13]. (i) The sparsity-based method. (j) Ground truth HR face image.

from different methods are almost the same, even for the oldest method [1]. There are distinctive ringing artifacts in [8], [10] and [13]. This is because the global face is reconstructed by the linear superposition of many basis element, for PCA or for NMF. In contrast, although the sparsity-based method also uses a linear superposition model, the sparsity constrains the involved basis elements as few as possible, to surpress the ringing effect much better.

3.3   Face Hallucination with Inaccurate Landmark Localization

The Experiment 2 is to test the face images with inaccurate landmark localization. We use the same testing images in Experiment 1 but with 1-2 pixels localization error from the ground truth coordinate for each eye center. We do not test on larger error because over 2-pixel error for each landmark will cause terrible face distotion and feature loss. The results are shown in Figs. 2, 3 and 4. As the increase of the alignment error, the visual quality of all existing methods is less good in general. The ringing effect is

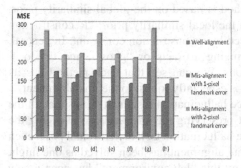

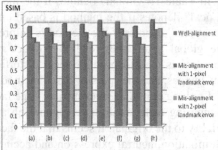

Fig. 3. The MSE comparison results of Experiment 2. (a) Baker and Kanade [1]. (b) Wang and Tang [8]. (c) Liu et al. [10]. (d) Zhuang et al. [12]. (e) Ma et al. [15]. (f) Hu et al. [17]. (g) Yang et al. [13]. (h) The sparsity-based method.

Fig. 4. The SSIM comparison results of Experiment 2. (a) Baker and Kanade [1]. (b) Wang and Tang [8]. (c) Liu et al. [10]. (d) Zhuang et al. [12]. (e) Ma et al. [15]. (f) Hu et al. [17]. (g) Yang et al. [13]. (h) The sparsity-based method.

more severe in [8], [10], [12] and [13], and the other pure local methods such as [1], [15] and [17] produce obvious local distortions. Note that Hu et al.'s method [17] produces the fewest artifacts due to the re-alignment process, but the results are too smooth. With 1-pixel error, [15] gives the best MSE and SSIM. However, with 2-pixel error, [15] is not robust anymore as if there are two faces that overlap, while the sparsity-based method maintains good performances even is better than 1-pixel error case as shown in Fig. 4 (h).

Table 1. A list of the method feature and the subjective strengths and weaknesses

	[1]	[8]	[10]	[12]	[13]	[15]	[17]	Sparsity
Global	No	Yes	Yes	Yes	Yes	No	No	Yes
Local	Yes	No	Yes	Yes	No	Yes	Yes	Yes
Reconstruction constraint	Yes	Yes	Yes	No	Yes	No	Yes	Yes
Sharpness	−	+	+	−	−	+ +	− −	+ +
Ringing effect	− −	+ +	+	+	+ +	−	− −	−
Local distortion	+ +	+	+	−	+ +	+	−	− −
Robustness to mis-alignment	+	− −	− −	−	− −	−	+	+ +

4   Conclusions

An overview of the method feature and the subjective strengths and weaknesses are presented in Table 1 using a four step scale consisting of − −, −, +and + + from low to high.

In Table 1, "Global" denotes if the method is based on the global similarity prior; "Local" denotes if the method is based on the local similarity prior; "Reconstruction constraint" denotes if the method is enforced by reconstruction constraint. In general, the global approaches tend to produce ringing artifacts or "ghost", and the local approaches tend to produce local distortions. We can see that each method has its advantages, and the sparsity-based method is especially robust to the mis-alignment.

Looking at in the Experimental 1 the face hallucination results, it seems that all the comparing methods do a very good job at preserving the sharpness and keeping the fidelity to the original. It seems that the face hallucination task under frontal pose, even illumination, neutral expression and accurate alignment has been solved as one might expect. Maybe it is time to seal the study on this "lab environment" but open a new research field in more complicated conditions. To the best of our knowledge, there have been related studies for hallucinating HR face images across multiple modalities, achieving generalization to variations in expression and pose [25]. The further development of face hallucination technique should be focusing on overcoming a variety of complicated interferences in practical applications.

Acknowledgments. This research is supported by the 12th Five-year Plan China S & T Supporting Programme (No. 2012BAK16B06), the National Science Foundation of China under Grant 61173084 and Grant 61128009, and the open fund from Key Lab of Digital Signal and Image Processing of Guangdong Province (No. 54600321).

References

1. Baker, S., Kanade, T.: Hallucinating Faces. In: Proc. IEEE Int. Conf. Automatic Face and Gesture Recog., pp. 83–88 (2000)
2. Schyns, P.G., Bonnar, L., Gosselin, F.: Show Me the Features! Understanding Recognition from the Use of Visual Information. Psychological Science (2002)
3. Baker, S., Kanade, T.: Limits on Super-Resolution and How to Break Them. IEEE TPAMI 24(9), 1167–1183 (2002)
4. Penev, P.S., Sirovich, L.: The Global Dimensionality of Face Space. In: Proc. IEEE Int. Conf. Automatic Face and Gesture Recognition, pp. 264–270 (2000)
5. He, X.F., Niyogi, P.: Locality Preserving Projections. In: Advances in Neural Information Processing Systems, Vancouver, Canada (2003)
6. Lee, D.D., Seung, H.S.: Learning the Parts of Objects by Non-negative Matrix Factorization. Nature 401(6755), 788–791 (1999)
7. Shan, S., Chang, Y., Gao, W., Cao, B., Yang, P.: Curse of Mis-alignment in Face Recognition: Problem and a Novel Mis-alignment Learning Solution. In: Proc. IEEE Int. Conf. Automatic Face and Gesture Recognition (2004)
8. Wang, X.G., Tang, X.O.: Hallucinating Face by Eigentransformation. IEEE Trans. Systems Man and Cybernetics (Part C) 35(3), 425–434 (2005)
9. Park, J.-S., Lee, S.-W.: An Example-based Face Hallucination Method for Single-frame, Low-resolution Facial Images. IEEE Trans. Image Processing 17(10), 1806–1816 (2008)
10. Liu, C., Shum, H.-Y., Freeman, W.T.: Face Hallucination: Theory and Practice. IJCV 75(1), 115–134 (2007)

11. Chakrabarti, A., Rajagopalan, A.N., Chellappa, R.: Super-resolution of Face Images Using Kernel PCA-based Prior. IEEE Transactions on Multimedia 9(4) (2007)
12. Zhuang, Y., Zhang, J., Wu, F.: Hallucinating Face: LPH Super-resolution and Neighbor Reconstruction for Residue Compensation. Pattern Recognition 40(11), 3178–3194 (2007)
13. Yang, J., Wright, J., Huang, T., Ma, Y.: Image Super-resolution via Sparse Representation. IEEE Trans. Image Processing 19(11), 2861–2873 (2010)
14. Su, C., Zhuang, Y., Huang, L., Wu, F.: Steerable Pyramid-based Face Hallucination. Pattern Recognition 38, 813–824 (2005)
15. Ma, X., Zhang, J., Qi, C.: Hallucinating Face by Position-patch. Pattern Recognition 43(6), 2224–2236 (2010)
16. Zou, W.W.W., Yuen, P.C.: Very Low Resolution Face Recognition Problem. IEEE Transactions on Image Processing 21(1), 327–340 (2012)
17. Hu, Y., Lam, K.-M., Qiu, G., Shen, T.: From Local Pixel Structure to Global Image Super-resolution: A New Face Hallucination Framework. IEEE TIP 20(2), 433–445 (2011)
18. Schulz, R.R., Stevenson, R.L.: A Bayesian Approach to Image Expansion for Improved Definition. IEEE TIP 3(3), 233–242 (1994)
19. Freeman, W.T., Pasztor, E.C., Carmichael, O.T.: Learning Low-level Vision. IJCV 40(1), 25–47 (2000)
20. Chang, H., Yeung, D.-Y., Xiong, Y.: Super-resolution through Neighbor Embedding. In: Proc. IEEE Conf. Computer Vision and Pattern Recognition (2004)
21. Wright, J., Yang, A.Y., Ganesh, A., Sastry, S.S., Ma, Y.: Robust Face Recognition via Sparse Representation. IEEE Trans. PAMI 31(2) (2009)
22. Yang, J., Jiang, Y.-G., Hauptmann, A., Ngo, C.-W.: Evaluating Bag-of-visual-words Representations in Scene Classification. In: Workshop on Multimedia Information Retrieval (MIR), in Conjunction with ACM Multimedia (2007)
23. Gao, W., Cao, B., Shan, S., Chen, X., Zhou, D., Zhang, X., Zhao, D.: The CAS-PEAL Large-scale Chinese Face Database and Baseline Evaluations. IEEE Trans. SMC, 149–161 (2008)
24. Wang, Z., Bovik, A.C., Sheikh, H.R., Simoncelli, E.P.: Image Quality Assessment: From Error Visibility to Structural Similarity. IEEE TIP 13(4), 600–612 (2004)
25. Jia, K., Gong, S.: Generalized Face Super-Resolution. IEEE TIP 17(6), 873–886 (2008)

Active Shape Model Based
on Sparse Representation

Yanqing Guo[1,4], Ran He[2], Wei-Shi Zheng[3], and Xiangwei Kong[1]

[1] Dalian University of Technology, Dalian 116024, China
[2] Institute of Automation, Chinese Academy of Sciences, Beijing 100190, China
[3] Sun Yat-Sen University, Guangzhou 510275, China
[4] State Information Center, Beijing 100045, China

Abstract. Active shape model (ASM), as a method for extracting and representing object shapes, has received considerable attention in recent years. In ASM, a shape is represented statistically by a set of well-defined landmark points and its variations are modeled by the principal component analysis (PCA). However, we find that both PCA and Procrustes analysis are sensitive to noise, and there is a linear relationship between alignment error and magnitude of noise, which leads parameter estimation to be ill-posed. In this paper, we present a sparse ASM based on l^1-minimization for shape alignment, which can automatically select an effective group of principal components to represent a given shape. A noisy item is introduced to both shape parameter and pose parameter (scale, translation, and rotation), and the parameter estimation is solved by the l^1-minimization framework. The estimation of these two kinds of parameters is independent and robust to local noise. Experiments on face dataset validate robustness and effectiveness of the proposed technique.

1 Introduction

Statistical shape analysis is an active research area in statistics and computer vision. It involves methods for automatic analysis and processing of geometrical objects where location, rotation, scale and variation information can be learned. A number of approaches have been proposed over the past decades, among which, Active Shape Model (ASM) [1] is one of most flexible methodologies. In ASM, there are three important parts: 1) model selection, 2) optimal features to model local texture structure, and 3) estimation of pose and shape parameters. The principal component analysis (PCA) is often used in ASM to model both shape variations and local texture structures. Some other modeling methods could resort to mixture of Gaussians [2], multiple statistical models [3], hierarchical models [4], and regularized models [5]. During the searching process, optimal features [6] are used to decide the movements of landmarks at each step, after which both pose and shape parameter are estimated in order to constrain these movements to a variation of shape under the learned model. To deal with in-plane rotation, translation and scaling of a shape, Procrustes analysis [7] is often used to estimate the pose parameter. Probabilistic methods, especially the Bayesian

W.-S. Zheng et al. (Eds.): CCBR 2012, LNCS 7701, pp. 94–103, 2012.

inference, are often used for shape parameter estimation [8][9]. Electric flows [10] and affine-invariant geometric shape priors [11] are also introduced into ASM to further improve alignment accuracy.

Due to local noise and the independent movement of each landmark, some movements predicted by the optimal features may be inaccurate. The errors incurred by inaccurate movements often make ASM fail at the stage of parameter estimation. Hence robust ASM draws more attention recently [12]. A common way is using shape prior knowledge. In the robust methods [13], M-estimator and randomly sampling approaches are used to estimate the shape parameter of ASM. In the Bayesian methods [14][15][16], Bayesian inference framework is developed for parameter estimation, where PCA is formulated by a probabilistic model. By maximizing a posterior probability, they can yield a good linear approximation to the general shape space.

The above methods mainly depend on PCA model as well as its shape prior for estimation of shape parameter, or Procrustes analysis to estimate pose parameter. However, the alignment error based on PCA or Procrustes analysis is linearly related to the magnitude of local noise [17][18]. The larger the magnitude of local noise is, the higher the alignment error tends to be. Since the noise of each landmark may be different due to partial occlusion, complex background or other effects in practical applications, it is unsuitable to assume that noisy residuals follow Gaussian distribution [13]. Such assumption may be inaccurate so that ASM fails to match the given shape contour when the magnitude of noise is large.

This paper presents a sparse ASM for shape alignment under the l^1 framework, which has attracted a lot of attentions in the signal and image processing communities [19][20]. Different from previous sparse methods, this work focuses on harnessing the l^1 optimization to select an effective group of principal components to represent a given shape and to estimate a robust pose parameter during searching in ASM. Firstly, the shape representation problem is formulated as a sparse representation problem. We aim to find a set of effective principal components from a shape basis to represent a smooth shape. A noisy item is introduced in the sparse framework to make the shape parameter estimation robust to noise. Instead of the assumption that the distribution of observed noise is Gaussian, we assume that noise has a sparse representation. Secondly, a sparse method is proposed to estimate the pose parameter (scale, translation, and rotation), which is generalized by appending a noisy vector. As analyzed later, the generalized pose parameter is also modeled by an l^1 optimization. Compared with the Procrustes analysis, the proposed method can alleviate the effect of noise. Experimental results on face alignment show that the proposed sparse framework performs better than other related ASM methods.

2 Concepts of ASM

This section briefly reviews modeling and parameter estimation in ASM. In ASM, an object is described in points, referred as landmark points. The landmark points are (manually) determined by a set of K training images. From these collections of landmark points, a point distribution model (PDM) is constructed as follows: the landmark points $(x_1, \ldots, x_n, y_1, \ldots, y_n)$ are stacked in shape vectors.

$$D_k = (X, Y) = (x_1, .., x_n, y_1, .., y_n)^T \tag{1}$$

where T denotes the transpose. PCA is then applied to the shape vectors D_k by computing the mean shape and covariance matrix: $\bar{D} = (1/K) \sum_{k=1}^{K} D_k$ and $S = (1/(K-1)) \sum_{k=1}^{K} (D_k - \bar{D})(D_k - \bar{D})^T$.

Then, $\{F_i\}$, the eigenvectors of S corresponding to the N largest eigenvalues λ_i, are retained. By defining $F = [F_1, \ldots, F_N]$, a shape can be approximated by

$$D \approx \bar{D} + Fb \tag{2}$$

where shape parameter b is a N-dimensional vector, and can be computed by

$$b = F^T(D - \bar{D}) \tag{3}$$

The shape parameter b defines a deformable model in (2). By varying b, one can obtain different shapes via (2). Since discontinuous calculation on b may result in an unstable estimation, regularized estimation of shape parameter is introduced to generate a valid shape. In [8], each entry b_i of b is updated by

$$b_i = (\lambda_i/(\lambda_i + \sigma^2))b_i \tag{4}$$

where σ^2 represents the PCA residual variance. We denote this Bayesian regularization method by **BR1**.

Slightly different from BR1, [15] regularizes each item b_i via

$$b_i = (\lambda_i/(\lambda_i + \rho))b_i \tag{5}$$

where $\rho = (1/n) \sum_{i=1}^{n} ((x_i^{old} - x_i)^2 + (y_i^{old} - y_i)^2)$ and (x_i^{old}, y_i^{old}) denotes the shape estimated in the last iteration and (x_i, y_i) denotes the updated landmarks. We denote this Bayesian regularization method by **BR2**.

In robust ASM (RASM) [13], M-estimator is introduced to perform a robust estimation of the shape parameter in context of ASM search. The shape parameter is computed by $b = K^T(D - \bar{D})$ where $K = (F^T W^T W F) F^T W^T W$ and W is a diagonal matrix whose diagonal element can be computed by Huber's rule.

Before estimating the shape parameter, a shape should be aligned by translating, rotating and scaling. We can express the initially estimated D of a shape as a scaled, rotated and translated version of the current shape D_0.

$$D = M(s, \theta)(D_0) + T \tag{6}$$

where $M(s, \theta)$ is a scaling and rotation matrix and $T = (t_x, t_y)^T$ is a translation matrix. The pose parameter is defined as a vector $p = (s, \theta, t_x, t_y)$ (See [1] for details). Procrustes analysis [7] and EM algorithm [8] are often used to estimate the pose parameter.

3   ASM Based on Sparse Representation

3.1   Sparse Shape Model

In ASM, each entry of the shape parameter b controls a particular variation along the principal components. The fewer the principal components are selected, the smoother the reconstructed shape tends to be; the more principal components are selected, more flexible ASM can be for detailed description of the shape [8]. Therefore, a subset of principal components is often (would be preferred to be) used to model a shape with shape variations.

In real-world shape alignment problem, many different groups of principal components are needed to reconstruct different shapes. Taking face contour alignment as an example, variations of a face contour could involve pose rotation, expression variation etc. We need a set of principal components to represent different possible face variations of different persons. We also need to select an appropriate group of these principal components to reconstruct a given shape for a particular segmentation task. However, to our best knowledge, it is still an unsolved problem.

Given a set of principal components and a new shape, we expect that the computer can automatically select the principal components . Such selection means that some entries of b will be zero while others are nonzero. A given shape can be accurately represented only by nonzero entries of the b. We say the principal components corresponding to the zero entries are irrelevant to the given shape. Thus we can treat the shape parameter estimation problem as an l^1-minimization problem:

$$\hat{b} = \arg\min_b ||D - \bar{D} - Fb||_2^2 + \lambda ||b||_1 \tag{7}$$

The optimization problem in (7) is the Lasso optimization problem and can be solved in polynomial time using standard linear programming methods.

During the local search in ASM, positions of landmarks may be inaccurate due to complex background, and differ due to different input backgrounds and are unknown to the computer. The errors may have arbitrary magnitude and make estimation of the shape parameter biased. Therefore, these errors cannot be ignored. Different from the traditional model that assumes a Gaussian noise, we extend the sparse representation method to deal with local noise. In this case, the above linear model (2) can be further modified as

$$D = D_0 + e_0 = \bar{D} + Fb + e_0 \tag{8}$$

where $e_0 \in R^{2n}$ is a noisy vector of errors. The nonzero entries of e_0 indicate that landmarks of shape D are inaccurately predicted. We assume that most of the landmarks' movements are reasonable so that variation of shape is in a suitable range and semantic information is held. Hence, those inaccurate landmarks are only a relatively small portion of a shape and we can assume that the noise vector e_0, like the parameter b, has a sparse representation with respect to the natural pixel coordinates. Then we can rewrite (8) as:

$$(D - \bar{D}) = [F, I] * [b^T, e_0^T]^T = Bb_0 \tag{9}$$

We call b_0 the generalized shape parameter. Then we obtain the following constrained optimization problem:

$$\widehat{b}_0 = \arg\min \|b_0\|_1 \; s.t. \; Bb_0 = D - \bar{D} \tag{10}$$

We can make use of the primal-dual algorithm to solve the above problem [1]. Given $\hat{b}_0$, we only use the b to reconstruct the desired shape.

To further illustrate the idea of sparse representation, we randomly perturb the ground truth shape D_g with a synthetic noise, i.e., $D = D_g + ae$ where a is a constant to control magnitude of noise and $e \in R^{2n}$ is a random vector whose nonzero entries are between 0 and 1. Fig. 1 (b) shows the shape parameter b yielded by PCA and the proposed sparse method respectively. It is easy to find that the two shape parameters computed by PCA are different. Local noise directly affects the estimation of shape parameter. For the sparse method, the shape parameter (solid line) calculated in D is similar to that (dash line) in D_g. This illustrates that the sparse method can efficiently deal with noise. We will further show its robustness in the experiment.

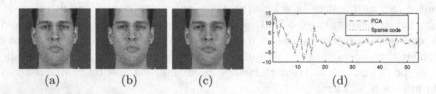

(a)   (b)   (c)   (d)

Fig. 1. Shapes reconstructed by PCA and sparse method. The y-axis is value of each shape parameter and x-axis is the index of shape parameter sorted by their corresponding eigenvalues. (a) Ground-truth shape (b) Shape reconstructed by PCA. (c)Shape reconstructed by the sparse method. (d) Shape parameter calculated by PCA and sparse method corresponding to the right two corresponding shapes respectively.

When noise is introduced, an important issue of the sparse method is that the estimated e_0 may be still nonzero on a ground truth shape. When noise does not exist or its magnitude is small, the reconstruction error of PCA is smaller than that of the sparse method, since the PCA method tries to minimize the reconstruction error (the distance between original shape vector and reconstructed one). However, in this case, it is difficult to evaluate which reconstructed shape (PCA or the sparse method) is the better one from human sense. As shown in Fig. 1 (b), the shape parameter yielded by PCA and that by the sparse method are slightly different. It shows that both reconstructed shapes in Fig. 1 are good enough as compared to the ground-truth one. Hence, the sparsity assumption of the shape parameter is suitable and using the sparse method to represent a shape is acceptable.

---

[1] http://www.acm.caltech.edu/l1magic/

3.2   Sparse Pose Parameter Estimation

Pose parameter in ASM includes the ones for scaling, translation, and rotation. Procrustes analysis is often used in ASM in both training stage and searching stage for their estimation. Procrustes analysis is a form of statistical shape analysis that uses pose parameter to find the best match between two or more landmark shapes. It calculates pose parameter by minimizing the distance between two shapes using the least squares technique. The merit of Procrustes analysis in ASM is that it can modify pose parameter step by step, which leads to a continuous update of a shape. However, on the other hand, small variations of landmarks will make Procrustes analysis find a different pose parameter. It shows that the estimation of pose parameter will be unstable when there is noise.

To handle noise, we also associate (6) with a noisy item similar in previous section. Then we get:

$$D = M(s, \theta)[D_0] + T + \varepsilon_0 \tag{11}$$

If we denote $(x_1, \ldots, x_n, y_1, \ldots, y_n)^T$ by (X, Y) where $X = (x_1, \ldots, x_n)^T$ and $Y = (y_1, \ldots, y_n)^T$, we can rewrite (11) as

$$D = \begin{pmatrix} X & -Y \\ Y & X \end{pmatrix} \begin{pmatrix} s\cos\theta \\ s\sin\theta \end{pmatrix} + \begin{pmatrix} 1 & 0 \\ 0 & 1 \end{pmatrix} \begin{pmatrix} tx \\ ty \end{pmatrix} + I e_0 \tag{12}$$

where $\mathbf{1}$ is an all-one column vector and I is a $2n \times 2n$ identify matrix. Eq. (12) can be further expressed as $D = B p_0$ where $B = \begin{pmatrix} X & -Y & 1 & 0 \\ Y & X & 0 & 1 \end{pmatrix} I$ and $p_0 = \begin{pmatrix} s\cos\theta & s\sin\theta & t_x & t_y & e_0 \end{pmatrix}^T$.

We denote the p_0 by the generalized pose parameter, and also assume that p_0 is sparse. This assumption mainly comes from the following fact in the searching stage of ASM. At each step of ASM searching, the searching step-length of each landmark is limited and most of the landmarks' movements are reasonable, so that the in-plane variation is within a suitable range. Hence, the change of pose parameter is small and the entries of noise item e_0 could be sparse (as in the last section, we assume only part of the landmark points that are inaccurately predicted). Therefore, we can formulate estimation of the pose parameter as an l^1-minimization problem:

$$\widehat{p}_0 = \arg\min \|p_0\|_1 \ s.t. \ B p_0 = D \tag{13}$$

Accordingly, the updating Equation of pose parameter is,

$$(\sqrt{p_0(1)^2 + p_0(2)^2}, \operatorname{atan}(p_0(2)/p_0(1)), p_0(3), p_0(4))$$

where $p_0(i)$ is the i-th element of p_0. The above problem can be solved by primal-dual algorithm based on convex optimization. We also call this estimation method as a sparse method.

4   Experiments

In this section, we perform experiments on face dataset to demonstrate robustness and accuracy of our sparse method as compared to three state-of-the-art robust ASM methods: BR1-ASM, BR2-ASM and RASM (See Section 2 for details). The setting of parameters of the three compared methods follows the suggestion of [13][8][15] respectively. To quantitatively compare the accuracy of different algorithms, we evaluate the segmentation error by a distance measure that is often used in comparing different ASM methods [8][21]. This measure is defined by an average distance between the searched landmarks and the ground truth landmarks as follows:

$$dist(A) = (1/N) \sum_{i=1}^{N} \sqrt{(x_i^A - x_i)^2 + (y_i^A - y_i)^2} \tag{14}$$

where $dist(A)$ denotes the estimation error of algorithm A (or reconstruction error), (x_i, y_i) is coordinate of the i-th ground-truth landmark and (x_i^A, y_i^A) is the searched coordinate of the i-th landmark by algorithm A.

We select 100 face images from the XM2VTS face database [18]. The average eyes-distance is 80 pixels for each facial image. All 96 face landmarks for each image are labeled manually. The five sense organs (F.S.O.) are composed of 71 landmarks and the cheek contour contains 25 landmarks. We follow Hamarneh ASM [2] and implement the ASM based on his code. A three level image pyramids is formed for an input image by repeated sub-sampling. The PCA threshold is set to 97.5% for each ASM. All algorithms in the comparison experiment only differ in the scheme for parameter estimation. Although the images in XM2VTS have good quality, the selected data set is still challenging for precise alignment due to mustache, eyebrow and glasses.

Please note that our goal is not to achieve the best segmentation performance on the XM2VTS dataset. Instead, we aim to illustrate the efficiency of the sparse method as compared to traditional methods.

Table 1. Comparison results of different methods on face alignment

	Face				F.S.O.				Cheek Contour			
	mean	min	max	std	mean	min	max	std	mean	min	max	std
ASM	5.7	2.8	11.7	2.0	5.3	2.3	12.5	2.1	6.8	3.0	18.4	3.1
BR1-ASM	5.6	3.0	11.7	1.9	5.3	2.4	12.5	2.0	6.6	3.2	17.5	2.9
BR2-ASM	5.3	2.8	13.5	2.1	4.9	2.3	13.5	2.1	6.4	2.9	19.8	3.3
RASM	5.2	2.5	11.7	1.8	5.1	2.5	10.6	1.8	5.6	1.9	15.4	3.1
SASM	4.5	2.0	8.3	1.4	4.2	2.2	8.0	1.0	5.5	2.1	16.4	2.9

Face Alignment Accuracy. In previous sections, we focus on the comparison at the stage of parameter estimation in ASM. In this section, we integrate the

---

[2] http://www.cs.sfu.ca/~hamarneh/software/asm/index.html

proposed sparse method into the standard ASM and denote it by SASM. We would then compare it with standard ASM, RASM, BR1-ASM, and BR2-ASM, where BR1 and BR2 are used for parameter estimation in the latter two methods. For each input image, an initial shape is generated by the mean shape of training set. Table 1 reports different alignment results of different methods. Location error is measured in pixels by (14). The average improvement of SASM with respect to the RASM segmentation is 11.9%. For the F.S.O. and check contour, the improvements are 17.4% and 0.5% respectively. We see that both SASM and RASM can accurately match the cheek contour. But SASM can also match F.S.O. more accurately. It is shown that our algorithm is much more accurate as compared to other ASM methods.

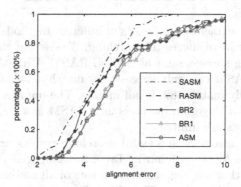

Fig. 2. Average shape alignment errors (regardless of pose parameter). The smaller the reconstruction error is, the more robust to noise the method is.

Fig. 2 shows the cumulative curve of alignment accuracy. The x-axis represents the alignment error and the y-axis represents the percentage (frequency) of all testing samples having the alignment error smaller than the corresponding value in x-axis. As shown in Table 1, SASM performs better than another methods. The Bayesian regulation method and RASM can also deal with noise and yield an improvement, but the sparse method can achieve more accurate alignment results. In some easy alignment cases, the sparse method can match the shape more accurately; for some difficult alignment cases, it can hold more accurate position and prevent the searching from trapping in local minima. Therefore, noise can be alleviated more effectively and accordingly a more accurate position can be found.

Rotation and Scaling. In shape alignment, a shape may be rotated and scaled in the input image. ASMs have potential risk to miss the correct position during searching. We simulate this scenario by giving a random initialization of pose parameters. To fairly compare different methods, we use a random strategy to initialize the mean shape. For each test image, an initial shape is generated by randomly rotating (from -20 to 20) and scaling (from 0.9 to 1.1) the mean shape, and then it is fed into different algorithms. Because all ASMs may lose the correct position during segmentation, we set a threshold to judge this scenario. When the segmentation error of searching results is larger than 10, we consider that this searching fails, otherwise, the searching succeeds.

Table 2. Comparison results under randomly initialized pose parameter

	Face	F.S.O.	Cheek	Success
ASM	6.65	5.88	8.54	47%
BR1 -ASM	6.19	5.54	8.20	49%
BR2 -ASM	5.71	4.98	7.11	53%
RASM	5.54	4.99	7.01	55%
SASM	5.15	4.81	6.10	58%

Table 2 shows the segmentation results of different methods. The last column of Table 2 shows the rate of successful searching. We see that the methods can be ordered in descending success rates as SASM, RASM, BR2 -ASM, BR1 -ASM, ASM. The classical ASM can only successfully match 47.4% facial images. But SASM can successfully match 58% facial images. The improvement is nearly 10 percent. Although two Bayesian methods and RASM can also improve success rate, the improvements are limited.

The segmentation errors of successful searching results are listed from the second column to the fourth column in Table 2. Compared with the results in Table 1, we can find that the segmentation errors of all methods become larger. Although the segmentation errors of SASM in Table 2 are also larger than those of SASM in Table 1, segmentation errors of SSAM in Table 2 are still smaller than those of other methods in Table 1. This illustrates that SASM can still outperform other ASM methods.

5   Conclusion

This paper addresses model selection and parameter estimation in ASM under noise and presents a novel method for shape alignment problem under the l^1-minimization framework. By formulating shape parameter estimation as an l^1-minimization problem, we have built a sparse model describing statistical shapes. Furthermore, the pose parameter estimation is also formulated as the l^1-minimization problem. Experimental results illustrate that the two sparse methods are more robust to noise and can estimate the true parameter from noise. When the two methods are applied in ASM, we get a new ASM method called SASM. Comparison between SASM, classical ASM algorithm, robust ASM, and Bayesian regularization ASM methods has demonstrated the promising results of our proposed methods.

Acknowledgment. This work is funded by China Postdoctoral Science Foundation (NO. 20110490343) and National Natural Science Foundation of China (No. 60971095, 61103155, 61102111).

References

1. Cootes, T.F., Taylor, C.J., Cooper, D., Graham, J.: Active shape models-their training and application. CVIU 61(1), 38–59 (1995)
2. Cootes, T.F., Taylor, C.J.: A mixture model for representing shape variation. In: British Machine Vision Conference, pp. 110–119 (1997)
3. Butakoff, C., Frangi, A.F.: A framework for weighted fusion of multiple statistical models of shape and appearance. IEEE TPAMI 28(11), 1847–1857 (2006)
4. Lee, S.W., Kang, J., Shin, J., Paik, J.: Hierarchical active shape model with motion prediction for real-time tracking of non-rigid objects. IET Computer Vision 1(1), 17–24 (2009)
5. Yu, T., Luo, J., Ahuja, N.: Search strategies for shape regularized activen contour. Computer Vision and Image Understanding 113(10), 1053–1063 (2009)
6. Sukno, F., Ordas, S., Butakoff, C., Cruz, S., Frangi, A.: Active shape models with invariant optimal features: application to facial analysis. IEEE Trans. on Pattern Analysis and Machine Intelligence 29(7), 1105–1117 (2007)
7. Goodall, C.: Procrustes methods in the statistical analysis of shapes. Journal of the Royal Statistical Society 53(2), 285–339 (1991)
8. Zhou, Y., Gu, L., Zhang, H.: Bayesian tangent shape model: Estimating shape and pose parameters via bayesian inference. In: CVPR, pp. 109–116 (2003)
9. Yan, S., Li, M., Zhang, H., Cheng, Q.: Ranking prior likelihood distributions for bayesian shape localization framework. In: ICCV, pp. 453–468 (2003)
10. Chang, H.H., Valentino, D.J., Chu, W.C.: Active shape modeling with electric flows. IEEE TVCG 16(5), 854–869 (2010)
11. Foulonneau, A., Charbonnier, P., Heitz, F.: Affine-invariant geometric shape priors for region-based active contours. IEEE TPAMI 28(8), 1352–1357 (2006)
12. Lekadir, K., Merrifield, R., Yang, G.Z.: Outlier detection and handling for robust 3-d active shape models search. IEEE TMI 26(3), 212–222 (2007)
13. Rogers, M., Graham, J.: Robust Active Shape Model Search. In: Heyden, A., Sparr, G., Nielsen, M., Johansen, P. (eds.) ECCV 2002, Part IV. LNCS, vol. 2353, pp. 517–530. Springer, Heidelberg (2002)
14. Blanz, V., Mehl, A., Vetter, T., Seidel, H.: A statistical method for robust 3d surface reconstruction from sparse data. In: 3D Data Processing, Visualization and Transmission (2004)
15. He, R., Li, S., Lei, Z., Liao, S.: Coarse-to-Fine Statistical Shape Model by Bayesian Inference. In: Yagi, Y., Kang, S.B., Kweon, I.S., Zha, H. (eds.) ACCV 2007, Part I. LNCS, vol. 4843, pp. 54–64. Springer, Heidelberg (2007)
16. Huang, Y., Liu, Q., Metaxas, D.: A component based deformable model for generalized face alignment. In: ICCV, pp. 1–8 (2007)
17. He, R., Hu, B., Yuan, X.: Robust Discriminant Analysis Based on Nonparametric Maximum Entropy. In: Zhou, Z.-H., Washio, T. (eds.) ACML 2009. LNCS, vol. 5828, pp. 120–134. Springer, Heidelberg (2009)
18. He, R., Hu, B.G., Yuan, X., Zheng, W.S.: Principal component analysis based on nonparametric maximum entropy. Neurocomputing 73, 1840–1952 (2010)
19. Wright, J., Ma, Y., Mairal, J., Sapiro, G., Huang, T.S., Yan, S.: Sparse representation for computer vision and pattern recognition. Proceedings of IEEE 98(6), 1031–1044 (2010)
20. He, R., Zheng, W.S., Hu, B.G., Kong, X.W.: A regularized correntropy framework for robust pattern recognition. Neural Computation 23(8), 2074–2100 (2011)
21. Liang, L., Wen, F., Tang, X., Xu, Y.: An Integrated Model for Accurate Shape Alignment. In: Leonardis, A., Bischof, H., Pinz, A. (eds.) ECCV 2006. LNCS, vol. 3954, pp. 333–346. Springer, Heidelberg (2006)

On the Influence of Fingerprint Area in Partial Fingerprint Recognition

Fanglin Chen[1] and Jie Zhou[2]

[1] Department of Automatic Control, College of Mechatronics and Automation,
National University of Defense Technology, Changsha, Hunan 410073, P.R. China
[2] Department of Automation, Tsinghua University, Beijing 100084, P.R. China
fanglinchen@nudt.edu.cn, jzhou@tsinghua.edu.cn

Abstract. Conventional algorithms for fingerprint recognition are mainly
based on minutiae information. However, the small number of minutiae
in partial fingerprints is still a challenge in fingerprint matching. In fingerprint recognition systems, there are frequently appeared partial fingerprints, such as incompletely touching in fingerprint scanning or latent
fingerprints. In this paper, we studied the influence of the fingerprint
area in partial fingerprint recognition. First, a simulation scheme was
proposed to construct a serial of partial fingerprints with different area.
Then, the influence of the fingerprint area in partial fingerprint recognition is studied. By comparing the performance of partial fingerprint
recognition with different fingerprint area, some useful conclusions can
be drawn: (1) The decrease of the fingerprint area degrades the performance of partial fingerprint recognition; (2) When the fingerprint area
decreases, the genuine matching scores will decrease, whereas the imposter matching scores will increase; (3) When the area of partial fingerprints is smaller than 20,000 pixels (about fifth of the normal full
fingerprints), the performance of partial fingerprint recognition becomes
very poor; (4) The threshold value of a given false accept rate increases
when the area of partial fingerprints decrease a lot, but it remains almost the same if the area of partial fingerprints decrease not so much,
e.g., greater than 50,000 pixels (about half of the normal full fingerprint). These observations can be helpful in improving the performance
of partial fingerprint recognition in the future.

Keywords: Fingerprint recognition, partial fingerprint, fingerprint
area, minutiae, fingerprint matching.

1 Introduction

Recently, biometric technologies have shown more and more importance in various applications. Among them, fingerprint recognition is considered one of
the most reliable technologies and has been extensively used in personal identification. In the recent years this technology has received increasingly more
attention [1].

A fingerprint is the pattern of ridges and valleys on the surface of a fingertip.
A microscopic feature of the fingerprint is called minutiae, which means ridge

W.-S. Zheng et al. (Eds.): CCBR 2012, LNCS 7701, pp. 104–111, 2012.
© Springer-Verlag Berlin Heidelberg 2012

endings and bifurcations. Most classical fingerprint verification algorithms [2, 3] take the minutiae, including their coordinates and direction, as the distinctive features to represent the fingerprint in the matching process. Minutiae extraction mainly includes the below steps: orientation field estimation, ridge extraction or enhancement, ridge thinning and minutiae extraction. Then the minutiae feature is compared with the minutiae template; if the matching score exceed a predefined threshold, these two fingerprints can be regarded as belonging to a same finger.

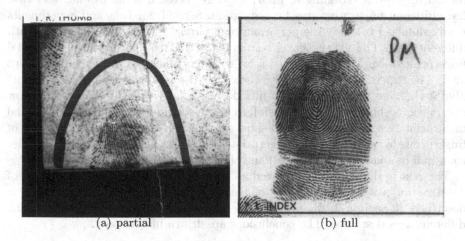

(a) partial   (b) full

Fig. 1. Example of a partial fingerprint and its matching full fingerprint

However, the small number of minutiae in partial fingerprints is still a challenge in fingerprint matching. For partial fingerprint images, existing minutiae based algorithms are likely to detect few minutiae. As a result, the recognition rate of the fingerprint identification would decrease. Specially, many researchers reported that the performance of the minutiae-based algorithms degraded heavily in partial fingerprint recognition [4–8]. In fingerprint recognition systems, there are frequently appeared partial fingerprints, such as incompletely touching in fingerprint scanning or latent fingerprints (see Fig. 1 for an example). Therefore, it is a challenging problem of how to improve the performance for partial fingerprint. Jea et al. [4] presented an approach that uses localized secondary features derived from relative minutiae information for partial fingerprint recognition. Milshtein et al. [7] studied fingerprint recognition algorithms for partial and full fingerprints. They used minutiae classification scheme to reduce the reference base for given tested finger. Girgis et al. [8] defined a new representation to encode the local neighborhood of each minutiae, then employed a dynamic programming which is based on genetic algorithm to find the global optimized transformation. All these algorithms were depending on the extracted minutiae, and still cannot perform well when there are a few minutiae in partial fingerprint.

In this paper, we addressed the topic of partial fingerprint recognition. Since the size of different fingerprint acquisition equipment is not the same, and the pressure of different people when acquiring fingerprints differs in thousand ways, the area of acquired fingerprints differs a lot with each other. Some of the existed algorithms consider the factor, but they just account the number of minutiae. Though the number of minutiae has some relation with the area of a fingerprint, it is not absolutely causal. What is more, due to spurious minutiae and missing detection in fingerprints with poor quality, the real number of minutiae is hard to obtain. Thus we considered the area information of partial fingerprints in fingerprint recognition, and studied the influence of the fingerprint area in partial fingerprint recognition. First, we constructed a serial of data sets that have different fingerprint area by simulation. Second, analysis and experiments were conducted to study the performance of partial fingerprint recognition with different area. The experimental results show that the performance of partial fingerprint recognition is degraded a lot with much decreasing of the fingerprint area. The experimental results also show that the performance remains acceptable if the area of partial fingerprints decrease not so much. These important observations show that the area information should be considered in partial fingerprint recognition. They also show that we can improve the acquisition of fingerprints by refusing partial fingerprints whose area are too small (e.g., smaller than half of a normal fingerprint), and then re-acquire.

The rest of the paper is organized as follows: in Section 2, the simulation of constructing a serial of data sets of partial fingerprints with different area is described; in Section 3, the performance of partial fingerprint recognition with different area is studied. The conclusions are drawn in Section 4.

2   Data Sets Construction

Though there are partial fingerprints in many databases, the scale of partial fingerprint is not big enough for statistics analysis. What is more, the area of these partial fingerprints is different with each other, and thus is not appropriate for studying the influence of area in partial fingerprint recognition.

In this section, we will introduce the simulation based method to construct a serial of data sets with different fingerprint area. The partial fingerprints are cut from the full fingerprints to the desired area S_d. Thus the first step is to select full fingerprint from a database. This can be done very quickly by manual. The second step is to cut the full fingerprint to partial fingerprint with desired area S_d. This is conducted by the following steps:

1. Generate a random point (x, y) in the full fingerprint.
2. Generate a random direction $\theta \in [0, 2\pi)$ at point (x, y).
3. Cut the fingerprint with random depth d perpendicular to the direction θ.
4. Repeat step 2 and 3 until the area of the fingerprint S approximately reach the desired area S_d by the following stopping principle:

$$abs(S - S_d) < \delta, \tag{1}$$

where δ is a pre-defined threshold. In this study, $\delta = 200$ pixels.

If the area of the cut fingerprint is smaller than S_d after step 3, then go back to step 2 and cut again with a smaller d. Fig. 2 shows the scheme of cutting a full fingerprint to a partial one. Here, we put the cut parts together with the remain partial fingerprint for the convenience to give a visual sense.

Fig. 2. The scheme of cutting a full fingerprint to a partial one

3   Comparing the Performance of Partial Fingerprint Recognition with Different Area

In this section, the experiments of comparing performance of partial fingerprint recognition with different fingerprint area have been carried out. The databases will be first described. Then the experimental results are reported and some interesting observations are summarized.

3.1   Database Description

The experiments are conducted on three databases, including three public collections, FVC02 DB1 and DB2 [9], and the THU database [10].

Both DB1 and DB2 from FVC02 contain 800 fingerprints, that is, 100 fingers and 8 prints for each finger respectively. The FVC02 database has following features: (1) fingerprints collected in three sessions with at least two weeks' time separating each session; (2) no efforts were made to control image quality and the sensor platens were not systematically cleaned; (3) at each session, four impressions were acquired of each of the four fingers of each volunteer; (4) during the second session, individuals were requested to exaggerate displacement (impressions 1 and 2) and rotation (3 and 4) of the finger, not to exceed 35 degrees; (5) during the third session, fingers were alternatively dried (impressions 1 and 2) and moistened (3 and 4). DB1 were collected by sensor "TouchView II" of Identix with size=388×374, and DB2 were collected by sensor "FX2000" of Biometrika with size=296×560. The qualities of fingerprints in DB1 is much worse than those in DB2.

The THU database consists of 6616 fingerprint impressions, which are captured by sensor of Digital Persona (image size=320×512). All these fingerprints are from 827 different fingers, and 8 fingerprints per finger. These fingerprint images have different sizes and vary in different qualities. In them, more than 40% of these images are suffering the affection from creases, scars and smudges in the ridges or dryness and blurs of the fingers.

Using the full fingerprints of these three databases, we generated three serials data sets. Each serial data set has the same number of partial fingerprints with different fingerprint area. The fingerprint area changes from 10,000 pixels to 100,000 pixels with the interval of 10,000 pixels.

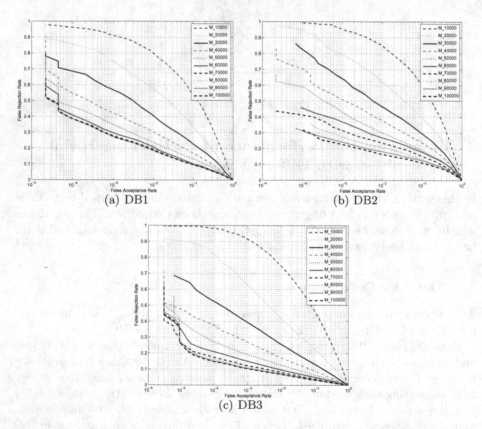

(a) DB1　　　　　(b) DB2

(c) DB3

Fig. 3. ROCs of different areas on DB1, DB2, and THU database, respectively

3.2   Results and Analysis

The receiver operating curve (ROC) plots FAR versus FRR of fingerprint recognition system. False Rejection Rate (FRR) is defined as the percentage of imposter matches in all genuine pairs, while False Acceptance Rate (FAR) is defined as the percentage of genuine matches in all imposter pairs. Fig. 3 shows the ROCs of the partial fingerprint recognition with different fingerprint area in three data sets. From the results, it can be drawn that the performance of partial fingerprint recognition degrades with the decreasing of the fingerprint area. And when the area of partial fingerprints is smaller than 20,000 pixels (about fifth of the normal full fingerprints), the performance of partial fingerprint recognition becomes very poor.

Why the decreasing of fingerprint area degrades the performance of partial fingerprint recognition? The main reason is that the number of minutiae is very small when the fingerprint area decreases. Thus the discrimination of minutiae matching declines. Fig. 4 shows the threshold values with different given false

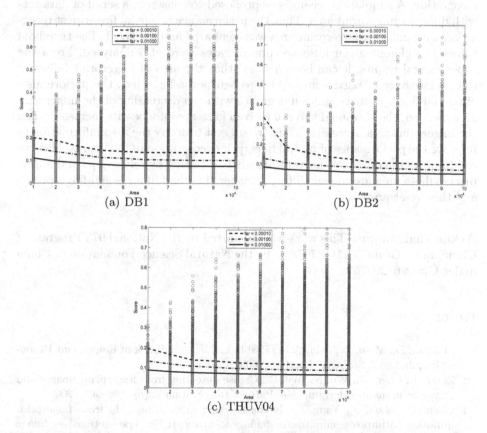

Fig. 4. The threshold of different given false acceptance rates on DB1, DB2, and THUV04, respectively. The red circles represent genuine matching scores, while the green cross stand for the imposter matching scores.

acceptance rates. From the results, it can be concluded that the threshold valve increases when the fingerprint area decreases. It also shows that when the fingerprint area decreases, the genuine matching scores will decrease, whereas the imposter matching scores will increase. However, scores and the threshold value remain almost the same if the area of partial fingerprints decrease not so much, e.g., greater than 50,000 pixels (about half of the normal full fingerprint). This indicates that when the area of partial fingerprints decrease not so much, the minutiae matching is robust. But the performance becomes very poor if the area of partial fingerprints decrease a lot, and more information is needed to improve the robustness of the minutiae-based system. All these observations reflect the declination of the discrimination of minutiae matching.

4   Conclusion

In this paper, we studied the influence of fingerprint area in partial fingerprint recognition. A simulation scheme was proposed to construct a serial of data sets with different fingerprint area. Then the performance of partial fingerprint recognition with different fingerprint area was compared and analyzed. The threshold values of different given false acceptance rates were also analyzed. From the experimental results, it can be concluded that the area of fingerprint influence the performance of partial fingerprint recognition a lot. First, the performance of partial fingerprint recognition degrades with the decreasing of the fingerprint area. Second, the threshold valve of a given false acceptance rate increases when the fingerprint area decreases. Thus, we suggest utilizing the area information to improve the performance of partial fingerprint recognition in the future. Also, we can improve the quality of fingerprints when acquiring by refusing partial fingerprints whose area are too small (e.g., smaller than half of a normal fingerprint), and then re-acquire.

Acknowledgement. This work was supported by the National 973 Program of China under Grant 2011CB707802, by the Natural Science Foundation of China under Grant 61203263.

References

1. Maltoni, D., Maio, D., Jain, A.K., Prabhakar, S.: Handbook of Fingerprint Recognition, 2nd edn. Springer, London (2009)
2. Zhou, J., Chen, F., Wu, N., Wu, C.: Crease detection from fingerprint images and its applications in elderly people. Pattern Recognition 42(5), 896–906 (2009)
3. Chen, F., Zhou, J., Yang, C.: Reconstructing orientation field from fingerprint minutiae to improve minutiae-matching accuracy. IEEE Transactions on Image Processing 18(7), 1665–1670 (2009)
4. Jea, T.Y., Govindaraju, V.: A minutia-based partial fingerprint recognition system. Pattern Recognition 38(10), 1672–1684 (2005)

5. Jea, T.Y.: Minutiae-based partial fingerprint recognition. PhD thesis, State University of New York at Buffalo (2006)
6. Fang, G., Srihari, S.N., Srinivasan, H., Phatak, P.: Use of ridge points in partial fingerprint matching. In: Proc. of SPIE: Biometric Technology for Human Identification IV, pp. 65390D1–65390D9 (2007)
7. Mil'shtein, S., Pillai, A., Shendye, A., Liessner, C., Baier, M.: Fingerprint recognition algorithms for partial and full fingerprints. In: 2008 IEEE Conference on Technologies for Homeland Security, pp. 449–452. IEEE (2008)
8. Girgis, M.R., Sewisy, A.A., Mansour, R.F.: A robust method for partial deformed fingerprints verification using genetic algorithm. Expert Systems with Applications 36(2), 2008–2016 (2009)
9. Maio, D., Maltoni, D., Cappelli, R., Wayman, J., Jain, A.: FVC2002: Second Fingerprint Verification Competition. In: International Conference on Pattern Recognition, vol. 16, pp. 811–814 (2002)
10. Zhou, J., Gu, J.: A model-based method for the computation of fingerprints' orientation field. IEEE Transactions on Image Processing 13(6), 821–835 (2004)

Fingerprint Identification Based on Semi-supervised *FSS*

Xuzhou Li[1,2], Ying Li[1], Yilong Yin[1,*], and Gongping Yang[1]

[1] School of Computer Science and Technology, Shandong University, Jinan, 250101, China
[2] Shandong Youth University of Political Science, Jinan, 250103, China
lixuzhou@126.com, vicky71222008@hotmail.com,
{ylyin,gpyang}@sdu.edu.cn

Abstract. Fingerprint images captured in real world applications always include some variations, called intra-class variations, due to various uncontrolled conditions like scratching, aging, moisting, drying, etc. It is important for current fingerprint identification systems to adaptively deal with these variations. In this paper, we propose a semi-supervised *FSS* based fingerprint identification method. We use unlabeled samples to train *FSS Center* for each finger in a semi-supervised setting, which significantly improves the robustness of the *FSS* based method. We evaluate our method on the DIEE Fingerprint database. The experimental results show favorable performance of our method as compared to state-of-the-art.

Keywords: fingerprint identification, *FSS*, template update.

1 Introduction

An automatic fingerprint identification system (AFIS) normally consists of two main stages: the enrollment stage and the identification stage. During enrollment, fingerprint images are acquired and processed to extract feature sets. One or more feature sets are then saved as enrollment templates in a template database. During identification, a new fingerprint image is received for identification. We first extract the feature set. The system then compares the feature set against templates in the template database to determine the identity of the new fingerprint image [4]. However, as mentioned before, there always exist intra-class variations for fingerprint images captured in uncontrolled conditions like scratching, aging, moisting, drying, etc. Thus, in real-world applications, the captured fingerprint images of an identity can be different from the enrolled ones, resulting in a declined identification performance. Given this fact, it is of great benefit to solve the problem incurred by intra-class variations. The related research is becoming a hot topic in fingerprint recognition.

Currently, most solutions focus on updating fingerprint templates. In particular, the template updating methods normally consist of the following two steps: (1) inserting of a novel template into the gallery, (2) fusing the new template with an existing one or replacing an existing template with the new one [3],[9],[1],[2]. Uludag et al. [8]

---

* Corresponding author.

W.-S. Zheng et al. (Eds.): CCBR 2012, LNCS 7701, pp. 112–119, 2012.

proposed two automatic template selection methods called DEND and MDIST. The goal is to select prototype fingerprint templates for a finger from a given set of fingerprint impressions. Yin. et al. [11] proposed a template update method to better represent a given finger. MDIST and Yin's method have better performance than other template update methods [3], [11].

In this paper, we propose a semi-supervised *FSS* based fingerprint identification method, called "FSS semi-supervised". Our method utilizes a two-stage process. In the first enrollment stage, *FSS Center* of each finger is trained by the *FSS* based fingerprint identification method. In the second identification stage, we collect a large number of unlabeled fingerprint images, based on which the *FSS Center* is retrained in a semi-supervised setting. Experimental results on the DIEE fingerprint database indicate that the proposed method outperforms state-of-the-art methods including the MDIST method and Yin's method.

2   Prior Work

The *FSS* based identification method, called "FSS", include two stages: enrollment stage and identification stage [10].

2.1   Enrollment Stage

Suppose in a fingerprint identification system there are N ($N > 1$) fingers and each finger has M templates, which is shown in Fig. 1.

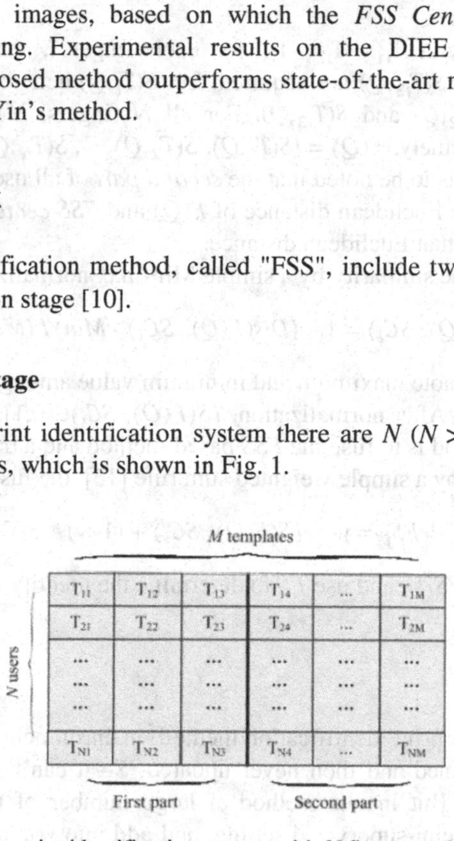

Fig. 1. A fingerprint identification system with N fingers and M templates

To each finger, its M templates are divided into two parts: *first part* and *second part*. As shown in Fig.1, T_{i1}, T_{i2}, T_{i3} ($i = 1,...,N$) as the *first part* and the remaining M-3 templates as the *second part*. The *first part* is used as base templates and the *second part* is used as queries. Take finger 1 for example, by matching T_{14} with T_{i1}, T_{i2}, T_{i3} for each finger i, three matching scores can be acquired, then the maximum score of the three ones is selected as the matching score corresponding to T_{14} with templates of finger i. As a result, for finger 1, a *FSS* including N scores is produced. In the same manner, for finger 1, T_{14}, T_{15}, ..., T_{1M} are used to match with the *first part* of each finger, and *M-3 FSSs* can be acquired. Each *FSS* is a *N* dimensional vector. In *N* dimensional space, *M-3 FSSs* can be expressed by *M-3* points. The average value of *M-3 FSSs* of finger 1 is calculated as a *FSS center* named SC_1. In this way, for each finger *i*, *M-3 FSSs* can be acquired and the corresponding *FSS center* SC_i can be calculated and stored in the database.

2.2   Identification Stage

To a query fingerprint *Q*, the process of *FSS* based fingerprint identification method is described as following:

Step1: Match *Q* with T_{i1}, T_{i2}, T_{i3} for each finger *i*, three matching scores $S(T_{i1},Q)$, $S(T_{i2},Q)$ and $S(T_{i3},Q)$ are acquired. Let $S(T_i,Q)$ denote the maximum score among $S(T_{i1},Q)$, $S(T_{i2},Q)$ and $S(T_{i3},Q)$. For all *N* fingers, *N* maximum matching scores are acquired, namely, $F(Q) = (S(T_1,Q), S(T_2,Q),\ldots, S(T_N,Q))$, which is the *FSS* corresponding to *Q*. It is to be noted that the *second part* of all users are not used here.

Step2: Calculate the Euclidean distance of *F(Q)* and *FSS center* SC_i, *i*=1,...,*N*. Let $Dis(F(Q), SC_i)$ denote that Euclidean distance.

Step3: Normalize the similarity by a simple Min-max normalization method [12].

$$TS(F(Q), SC_i) = 1 - (Dis(F(Q), SC_i) - Min) / (Max - Min) \qquad (1)$$

Here, *Max* and *Min* denote maximum and minimum value among $Dis(F(Q), SC_i)$, *i*=1,...,*N*, respectively. After normalization, $TS(F(Q), SC_i) \in [0,1]$.

Step4: Fusion method is to fuse the *FSS* based method and a traditional identification method by a simple weighted sum rule [13], the fused similarities is:

$$FS_i = w * TS(F(Q), SC_i) + (1-w) * S(T_i, Q) \qquad (2)$$

Step5: Let $FS = Max\{FS_i\}$, and use *FS* to determine the identity of the query *Q*.

3   Our Work

In the *FSS* based fingerprint identification method, in enrollment stage, *FSS Center* of each finger is determined and then never updated. So it can't solve the problem of intra-class variations. But in our method, a large number of unlabeled fingerprint images are used in a semi-supervised setting, and add into *second part* to retrain *FSS Center*. So, the intra-class variations problem is solved.

Our method is described as follows (see Fig.2):

In the enrollment stage, each finger only need to enroll a small amount of labeled fingerprint images. These labeled samples are also divided into two parts: *first part* and *second part*. The *first part* is used as base templates, and the *second part* is used to calculate *FSS Center* of each finger. As shown in Fig.2, there are *N* fingers, let T_i denote the *first part* of the ith finger, let D_l denote the *second part*, T_i and D_l are acquired during enrollment stage. Let D_u denote unlabeled fingerprint images, and D_u are obtained during the system operation process. Let *SC* denote *FSS Center* of all fingers.

Algorithm 1.   The semi-supervised *FSS* based fingerprint identification method.

require:
— N be the number of fingers
— T_i be base templates as *first part*
— D_l be labeled fingerprint images as *second part*
— D_u be unlabeled fingerprint images
— SC be *FSS Center* of all fingers
repeat:
 Estimate *threshold* on all T_i ($i = 1,...,N$) and SC
 for each query fingerprint Q, $Q \in D_u$
  for each finger i, $i=1,...N$
   Acquire the maximum matching score MS_i between Q and template T_i.
   Acquire the *FSS* corresponding to Q.
   Calculate the Euclidean distance Ed_i of *FSS* and *center* SC_i.
   Normalize Ed_i by a simple Min-max normalization method.
   Acquire FS_i by a fusion method to fuse Ed_i and MS_i.
   if FS_i > *threshold*,
    Assign the ith identity label to Q
    Increase the labeled fingerprints $D_l \leftarrow Q$
    $D_u = D_u - Q$
    break
   end if
  end for
 end for
 Update SC using the augmented labeled set D_l
until (no new unlabeled image is added into D_l or $D_u=\emptyset$)

Fig. 2. The semi-supervised *FSS* based fingerprint identification method

In the identification stage, firstly, threshold is estimated on all T_i ($i = 1,...,N$) and SC, and *FAR* (False Accept Rate) is 0. Then, for each fingerprint Q ($Q \in D_u$), it will be matching to T_i. The processing as follows: (1) the maximum matching score MS_i between Q and templates T_i is acquired. (2) The *FSS* based fingerprint identification method is used to acquire the *FSS* corresponding to Q. (3) Calculate the Euclidean distance Ed_i of *FSS* and SC_i. (4) Normalize Ed_i by a simple Min-max normalization method. (5) Acquire FS_i by a simple weighted sum rule to fuse Ed_i and MS_i. (6) Compare FS_i with threshold. If FS_i is bigger than threshold, assign the ith identity label to Q, and add Q into D_l, and then delete Q from D_u.

When every query fingerprint of D_u has been processed, a number of new images are added into D_l to update SC using the augmented labeled set D_l. Then we estimate threshold on all T_i and SC again. When no new unlabeled image is added into the second part D_l, or $D_u=\emptyset$, the process would be stopped.

4   Experiments

4.1   Database

It is necessary to acquire several fingerprint images per finger over a period of time to study our method. Standard fingerprint databases, such as FVC2002, don't contain a large number of images per finger. Therefore, we use the fingerprint dataset of DIEE multi-modal database [7] collected by F.Roli laboratory.

These fingerprint images are collected by varying moisture, pressure, and position with respect to the scanner surface, and Biometrika FX2000 is adopted as a fingerprint scanner. 40 fingers with 100 samples per finger are used in this paper.

These 100 samples are acquired in 10 sessions with 10 samples per session, and the time interval of two consecutive sessions is at least three weeks. The whole collection process spanned a period of 2 years.

4.2   Experimental Results

To compare fingerprints, we use a minutiae-based fingerprint identification method [6], called "Base". Using this comparator, different approaches to update the samples of enrolled users, called "MDIST", "Yin", "FSS", "FSS semi-supervised", are tested. So "Base" is the comparator used for identification, and other methods are strategies for template update built on "Base".

In this paper, we perform five experiments: "Base", "MDIST", "Yin", "FSS", "FSS semi-supervised". For each method, we set the number of base templates as 1, 2, 3, and get the experiment results respectively. For "Base", "FSS" and "FSS semi-supervised", we use the first one, the first two and the first three images as base templates, and those base templates have no longer updated. For "MDIST" and "Yin", base templates are selected and then updated using the MDIST and Yin's method. We use Equal Error Rate (EER) to evaluate the performance in our experiments [5].

Samples in DIEE fingerprint database are acquired in 10 sessions with 10 samples per session. In order to express changes of recognition rate, we carried out our experiments as follows:

(1) 10 samples from session 1 are used as the labeled fingerprint images. For "Base", "MDIST" and "Yin", we only use base templates. But for "FSS" and "FSS semi-supervised", we need to train the *FSS Center* using the *second part* which is the remaining images of session 1.

(2) 10 samples from session 2 are used as the test set to evaluate performances of five methods, and then used as unlabeled fingerprint images to update the fingerprint database. Using the augmented database, we update templates for "MDIST" and "Yin", and update *FSS Center* for "FSS semi-supervised".

(3)   For session 3,…,9, the process is the same as (2).

(4) 10 samples from session 10 are used as the test set to evaluate performances of above five methods.

Table 1. The average EERs(%) of five methods

The number of templates	1	2	3
Base	4.137	3.803	1.707
MDIST	2.489	1.898	1.633
Yin	2.489	1.819	1.376
FSS	2.267	1.711	1.165
FSS semi-supervised	*1.621*	*1.074*	*0.691*

As shown in Table 1, the average EERs of our method "FSS semi-supervised" are 1.621%, 1.074%, 0.691% when the number of base templates is 1, 2, 3, respectively. Compared to "MDIST", the average EERs of "FSS semi-supervised" reduced 0.868%, 0.824%, 0.942%, respectively; and compared to "Yin", reduced by 0.868%, 0.745%, 0.685%, respectively.

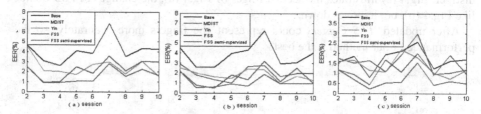

Fig. 3. Performance curves in the different numbers of base templates. (a) the number of templates is 1; (b) the number of templates is 2; (c) the number of templates is 3.

Fig.3 illustrates the performance curves of five methods. As shown in Fig.3, the performance of base method "Base" is poor, because the fingerprint images are acquired using two years, due to scratches, increase of moisture or dryness, aging etc, the later images are different from the previous, and the templates have never been updated. "MDIST" updates templates, so the performance is better than "Base". When the number of base templates is 1, "MDIST" and "Yin" select the same fingerprint template, so the performance of two methods is the same. But when the number of base templates is 2 or 3, "Yin" chooses more complementary fingerprint templates, so the performance is better than "MDIST". The *FSS* based fingerprint identification method "FSS" uses large numbers of heterogeneous matching score, and the performance increases. The performance of our method "FSS semi-supervised" achieves the best, because *FSS Centers* is updated, and after updated, *FSS Centers* could represent the fingers more accurately.

4.3   Analysis

In this paper, the semi-supervised *FSS* based fingerprint identification method is better than MDIST and Yin's method. In order to prove the effectiveness of our method proposed, we choose randomly two fingers from 40 fingers, and show how *FSS Centers* change when more unlabeled samples are used to update *FSS Centers*.

Initially, we choose the front 3 images of session 1 as *first part*, and the remaining 7 images as *second part* and the initial *FSS Center* is trained. As shown in Fig.4, "•"denotes the *FSS* of the first finger, "*" denotes the *FSS* of the second finger, and "•" denotes the *FSS Center*.

Fig.4 (b) illustrates the first finger of Fig.4 (a), In session 1, the blue "•" denotes the *FSS* feature distribution of the first finger, the blue "•" denotes the initial *FSS Center*. For session 2, let green "•" denote the *FSS* feature distribution of the first finger, 10 images of session 2 with high confidence are added into the *second part*, and then the *FSS Center* is updated and denoted by green "•". For session 3,...,10, we do the same processing. We could find out that the position of *FSS Center* has always moved to left, and the changes of position are very distinct at the beginning, but at last the changes are not distinct. Due to intra-class variations, the matching score between unlabeled images and templates will become lower, so the position of *FSS Center* moves to left. But the number of *second part* is bigger, so the changes will be not distinct. Fig.4 (c) illustrates the second finger of Fig.4 (a), the changes of *FSS Center* like Fig.4 (b), but it moves down.

After updated, *FSS Centers* could represent the fingers more accurately, so the performance of our method is the best.

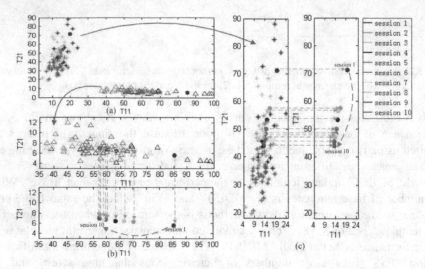

Fig. 4. (a)FSS distribution of two fingers (b) *FSS Center* changes of the first finger; (c) *FSS Center* changes of the second finger

5   Conclusion and Future Work

In this paper, we proposed a fingerprint identification method based on semi-supervised *FSS*. Using semi-supervised learning, unlabeled fingerprint images with high confidence were added into the fingerprint database to optimize *FSS Centers*. The main contributions of this paper are: (1) we employed a semi-supervised learning framework to update the *FSS Center*; (2) we proposed a semi-supervised *FSS* method for fingerprint identification to adaptively deal with intra-class variations; and (3) we evaluated our method on the DIEE fingerprint database, and the experimental results showed that our method outperforms MDIST and Yin's method.

Future work will focus on two aspects. (1) We have proposed a general framework for dealing with intra-class variations based on semi-supervised learning. It is potential to apply our framework to other fields of biometric identification. (2) It is interesting to test the performance of AFIS with increasing number of template.

Acknowledgements. This research is supported in part by National Natural Science Foundation of China under Grant No.61070097, 61173069, the Research Found for the Doctoral Program of Higher Education under Grant No.20100131110021, and Shandong Province Higher Educational Science and Technology Program under

Grant No.J11LG28. The authors would like to thank F.Roli laboratory, Guangtong Zhou and Dongmei Sun for their help.

References

1. Rattani, A., Freni, B., Marcialis, G.L., Roli, F.: Template Update Methods in Adaptive Biometric Systems: A Critical Review. In: Tistarelli, M., Nixon, M.S. (eds.) ICB 2009. LNCS, vol. 5558, pp. 847–856. Springer, Heidelberg (2009)
2. Rattani, A., Marcialis, G.L., Roli, F.: Temporal Analysis of Biometric Template Update Procedures in Uncontrolled Environment. In: Maino, G., Foresti, G.L. (eds.) ICIAP 2011, Part I. LNCS, vol. 6978, pp. 595–604. Springer, Heidelberg (2011)
3. Freni, B., Marcialis, G.L., Roli, F.: Replacement Algorithms for Fingerprint Template Update. In: Campilho, A., Kamel, M.S. (eds.) ICIAR 2008. LNCS, vol. 5112, pp. 884–893. Springer, Heidelberg (2008)
4. Maltoni, D., Maio, D., Jain, A.K., Prabhakar, S.: Handbook of Fingerprint Recognition. Springer, London (2009)
5. Wayman, J.L., Jain, A.K., Maltoni, D., Maio, D.: Biometric Systems-Technology, Design and Performance Evaluation. Springer, New York (2005)
6. Jiang, X., Yau, W.: Fingerprint minutiae matching based on the local and global structures. In: 15th International Conference on Pattern Recognition, vol. 2, pp. 1042–1045 (2000)
7. Diee multimodal database (2008), http://prag.diee.unica.it/pra/eng/home
8. Uludag, U., Ross, A., Jain, A.: Biometric template selection and update: a case study in fingerprints. Pattern Recognition, 1533–1542 (2004)
9. Li, Y., Yin, J., Zhu, E., Hu, C., Chen, H.: Score based biometric template selection and update. In: 2nd International Conference on Future Generation Communication and Networking, vol. 3, pp. 35–40 (2008)
10. Ning, Y., Yin, Y., Li, Y., Yang, G.: Full Matching Score Sequence based Identification Method for Biometrics. Technical Reports (2012), http://mla.sdu.edu.cn/PeopleInfo/ningyanbin/ningyanbin.html
11. Yin, Y., Ning, Y., Ren, C., Liu, L.: A Framework of Multi-Template Ensemble for Fingerprint Verification. EURASIP Journal on Advances in Signal Processing (2012)
12. Ross, A., Nandakumar, K., Jain, A.K.: Handbook of multibiometrics. Springer (2006)
13. Jain, A., Nandakumar, K., Ross, A.: Score normalization in multimodal biometric systems. Pattern Recognition 38(12), 2270–2285 (2005)

A Performance Improvement Method for Existing Fingerprint Systems

Chunxiao Ren[1], Yilong Yin[2,*], and Yanbin Ning[2]

[1] Administration Center, Shandong Academy of Information & Communication Technology, 1768 Xinluo Street, High-Tech Development Zone, Jinan 250101, China
renchunxiao@gmail.com
[2] School of Computer Science and Technology, Shandong University, Shunhua Road, Jinan, 250101, P. R. China
ylyin@sdu.edu.cn, ningyanbin009@163.com
http://mla.sdu.edu.cn

Abstract. How to improve the performance of an existing fingerprint system is an interesting and meaningful problem. Considering the widespread deployment of fingerprint systems, the performance improvement method is very practical and instructive to not only the existing fingerprint systems but also the next biometric systems. In this paper, we propose a novel performance improvement method based on fingerprint's Möbius representation and Choquet integral for an existing fingerprint system. The basic idea of our method is to map the fingerprint similarity as a distance in a geometric space firstly, and then transform the similarity problem between the impressions into a geometric problem through using multiple impressions, and last, map the results obtained in geometric space back to solve the fingerprint similarity problem. The experiments show that the performance achieved by using this method is better than that of other methods.

Keywords: biometric, non-additive measures, Choquet integral, Bayesian inference, maximum likelihood estimation (MLE).

1 Introduction

Biometric systems are rapidly gaining acceptance as one of the most effective technologies to identify people. A biometric system is essentially a pattern recognition system that acquires raw data from an individual, extracts a notable feature set from the raw data, compares this feature set against the feature sets stored in the database, and executes an action according to the result of the comparison. In biometric community, fingerprint recognition is the most popular technology. With the development of fingerprint recognition technology, many fingerprint recognition systems based on various algorithms have been developed and deployed. Nowadays, there are a lot of fingerprint recognition systems existing in a wide range of applications: from physical access control to criminal

---

* Corresponding author.

W.-S. Zheng et al. (Eds.): CCBR 2012, LNCS 7701, pp. 120–127, 2012.
© Springer-Verlag Berlin Heidelberg 2012

investigation and from inmates managing to corpse identification. Most of these systems are developed based on a certain out-fashion algorithm. The performance of these systems is usually worse than that of present systems. So how to improve the performance of an existing fingerprint system is an interesting and meaningful problem.

In fingerprint recognition community, most researches work on developing new technologies to improve each stage in recognition, including sensing, feature extraction, matching, classification, indexing and so on. Few work aims at improving the performance of an existing system. Obviously, this kind of method is system level one. When we talk about system level method, we usually considered a multibiometrics technology. Many researchers try to use multibiometrics systems to achieve better performance by consolidating the evidence presented by multiple biometric sources [1]. For example, by combining the fingerprint system and face system or several fingerprint systems using deferent type of algorithm, the performance of system can be enhanced. However, these methods, the way to enhance the performance of system through introducing another biometric system, are very costly in all aspects. On the other hand, many researches have shown that the performance of system based on single fingerprint, single feature or single classifier encounters some drawbacks in some applications, and multimodal fingerprint-based methods, including multiple features, multiple matchers, multiple fingers and multiple impressions of the same finger [2], have received more and more attention.

Considering the widespread deployment of fingerprint systems, the performance improvement method is very practical and instructive to not only the existing fingerprint systems but also the next biometric systems. In this paper, we propose a novel performance improvement method based on fingerprint's Möbius representation and Choquet integral for an existing fingerprint system. The basic idea of our method is to map the fingerprint similarity as a distance in a geometric space firstly, and then transform the similarity problem between the impressions into a geometric problem through using multiple impressions, and last, map the results obtained in geometric space back to solve the fingerprint similarity problem. The experiments show that the performance achieved by using this method is better than that of other methods. This idea was briefly introduced in an earlier work [3]. In this paper, the whole approach we improved is described, and the results of systematic experiments are reported.

2   System Analysis and Related Work

2.1   System Analysis

A typical fingerprint verification system involves two stages: during enrollment, the user's fingerprint is acquired and its distinctive features are extracted and stored as a template; and during verification, a new fingerprint is acquired and compared to the stored template to verify the user's claimed identity. Suppose there is an existing fingerprint system. That means there are a database, an enrollment module and a verification module we can utilize. Using the enrollment module, an impression can be extracted as a feature set named template. Using the verification module, we can compute the similarity between two impressions or templates.

In enrollment stage, the fingerprint system usually needs to acquire several impressions of the same finger for checking eligibility of the finger. However, in verification stage, not all the impressions are utilized for comparison. Traditionally, only one typical impression or template stored in the database is selected as user's standard template. Other impressions or templates will never be used after eligibility checking stage. When a query image is imputed, the system compares the query image and standard template using verification module, then determines the result whether the query is the claim itself through considering the similarity.

Clearly, the multiple impressions are utilized insufficiently in traditional fingerprint systems excepting eligibility checking. We address that the performance of the system can be enhanced if the relationships among all enrolled impressions and query image were fully utilized.

2.2 Similarity

In the previous work [3], we propose that the matching score, as a similarity measure of two impressions, can be transformed to a distance in geometry. A better performance of fingerprint system can be achieved through transforming the similarity problem between the impressions into a geometric problem by using multiple impressions. More details can be found in [3].

2.3 Möbius Representation of Impression

We propose that the impression can be represented by Möbius transform. The Möbius representation is defined as follow:

Definition 1. Any set function ν: $P(N) \rightarrow R$ can be uniquely expressed in terms of its Möbius representation [4] by

$$\nu(T) = \sum_{S \subseteq T} m_\nu(S), \forall T \subseteq N \tag{1}$$

where the set function $m_\nu : P(N) \rightarrow R$ is called the Möbius transform or Möbius representation of ν and is given by

$$m_\nu(S) = \sum_{T \subseteq S} (-1)^{s-t} \nu(T), \forall S \subseteq N \tag{2}$$

Using the Möbius representation, we can treat fingerprint impressions from a novel perspective. An impression can be regarded as a combination of several regions. Each region contains the overlap with other impressions respectively. Therefore, the importance of each region for recognition performance is vary. Through the introduction of importance parameters, we can describe in detail the effect of each region for recognition to gain a better expression of fingerprint. Naturally, we will introduce the non-additive measure to get the job done.

2.4   Choquet Integral Based Similarity Measure

Within the fields of economics, finance, computer science and decision theory there is an increasing interest in the problem how to replace the additivity property of probability measures by that of monotonicity or, more generally, a non-additive measure. Several types of integrals with respect to non-additive measures, also known as fuzzy measures, were developed for different purposes in various works. The Choquet integral, as a popular representation of the non-additive measure, has been successfully used for many applications such as information fusion, multiple regressions, classification, multicriteria decision making, image and pattern recognition, and data modeling.

Using Choquet integral, we can link the Möbius representation of fingerprints and recognition performance. Typically, we can calculate the utility parameters through regression algorithms. Thus, a fingerprint recognition problem can be converted to a distance computation problem in geometry space by using the Choquet integral based similarity measure.

3   Our Method

3.1   Overview

Let Q be a query image and t be the tth impression used as template. The existing fingerprint system can be regarded as determining the result whether the query is the claim itself depended on $S(Q, I^t)$. A key different between original and improved system is that there is an additional module used to build a model for query image and multiple impressions, as illustrated by Fig. 1 and Fig. 2. An input of the module is similarity set M, where M is defined as

$$M = \left\{ S(I^i, I^j) | I^i, I^j \in Q \cup F \right\}$$

In this work, we propose a novel model based on Choquet integral to acquire a better recognition result.

As described above, our method is a performance improvement method based on the Möbius representation of fingerprints and the Choquet integral. In the initialization stage of the fingerprint system, the utility parameters are estimated by regression algorithms. In the identification stage, we calculated the Möbius representation for each impression firstly. Then, we calculate and output the Choquet integral of the input fingerprint image as result.

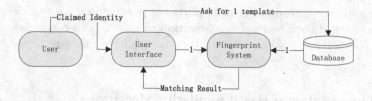

Fig. 1. A framework of an existing fingerprint system

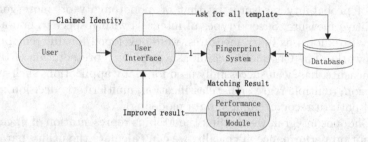

Fig. 2. A framework of the performance improvement method

3.2   Performance Improvement Method

Our method is divided into four parts. The first part is to estimate the position of the fingerprint, the second part is to calculate the Möbius representation of fingerprint impression, the third part is to estimate the utility parameters using regression algorithms, and the fourth part is to calculate the Choquet integral of the fingerprint. These four parts are described in detail as follows.

Estimation of the Position. As mentioned in 2.2, suppose the fingerprint is represented as a circle of radius r, and all distances between any pair of centers of the circle are known. We develop a model to estimate a reasonable two-dimensional position for center of the circle as illustrated in Fig. 3. In this paper, our model is established by Alg. 1.

The Möbius Representation of Fingerprint Impressions. In this work, we use the percentage of each region as the Möbius representation of fingerprint impression. We use Monte Carlo (MC) algorithm to establish the estimation of each region's size. Monte Carlo algorithm is relatively simple and easy to implement [5]. In this paper, we use the 1000 samples for each model.

Estimation of the Utility Parameters. As mentioned in 2.4, given the observation data, the optimal regression coefficients μ can be determined by using regression methods. In this work, we use a maximum likelihood estimation (MLE) [6] method to estimate μ. The MLE method is:

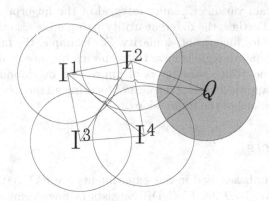

Fig. 3. An illustration of estimation for two-dimensional position. There are four fingerprint impressions in F, Q is the query image.

Alg. 1. Estimation of the Two-dimensional Position

Input: similarity set M

Output: the coordinates of $I^i \in Q \cup F$

- Convert all the similarity measure $S(I^i, I^j)$ to distance $D(I^i, I^j)$
- Find the biggest $D(I^m, I^n)$ among all $D(I^i, I^j | I^i, I^j \in F)$
- Set the coordinate of m as $(0,0)$ and n as $(D(I^m, I^n), 0)$
- For all $I^i \in F$ and $i \neq m, n$
  1. Find $D(I^i, I^m)$ and $D(I^i, I^n)$
  2. Compute the possible position of I^i using a triangle relationship of m, n and I^i
  3. Decide the most reasonable side of I^i via other impressions
- Find the most reasonable position of Q using the coordinates of F and all distance $D(I^i, Q)$

$$\mu_{ML} = \left(\Phi^T \Phi \right)^{-1} \Phi^T \mathbf{t} \tag{3}$$

Here Φ is an $N \times M$ matrix whose elements are given by $\Phi_{nj} = \phi_j(f_n)$ [7], so that

$$\Phi = \begin{pmatrix} \phi_0(f_1) & \phi_1(f_1) & \cdots & \phi_{M-1}(f_1) \\ \phi_0(f_2) & \phi_1(f_2) & \cdots & \phi_{M-1}(f_2) \\ \vdots & \vdots & \ddots & \vdots \\ \phi_0(f_N) & \phi_1(f_N) & \cdots & \phi_{M-1}(f_N) \end{pmatrix} \tag{4}$$

The Choquet Integral of the Fingerprint Similarity. Based on the Möbius representation of the fingerprint, a novel perspective, we can use different utility parameters to obtain various Choquet integral of the fingerprint similarity, as mentioned in 2.4. Further, the different utility parameters also imply the different interpretations for fingerprint similarity. For example, the fully equal utility parameters mean that all regions have the same importance to fingerprint identification; and if the utility parameters of impression overlapping regions were assigned to 0, this approach means the idea of focusing all the recognition method on the separate regions of the impressions.

4   Experiments

The fingerprint databases used in our experiments are FVC2000 DB1, DB2 [8] and FVC2002 DB1, DB2 [9]. FVC DB consists of fingerprint impressions obtained from 100 non-habituated, cooperative subjects. Every subject was asked to provide 8 impressions of the same finger. We select 1st to 4th impressions of every subject as templates and 5th to 8th impressions as query image. Therefore, for each fingerprint, there are four training samples and four test samples.

In this work, we use a minutiae-based automatic fingerprint identification system to complete one to one comparison. For each fingerprint, we match the 5th impression to each of 4 impressions in training set, so a total of 400 homologous match; and match the 5th impression to 4 randomly selected heterologous impressions, so a total of 400 heterologous match.

The performance of a fingerprint verification system is mainly described by two values, i.e., false acceptance rate (FAR) and false rejection rate (FRR). FAR and FRR are defined as

$$FAR = P(D_1|\omega_2) \tag{5}$$

and,

$$FRR = P(D_2|\omega_1) \tag{6}$$

where ω_1 and ω_2 represent the classes of true genuine matches and impostor matches, respectively, D_1 and D_2 denote the decisions of genuine matches and impostor matches, respectively. The Equal Error Rate (EER) is computed as the point where $FAR(t) = FRR(t)$, usually we use EER to evaluate the biometric system.

In this work, we used $\frac{1-S(I^i,I^j)}{1+S(I^i,I^j)}$ as the conversion method from the similarity to the distance. The experimental results show that the performance achieved by using our method is better than that of the original fingerprint system. The average EER of this method is observed to be 1.94%, while that of the original fingerprint system is 4.56%, as shown in Table 1.

Table 1. The experimental results (EER) of performance improvement

	2000-DB1	2000-DB2	2002-DB1	2002-DB2	Average
Original	8.5%	3.75%	4.25%	1.75%	4.56%
Our Method	3.75%	1.5%	1.5%	1.0%	1.94%

5 Conclusion

In this paper, we propose a novel performance improvement method based on fingerprint's Möbius representation and Choquet integral for an existing fingerprint system. The basic idea of our method is to map the fingerprint similarity as a distance in a geometric space firstly, and then transform the similarity problem between the impressions into a geometric problem through using multiple impressions, and last, map the results obtained in geometric space back to solve the fingerprint similarity problem. The experiments show that the performance achieved by using this method is better than that of other methods.

Acknowledgments. This research is supported in part by National Natural Science Foundation of China under Grant No. 61070097 and 61173069.

References

1. Ross, A., Nandakumar, K., Jain, A.: Handbook of multibiometrics. Springer-Verlag New York Inc. (2006)
2. Yang, C., Zhou, J.: A comparative study of combining multiple enrolled samples for fingerprint verification. Pattern Recognition 39(11), 2115–2130 (2006)
3. Ren, C., Yin, Y., Ma, J., Yang, G.: A novel method of score level fusion using multiple impressions for fingerprint verification. In: IEEE International Conference on Systems, Man and Cybernetics, SMC 2009, pp. 5051–5056. IEEE (2009)
4. Rota, G.: On the foundations of combinatorial theory i. theory of möbius functions. Probability Theory and Related Fields 2(4), 340–368 (1964)
5. Walsh, B.: Markov chain monte carlo and gibbs sampling. Lecture notes for EEB, vol. 581 (2004)
6. Golub, G., Van Loan, C.: Matrix computations. Johns Hopkins Univ. Pr. (1996)
7. Bishop, C., et al.: Pattern recognition and machine learning. Springer, New York (2006)
8. Maio, D., Maltoni, D., Cappelli, R., Wayman, J., Jain, A.: FVC2000: Fingerprint verification competition. IEEE Transactions on Pattern Analysis and Machine Intelligence 24(3), 402–412 (2002)
9. Maio, D., Maltoni, D., Cappelli, R., Wayman, J., Jain, A.: FVC2002: Second fingerprint verification competition. In: International Conference on Pattern Recognition, Citeseer, vol. 16, pp. 811–814 (2002)

The Location Method of the Main Hand-Shape Feature Points

Weiqi Yuan and Lantao Jing

Computer Vision Group, Shenyang University of Technology
No. 111, Shenliao West Road, Economic & Technological Development Zone, Shenyang,
110870, P.R. China
yuan60@126.com, letalaura@qq.com

Abstract. While locating the points used for obtaining the hand-shape features with high class separability, the stability of the point positions is easily influenced by the hand positions and the wearing decorations. This paper improves the linear fitting accurate location method through removing the interference of parts of the experience values. It can reduce the impact of fingers flexibility and improve the accuracy of the finger-tip and finger-root points. In addition, the paper proposes a revised method to locate the wrist point. And the palm length can be used for automatic identification as one of the features in the vector. The experiments can verify the stability of the method through the standard deviation mean. Through the contrast of the matching results between the automatic and artificial measurement, the D-value is 0.7% of the 3-feature vector and 0.4% of 6-feature vector. It can prove the feasibility of the location method used the peg-free images.

Keywords: Hand-shape feature, linear fitting, angle of curvature, wrist point.

1 Introduction

The advantages of the hand-shape feature are easy acquisition, simple features, small computation and so on[1-3]. In order to improve the acceptance of the users, the application direction of the hand-shape identification device is peg-free and non-contact acquisition[4-5]. In this case, the robustness of the recognition algorithm needs to be improved.

The traditional location methods of hand-shape feature points contain curvature method[6], disc method[7], linear fitting method[8], etc. In the case of putting the hand freely or wearing decorations, the accuracy of the feature point location will be reduced. For example, the curvature method is hard to locate the points if the hand in images wears decorations or has prominent joint. The disc method is hard to choose the threshold of the area. The traditional linear fitting method can not locate the finger-root points accurately when the finger gaps are different. And it is easy to be influenced by parts of the experience results.

In order to solve the above problems, the paper proposes a point location method used for obtaining the better distinguishable features in literature [9]. The linear fitting

W.-S. Zheng et al. (Eds.): CCBR 2012, LNCS 7701, pp. 128–135, 2012.

method can be improved for locating the finger-tip and finger-root points. Firstly, the tangent points can be acquired as the reference. Secondly, parts of the experience results can be removed for locating the precise points in order to improve the accuracy. Thirdly, the upper wrist point can be obtained by the way of locating the maximum of the curvature, and then the downer point and the wrist point can also be located so that the palm length can be used for fast and effective recognition.

2   Image Preprocessing

Because the background of the images used in the experiments is single black, the image preprocessing includes binarization, denoising and contour extraction.

Binarization: Because of the black background, the processing chooses the fixed threshold method. The method of determining the threshold is to locate the lowest gray level between the target area and the background area in the grey level histogram of the hand images.

Denoising: The main source of the noise is the effect of non-uniform illumination and the sensor. It may causes holes in the binary images. The smaller holes can be eliminated by the morphologic method, and the bigger ones can be eliminated by filling the connected regions except the largest one which is the hand area. That is set the whole hand area to 1, the others to 0.

Contour Extraction: The paper uses the directional tracking algorithm[10]. The method is described briefly as follows. Firstly, the starting point of the contour is in the last column, which is the first pixel with 1 as the gray value in the up-down scanning sequence. Secondly, the candidate points of the contour are according to the positional relation between the current point and the previous point. It chooses the 5 points on the connective and the vertical direction. The next contour point is the first 1-gray-value point on the clockwise direction. Finally, if the column of the candidate points is equal to the width of the image, the tracking is over. The result is in Fig.1.

Fig. 1. The binary image and the contour image

3   Feature-Point Location Algorithm

According to the discussion about the separability of each hand-shape feature in literature [9], the feature points of the better distinguishable features are needed to be located accurately. These points include the finger-tip and finger-root points used for measuring the finger length, the boundary points used for measuring the palm width and the wrist point used for measuring the palm length.

3.1   Location Method of the Finger-Tip and Finger-Root Points

Rough Location of the Finger-Tip and Finger-Gap Points:
In the actual circumstances, the thumb is hard to measure because of its flexibility. In order to avoid the interference of the thumb, it can be cut off in the contour images. Then the 4 finger-tip points (P1, P2, P3, P4) and 3 finger-gap points (Q1, Q2, Q3) can be located roughly by determining the tangent points, as shown in Fig.2.

The specific procedure is as follows:

(1) Reset the accumulator sum, *scan the contour image in right-to-left and up-to-down direction. When the D-value in the same column between the current line and the last line is* -1, *sum plus* 1. *In a column, if* sum *reaches to 3 for the first time, record the column and the row coordinates when* sum=2. *It stands for the coordinates of the thumb root point* TH, *and stores in 2D-array* thumb.

(2) Use the directional tracking method to detect the thumb border points of which column coordinates are less than TH. *Set the gray value of these points to 0. Obtain the non-thumb contour image* CT.

(3) Reset the accumulator sumer, *scan the column before* TH *in right-to-left and up-to-down direction. In a column, if the gray value of a point is 1 and the gray value summation in the top and left neighborhoods is 0, store the coordinates in a 2D-array* TP, *and* sumer *plus* 1. *When* sumer=4, *the scanning stops.*

(4) Reset the accumulator summer, *start with the column before* TH *and scan in right-to-left and up-to-down direction. In a column, if the gray value of a point is 1 and the gray value summation in the top and right neighborhoods is 0, store the coordinates in a 2D-array* TV, *and* summer *plus* 1. *When* summer=3, *the scanning stops.*

(5) Re-order the coordinates per row in TV *and* TP *by bubble sort with the order of the row coordinates from small to large.*

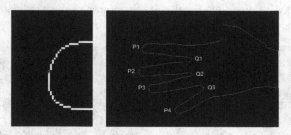

Fig. 2. Rough location of the finger-tip and finger-gap points

Accurate Location of the Finger-Tip and Finger-Root Points:
The paper proposes the improved linear fitting method for accurate location. According to scanning the boundary points near the tangent points, 16 boundary intersections can be determined. Then, the finger centerlines (L1, L2, L3, L4) and finger-gap centerlines (M1, M2, M3) can be drawn. According to the intersections of these lines and the contour lines, the finger-tip (T1, T2, T3, T4) and finger-gap points (V1, V2, V3) can be located accurately and the finger-root points (H1, H2, H3, H4) can be obtained, as shown in Fig.3.

The specific procedure is as follows:

(1) *Starting with the row coordinate of each finger-tip point, scan along the up and the down direction in the 15th column latter. If the D-value of the adjacent gray level is 1, the coordinates of the corresponding points can be obtained and stored in the 2D-array* fit1 *with the order of the row coordinate from small to large.*

(2) *Starting with the row coordinate of each finger-gap point, scan along the up and the down direction in the 15th column before. If the D-value of the adjacent gray level is 1, the coordinates of the corresponding points can be obtained and stored in from the 2nd to the 7th row of the 2D-array* fit2 *with the order of the row coordinate from small to large. Scan along the up direction in the column of Q1, obtain the coordinate of the point with 1 D-value gray level, and store in the first row of* fit2. *Scan down in the column of Q3, obtain the coordinate of the point with 1 D-value gray level, and store in the last row of* fit2.

(3) *According to the midpoints of the lines connected with the corresponding points in* fit1 *and* fit2, *the finger centerlines can be obtained. Scan these lines from right to left, accurately determine the finger-tip points T1, T2, T3, T4, store the coordinates in array* TL.

(4) *According to the corresponding points in* fit1 *and* fit2, *the finger-gap centerlines can be obtained. Scan these lines from left to right, accurately determine the finger-gap points V1, V2, V3, store the coordinates in array* VL.

(5) *Draw a line through V1 perpendicular to L1, the foot of the perpendicular is the finger-root of the index finger H1. The intersection of L2 and line V1V2 is the finger-root of the middle finger H2. The intersection of L3 and line V2V3 is the finger-root of the ring finger H3. Draw a line through V3 perpendicular to L4, the foot of the perpendicular is the finger-root of the little finger H4. Store the 4-point coordinates in array* HL.

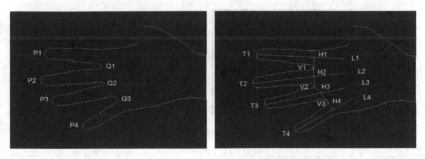

Fig. 3. The boundary intersections image and the finger-tip and finger-root location image

3.2   Location Method of the Palm width Boundary Points

The palm width boundary points include upper boundary point PW1 and the lower boundary point PW2.

The location method is as follows and shown in Fig.4.

(1) *Connect TH and H1, gain the midpoint PM, and then store in the array* TM.

(2) Draw a line through PM parallel to line H1H4, the intersections of the line and the boundary are the palm width boundary points. The one with smaller row coordinate is PM1, the other is PM2. Then store the coordinates in array PW.

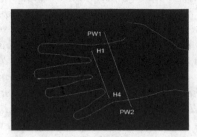

Fig. 4. Location image of palm width boundary points

3.3   Location Method of the Wrist Point

Because the curve extent of the wrist contour region is bigger, the upper wrist points can be determined by improved curvature method. The curvatures of the upper boundary wrist points need to be calculated one by one, and the point with the maximum is the upper wrist point. Further, the lower point and the wrist point can be obtained. In order to simplify the calculation, the angle of curvature is chosen as the parameter. The formula is (1) and the parameters are shown in Fig. 5.

$$\zeta(s) = \arccos\left(\frac{\overrightarrow{W_1W_1'} \bullet \overrightarrow{W_1W_2'}}{\left|\overrightarrow{W_1W_1'}\right| \bullet \left|\overrightarrow{W_1W_2'}\right|}\right) \tag{1}$$

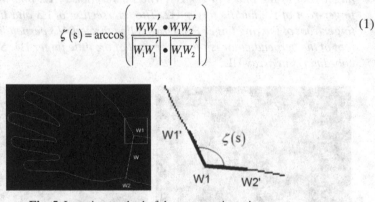

Fig. 5. Location method of the upper wrist point

The specific procedure is as follows:

(1) Scan the last column from up to down, if the gray gradient of the point is 1 for the first time, it is the starting point of the upper boundary candidate points. Starting with TH, the intersection with the contour in the right direction is the end point.

(2) Through formula (1), the curvature angles of candidate points can be calculated, and the corresponding point of the minimum angle is the upper wrist point W1.

(3) Scan the last column from down to up, if the gray gradient of the point is 1 for the first time, it is the starting point of the lower boundary candidate points. In the column of TH, the intersection with the lower contour is the end point.

(4) Calculate the European distance between W1 and each lower candidate point, the corresponding point of the minimum distance is the lower wrist point W2.

(5) Determine the midpoint W of the line W1W2.

4   Analysis of Experimental Results

In this paper, the experiments use the database from the Hong Kong university of science and technology. The images are from the first 100 persons of the database, and 10 right hand images each person, 1000 images in all. The resolution of the image is 640×480. In the image, the hand is put on the desktop with a black background and keeps the fingers natural open. The distance between the camera and the desktop is about 23cm[11]. In this paper, the experiments contain two parts, the verification experiments for proving the stability and the validity of the location method.

4.1   Stability Experiments

The purpose of the stability experiments is to prove the stability of the feature point location method. Because there are 10 images every person, one feature for each person can obtain 10 different values. Make the same feature as a sample space, store the values of all the features, and then obtain the sample standard deviation. The smaller the standard deviation is, the closer the values are. It means that the stability of the location method is better. On the contrary, if the standard deviation is bigger, the stability is poorer. The means of the standard deviation (MSD) are in Table 1.

Table 1. The means of the standard deviation

Feature	The means of the standard deviation
Hand length	3.8
Palm length	3.8
Palm width	1.6
Index finger length	2.4
Ring finger length	1.8
Little finger length	2.5

From the table, the values of hand length and palm length are bigger, because some images lack the wrist region. But the values of each feature are all less than 4 pixels. Therefore, the location method is stable.

4.2   Validity Experiments

The method of the validity experiments is to do the matching experiments respectively using the features by automatic and artificial measurement. Finally, the results can be used for contacting the precision of the same feature vector.

When the matching experiments selected a feature vector, the user's registration feature vector is represented as $f = \{f_i, i = 1, 2, \ldots, n\}$, and the recognition feature vector is represented as $f' = \{f_i', i = 1, 2, \ldots, n\}$. i is the number of the features in the vector. The Euclidean distance between the registration feature vector and the recognition feature vector is represented as *Distance*. When the distance is less than a certain threshold T, they are the same person. On the contrary, they are different persons. The formula is (2):

$$Distance = \sqrt{\sum_{i=1}^{n} \left(f_i - f_i' \right)^2} \qquad (2)$$

The smaller the Euclidean distance is, the more similar the two feature vectors are. If the distance is smaller than the threshold T, they are achieved the matching standard. In the experiments, the threshold T is selected when the false accept rate (FAR) and the false reject rate (FRR) are equal. Because of the procedures, the error was existed.

The experiments consist of 499500 matching times, including 4500 times Intra-class matching, and 495000 times Inter-class matching. According to the results by automatic measurement, the Euclidean distance distribution and the curve of FAR&FRR can be obtained in Fig.6. And the recognition results are in Table 2.

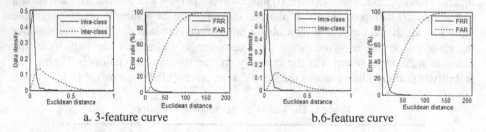

a. 3-feature curve   b.6-feature curve

Fig. 6. 3-feature and 6-feature classification curve

Table 2. The contrast of the recognition results

Measuring method	Features number	Recognition rate
Automatic measurement	3	91.0%
Automatic measurement	6	93.8%
Artificial measurement[9]	3	91.7%
Artificial measurement[9]	6	94.2%

According to the experimental results, when the experiments use the same feature vector, the recognition results by automatic measurement are close to the artificial measurement ones. It means that the hand-shape feature values with higher precision can be obtained through the automatic location method. So, it is valid.

5　Conclusion

The images used in this paper are taken by the peg-free device. After determining the tangent points, the finger-tip and finger-root points can be located through the improved linear fitting method. It can avoid the interference of the decorations and the open degree of the fingers. Furthermore, the upper wrist point can be determined by the improved curvature method. Then, calculate the hand length and the palm length through the wrist point. The two features can be used for recognition in order to achieve the effective identification with fewer features. However, the location method of the wrist point is less accurate than the finger-tip and finger-root points, it still needs to be further improved.

Acknowledgement. This work is supported by National Natural Science Foundation of China (60972123), Specialized Research Fund for the Doctoral Program of Higher Education (20092102110002) and Shenyang Science and Technology Development Program (F10-213-1-00).

References

1. Sanchez, R., Sanchez, A., Gonzalez, M.: Biometric identification through hand geometry measurements. IEEE Transactions on Pattern Analysis and Machine Intelligence 22(18), 1168–1171 (2002)
2. Dong, Q.: Research on Character Extraction and Recognition Method of Hand Shape. Shenyang University of Technology (2011) (in Chinese)
3. Yuan, W.Q., Ke, L., Bai, Y.: Biometrics Technology. Science Press, Beijing (2009)
4. Amayeh, G., Bebis, G., Erol, A., Nicolescu, M.: Peg-free hand shape verification using high order Zernike moments. In: Proceedings of the IEEE Workshop on Biometrics at CVPR 2006, New York, USA (2006)
5. Xin, C., Wu, X.Q., Zhao, Q.S.: A Contactless Hand Shape Identification System. In: 3rd International Conference on Advanced Computer Control, pp. 561–565. IEEE, Harbin (2011)
6. Xiong, W., Toh, K.A., Yau, W.Y.: Model-Guided Deformable Hand Shape Recognition without Positioning Aids. Pattern Recognition 38, 1651–1664 (2004)
7. Chen, Y.X., Qi, F.H.: A New Approach to Extract Feature Points on the Boundary. J. Infrared Millim. Waves 17(3), 171–176 (1998) (in Chinese)
8. Zanuy, M.F., Elizondo, D.A.: Authentication of Individuals using Hand Geometry Biometrics: A Neural Network Approach 26, 201–216 (2007)
9. Yuan, W.Q., Jing, L.T.: Hand-Shape Feature Selection and Recognition Performance. In: 2011 International Conference on Hand-Based Biometrics (ICHB), pp. 153–158. IEEE, Hong Kong (2011)
10. Li, Y.: Research on Methodology of Fuzzy Hand Feature Extraction. Shenyang University of Technology (2011) (in Chinese)
11. Kumar, A., Wong, D.M., Shen, H., Jain, A.: Personal Verification Using Palmprint and Hand Geometry Biometric. In: Kittler, J., Nixon, M.S. (eds.) AVBPA 2003. LNCS, vol. 2688, pp. 1060–1067. Springer, Heidelberg (2003)

Palmprint Feature Extraction Based on Improved Gabor Wavelet Combing LBP Operator

Anna Wang[1], Hongrui Zhang[1], Maoxiang Chu[1], and Zi Wang[2]

[1] College of Information Science and Engineering, Northeastern University, Shenyang, Liaoning, China
wanganna@mail.neu.edu.cn
[2] Dongbei University of Finance and Economics, Dalian, Liaoning, China

Abstract. We proposed in this paper an accurate and efficient approach for palm-print feature extraction based on improved Gabor wavelet combing LBP operator. Firstly, the spectrum measured is used to accurately select the direction of Gabor filter, where the amplitude of the Gabor wavelet is directly convolved with the palmprints to obtain Gabor images. Secondly, LBP operator is applied to get the texture images, while the histogram information is extracted as the characteristics of the palmprints. The experiments based on CASIA Palmprint Database show that this method can achieve higher recognition accuracy, more effective and more feasible.

Keywords: Plamprint, Feature extraction, Gabor wavelet, LBP.

1 Introduction

In recent years, biometric identification technology has been widely used in daily life. What's more, the palm's line features, point features, texture features and geometry features can completely be used to identify a person's identity. Compared with other biological characteristics, palmprint, as a new biometric, has many unique advantages: 1) collect conveniently: palmprint images are easier to acquisition; 2) stability: palmprint features are hard to be forged; 3) uniqueness: studies have shown that even identical twins' palmprint features are not same exactly because of the differences of the genetics; 4) good recognition results of the low-resolution images. In a word, using palmprint to identify personal authentication has attracted more and more researchers' attention [1-2].

How to extract the palmprint features rationally and effectively is the key in the palmprint recognition, but single palmprint feature extraction methods have some limitations. This paper proposed a new method of feature extraction combing the modified Gabor filter and LBP (Local Binary Pattern).

2 Improved Gabor Filter

As an approximation of the texture image, palmprint's three main lines have certain directions. However, palm is not a straight line, so it is difficult to determine the

W.-S. Zheng et al. (Eds.): CCBR 2012, LNCS 7701, pp. 136–142, 2012.
© Springer-Verlag Berlin Heidelberg 2012

specific direction of its main lines in airspace. The Fourier spectrum of texture images can be used to describe the directionality of the texture.

Suppose $f(x,y)$ denotes an image of size $M \times N$, where $x = 0,1,\cdots,M-1$ and $y = 0,1,\cdots,N-1$. 2D discrete Fourier transforms of f can be expressed $F(u,v)$.

$$F(u,v) = \frac{1}{\sqrt{MN}} \sum_{x=0}^{M-1} \left[\sum_{y=0}^{N-1} f(x,y)e^{-j2\pi y/N} \right] e^{-j2\pi x/M} \tag{1}$$

Assume that the texture image matrix as: $I = \begin{bmatrix} 0 & 0 & 0 \\ 1 & 1 & 1 \\ 0 & 0 & 0 \end{bmatrix}$ and its Fourier transform is

A, then its Fourier transformed spectrum is: $abs(A) = \begin{bmatrix} 0 & 1 & 0 \\ 0 & 1 & 0 \\ 0 & 1 & 0 \end{bmatrix}$. It can be seen that

the spectrum matrix of the Fourier transform and the original image matrix are vertical on the contours, which is shown in Fig. 1.

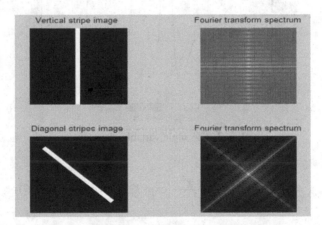

Fig. 1. Fringe spectrogram

In order to reflect the directionality of the palmprint texture, the spectrum after Fourier transform is made the polar coordinate transformation to get the spectral characteristics of a circle cantered at the origin, shown in Fig. 2. Then count the centralized directions of the spectral energy, mark the extreme value of the spectrum in the charts and return the corresponding angle values, shown in Fig. 3. The directions of palm's main lines can be obtained for the vertical relationship and as the direction parameters of the Gabor filter [3].

In the spatial domain, a 2D Gabor wavelet is a Gaussian kernel function modulated by a sinusoidal plane wave:

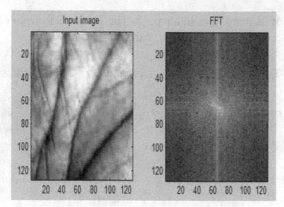

Fig. 2. Palmprint spectrogram

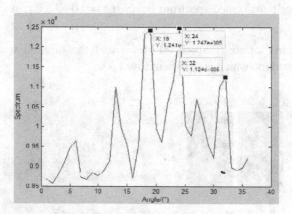

Fig. 3. The angle variable charts

$$\varphi_{(f,\theta,\sigma)} = \frac{1}{2\pi\sigma^2}\exp\left(-\frac{(x^2 + y^2)}{\sigma^2}\right)\exp(j2\pi f(x\cos\theta + y\sin\theta)) \qquad (2)$$

f is the central frequency of the sinusoidal plane wave, θ is the anti-clockwise rotation of the Gaussian and the plane wave and σ is the scale of the Gaussian function. The Gabor wavelets are self-similar — all wavelets can be generated from one mother wavelet by dilation and rotation. Due to its high resolution in both spatial and frequency domain, Gabor wavelet has been successfully used in biometrics like face and palmprint. Normally, the wavelets with different orientations and frequencies are used for feature extraction. In this paper, the method of spectrum measured is used to determine the direction of the Gabor filter and a group of Gabor filters are designed with 3 directions and 4 scales (f =1/2, 1/4,1/6,1/8). The palmprint images after Gabor transform are shown in Fig. 4.

Fig. 4. 3×4 Gabor transform

3   LBP Operator

LBP operator was firstly introduced by Finnish scientists Timo Ojala, etc., and used to describe the image texture features. The operator labels the pixels of an image with the binary sequences by comparing the neighbourhood of each pixel with itself, then convert the sequences into decimals. For example, the operator can be used to the image shown in the left of Fig. 5, we can get the binary code 11011000 and the decimal code 216 [4].

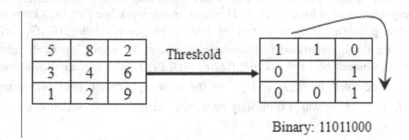

Fig. 5. LBP operator

By change the radius and the number of pixels in the neighbourhood, we can get the neighbourhoods of different sizes and shapes, and thus extend the common LBP algorithm to the variable regions. In this paper, we focus on the 3×3 neighbourhood. Palmprint images in the treatment of LBP operator shown in Fig. 6.

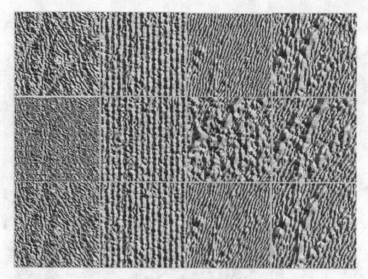

Fig. 6. LBP treatment palmprint

4   Feature Extraction Combing Gabor Filter and LBP

Once the convolution result of a palmprint image with the Gabor filter is obtained, LBP operator can be applied to encode texture information. LBP labels the pixels by threshold conversion for each pixel and its neighbourhood pixels. Therefore, the codes show the relationship of the amplitude of wavelet response at the centre pixel with that of its neighbours. The descriptor thus not only calculates simple and describes the local characteristic effectively, but also has more robust against rotation, which can reduce the influence of light and direction change. LBP has been successfully applied in texture image classification, face recognition etc. In those works, images are divided into many small blocks and histograms of the LBP response are used for extraction. However, in our work, we first use Gabor filter to process palmprint images, getting M feature images of Gabor $(G_1, G_2, \cdots G_m)$, then use the 8 neighbourhood LBP operator to process M images separately, getting M feature images of LBP $(GLBP_1, GLBP_2, \cdots GLBP_m)$, and extract the histogram sequences, de-noted by $H_1, H_2, \cdots H_m$, so the whole palmprint joint histogram is $H = \{H_1, H_2, \cdots H_m\}$, which ultimately be used to identify [5-6], which is shown in Fig. 7 as.

5   Experimental Results and Analysis

In order to verify the effectiveness of the proposed algorithm, we used CASIA Palmprint Database to found a new palm database, including 100 people and 8 images per everyone. Each image size is 640×480. After processing, 128×128 size of ROI (Region of Interest) was extracted. To test the approach, 5 selected images are captured from 100 people as training templates, while the rest 3 images of each person as used as testing images. To compare the results, we made two experiments respectively: the first group implemented the traditional Gabor approach and our method, shown in Table 1; the second group was the traditional LBP and paper's method contrast, shown in Table 2.

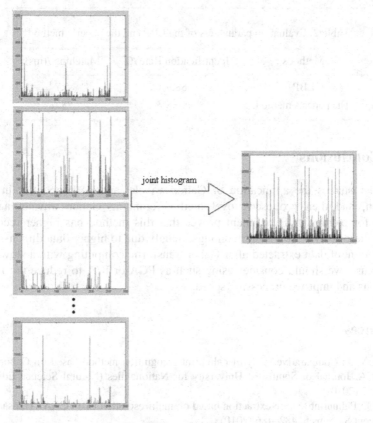

joint histogram

Fig. 7. Feature extraction

From Table 1, when using the traditional Gabor filter with fixed directions (0°,45°,90°,135°), the recognition rate is lower than the proposed method and takes longer time. So we can observe the direction of the Gabor filter set influence on the identify result. From Table 2, when using the traditional LBP method, namely direct apply of LBP operator for images, it consumes less time, but the recognition rate is not as well as paper's method. That is because the conventional LBP can only describe the overall profile characteristics of images, while ignoring the texture details. However, the proposed method, extracting multilevel LBP histogram sequence characteristics of palmprint images after Gabor transform, can describe the details and the overall characteristics, as well as good results.

Table 1. Evaluation parameters of the Gabor transform and the paper's method

Angle Selection/(°)	Identification Rate/%	Matching/(ms)
0,45,90,135	92.1	81.2
The paper's method(3 directions)	96.8	78.6

Table 2. Evaluation parameters of the LBP and the paper's method

Methods	Identification Rate /%	Matching /(ms)
LBP	88.9	5.7
The paper's method	96.8	78.6

6   Conclusions

This paper studies the application of Gabor wavelet and LBP operator in texture extraction, and then proposed novel method combing Gabor wavelet and LBP operator for palmprint. Experiment proves that this method has higher recognition rate, but there are also some shortcomings, mainly due to higher data dimensions and larger amount of data extracted after Gabor transform, computing with a slower pace. In the future, we should consider using such as PCA or ICA to reduce the features' dimensions and improve processing speed.

References

1. Xiang, W.J.: Comparative study of palmprint recognition method based on Gabor wavelet and PCA. Journal of Southwest University for Nationalities (Natural Science Edition) 36, 450–453 (2010)
2. Li, R.Q.: Palmprint feature extraction based on multiresolution LBP. CAAI Transactions on Intelligent Systems 5, 482–486 (2010)
3. Zhang, W., Liu: A Method of Gabor Filter Direction Selection Using for Palmprint Recognition. Journal of South-Central University for Nationalities (Natural Science Edition) 29, 77–81 (2010)
4. Wang, H.F., Li, F.H.: Face description and recognition using multi-scale LBP feature. Optics and Precision Engineering 16, 696–704 (2008)
5. Gao, H.M., Dai, B.: Face Recognition Using Multi-level Histogram Sequence Local Binary Pattern. Journal of Image and Graphics 14, 202–207 (2010)
6. Chen, C.S., Chen: A Face Recognition Algorithm Based on Gabor Wavelet and LBP. Journal of Jimei University (Natural Science) 15, 77–80 (2010)

The Research of Multi-spectral Hand Texture Fusion Method under a Non-constraint Condition

Weiqi Yuan, Yonghua Tang, and Ting Fang

Computer Vision Group Shenyang University of Technology Shenyang, 110870, China
sdsgtyh@163.com

Abstract. As different ways of Biometric Identification, palm print, palm veins and palm shapes identification have their own characteristics. The main stream of research is forming especially in the fields of none or low constraint conditions in this area. The palm print and shape is easy to be acquired to get pictures of high qualities by which we can make further research. However, under the same infrared band, one is hard to extract clear images of the hand veins of different individuals. This article is aim to solve this problem. Base on a method of multiband and multispectral palm print extracting, we could reach the aim letting quite a few people's hand under permission. Considering the fact that the None/Low constraint condition extracting could break the parallel position between the hand and the imaging sensor and cause affine deformation. Using the outline of the palm to revise and uniform the hand, we can realize the correction registration and the normalization of the palm print image. The experimental result will prove the advantage of this method we implemented.

Keywords: Multispectral imaging, Palm vein, Data fusion, Biometrics identification, Normalization.

1 Introduction

Among all the methods based on single model of Biometrical Identification, there is not a perfect one; every single method has downsides when they are implemented. Hence, using multi-model techniques, which means extracting and identifying two or more characteristics of the hand at the same time, could improve the overall property of the system, increase the robustness, and lower the requirement and the detecting complexity, so that a better performance could be fetched.

As a newly emerging technique, analyze the palm veins has gained the attention of more and more scholars and researchers for its several properties: hard to fake, highly classified, living collection and etc. But before all the method and techniques were implemented, there must be a reliable way to attain the pictures. To do this, we have to receive the signals radiated from the palm veins that have an appropriate wave length and brightness by an imaging sensor. As a matter of fact, the skin of the palm is among the thickest of the human body. Different people shares different skin properties such as the thickness of the outer layer skin or the fat, and the texture precision and so on. Thus, what would be the perfect wave length and brightness of light to

W.-S. Zheng et al. (Eds.): CCBR 2012, LNCS 7701, pp. 143–150, 2012.

transmit the info has been long a topic among the scholars, and they have had some researches. For instance, the optical reflection characteristics of living cells of human body have been studied since the last century by Guanghuang Gao's group. His final result shows that women's reflectivity is higher than men's, which means there will be less information of the veins under the skin of a women being transmitted to the imaging sensor, and that will make its quality lower. The same result comes from Jianmin Tang's group when he measured the regular pattern of the skin's optical property which also proved that acquiring the palm vein's image under visible light lacks brilliance. Moreover, the absorption and dissipation coefficient measure work has been done by Lianshun Zhang; Rong Chen has researched in the area of strong scatter optical perimeters of biological tissues; Wenbo Wan and Weiqi Yuan's group put the different kinds of palm skin into 4 categories, and also did researches narrated the principle of vein image-forming and done a number of works concentrating on the selection of wave length. They also created the image acquisition device to capture the palms. People like Weiqi Yuan and Dapeng Zhang suggested that the wave length around 850 nm is optimal for palm vein capture. Several experiments had made to prove their point. Yet, like we have discussed before, there is not a fixed wave length that could make all the hands appears clearly (Demonstrated in Figure 1). Therefore, the author implemented a multiband image forming strategy and using data fusion method to generate a picture that could be identified.

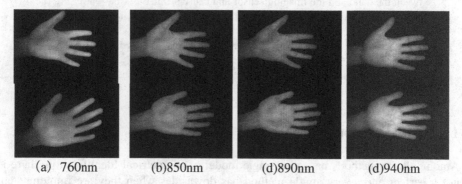

(a) 760nm   (b)850nm   (d)890nm   (d)940nm

Fig. 1. Images of different palms under different infrared wavelength

It is because the palm print is located on the surface of the hand, getting the image of it could be simple especially under the wave length of a blue ray [11], which is 430nm, and yet, easy to fake and also have a poor confidentiality. This article used the method to capture several pictures under different wave length and using some image processing techniques to fuse them into one picture to create an ideal image. In the following passages, we call this image in unification as Palm Texture Image, it contains the shape information at the same time and possesses the qualities such as the good confidentiality, accessibility and practical applicability. In figure 1, same hand in a line and same wavelength in a row.

2   The Model of Multispectral Palm Print Fusion Process

Using the non/low constraint hand imaging devise developed autonomously shown in Figure 2, this article contains the experiment collecting images from the same group of people (100 graduates of our department) in different times, and we created a non/low constraint image bank by doing that.

The non/low constrained in this article means that the person whose palm image was being extracted need to stretch his/her hand naturally and keep paralleled a distance from the camera of about 20-30 cm. Judging from a vast experimental results we can easily dictate that the palm images we get at the same time but different wavelengths have a good outline unity; but the palm images of different times shows a considerable distinctions on the positions, directions, distances and the parallelism, shows in the figure 3. For getting a good quality of the image in different wavelength, different brightness of the light is implemented. Consequentially, the gray level differences between images are considerable.

It is because there is no distance standard between the hand and the camera under the circumstance of non/low constraint and so are the parallelism and the stretch of hand, we stipulate that the first band we capture when registered and also all the 430 nm ranges are considered to be the standards. All the other images would be adjust and process by them.

Considering all the facts narrated above, we come up with a fusion model to fully highlight the efficient information in different bands, shows in figure 4.

Fig. 2. Multispectral palm imaging device

Fig. 3. Picture of same person at different time

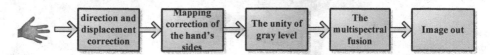

Fig. 4. Fusion of the multispectral palm vein image

3   Image Direction and Displacement Correction of Each Band

Before any kinds of correction take place, the direction and displacement correction is the premise of all. As for the whole hand, the direction of the fingers and their approach degree is not as stable as the palm. So we decided to use the line starts from the midpoint of the middle finger to the midpoint of wrinkle to be the palm position reference standard. All the images whether they are of different wavelength or different time, take this standard as unity.

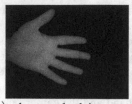 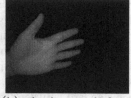 

(a) the standard image   (b) the images before correction (c) the images after correction

Fig. 5. The standard image and the images before and after correction

4   Mapping Correction of the Hand's Sides

The fingers of a hand are the easiest part to emerge a distortion, especially for women, as their hands' joint between palm and fingers could appear an apparent distortion. In that way, the final image will be influenced. To tackle that problem, hands are separated into two independent parts, say, the finger part and the palm part, which will be adjusted separately. However, we have yet considered the differences if the fingers adducted.

Shown in figure 6, we use the method of mapping to achieve the correction of palm and fingers separately. Figure 6 shows how it works. We define the real length of palm is Lpa, the real measure length is Lpn, the length after correction is Lph, the real length of finger is Lfa, the real measure length is Lfn, and the length after correction is Lfh.The contrast between images before correction and images after correction is shown in figure 7.

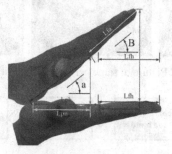

Fig. 6. Backward tilting measure techniques

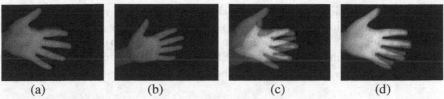

(a)   (b)   (c)   (d)

(a) standard image (b) target registration image before treatment

(c) direct registration image before treatment   (d) registration image after treatment

Fig. 7. contrast between image before registration and after registration

5   The Unity of Gray Level on Multispectral Palm Print

Among all the bands of the image collection, no specific background color was defined. But the image sensor we were using was extremely sensible to near-infrared wave band and could filter the visible light, hence, all the background turns into black without strong illumination from the outside, shows in figure 1. Yet, because of the difference of the brightness of the illuminator we were using can't be ignored, we cannot fusion all the images from different wave bands, or it will decrease the influence of the Affected texture characteristics. So we have to normalize the image by standard on the front part, which means the background part is not in consideration.

In this paper, according to the acquisition of the palm and the band palm-vein image, it will conduct the vein image fusion, and then with the palmprint image fusion. In the palm of the hand vein image fusion process,the image configuration can be generally divided into two kinds, one is in accordance with the image size, this paper is according to the palm contour,as shown in figure 7 (a) below. This method is simple, but it will make the palm vein configuration is inaccurate.This method not only makes the actual existence of a vein texture in configuration appear two veins,and due to the superimposed effects of the image peaks and troughs, but also makes the vein texture significantly weakened, as shown in Figure8 (a) below. In order to avoid this phenomenon, retain the original palm vein texture structure, this paper is in accordance with the palm of the hand contour registration, followed by the second registration.That means the sreach will be in a certain range in accordance with the palm vein texture to achieve the best principle of the vein texture registration, as shown in figure 8 (b) below.

(a)in accordance with the palm contour image (b) in accordance with the vein trend image

Fig. 8. Vein image registration results

After the registration, the palm-vein image continue to fuse with the palmprint image.Because palmprint image and palm-vein image are quite different in the gray level distribution(the histogram in Figure 9 (a) (b) as shown), direct integration is difficult to fully retain the original texture features of two images.The two images are firstly processed to gray scale stretch, as shown in Figure9 (c)、 (d) below.

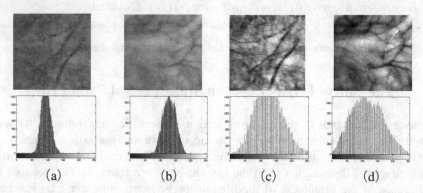

(a)   (b)   (c)   (d)

Fig. 9. The unnormalized and normalized palm image, palm-vein image and its histogram

6   The Multispectral Fusion and Identification of the Palm Print

We now can fusion the image after the steps we've done above. This article will undergo a series of processing of the vein and palmprint image of various pixel level data fusion experiments, found that the palm and palm-vein image fusion effect is the best in according to the gray in small principles, and the recognition results is the most accurate, fusion image and extraction of ROI results as shown in figure 10.

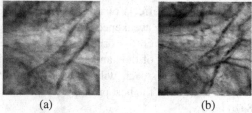

(a)   (b)

(a)   according to transparency 50% fusion results
(b)   fusion results according to the gray in small principles

Fig. 10. Palm, palm-vein fusion results

Figure 10 (a) is the data fusion according to the transparency way.The fusion principle is ˋC=d*A+(1-d)*B. Type A is a stair fusion image, and in this paper for the palmprint image,the value is the image pixel values / 255; Type B is a secondary fusion image, in this paper for the fusion of the palm-vein image,its meaning is equal to A; d is the transparency , its range is 0 to 1, adjusting its value can adjust the position

of the two image fusion results; C is the final fusion result, the corresponding fusion image is its value * 255. Figure 10 (a) is the results of 0.5 transparency d
Figure 10 (b) is the data fusion according to the Minimum gray value, that is
B<=A: C=B   B>=A: C=A

7   Experiment and Analysis

The ROI value needed to be extracted to compare with the condition where the fusion method was not implemented to judge if our fusion strategy could improve the recognition rate, through 2DPCA.

In this paper, the image library is obtained through the Institute's self-developed multi-band hand acquisition devices , collecting 10 images on the left hand of 100 people in the four near-infrared bands and Blu-ray respectively.A total of 5000(100*10*5) images formed the image library,and 5 for registration, 5 is used to test.Table 1 lists 10 persons recognition results under various bands and the fusion results.

Table 1. Parts of image library object recognition results

The object code	760nm	850nm	890nm	940nm	Palm print	Image fusion
1	97.25	99.01	98.38	98.57	98.80	99.35
2	97.56	99.11	99.05	99.02	98.67	99.38
3	97.98	98.97	99.06	99.10	98.54	99.32
4	98.02	99.09	99.11	98.88	98.90	99.40
5	97.53	99.13	98.85	98.68	98.72	99.31
6	97.28	99.06	99.12	98.86	98.78	99.41
7	97.64	99.21	98.87	98.98	98.73	99.39
8	97.47	99.16	99.07	99.17	98.82	99.39
9	98.11	99.19	98.99	99.12	98.96	99.37
10	97.31	98.99	99.04	98.95	98.84	99.43

The experimental results show that the fusion image recognition results are generally better than single band multiple corresponding images. The main reason is the fusion texture of the palm-vein and palm prints can maximize the integrated multiple bands,increase the effective amount of information,and produce some new texture information were not in the single band images.

8   Conclusion

The fusion palm texture image have some advantage which were not in the single band images,so as to improve the image quality, increase the information in the image, improve biometric hand recognition rate. This paper's image library contains a complete palm outline, on the basis of this article can also add the hand shape recognition, and with the palm texture recognition results to make decision fusion will be able to further improve the overall recognition effect.

Acknowledgement. This work is supported by National Natural Science Foundation of China (60972123), Specialized Research Fund for the Doctoral Program of Higher Education (20092102110002) and Shenyang Science and Technology Development Program (F10-213-1-00).

References

1. Gao, G.H., Zhang, G.S.: Human skin in vivo laser reflectance characteristic research. Laser Journal 12(5), 253–256 (1991)
2. Gao, J.M., Fu, C.H.: The pilot study on the skin to light reflection, transmission and absorption of regular. Chinese Journal of Lasers 14(7), 440–443 (1987)
3. Zhang, L.S.: He-Ne laser irradiation of biological tissue measurement of the optical parameters. Laser Journal 28(6), 87 (2007)
4. Xu, T., Zhang, C.H., Wang, X.Y.: Time-resolved reflection to determine the optical parameters of biological tissue. Optoelectronic Laser Journal 15(1), 108–112 (2004)
5. Chen, R., Chen, S.H., Liu, J.H.: Strongly scattering biological tissue optical parameters of the reconstruction. Hubei University Journal (Natural Science Edition) 28(1), 45–47 (2006)
6. Xie, S.H., Gong, W., Li, H.: Selective photothermolysis effect of biological tissue. Laser and Photonics Progress 8(41), 48–51 (2004)
7. Wan, W.B.: The study of palm vein image capture and recognition system. Shenyang University of Technology (2007)
8. Yuan, W.Q., Yang, G.T., Li, W.: The study of palm vein harvesting system based on wavelength selection. Laser and Infrared Journal 41(2), 234–239 (2011)
9. Zhang, D.P., Lu, G.M., Guo, Z.H.: Based on the palm vein and the palm print near-infrared imaging device and an identification method. China 200710144916 (2008)
10. Zhang, D.P., Lu, G.M., Guo, Z.H.: Online palm, palm vein image identification method and its special collection instrument. China 200710144914 (2008)
11. Yuan, W.Q., Sun, H.: Non-contact palm image capture light design. Application Research of Computers 28(5), 1965–1967 (2011)

Rotation Invariant Finger Vein Recognition[*]

Shaohua Pang, Yilong Yin[**], Gongping Yang, and Yanan Li

School of Computer Science and Technology, Shandong University,
Jinan, China
pangshaohua11271987@126.com, ylyin@sdu.edu.cn,
sduygp@gmail.com, lyn19890505@163.com

Abstract. Finger vein patterns have recently been recognized as an effective biometric identifier and many related work can achieve satisfied results. However, these methods usually suppose the database is non-rotated or slightly rotated, which are strict for preprocessing stages, especially for capture. As we all know, user-friendly capture tends to cause the rotation problem, which degrades the recognition performance due to the unregulated images or feature loss. In this paper, we propose a new finger vein recognition method to solve the common rotation problem of finger vein images. Two experiments are designed to evaluate the recognition performance in both verification mode and identification mode and to demonstrate the advantages and robustness of our method in different rotated databases compared with pattern binary based method like LBP. Experimental results show that the proposed method can not only achieve a lower EER (1.71%) than LBP (2.67%), but also can overcome the difficulties of rotation in rotated databases. The EERs of proposed method in three different rotated databases are 2.15%, 2.98% and 2.75% respectively, which shows that our method has better robustness in rotation than LBP.

Keywords: Finger Vein Recognition, Scale Invariant Feature Transform (SIFT), Rotation Invariance, Local Binary Pattern (LBP).

1 Introduction

Biometric recognition has been used in many areas such as border crossing, national ID cards and e-passports due to its efficiency and high security. Hand-based biometrics normally include fingerprint recognition, finger knuckle print recognition and palm recognition, in which fingerprint recognition is mature and has been widely researched [1]. However, the hand-based biometrics such as fingerprint, palm print and finger knuckle are easy to be forged and the surface conditions can influence the performance significantly [2]. To overcome the shortages of hand-based biometric systems, finger vein recognition is proposed and well studied these years [3]. The distinctive property of finger vein is non-contact [4] [5], which can overcome the difficulties mentioned before.

---

[*] This work is supported by National Natural Science Foundation of China under Grant No. 61173069 and 61070097.

[**] Corresponding author.

W.-S. Zheng et al. (Eds.): CCBR 2012, LNCS 7701, pp. 151–156, 2012.

Feature extraction is important for finger vein recognition and many finger vein recognition methods utilize the features of blood vessel network [6]. However, the performance of recognition will degrade significantly, if the images have low quality and can not be segmented correctly. To solve this problem, binary pattern based methods such as LBP, LDP [7] and PBBM [8] have been proposed, and experiments show these methods have high accuracy of recognition. Although the binary pattern based methods can somewhat make up the deficiency of low quality and incorrect segmentation of finger vein images, the rotation problem of images remains unsolved. With slight rotation, the performance of binary pattern based methods will degrade severely due to unregulated images or feature loss. However the the rotated finger vein images are usually in user-friendly recognition system, and in a practical system the rotation problem is inevitable. To solve the problem, we proposed a new rotation invariant finger vein recognition method.

The rest of this paper is organized as follows: Section 2 describes the proposed method. In section 3, experiments and analysis will be presented and in the last section conclusions will be given.

2   Proposed Method

2.1   Preprocessing

The captured finger vein images usually have problems such as low contrast, non-uniform illumination and background noise, thus preprocessing is necessary for feature extraction and matching. In our method, segmentation and enhancement will be used in preprocessing stage. To exclude the influence of background noise, segmentation will be implemented. First with Sobel edge detection, we can get the edge outline of finger vein, and then inner rectangle will be used to intercept the finger vein image (Fig.1 (b)). Just as Fig.1shows, our preprocessing includes segmentation and enhancement. With suitable segmentation, the background is removed and with enhancement the contrast of venous regions and non-venous regions improve effectively. The finger-vein images are captured with infrared ray, and the background and the finger vein features can not distinguished without histogram equalization. By this preprocess, details of finger-vein can be shown clearly which is illustrated in Fig.1. It can effectively deal with the degradation. So we enhance the images with histogram equalization, which can overcome the difficulties caused by low contrast and non-uniform illumination. The enhanced finger vein image is shown in Fig.1 (c).

(a) The captured image　　(b) Segmentation　　(c) Enhancement with histogram equalization

Fig. 1. Preprocessing of finger vein images

2.2   Feature Extraction and Matching

After preprocessing, SIFT[9] will be used for feature extraction and matching. The reason that we choose this algorithm is the vantage in rotation-invariance. SIFT was first introduced by D.G Lowe to get better performance in object recognition. Due to its advantages of invariance to scale, rotation and affine transformation, SIFT is soon used in many application areas, especially in biometrics.

The principle of SIFT is to find extreme points in scale-space and filter them to get stable ones, and then local features of the images around these stable points are extracted, thus local descriptors are generated from these local features for matching. Four stages of SIFT algorithm can be described as follows: (1) Use a difference-of-Gaussian function to implement scale-space extrema detection; (2) Select stable keypoints from extreme points; (3) Assign orientations to each keypoint; (4) Generate local keypoint descriptors. With stable features are extracted from SIFT, influence of angles will be excluded and problems caused by rotation will be solved.

Feature points extracted from images are selected as matching pairs, and the number of matching pairs is used to measure the similarity of two finger vein images. Then the suitable threshold T (the number of matching pairs) is selected after testing the matching results of the whole database. For example, two finger vein images will be classified as the same class if the number of matching pairs is bigger than T, otherwise these two finger vein images will be classified as different classes. The matching result is shown in Fig.2.

Fig. 2. Matching result of two finger vein images

3   Experimental Results and Analysis

3.1   Database and Experiment Setting

We construct our database with 95 individuals (classes) and each class has 11 finger vein pictures with slightly rotation. All the captured finger vein images are stored by BMP format with resolution 320*240. All experiments are implemented by Visual C++ and MATLAB, and executed on a machine with 2.93GHz CPU and 4G memory. In this paper, two experiments are designed to evaluate the performance and robustness of proposed method: (a) Experiment 1 evaluates the performance of the proposed method with verification mode and identification mode respectively, and compare the results with LBP [7] based method; (b) Experiment 2 is conducted to show the advantages of our method in solving the rotation problem compared with LBP [7] based method.

3.2   Experiment 1

We perform experiments in verification mode and identification mode respectively. In verification mode, the class of each test sample is claimed and each test sample will be matched with templates of the claimed class by both SIFT and LBP. If the number of matching pairs is bigger than threshold, matching is successful. The successful matching is called intraclass matching or genuine matching. Otherwise, the unsuccessful matching is called interclass matching or imposter matching. In the experiments, we get $95*C_{11}^2$ intraclass matching results (each class has C_{11}^2 matching results); also, we choose the first sample to perform interclass matching and get C_{95}^2 matching results. The performance of the proposed method and LBP is evaluated by EER (Equal Error Rate). The EERs of proposed method and LBP are 0.0171 and 0.0267 respectively, and the ROC curves are shown in Fig.3.

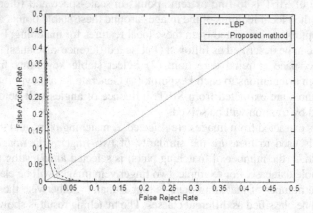

Fig. 3. ROC curves of different methods

In the identification mode, we conduct experiments in the close-set database (all the samples are in the enrollment database). We do not know the class of input finger vein and want to identify which class it belongs to. We choose the first sample in each class as template and use other ten samples in each class as test samples (probes). Therefore, we get 95 templates and 95*10 probes totally. Each probe will be matched with all the templates. For each probe, the matching result will be ranked based on the matching score. The CMC (cumulative match curves) is shown in Fig.4, and the rank-one recognition rate and lowest rank of perfect recognition is given in Table 1. From the experimental results we can see the proposed method is better than LBP based method.

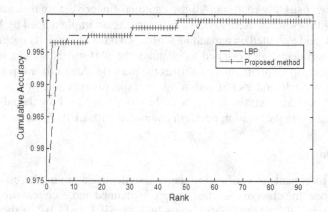

Fig. 4. Cumulative match curves by different methods

Table 1. Identification performance by different methods

	rank-one recognition rate	lowest rank of perfect recognition
LBP[7]	0.9778	55
Proposed method	0.9883	47

3.3 Experiment 2

We conduct experiment to show the advantage of the proposed method in rotation and analyze the advantage in translation compared with LBP.

LBP is based on the computation on pixel level. LBP solves problem of translation by translating corresponding pixels to generate feature vectors and measuring similarities of these vectors. Although the problem in translation of images can be solved, the system is time-consuming. However, SIFT method extracts key points from scale-space and the extracted key points are independent of coordinate, which can overcome the problem in translation.

To verify the robustness in rotation invariance, we construct three simulated rotated databases based on the source database. We rotate all the samples in the source database with different rotated ranges to construct three rotated databases. The three rotation ranges are $\pm 1^0, \pm 3^0$ and $\pm 5^0$. For example, in the simulated $\pm 5^0$ database, the rotated degrees may range from -5^0 to $+5^0$.

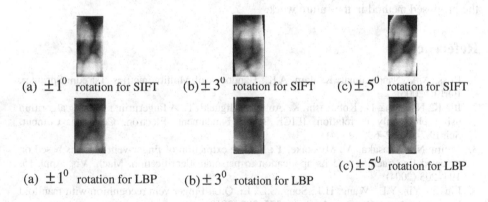

(a) $\pm 1^0$ rotation for SIFT   (b) $\pm 3^0$ rotation for SIFT   (c) $\pm 5^0$ rotation for SIFT

(c) $\pm 5^0$ rotation for LBP

(a) $\pm 1^0$ rotation for LBP   (b) $\pm 3^0$ rotation for LBP

Fig. 5. Different preprocessing samples of two methods with different rotated degrees

We evaluate the performance of different methods in three rotated databases. Fig.5. shows different preprocessing samples with different rotated degrees. Table 2. shows the EERs of proposed method and LBP in different rotated databases. From Table.2, we can see the proposed method can overcome rotation problem better compared with LBP based method.

Table 2. EERs in different rotated databases with the proposed method and LBP

Degrees	LBP [7]	Proposed method
$\pm 1^0$	2.70%	2.15%
$\pm 3^0$	3.33%	2.98%
$\pm 5^0$	4.81%	2.75%

4   Conclusions

In this paper, a new finger vein recognition method is proposed to overcome the difficulties in rotation of images. Although SIFT has been used in finger-vein recognition, to the best of my knowledge, SIFT usually is only used in feature extraction. Our work mainly focus on the counter-rotation property of this algorithm. And also our experiments on the rotated databases verify the efficiency of proposed method. Experiments are conducted in different rotated databases to verify the efficiency and robustness in rotation invariance and it is suitable for a user-friendly system. Although the experimental results are satisfactory, the number of individuals is limited in constructed database. So, a large-scale real-world database will be applied in the proposed method in the future work.

References

1. Ross, A.A., Nandakumar, K., Jain, A.K.: Handbook of Multibiometrics, 1st edn. Springer, Berlin (2006)
2. Ito, K., Nakajima, H., Kobayashi, K., Aoki, T., Higuchi, T.: A fingerprint matching algorithm using phase-only correlation. IEICE Trans. Fundament. Electron. Commun. Comput. Sci. E87-A, 682–699 (2004)
3. Miura, N., Nagasaka, A., Miyatake, T.: Feature extraction of finger-vein patterns based on repeated line tracking and its application to personal identification. Mach. Vis. Appl. 15, 194–203 (2004)
4. Liu, Z., Yin, Y.L., Wang, H.J., Song, S.L., Li, Q.L.: Finger vein recognition with manifold learning. J. Netw. Comput. Appl. 33, 275–282 (2010)
5. Wu, J.D., Ye, S.H.: Driver identification using finger-vein patterns with radon transform and neural network. Expert Syst. Appl. 36, 5793–5799 (2009)
6. Rosdi, B.A., Shing, C.W., Suandi, S.A.: Finger vein recognition using local line binary pattern. Sensors 11, 11357–11371 (2011)
7. Lee, E.C., Jung, H., Kim, D.: New finger biometric method using near infrared imaging. Sensors 11, 2319–2333 (2011)
8. Yang, G.P., Xi, X.M., Yin, Y.L.: Finger Vein Recognition Based on a Personalized Best Bit Map. Sensors 12, 1738–1757 (2012)
9. David, G.L.: Distinctive Image Features from Scale-Invariant Keypoints. International Journal of Computer Vision 60(2), 91–110 (2004)

Hand Dorsal Vein Recognition Based on Hierarchically Structured Texture and Geometry Features

Xiangrong Zhu and Di Huang

IRIP, School of Computer Science and Engineering, Beihang Univ., Beijing, 100191, China
xiangrong.zhu@gmail.com, dhuang@buaa.edu.cn

Abstract. In recent years, hand dorsal vein has attracted increasing attentions of researchers in the domain of biometrics. This paper proposes a novel approach for hand dorsal vein identification, making use of both the texture and geometry features. The proposed approach works in a hierarchical way: 1) the coarse step segments the vein region and calculates its skeleton to feed the following operations, and the Energy Cost extracted in the Thinning process (TEC) is also used to reduce a large number of false candidates, greatly improving the efficiency; 2) in the fine step, both texture and geometry clues are represented by Local Binary Patterns (LBP) and the graph composed by the crossing points and endpoints of vein pattern respectively, and the two modalities are finally combined for decision making. The proposed method is evaluated on the NCUT dataset containing 2040 hand dorsal vein images of 102 subjects, and the experimental results clear highlight its effectiveness.

Keywords: hand vein recognition, graph matching, local binary patterns.

1   Introduction

The hand vein pattern, as a biometric trait, was first proposed for people identification elated applications in 1990s and in recent years has drawn increasing attentions in this research community. Anatomically, veins are blood carrying vessels interweaved with muscles and bones, and their fundamental function of the vascular system is to supply oxygen to each part of the body [1]. Similar with other biometrics, e.g. iris, face and fingerprint, the hand vein pattern provides a significant uniqueness since vein patterns of individuals are different, even between the identical twins [1]. Besides, it possesses some other important advantages that can be summarized as follows:

(1) As hand veins are imaged by using far or near infrared lighting resources to capture temperature differences between the blood flow in the veins and surrounding skin, they can only be obtained from live bodies, thereby offering a natural and convenient manner for live-ness detection.

(2) Blood vessels are distributed underneath the skin, and it is thus much more difficult for intruders to forge than other biometrics.

(3) Hand vein patterns are quite stable, and they generally keep constant from 14 to 60 years old, in contrast to face whose appearance varies along with the aging process of human beings.

W.-S. Zheng et al. (Eds.): CCBR 2012, LNCS 7701, pp. 157–164, 2012.

(4) Unlike fingerprint, hand vein images are acquired by contactless devices, avoiding infectious diseases and bringing better user experience.

Due to these above merits and the simplicity in processing, there exist an increasing amount of tasks in the last decade, based on hand vein patterns of the palm part [2] [3], dorsal part [4] [5] [6] and finger part [7]. Most tasks in the literature followed the way that firstly segments region of interest (ROI), i.e. hand subcutaneous vascular network, from hand vein images, and then extracts local geometric features for matching, such as the positions and angles of short straight vectors [8], endpoints and crossing points [9], dominant points [4], vein minutiae and knuckle shape [6]. All these studies report reasonable performance; however, when regarding dorsal hand vein recognition, these techniques tend to suffer from limited local features since compared with the palm or finger part, the number of vein minutiae on dorsal part is really few, leading to a deficiency in capturing vein pattern difference between subjects. On the other hand, some investigations turn to utilize the texture of entire hand dorsal parts [5] [10], which also leaves space in accuracy improvement.

In contrast to the tasks in the literature of hand dorsal vein recognition that are dependent on single modality, either geometry or texture, in this paper, we claim that the joint use of both types of information contributes to improved performance. Therefore, a novel hierarchical method is proposed. As depicted in Fig. 1, in the coarse phase, it segments vein areas and calculates its skeleton for the following operations, and Energy Cost in the Thinning process (TEC) is also applied to eliminate a large number of false candidates to be matched, greatly reducing the computational cost of the system. The texture and geometry clues are further in the fine stage described by Local Binary Patterns (LBP) and the graph composed by the crossing and ending points in the vein region respectively, and the similarity measurements are finally combined for decision. The results achieved on the NCUT dataset clearly demonstrate the effectiveness of the proposed approach to recognize hand dorsal vein patterns.

The remainder of the paper is organized as follows: Section 2 presents the Thinning Energy Cost (TEC) based coarse classification and the fine step is presented in section 3 including the methods of texture and geometry feature extraction. The NCUT database and experimental result are presented in Section4. Section 5 concludes the paper.

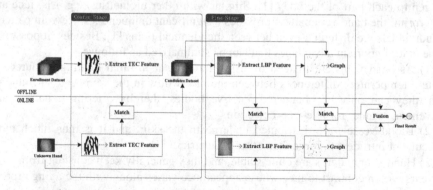

Fig. 1. The framework of the proposed hand vein recognition approach

2   Thinning Energy Cost (TEC) Based Coarse Classification

In order to utilize geometry features of dorsal hand vein patterns, repeatable keypoints (e.g. endpoints and crossing points) are required to be located in their skeleton images. Intuitively, the skeleton images of the hand vein pattern of the same individual should have more similarity to each other than the ones of different individuals, and inspired by the fact, in this study, we propose a novel feature, extracted in the thinning process of hand vein skeleton generation and thus named as Thinning Energy Cost (TEC). It's quite different from existing methods only concentrating on detected minutiae of hand dorsal vein images.

Specifically, after the preprocessing pipeline consisting of de-noising and ROI (Region of Interest) cropping, we make use of the method as in [12] to do binaryzation on images to separate vein region from dorsal hands. The thinning method is then used to obtain the vein skeleton. The thinning operation can remain key information and eliminate unimportant information as well as noise for recognition applications [13]. Some thinning algorithms have been proposed and they can be divided into two broad classes: i.e. iterative algorithms and non-iterative ones. Non-iterative algorithms generally run faster but they do not always produce accurate results. The approach [11] that we adopted is an iterative parallel algorithm. For each iteration, every pixel of the binary image is checked whether it is on the vein boundary according to certain pre-defined rules and the configuration within its 3-by-3 neighborhood [13]. If so, the pixel will be deleted. The process lasts until the skeleton width becomes no larger than one pixel. Considering that the mediate result of the same individual generated at each iteration during the thinning process should be more similar than the ones of different subjects, we record the number of the deleted points for each iteration and thus obtain a vector whose elements are the numbers of deleted pixels at each iteration and dimensions are the numbers of iterations. This vector is used as a feature for the coarse classification which we call Thinning Energy Cost (TEC). Some examples are shown in Fig. 2.

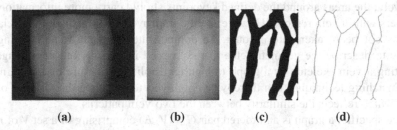

(a)   (b)   (c)   (d)

Fig. 2. (a): the original 480-by-640 hand dorsal vein image; (b): the 451-by-352 region of interest; (c): the result of binaryzation; and (d) the skeleton of the vein region

3   Texture and Geometry Feature Fusion Based Fine Classification

3.1   Improved LBP Method for Vein Pattern

The LBP operator is a powerful manner of texture description. The operator labels the pixels of a given image by thresholding its neighbors within a rectangular or a circular area and considering the corresponding binary number as a decimal value, and Fig. 3 depicts the basic LBP operator. The histogram of the labels is finally used as a texture descriptor [14].

Fig. 3. An illustration of the basic LBP operator

In [5], LBP has been investigated for texture description in dorsal hand vein recognition. A given dorsal hand vein image is firstly divided into several sub-regions from each of which LBP histograms are extracted, and these histograms are finally concatenated as a comprehensive representation of the texture information of the entire vein area. In order to use texture information of dorsal hand veins, we follow this approach but make a further improvement. Considering that vein regions in a hand vein pattern convey more discriminative information than the others, we introduce the above technique by assigning a weight to each sub-region. The weight is equal to the percentage of vein pixels in the region which can be calculated from the binary image.

The distance of two histograms in the gallery and probe set respectively, denoted as S and M is calculated by Chi square statistic as:

$$X(S, M) = w_j \sum_{i,j} \frac{(S_{i,j} - M_{i,j})^2}{S_{i,j} + M_{i,j}}, \tag{1}$$

where j is the region index and w_j is its corresponding weight for pattern matching.

3.2 Graph Matching Method for Vein Patterns

Intuitively, the areas around the defined keypoints should carry more information than the others within vein regions. However, in the improved LBP method, their relationship has not been taken into account. To compensate for such a shortcoming, we propose to describe the geometry clue that conveyed in dorsal hand vein images by presenting a vein skeleton as a graph to highlight holistic structure of a pattern, and graph matching techniques can thereby be employed to calculate the distance of two graphs which reflects the similarity between the two vein patterns.

To be specific, a graph is an ordered pair $G = (V, E)$ comprising of a set V of nodes together with a set E of edges. We use an undirected and weighted graph to present a skeleton image. The nodes of the graph are the minutiae of the vein area and the edges are the skeleton lines (See details in Fig. 4). The graph $G = \{a_{ij}\}$ is defined as follows:

$$a_{ij} = \begin{cases} (x, y), i = j \\ p, i \neq j \end{cases} \tag{2}$$

In the above equation, (x, y) is the position of the located keypoints in the dorsal hand vein image and p is the number of pixels on the skeleton line between the node i and j. If there is no skeleton line between node i and node j, then p=0.

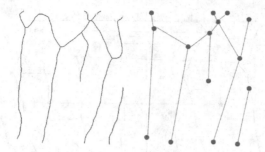

Fig. 4. A skeleton image (left) and its corresponding graph (right)

Graph matching techniques can be divided roughly into two categories: the first requires a strict correspondence among the two objects being matched or at least among their subparts, while the second defines inexact matching methods, where a matching can occur even if two graphs to be compared are structurally different to some extent [15]. Considering the distortions of the vein skeleton images, an inexact graph matching method is more suitable.

We choose an inexact matching method proposed in [16] for the problem of dorsal hand vein recognition. The method is based on the concept of graph edit distance: two graphs, G_1 and G_2, G_1 can be changed into G_2 in a finite sequence of graph edit operations. We define three types of operations: i.e. substituting a node or an edge; deleting a node or an edge; and inserting a node or an edge. Each operation takes a pre-defined cost and the total cost of the whole transforming process is obtained by accumulating the ones of all edit operations. The minimum total cost of all possible sequences is the graph editing distance between graphs being compared. The process to find the minimum operation sequence can be regarded as an assignment problem. We define three assigning ways considering the difference in node numbers between G_1 and G_2: assigning (or changing) the node i in G_1 to the node j in G_2 which corresponds to the substitution operation or the deleting operation that is followed by an inserting operation; assigning the node i in G_1 to null which corresponds to the deleting operation; assigning null to j in G_2 which corresponds to the inserting operation. The cost of each assignment is equal to the cost of its corresponding edit operations. The cost of each edit operation is defined as flows:

- The cost of deleting a node or inserting a node is the sum of the values of all the edges connected to the node;
- The cost of substituting node A with node B is the sum of Euclidean distance between them and the cost of the assignment of edges connected to A and B;
- The cost of deleting an edge or inserting an edge is the weight of the edge defined in the second rule;
- The cost of the assignment of edges is seen as an assignment problem in the same way with the nodes.

Then Munkres' algorithm [16] is applied to seek the minimum assignment cost that is seen as the distance of the two graphs. Figure 5 shows an assignment between two graphs.

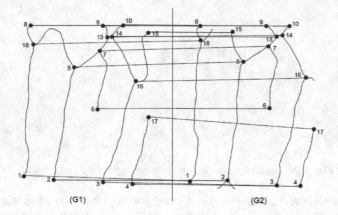

Fig. 5. Assignment between two graphs (The matched nodes are connected by lines and labeled the same numbers)

4   Experimental Results

We adopt the NCUT dataset [5] which consists of 102 subjects in our experiments for method evaluation. Each subject contains 20 dorsal hand images; half of them are of right hands while the other half are of left hands. We regard that samples of left hands and right hands are from different subjects as if we had 204 classes.

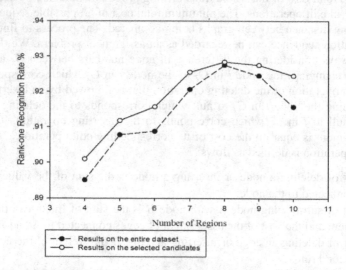

Fig. 6. Accurate rates under different divisions and matching samples

As illustrated in the framework of the proposed approach, TEC feature is first used. Even though its rank-one recognition rate is only 57.45% by a nearest neighbor classifier, a recognition rate of 99.71% can be achieved as the first 200 candidates are considered. The enrolled hand vein images in these 200 candidate classes will take part in the classification in the next level while the others are eliminated. By this means, the average match number is reduced to 377 from 1020. On the other side, the maximum value of the dimension of all the TEC vectors is 132, and the classification can thus be finished in a very short time.

Then the improved LBP method and graph matching method are used respectively. The uniform pattern of LBP with circular neighborhood is employed. The radius value of the neighborhood is set at 1 and the number of neighboring points is set at 8 as [5]. Figure 6 shows classification performance by the improved LBP method on the whole database and only on the candidates with different division strategies respectively. We can see that coarse classification ameliorates recognition rates when only utilizing the texture information. The best result is achieved with an accurate rate of 92.84% when vein images are divided into 64 (8-by-8) regions, while the one produced by the LBP method with no weights is only 91.86%. The accuracy of graph matching method on the candidates is 88.33%, and since this process is quite time consuming, the result on the entire dataset is not provided.

From Table 1, it can be seen that when we fuse the texture and geometry features at the matching score level by a multiply rule, the final accuracy is improved to 96.67%, which is better than either of the single modality based one, illustrating the effectiveness of the combination of both clues. At the same time, we also compare the accuracy with the ones dependent on the same dataset, and we can see that our method outperforms [3] by about 5 points. Although the result is slightly lower than [2], it should be noted that only a small subset of 15 persons is used.

Table 1. Comparison with the state of the art

Methods	Num. of Class	Database Size	Accuracy
M-LBP [2]	15	150	97.30%
LCP [3]	204	2040	90.88%
Texture based	204	2040	92.55%
Geometry based	204	2040	88.33%
Feature Fusion	204	2040	**96.67%**

5   Conclusions and Perspectives

In this paper, we proposed a novel hierarchical approach for hand dorsal vein identification, making use of both texture and geometry features. The system firstly adopts a weak feature, namely TEC, to reduce match range rapidly and output the candidates. The fusion of similarity scores of both modalities by LBP and global graph matching gives final decision. The recognition rate is up to 96.67% on the NCUT dataset which clearly demonstrates the effectiveness of the proposed method.

Acknowledgments. This work was funded in part by the National Basic Research Program of China under grant No. 2010CB327902; the National Natural Science Foundation of China (NSFC, No. 61273263, No. 61202237); and the Fundamental Research Funds for the Central Universities.

References

1. Kumar, A., Hanmandlu, M., Gupta, H.M.: Online biometric authentication using hand vein patterns. In: IEEE Symposium on Computational Intelligence for Security and Defence Applications (2009)
2. Malki, S., Spaanenburg, L.: Hand veins feature extraction using DT-CNNs. In: SPIE International Symposium on Microtechnologies for the New Millennium (2007)
3. Ladoux, P., Rosenberger, C., Dorizzi, B.: Palm vein verification system based on sift matching. In: IEEE International Conference on Biometrics (2009)
4. Lin, C., Fan, K.: Biometric verification using thermal images of palm-dorsa vein patterns. IEEE Transactions on Circuits and Systems for Video Technology 14, 199–213 (2004)
5. Zhao, S., Wang, Y., Wang, Y.: Biometric identification based on low quality hand vein pattern images. In: IEEE International Conference on Machine Learning and Cybernetics (2008)
6. Kumar, A., Prathyusha, K.: Personal authentication using hand vein triangulation and knuckle shape. IEEE Transactions on Image Processing 18, 2127–2136 (2009)
7. Miura, N., Nagasaka, A., Miyatake, T.: Feature extraction of finger-vein pattern based on repeated line tracking and its application to personal identification. Machine Vision and Applications 15, 194–203 (2004)
8. Cross, J., Smith, C.: Thermographic imaging of the subcutaneous vascular network of the back of the hand for biometric identification. In: IEEE International Carnahan Conference on Security Technology (1995)
9. Wang, K., Yuan, Y., Zhang, Z., Zhuang, D.: Hand vein recognition based on multisupplemental features of multi-classifier fusion decision. In: IEEE International Conference on Mechatronics and Automation (2006)
10. Wang, Y., Li, K., Cui, J., Shark, L., Varley, M.: Study of hand-dorsa vein recognition. In: IEEE International Conference on Intelligent Computing (2007)
11. Ding, Y., Zhuang, D., Wang, K.: A study of hand vein recognition method. In: IEEE International Conference on Mechatronics and Automation (2005)
12. Li, X., Liu, X., Liu, Z.: A dorsal hand vein pattern recognition algorithm. In: International Congress on Image and Signal Processing (2010)
13. Lam, L., Lee, S., Suen, C.Y.: Thinning methodologies - A comprehensive survey. IEEE Transactions on Pattern Analysis and Machine Intelligence 14, 869–885 (1992)
14. Ahonen, T., Hadid, A., Pietikäinen, M.: Face Recognition with Local Binary Patterns. In: Pajdla, T., Matas, J(G.) (eds.) ECCV 2004. LNCS, vol. 3021, pp. 469–481. Springer, Heidelberg (2004)
15. Conte, D., Foggia, P., Sansone, C., Vento, M.: Thirty years of graph matching in pattern recognition. IEEE Transactions on Pattern Analysis and Machine Intelligence 18, 265–298 (2004)
16. Riesen, K., Neuhaus, M., Bunke, H.: Bipartite Graph Matching for Computing the Edit Distance of Graphs. In: Escolano, F., Vento, M. (eds.) GbRPR. LNCS, vol. 4538, pp. 1–12. Springer, Heidelberg (2007)

Hand Vein Recognition Based on Feature Coding

Yiding Wang[1] and Weiping Liao[2]

[1] College of Information Engineering, North China University of Technology, Beijing, China
wangyd@ncut.edu.cn
[2] College of Information Engineering, North China University of Technology, Beijing, China
ncut564227621@gmail.com

Abstract. A novel feature coding scheme based on back propagation neural network (BP) is proposed in this paper for accurate hand dorsal vein recognition. Feature vector is converted to a binary sequence, which can improve the performance of classification. Partition local binary pattern (PLBP) is extracted as the input of BP encoder and orthogonal Gold code is selected as the output code for BP encoder. Thanks to the orthogonal characteristic, Gold code can decrease relevance between different classes while enhancing the relevance within the same classes. Besides single-encoder by BP, the error correcting coding (ECC) is adopted in the combination-encoder to reduce the rate of error codes. Correlation classifier is taken as the final classifier. Experimental results show that feature coding strategy by BP combination-encoder achieves a high recognition rate of 97.60%.

Keywords: Hand dorsa vein, Feature coding, Combination-encoder, BP network encoder.

1 Introduction

Biometric authentication based on hand vein patterns has grown in popularity as a way to confirm personal identity. Hand vein pattern is more reliable and robust comparing to the traditional biometric authentication methods. Block diagram for our hand vein recognition system is shown in Fig. 1.

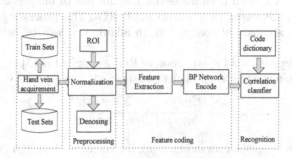

Fig. 1. Block Diagram for our system

W.-S. Zheng et al. (Eds.): CCBR 2012, LNCS 7701, pp. 165–175, 2012.
© Springer-Verlag Berlin Heidelberg 2012

The device to acquire hand vein images is shown in Fig. 2 (a). A CCD camera and near IR light source are employed for image acquisition. Some image samples acquired from our device are displayed in Fig. 2 (b).

(a)Vein image acquisition device

(b) Samples obtained by our device

Fig. 2. Device and samples

The key contributions from this paper can be summarized as follows. First, feature coding is investigated as a novel approach for hand vein recognition. Orthogonal Gold code is selected as the output of encoder for efficient representation. Second, both signal-encoder and combination-encoder are proposed and compared. In addition, correlation classifier is put into use for classification.

The rest of this paper is organized as follows. Preprocessing is introduced in section 2. Section 3 describes PLBP method for hand vein feature extraction. Construction of BP encoders for feature coding is detailed in section 4. Experimental results are demonstrated in section 5. Conclusion and future work are given at last.

2   Vein Image Preprocessing

2.1   Regions of Interest Extraction (ROI)

Hand vein images captured from the device contain lots of unnecessary information. The main goal of this step aims to extract stable ROI. This processing has significant influence on the accuracy of recognition. In addition, it will be helpful for saving recognition time.

Centroid strategy is used for extraction of ROI as applied in [3] [4]. Let (x_0, y_0) be the centroid of vein image $f(x, y)$ calculated using:

$$x_0 = \frac{\sum_{i,j} i \times f(i,j)}{\sum_{i,j} f(i,j)}; \quad y_0 = \frac{\sum_{i,j} j \times f(i,j)}{\sum_{i,j} f(i,j)} \tag{1}$$

For the hand vein images shown in Fig. 3 (a), the corresponding ROI images extracted are shown in Fig.3 (b).

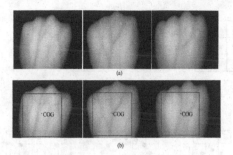

Fig. 3. (a) Hand dorsal vein images of different individuals (b) The corresponding ROI located in the rectangle area COG stands for the center of gravity

2.2   Normalization and De-noising

Since the light intensity may vary at different time, the gray levels of vein images are distributed over different ranges. To reduce the difference, gray level normalization based on the following equation is carried out.

$$y = ((x - \min) \times 255)/(\max - \min) \tag{2}$$

where x and y denote the gray level values of the original and normalized images respectively; min and max denote the minimum and maximum gray level values of the original image respectively.

The original hand vein usually contains noise. Generally, the presence of noise makes the feature extraction and classification less accurate. Traditional median filter can be used to effectively reduce noise.

3   Feature Extraction

A texture descriptor based on Partition Local Binary Patterns (PLBP) was previously proposed by the authors for improved vein pattern recognition [1]. Proposed by Ojala et al [5], Local Binary Patterns (LBP) provides an efficient rotation-invariant texture descriptor, and an illustration of the basic LBP operator is shown in Fig. 4 (a). For each pixel in an image, its value is compared with all the neighboring pixel values. The result of each comparison is coded as binary 0 if the center pixel value is smaller and binary 1 otherwise. The binary bits are then grouped in the clockwise direction starting from the top left pixel, and the arranged binary string is converted to a decimal number as the LBP label of the center pixel.

The LBP operator can be extended to neighborhoods of different sizes. For circular neighborhoods, the pixel values can be interpolated to allow any radius and number of pixels in the neighborhoods. With $LBP_{P,R}$ denoting P sampling points on a circle with a radius of R, some examples of the circular neighborhoods are shown in Fig. 4 (b).

To remove the effect of image rotation resulting in different binary patterns to be generated, each LBP is rotated to a position that acts as the common reference for all rotated versions of the binary patterns, and this involves the use of the rotation invariant LBP operator $LBP_{P,R}^{ri}$ defined as

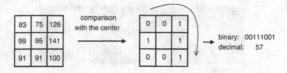

(a)   Example of basic LBP operator

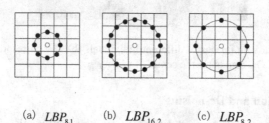

(a) $LBP_{8,1}$ (b) $LBP_{16,2}$ (c) $LBP_{8,2}$

(b)   Circular neighborhoods for LBP

Fig. 4. LBP algorithm

$$LBP_{P,R} = \min\{ROR(LBP_{P,R}, i \mid i = 0,1,2,...,P-1)\} \qquad (3)$$

Where $ROR(x, i)$ performs the circular bit-wise right shift i times on the P-bit binary number denoted by x.

A circular binary pattern is considered to be uniform if it contains at most two bit-wise transitions from 0 to 1, or vice versa [5]. For example, circular binary patterns of 00000000, 00011110 and 10000011 are uniform patterns. Rotation invariant and uniform LBP based on the circular neighborhood shown in Fig. 4 (b) (c), which are denoted collectedly by $LBP_{8,2}^{riu2}$, is used in this work to represent the features in the vein images.

To allow not only micro-patterns but also macro-patterns in a vein image to be represented, Partition LBP (PLBP) is used in the implementation; where by each vein image is divided into 64 non-overlapping rectangular regions as shown in Fig.5.

Fig. 5. Rectangular partition

4   Feature Coding

Feature coding is the most significant innovation in our work. This scheme is accomplished by back propagation artificial neural network. The core idea of this strategy can be explained in Fig. 6. For the sake of simplicity, we demonstrate it in three-dimensional space.

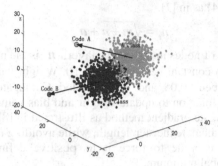

Fig. 6. Illustration of BP encoder strategy idea

The blue points set represents class B and green points set represents class A. Code A and Code B are the corresponding code after BP encoder. BP encoder can map a set of points to a specified code. The scheme aims to further enlarge the distance between Class A and Class B as well as enhance relevance within classes.

The process of this part can be summarized below. Firstly, we construct a BP network structure, which can well map high-dimensional to low-dimensional. Secondly, selecting an appropriate output code for BP encoder, which can increase relevance within same classes and reduce relevance between different classes. Furthermore, both single-encoder and combination-encoder are studied in this part.

4.1   BP Network Encoder

First, a 3 layers BP network is constructed for the feature encoding. BP network method has been wildly used as the encoder [6]. It has very strong computing capability and is suitable to be applied in complicated non-linear environment. Framework of BP network with 3 layers is shown in Fig. 7. Large amounts of researches have proved that three-layer feed forward network can well map high-dimensional to low-dimensional.

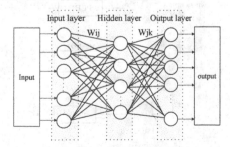

Fig. 7. Framework of BP network

Where W_{ij} is the weight between input layer and hidden layer. W_{jk} is the weight between hidden layer and output layer.

Determining the number of each layer, we take the following rules: The number of input layer neurons and output layer neurons are determined by dimension of input vector and output vector respectively. The numbers of nodes n_t in the hidden layer is determined in formula (4) as in [7].

$$n_t = \sqrt{m+n} + a \tag{4}$$

Here m is the number of nodes in the output layer, n is the number of nodes in the input layer, and a is a constant between 1 and 10. Weight values are initiated with random numbers between -0.05 and 0.05. Scaled Conjugate Gradient (SCG) is selected as the training function to update weight and bias values. SCG algorithm is an adaption to the conjugate gradient method as illustrated in [8] by Moller. It uses an estimate of Hessian to calculate the step length, while avoiding its explicit calculation. The Hessian estimate is scale to force it to positive definite to guarantee the approximation has a global minimum.

Diagrams of combination-encoder and single-encoder are shown in Fig. 8.

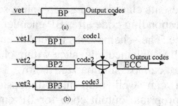

Fig. 8. (a)single-encoder (b)combination-encoder

Where feature vectors (vet, vet1, vet2 and vet3) are put into BP encoders and the ECC is the error correcting coding module. vet in single-encoder is an PLBP feature vector of a single scale hand vein image. While vet1, vet2 and vet3 are the corresponding PLBP vectors of different scale images (256, 360 and 180) and M1, M2, M3 are number of blocks. In the combination-encoder, extraction of feature vectors is demonstrated as Fig. 9.

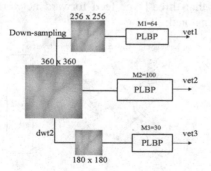

Fig. 9. Multi-scale PLBP feature vector

We specify the same hand vein in different scales can acquire the same output code during BP encoder training steps. Down-sampling means using bilinear interpolation algorithm to obtain the specified scale (256×256) image. Dwt2 represents using haar wavelet to decompose the original image for one-level. And finally we select the approximation coefficient (180 x 180) as the image for vet3.

ECC module working principle is illustrated as formula (5), (6), (7), (8). It is something like voting strategy.

$$code1 = \{c_{11}, c_{12}, c_{13}, \ldots\ldots, c_{1n}\};$$
$$code2 = \{c_{21}, c_{22}, c_{23}, \ldots\ldots\ldots, c_{2n}\}; \qquad (5)$$
$$code3 = \{c_{31}, c_{32}, c_{33}, \ldots\ldots\ldots, c_{3n}\};$$

$$\begin{cases} num_{i0} = the \ number \ of \ 0 \ in \ \{c_{1i}, c_{2i}, c_{3i}\}; \\ \\ num_{i1} = the \ number \ of \ 1 \ in \ \{c_{1i}, c_{2i}, c_{3i}\}; \end{cases} \qquad (6)$$

$$Output \ Codes = \{c_1, c_2, c_3, \ldots\ldots, c_n\}; \qquad (7)$$

$$c_i = \begin{cases} 1 & if \ num_{i1} > num_{i0} \\ 0 & if \ num_{i0} > num_{i1} \end{cases} \qquad (8)$$

Where code1, code2, code3 and Output Codes are output binary sequence code showed in Fig. 8 (b). n is the length of output code and $i = \{1, \ 2, \ 3, \ldots\ldots, n\}$.

4.2 Orthogonal Gold Code

A Gold code, also known as Gold sequence, is a type of binary sequence, used in telecommunication. Gold codes have bounded small cross-correlations within a set, which is useful for classification. A set of Gold code sequences consists of $2^n - 1$ sequences each one with a period of $2^n - 1$. n is the number of registers. Gold code is produced from m-sequence [9]. Fig. 10 (a) shows block diagram of m-sequence generator.

Where $a_{n-1}, a_{n-2}, a_{n-3}, \ldots.. a_0$ and $c_n, c_{n-1}, c_{n-2}, \ldots\ldots c_0$ represent the states of registers and feedback ratio respectively. A preferred pair of m-sequence of length $N = 2^n - 1$ can be used to generate Gold codes by module 2 with every possible relative delay. Gold code generator is shown in Fig. 10 (b). If m1 and m2 are a preferred pair of m sequences then a set of Gold sequence can be represented as in (9):

$$Gold(m1, m2) = (m1, m2, m1 + m2, m1 + Tm2 + m1 + T^2 m2, \ldots.m1 + T^{N-1} m2) \qquad (9)$$

Where T represents cycle shift by 1 bit. T^2 represents cyclic shifts by 2 bits etc.

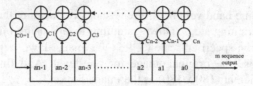

(a)   Diagram blocks of m-sequence generator

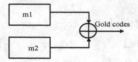

(b) Diagram blocks of Gold codes generator

Fig. 10. m-sequence generation and Gold sequence generation

4.3   Match Strategy and Database

Considering the orthogonality of the feature code shown in Fig. 11, we choose the correlation classifier to identify the hand vein. The correlation between the two binary sequences can be calculated as formula (10).

$$R_{xy}(n) = (A - D)/(A + D) \tag{10}$$

Where $R_{xy}(n)$ is cross-correlation between vector x and vector y, when y shifts n bits.

In this paper n is 0. A is the number of same bits between x and y. D is the number of different bits between x and y.

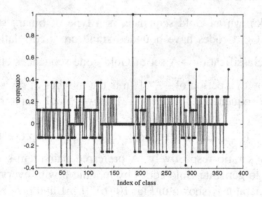

Fig. 11. Where peak value appears at its self-correlation

In our experiment, the database of hand vein images contains 10 images of each hand from 200 people with 97 females and 103 males. To evaluate the methods proposed, the database was divided into two sets, set A as the training database containing five images of every hand, and set B as the test images.

5   Experiment Results

To evaluate the effectiveness of the proposed method in our work, the experiments were conducted in two parts respectively. Results are shown in Table 1 and Table 2.

Table 1. Comparison recognition results with none encoder strategy and single-encoder strategy

Encoder strategy	Scale/blocks	Test images	Recognition (%)
none	360/100	1000	92.1
	256/64	1000	92.8
	180/30	1000	83
single	360/100	1000	94
	256/64	1000	93.1
	180/30	1000	86.2

Results from Table 1 show that it has been slightly improvement rate of recognition by single BP encoder.

Thanks to strong ability of BP encoder to deal with no-linear data, with single encoder strategy, feature vector can be well mapped into a specified Gold code sequence. As the orthogonal characteristic of Gold code, it is easy for classification.

However, some error bits may occur in output codes with single encoder. To reduce risk of error bits, combination encoder with ECC module is proposed in our work. Results in Table 2 suggest that combination-encoder exhibits better performance than single strategy, which achieves the accuracy of recognition at 97.60%.

Table 2. Comparison performance with single-encoder and combination-encoder

Encoder strategy	Scale/blocks	Test images	Recognition (%)
single	360/100	1000	94
	256/64	1000	93.1
	180/30	1000	86.2
combination	360/100		
	256/64	1000	97.60
	180/30		

6   Conclusion and Future Work

Feature coding strategy is proposed for hand vein recognition in this paper. The hand-dorsa vein images are captured by a CCD camera and near IR. The feature vector is a rotation invariation texture descriptor, which is extracted by PLBP algorithm. However, the main contributions in our work are the proposition of BP network as the encoder and the selection of Gold sequences as the output code for encoder. BP network maps a set of high-dimensional feature vectors into a specified low-dimension code sequence. SCG algorithm is selected as the training function. Both single-encoder and combination-encoder are researched in our work. The ECC module in combination-encoder performs more robustly to error coding. Orthogonal Gold sequence is selected as the outputs code for BP encoder. Orthogonal property of Gold sequence ensures low cross correlation between different sequences, which is good for classification. The combination-encoder strategy we took has achieved as high as 97.60%.

For future work, we will collect a larger scale database to further evaluate the performance of the proposed feature coding strategy. It is possible to exploit other coding schemes with high speed and accuracy.

Acknowledgments. This work is sponsored by National Natural Science Fund Committee (NSFC No.61271368). The authors would also like to thanks for Zhang Guangpeng and Amine for their constructive advices and grateful for comments from the anonymous associate editor and reviewers.

References

1. Wang, Y.D., Li, K.F., Cui, J.L.: Hand-dorsa vein recognition based on partition local binary pattern. In: Proceedings of 10th International Conference on Signal Processing (ICSP 2010), Beijing, China, October 24-28, pp. 1671–1674 (2010)
2. Zhao, S., Wang, Y.D., Wang, Y.H.: Biometric verification by extracting hand vein patterns from low-quality images. In: Proceedings of the 4th International Conference on Image and Graphics (ICIG), pp. 667–671 (August 2007)
3. Kumar, A., Prathyusha, K.V.: Personal authentication using hand vein triangulation and knuckle shape. IEEE Transactions on Image Processing 18(9), 2127–2136 (2009)
4. Lin, C.L., Fan, K.C.: Biometric verification using thermal images of palm-dorsa vein patterns. IEEE Transactions on Circuits and Systems for Video Technology 14(2), 199–213 (2004)
5. Ojala, T., Pietikäinen, M., Mäenpää, T.: Multiresolution gray-scale and rotation invariant texture classification with local binary patterns. IEEE Transactions on Pattern Analysis and Machine Intelligence 24, 971–987 (2002)
6. Zhang, X.: The application of BP type neural network in speed coding. In: Processing of the 3rd World Congress in Intelligence Control and Automation, Hefei China, vol. 4, pp. 2468–2470 (June 2000)
7. He, Y., Jin, B., Lv, Q., Yang, S.: Improving BP Neural Network for the Recognition of Face Direction. In: International Symposium on Computer Science and Society (ISCCS), Kota Kinabalu, pp. 79–82 (July 2011)
8. Moller, M.F.: A scaled conjugate-gradient algorithm for fast supervised learning. Neural Networks 6(4), 525–533 (1993)
9. Gold, R.: Optimal binary sequences for spread spectrum multiplexing (Corresp.). IEEE Transactions on Information Theory 13(4), 619–621 (1967)

Contact-Less Palm Vein Recognition Based on Wavelet Decomposition and Partial Least Square

Wei Wu[1,2,*], Wei-qi Yuan[1], Jin-yu Guo[3], Sen Lin[1], and Lan-tao Jing[1]

[1] Computer Vision Group Shenyang University of Technology Shenyang, China
[2] Information Engineering Department Shenyang University Shenyang, China
[3] Information Engineering Department, Shenyang University of Chemical Technology, Shenyang, China
wuwei429@163.com,yuan60@126.com, shandong401@sina.com,
lin_sen6@126.com, letalaura@qq.com

Abstract. To solve the problem of low recognition performance caused by contact-less imaging and poor palm vein image quality, a novel recognition method is proposed. Firstly, the ROI based on the thenar (a part of palm) is located; secondly, the palm vein features based on wavelet decomposition and partial least square are extracted; finally, the images are matched by Euclidean distance. In self-build palm vein database, the experimental result shows that the best recognition rate of this method reaches 99.86%. Comparing with the other typical palm vein recognition methods, the performance of proposed approach is the best. In conclusion, the scheme can improve the identification performance of contact-less palm vein recognition significantly.

Keywords: palm vein recognition, partial least square, wavelet decomposition, contact-less.

1 Introduction

Palm vein is a permanent and unique physiological feature [1]. It hides under the skin and its distribution is hard to be stolen, which makes the palm vein recognition to be a high security identification method. Contact-less imaging is welcomed for avoiding the spread of disease. However, some captured NIR palm vein images are not clear because of some physiological reasons. At the same time, contact-less imaging leads to a certain degree of image deformation. These two factors cause the low identification performance by traditional palm vein recognition methods.

According to the research literatures, feature extraction for palm vein images are divided into three categories: structure approaches[2,3], statistical approaches[4.5] and subspace approaches[6]. Structure approaches use either point detection or edge detection methods to extract vein lines. This kind of methods loose some information of palm vein and the recognition performance is not high. Statistical approaches transform images into another domain to recognition. Priori knowledge is needed in this kind of methods. Subspace approaches project a high-dimensional palm vein space into a low-dimensional space by a map. The redundant information in the image is removed and the sample points are more compact in the new space. The most popular

W.-S. Zheng et al. (Eds.): CCBR 2012, LNCS 7701, pp. 176–183, 2012.

techniques are principal component analysis (PCA) [7] and independent principal component analysis (ICA) [8]. PCA and ICA both can reconstruct the input sample well, but can not make use of the classified information. Compared with PCA and ICA, PLS[9] can decompose the input variable X and the output variable Y simultaneously, and extract principal components by utilizing the correlation between classes. So the features extracted by PLS contain more classified information of the image. It is very propitious to matching. This algorithm improves the identification rate. To solve the small sample size problem faced by PLS, wavelet decomposition is adopted.

The rest of the paper is arranged as follows. Image preprocessing is presented in Section 2. Algorithm for feature extraction based on wavelet decomposition and PLS is described in Section 3. In Section 4, some experiments are done to test the performance of the proposed method. Finally, our conclusion is given in Section 5.

2 Image Preprocessing

In order to reduce the influence of image deformation and increase the recognition accuracy, the region of interest (ROI) in the palm vein image is extracted. After low pass filter and binarization, we find the outline of the palm. Seek for the maximal inscribed circle nearest to the wrist side (WSMIC, Wrist Side Maximal Inscribed Circle) in the palm image outline. The radius of WSMIC is R.As shown in Fig.1, point A is the tangent point of WSMIC with thumb side outline. Point O is the center of WSMIC. Connect point A and point O, we obtain line AO. Take point O as middle point of DE, and then draw a square BCDE with side of $(2*\sqrt{5}*R/5)$ pass point B and C in WSMIC. Side of BE parallels with line AO. Extract the square BCDE and normalized it to the size of 128×128. The square is the ROI. The ROI is on the thenar of palm.

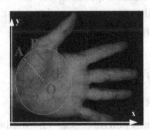

Fig. 1. Schematic diagram of ROI

3 Algorithm for Palm Vein Feature Extraction Based on Wavelet Decomposition and Partial Least Square

To solve the small sample size problem faced by PLS, wavelet decomposition is adopted firstly. The ROI is decomposed into sub-bands. Low-frequency sub-band is the approximation of original image, it describes global feature. High-frequency sub-band always relates with noise, it describes detail feature. In our recognition, we need more the low-frequencies. After K level wavelet decomposition, the resolution rates in different sub-image are reduced, so the data involve in computation is only 2^{-2K} of the original image. The K of decomposition is determined by the experiment.

Our scheme is described as following:

Step1: After K level wavelet decomposition, the palm vein image I decomposes into $3K+1$ sub-images, that is $\left[A_K, \{H_i, V_i, D_i\}_{i=1, \cdots, K} \right]$. A_K is the most approximate to the original image. H_i, V_i and D_i are the high-frequency information in horizontal direction, vertical direction and diagonal direction in the ith level wavelet decomposition.

Step2: Transform every sub-images of A_K into vector x_i. All vectors x_i $(i = 1, 2, \cdots, M)$ of train images compose data matrix of $X = \{x_1, x_2, \cdots, x_M\}^T$ as the input of PLS.

Step3: Construct output variable Y. As PLS algorithm extracts feature of palm vein, input variable X is train samples, output variable Y is category information of train samples. This paper constructs Y as following rules. Assume we have G class images to recognition, define G dimensions random vector $y = (y_1, y_2, \cdots, y_G)$. When image belongs to G class, $y_i = 1$, else when image belongs to class i-1, $y_i = 1 y_j = 0$, $j \neq i$, $i = 1, 2, \cdots, G$. For M pieces of train sample, observation matrix of class variables Y=$(y_1, y_2, \cdots, y_M)'$ is dimensions of M×G.

Step4: Extract feature of palm vein image based on PLS. Assume X and Y are normalized already, that is the value has been subtracted its mean value and divided its standard deviation. For further explaining the obtaining of output Y through input X, PLS adopts the following recursion algorithm:

Step4.1: Randomly initialize u

Step4.2: Exterior transformation $w = X^T u$

Normalize w: $w = w / \|w\|$ $t = Xw$ $c = Y^T t$

Normalize c: $c = c / \|c\|$ $u = Yc$

Iterate the above steps until convergence. The method of checking convergence is to compute the difference between t in this loop and t in last loop. If the difference is in the allowable scope, the loop stops.

Step4.3: Compute the coefficient of internal correlation: $b = w(p^T w)^{-1} c^T$, $p = X^T t / (t^T t)$. Project the palm vein image to coefficient b, so the feature vector β is obtained, that is the PLS feature vector.

4   Experiments and Results

4.1   Image Database

In order to test the performance of the proposed method, a palm vein database is built. The palm vein image is captured in the illumination of 850nm LED set. The database contains 300 palm vein images which belong to 50 individuals with 6 different images each left hand. 50 volunteers age from 20 to 60 years old include11 female.

Image acquisition requirement includes the wrist exposed region with more than 1.5cm. The image resolution is 768×554 pixels. Only rigid deformation is allowed in the collection process. Six images in our database are shown in Fig.2.

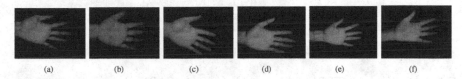

(a)   (b)   (c)   (d)   (e)   (f)

Fig. 2. Images from self-built image database

4.2   ROI Extraction

Extract the ROI from images in Fig.2 by method proposed in 2. The corresponding ROI are extracted and shown in Fig.3.

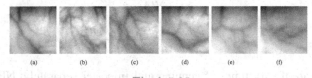

(a)   (b)   (c)   (d)   (e)   (f)

Fig. 3. ROI

4.3   Feature Extraction and Matching

The experiments are performed under the Matlab 2011b programming environment with Windows 7 system and Intel(R) Xeon(R) CPU X5687 CPU of 3.6GHz and 32GB. In the feature extraction stage, wavelet decomposition is applied to reduce the dimensionality of ROI firstly. For example, the image size is 16×16 after 3-level wavelet decomposition. The image is represented by a 1×256-dimensional vector. So X is a 300×256-dimensional vector. Then PLS is utilized to extract the features. The optimal wavelet type, level of decomposition and the component numbers are gained by experiments. The component numbers are chosen from 20 to 200. We choose the wavelet type from Db2, Haar and Bior2.2. The level of decomposition is chosen from 1 to 3.

After the feature extraction stage, feature matching stage is followed. A total of 44850 comparisons are performed, in which 750 comparisons are intra-class matching. According to the Euclidean distance distributions of inter-class matching and intra-class matching, the threshold value T will be gained for palm vein matching. Compute the Euclidean distance between two feature vectors from images, the formula is as following.

$$d(t_1, t_2) = \sqrt{\| t_1 \|^2 + \| t_2 \|^2 - 2t_1 t_2} \tag{1}$$

Fig.4 shows the Euclidean distance distribution of feature vectors after 3-level wavelet decomposition, when wavelet type of Haar is used and the component number is 140. T is 8.8975. If the distance less than 8.8975, the two images belong to the same hand else belong to different hand.

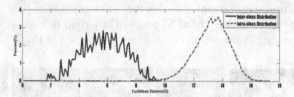

Fig. 4. Euclidean distance distribution of feature vectors

False rejection rate(FRR), false acceptation rate(FAR)and correct recognition rate(CRR)are used for recognition performance measurement[10].

$$FRR = \frac{NFR}{NAA} \times 100\% \tag{2}$$

$$FAR = \frac{NFA}{NIA} \times 100\% \tag{3}$$

$$CRR = \frac{the\ time\ of\ right\ result}{the\ total\ time\ of\ experiment} \times 100\% \tag{4}$$

NAA and NIA are the try times of genuine and imposter separately; NFR and NFA are the times of false rejection and false acceptation separately. The recognition performances of three wavelet types with 3 levels are shown in table 1-3. The time in the table represents the total of feature extraction and matching.

Table 1. The performance of recogniton by Db2+PLS

Component number	Level 1		Level 2		Level 3	
	CRR	Time	CRR	Time	CRR	Time
20	0.9027	0.00523	0.933	0.00133	0.931	0.000517
40	0.9107	0.0118	0.8975	0.00325	0.9355	0.00135
60	0.9314	0.0182	0.9053	0.00498	0.9041	0.00218
80	0.9906	0.0248	0.9538	0.0075	0.9307	0.0032
100	0.9869	0.0313	0.9905	0.0103	0.9671	0.00402
120	0.9974	0.0413	0.9979	0.0133	0.9842	0.00484
140	0.9991	0.0483	0.9991	0.0147	0.9971	0.00566
160	0.9989	0.0566	0.9992	0.0188	0.999	0.00729
180	0.9992	0.0684	0.9992	0.0213	0.9992	0.00791
200	0.9992	0.0763	0.9992	0.025	0.9992	0.00873

Table 2. The performance of recogniton by Haar +PLS

Component number	Level 1		Level 2		Level 3	
	CRR	Time	CRR	Time	CRR	Time
20	0.9082	0.00423	0.9123	0.0103	0.9054	0.000493
40	0.9227	0.0105	0.9226	0.00315	0.9276	0.00105
60	0.9389	0.0156	0.9367	0.00508	0.9211	0.00198
80	0.9716	0.0243	0.9596	0.0069	0.9623	0.0028
100	0.9918	0.0308	0.9866	0.0101	0.9817	0.00392
120	0.9981	0.0424	0.9978	0.0115	0.9938	0.00504
140	0.9992	0.0481	0.9988	0.0149	0.9986	0.00596
160	0.9992	0.0597	0.9991	0.0172	0.9991	0.00829
180	0.9992	0.0655	0.9991	0.0207	0.9992	0.00781
200	0.9992	0.0758	0.9992	0.0229	0.9992	0.00993

Table 3. The performance of recogniton by Bior2.2+PLS

Component number	Level 1		Level 2		Level 3	
	CRR	Time	CRR	Time	CRR	Time
20	0.8996	0.00513	0.9362	0.00143	0.9319	0.000617
40	0.9168	0.0116	0.9391	0.00356	0.9267	0.00125
60	0.8899	0.0186	0.9142	0.00518	0.9242	0.00198
80	0.9494	0.0237	0.9553	0.008	0.9333	0.0029
100	0.9841	0.0319	0.9859	0.011	0.9658	0.00352
120	0.9986	0.0388	0.9974	0.0132	0.9921	0.00494
140	0.9992	0.0517	0.9992	0.0157	0.9976	0.00576
160	0.9992	0.0572	0.9992	0.0181	0.9988	0.00689
180	0.9992	0.069	0.9992	0.0211	0.9991	0.00791
200	0.9992	0.0785	0.9992	0.0247	0.9992	0.00833

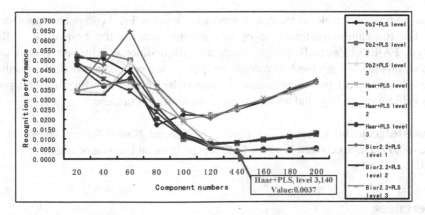

Fig. 5. Recognition performance comparison by three types of wavelet in three levels decomposition

To further evaluate the recognition performance by CRR and time, we use the formula 5.

$$Performance = \frac{(1 - CRR) + Time}{2} \tag{5}$$

The less the value of Performance is, the better the recognition performance is. From Fig.5, we find the performance is the smallest value: 0.0037, while using Haar wavelet with 3-level decomposition and component number of 140.

We compare the traditional palm vein recognition method of Gabor, SIFT, PCA, ICA, PCA+LPP with the method presented in this paper. Table 4 shows the recognition results for different algorithms.

From Table 4, we can see this method is super than the traditional method in FAR, FRR, CRR, Time and Performance, especially in FRR. Contact-less imaging makes the images of same hand discriminating and decreases the FRR of other algorithms. This algorithm explains the class information through input image uttermost. Wavelet decomposition not only reduces the noise in the image but also decreases complexity of compute.

Table 4. The performance comparison of different algorithms

Algorithm	FAR(%)	FRR(%)	CRR(%)	Time(s)	Performance
SIFT	4.00	8.57	95.93	0.0002	0.0205
Gabor	8.43	37.07	91.09	0.1519	0.1205
PCA	4.66	45.67	94.72	0.00151	0.0272
ICA	1.16	34.27	98.29	0.00404	0.0106
PCA+LPP	3.38	63.6	95.61	0.00224	0.0231
Wawelet+PLS	**0.14**	**0.67**	**99.86**	**0.00596**	**0.0037**

5   Conclusion

When the type of wavelet is Haar, decomposition level is 3 and component number is 140, the recognition performance of this scheme reaches the best value: CRR: 99.86%, FAR: 0.14%, FRR: 0.67%. Compare with traditional palm vein recognition method, this method get the best recognition performance. In conclusion, this method solves the poor recognition performance caused by contact-less imaging and poor palm vein image quality, and decreases the complexity of compute.

Acknowledgements. This work is supported by National Natural Science Foundation of China (60972123), Specialized Research Fund for the Doctoral Program of Higher Education (200921021100002).

References

1. Wang, L., Graham, L.: Near-and far-infrared imaging for vein pattern biometrics. In: IEEE International Conference on Video and Signal Based Surveillance, pp. 52–57 (2006)

2. Ladoux, P., Rosenberger, C., Dorizzi, B.: Palm Vein Verification System Based on SIFT Matching. In: Tistarelli, M., Nixon, M.S. (eds.) ICB 2009. LNCS, vol. 5558, pp. 1290–1298. Springer, Heidelberg (2009)
3. Toh, K., Eng, H., Choo, Y., et al.: Identity Verification Through Palm Vein and Crease Texture. In: The First IAPR International Conference on Biometrics 2005, pp. 546–553. IEEE Computer Society Press, Los Alamitos (2006)
4. Zhang, D., Guo, Z., Lu, G., et al.: An online system of multispectral palmprint verification. IEEE Transaction Instrumentation Measurement 59(2), 480–490 (2010)
5. Li, Q., Zeng, Y., Xiao, J., et al.: Curvelet-based palm vein biometric recognition. Chinese Optics Letters 8(6), 577–579 (2010)
6. Wang, J., Yau, W., Suwandy, A., et al.: Person recognition by fusing palmprint and palm vei images based on "Laplacian Palm" representation. Pattern Recognition (41), 1514–1527 (2007)
7. Lu, G., Zhang, D., Wang, K.: Palmprint Recognition Using Eigenpalms Features. Pattern Recognition Letters 24(9/10), 1463–1467 (2003)
8. Marian, S., Javier, R., Sejnowski, T.: Face recognition by independent component analysis. IEEE Transaction on Networks 13(6), 1450–1464 (2002)
9. Barker, M., Rayens, W.: Partial least squares for discrimination. Journal of Chemometrics 17(3), 166–173 (2003)
10. Wu, X., Zhang, D., Wang, K.: Palmprint Recognition, pp. 9–10. Science Press, Beijing (2006) (in Chinese)

Iris Image Deblurring Based on Refinement of Point Spread Function

Jing Liu[1,2], Zhenan Sun[2], and Tieniu Tan[2]

[1] Department of Automation, University of Science and Technology of China
[2] National Laboratory of Pattern Recognition
Chinese Academy of Sciences, Institute of Automation
liujing0@mail.ustc.edu.cn, {znsun,tnt}@nlpr.ia.ac.cn

Abstract. Blurred iris images are inevitable during iris image acquisition due to limited depth of field and movement of subjects. The blurred iris images lose detailed texture information for accurate identity verification, so this paper proposes a novel iris image deblurring method to enhance the quality of blurred iris images. Our method makes full use of the prior information of iris images. Firstly, benefiting from the properties of iris images, a set of initialization methods for point spread function (PSF) is proposed to obtain a better start point than that of common deblurring methods. Secondly, only the most reliable iris image regions which are obtained by structure properties of iris images are used to refine the initial PSF. Finally, the more accurate PSF is used to reconstruct the clear iris texture for higher accuracy of iris recognition. Experimental results on both synthetic and real-world iris images illustrate that the proposed method is effective and efficient, and outperforms state-of-the-art iris image deblurring methods in terms of the improvement of iris recognition accuracy.

Keywords: Iris recognition, deblurring, blind deconvolution.

1 Introduction

Current iris recognition systems always capture a large portion of blurred iris images, resulting from defocus or motion of imaging objects, or sometimes both of them. As shown in Figure 1, blurred iris images do not contain sufficient texture details for identification, resulting in high false reject rate. To improve system robustness and provide a good user experience, it is necessary to develop a deblurring method to enhance the quality of blurred iris images. For an observed image I, the shift-invariant blurring [1] can be expressed as

$$I = L \otimes f + n, \tag{1}$$

where L, f and n represent the latent unblurred image, blurring kernel (or PSF) and additive noise respectively, $\otimes$ denotes the convolution operator.

A few deblurring methods have been specially proposed for iris images [2,3,4]. To the best of our knowledge, most of them rely on the assumptions of parametric

W.-S. Zheng et al. (Eds.): CCBR 2012, LNCS 7701, pp. 184–192, 2012.

blurring kernels which are always overly simplified for actual blur. So these methods are only effective in one specific category of blur, either defocus or linear motion blurred iris images. As for nature-scene methods, they have been extensively investigated in the literature. Most state-of-the-art methods among them [5,1,6] apply a pixel-level PSF model rather than the extremely specific parametric models. They either enhance the edges in unblurred image, or use a complicated statistical prior of clear images to indirectly guide the iterative PSF optimization. However since the properties of iris images are not consistent with natura images, these methods are degraded or even invalid for blurred iris images.

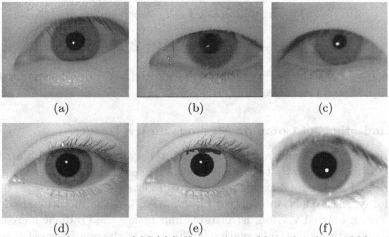

(a)   (b)   (c)

(d)   (e)   (f)

Fig. 1. Examples of iris image. (a)(b)(c) Clear, motion blurred and mixed blurred ones in our collected databases; (d)(e)(f) clear, clear with segmentation result and defocused ones in ICE'2005 [7].

In this paper, an automatic method named Iris image Deblurring with PSF Refinement (IDPR) is proposed to recover the separability between blurred iris images. It adopts a novel framework including two modules to resolve the problems of previous methods on blurred iris images. Firstly, IDPR initializes the PSF based on the parametric model, and obtains a more reasonable start point than the random value used in traditional methods. Secondly, IDPR takes into account both the structure characteristics of iris images and pixel-level PSF model, and updates the PSF by using our proposed rule-based method. These rules steer the selection of most reliable regions, with no need for unreliable edge enhancement and computationally expensive optimization mentioned above. Taken together, our method has two impressive aspects: 1) It can be used more extensively than pervious iris image deblurring methods which only work in a single blurring condition, since IDPR does not totally rely on the parametric PSF model; 2) Compared with nature-scene deblurring methods, IDPR is robust and more efficient by applying the initialized value and the proposed selection rules which are based on the distinct characteristics of iris images.

The remainder of this paper is organized as follows: In Section 2, background and limitations of common methods are introduced. In Section 3, overview of the proposed method and its details are presented. Experimental results are provided in Section 4. Section 5 concludes this paper.

2   Background

2.1   Image Deblurring

A successful approach for deblurring [5] is alternating the estimation of L and f in an iterative way. In these two steps, we respectively solve the equations as

$$\hat{f} = \arg\min_f \Phi(L \otimes f - I) + \alpha\Theta_1(f), \tag{2a}$$

$$\hat{L} = \arg\min_L \Phi(L \otimes f - I) + \beta\Theta_2(L), \tag{2b}$$

where $\Phi(L \otimes f - I)$ is the fidelity term, $\Theta_1(f)$ and $\Theta_2(L)$ denote the regularization terms on PSF and clear image respectively.

2.2   Limitations of Common Methods on Iris Images

If nature-scene deblurring methods are directly applied to restore blurred iris images, the results show that they will be invalid or even ruined. The encountered problems and some explanations are listed as follows.

Primarily, the prediction of latent clear image, i.e., the intentional edge enhancement in blurred version, is unstable and makes the gradient increase too fast to damage the ordinal information [8]. Especially, the prediction of sharp and dense edges, such as the eyelash regions in iris images, inevitably create a bad influence for PSF estimation in traditional methods. Otherwise, rigorous statistical prior which is difficult to be described and varies according to the contents, usually makes the deblurring results unstable and complicated to be obtained. Additionally, outliers are the pixels which cannot be modeled using Equation (1), such as the overflow region. Since outliers are uncommon in nature-scene images, traditional methods commonly ignore or exclude them using an iterative estimation step which are not reliable and has low computing efficiency.

That is to say, the common methods attempt to predict the sharp edge in the latent clear image and the location of detrimental structures, such as outliers and strong edges with small scale. This prediction step can be regarded as an iteratively guessing process, which not only is time consuming but also can introduce spurious information. It is no doubt that these guessing processes may mislead a recognition procedure.

3   Iris Image Deblurring with PSF Refinement

Reliability and efficiency are significant for iris recognition, so an algorithm for reliable region selection is proposed in IDPR to make up the limits arisen from the prediction of clear image and the iterative optimizations both for complicated prior and detrimental structures. After obtaining the initial PSF, we draw a rule to select the preliminary effective region for PSF refinement based on the gradient image, and then extend this rule to exclude the detrimental structures without iteratively guessing process. Since the iris image segmentation and reflection detection are accurate and necessary for the recognition procedure, our proposed selection method built upon them can be more reliable and take much fewer calculation time than that using the guessing process.

3.1 PSF Initialization

An initialized PSF can make the deblurring method much more effective, but it is always neglected in nature scene applications due to the limited prior imformation. In the proposed method, the parametric PSF model and the iris image characteristics are taken into account for PSF initialization, they can guarantee both simplicity and efficiency. The initialization of PSF provides a reasonable starting point, and it is a large improvement compared with the general deblurring methods. The flowchart of PSF initialization is shown in Figure 2.

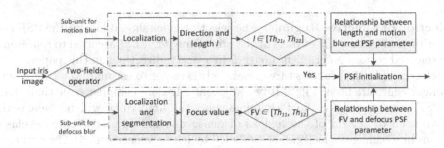

Fig. 2. The flowchart of initialization phase

Since the sensors in most iris recognition systems are interlacing, we apply the $(2 \times n)$ operator [9], where the amplitudes in the first and second row are -1 and 1 respectively, as a blur measurement to determine which sub-unit is applied. This measurement does not heavily influence the final result, because the initialized PSF will be further refined in the following phase. Afterwards, one of the two fields is extracted for subsequent processing. The kernels of defocus and linear motion blur are modeled as,

$$f_d(x, y) = \frac{1}{2\pi\sigma_h^2} e^{-\frac{x^2+y^2}{2\sigma_h^2}}, \tag{3a}$$

$$f_m(x, y) = \begin{cases} \frac{1}{d} & \text{if } x^2 + y^2 < d^2 \text{ and} \\ & \quad y = x\tan(\theta) \\ 0 & \text{otherwise} \end{cases} \tag{3b}$$

where σ_h^2 represents the variance, θ and d are the direction and length of motion respectively. For defocus blur, the focus value [10] of iris region is calculated and mapped to the parameter space based on the iris localization [11] and segmentation [12] results shown in Figure. 1(e). For motion blurred iris images, the main reflection region [4] is clipped and applied to estimate the direction θ using directional filter. The length of the specular reflection along motion direction is measured to obtain the length of motion d in Equation (3) according to the pre-trained relationship curve.

3.2 PSF Refinement

Based on the above rational starting point, PSF can be iteratively optimized instead of random searching. For refinement, PSF turns to be modeled on pixel-level and is refined by the way that L and PSF are optimized alternatively. A specialized selection scheme containing three rules is proposed to find the reliable regions for PSF estimation and reject the detrimental information without iterations. As a result, the probability of misleading a recognition procedure caused by guessing processes will be decreased. By using the final accurate PSF, clear texture can be recovered for higher accuracy of iris recognition.

Selection of Effective Regions. The selection rules should benefit the PSF estimation and exclude the outliers at the same time. $\{L_x, L_y\}$ are used to represent the selected regions on gradient image L in x and y directions in this paper.

Selecting $\{L_x, L_y\}$ follows three rules. 1) It is easier to estimate the PSF when stronger edges are used [13]. 2) If two adjacent edges in a smaller scale than that of PSF are selected for the PSF refinement, the ambiguity will be increased. So we need to get rid of the regions of dense and multiple edges, i.e., eyelash regions in iris images which can be excluded by iris segmentation. 3) The outliers, consisting principally of overflow regions in iris images, should not be applied, since their lost information will damage the PSF estimation.

These three rules are combined to select the reliable regions $\{L_x, L_y\}$ for PSF refinement, as the flowchart shown in Figure 3. Afterwards, the selection of $\{I_x, I_y\}$ can be accomplished by using $\{L_x, L_y\}$ and PSF in last iteration. For $I_i \in \{I_x, I_y\}$, the convolution of L_i and f are calculated, and then the regions with large values are selected as I_i.

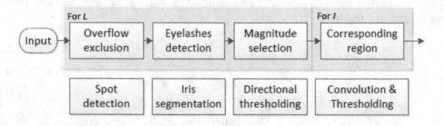

Fig. 3. The flowchart of reliable regions selection

PSF and L Estimation. In this step, only the reliable regions selected by the above algorithm are applied to iteratively estimate PSF and L. The noise model applied in IDPR is based on derivative constraint [6]. It can totally capture the spatial randomness. To increase the estimation robustness, an incremental regularization term $\triangle f = f - f_0$ is applied with a self-adaptive weight, where f_0 is the initial PSF. The regularization term of L takes the form of $\|\nabla L\|^2$. Taken together, Equation (2) can be rewrote into

$$E_f(f) = \sum_i \omega_i \|\partial_i L \otimes f - \partial_i I\|^2 + \alpha \|\triangle f\|^2, \tag{4a}$$

$$E_L(L) = \sum_i \omega_i \|\partial_i L \otimes f - \partial_i I\|^2 + \beta \|\nabla L\|^2, \tag{4b}$$

where $\partial_i \in \{\partial_x, \partial_y, \partial_{xx}, \partial_{yy}, \partial_{xy}\}$ and $\omega_i \in \{\omega_x, \omega_y, \omega_{xx}, \omega_{yy}, \omega_{xy}\}$ denote the partial derivative operator and weight in different directions and orders.

4   Experiments

The experiments are conducted both on artificial and real-world examples. Two kinds of deblurring methods for nature-scene and iris images are both compared. Four datasets shown in Figure 4 are collected using IrisGuard H100 [1] to ensure that blur is the only covariate in each set of datasets. As the performance metrics have to be compared step by step, IDPR-defocus/motion is used to denote IDPR only having defocus or motion sub-unit in PSF initialization respectively.

	Evaluation for motion blur		Evaluation for defocus blur	
Name:	MC-dataset	MB-dataset	DC-dataset	DB-dataset
Description:	clear	motion-blurred	clear	defocus-blurred
Number of images:	266	141	1117	1160

Fig. 4. Description of four datasets

4.1   Synthetic Data

A randomly selected clear iris image is applied to generate 3 blurred images, i.e., a defocus blur, a linear motion blur and a complex (or mixed) blur. The PSNRs and matching scores (MS) [8] of blurred images, deblurred images by using previous methods for nature-scene image [6] (denoted by NSI-1), [14] (NSI-2), [15] (NSI-3) and for iris image [4] (II-m), [2] (II-d) and our proposed method (IDPR) are compared in Figure 5.

   IDPR outperforms previous methods in term of MS, although the assumptions of parametric blurring kernel and convolution model can be perfectly abode on synthetic blurred images. However, the assumptions are so idealized that they are always broken in practice leading to the failure of those methods. Additionally, these methods are supposed to be unrobust based on the observation of unsteady performance in Figure 5.

---

[1] IrisGuard H100: www.irisguard.com

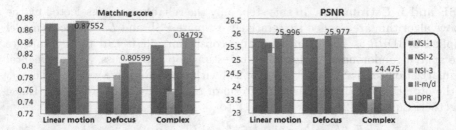

Fig. 5. MS and PSNR on synthetic images (where the overly simplified models and the specific assumptions are true).

4.2   Real Data

The first experiment is conducted on DC/DB-datasets and MC/MB-datasets to illustrate the decreasing performance caused by blurred iris images. The results are shown in Figure 6(a). Equal error rate (EER) and decidability index (d') are used to quantitatively measure the iris recognition performance.

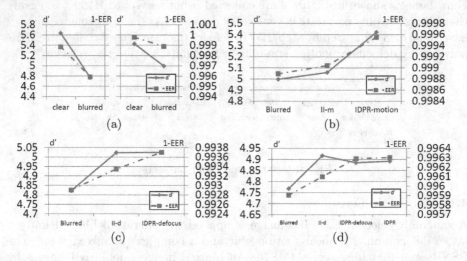

Fig. 6. d' and 1-EER on real-world images: (a) verification of decreasing performance on blurred iris images, DC/DB-dataset (left), MC/MB-dataset (right); (b) evaluation for motion blur (MC/MB-dataset); (c) evaluation for defocus blur(ICE'2005-Left [7]); (d) evaluation for complex blur (DC/DB-dataset).

The following three experiments are conducted to evaluate the performance of IDPR step by step. In the first one, MB/MC-datasets are used to evaluate the performance of IDPR-motion, while the state-of-the-art method [4] is taken as a comparison. All the images in MC-dataset are used for enrolled images. In the second one, IDPR-defocus is compared with the method [2] on

ICE'2005-Left [7] which contains many defocus blurred iris images. The DB/DC-datasets are used in the last experiment. We not only verify the effectiveness of IDPR-defocus again, but also test the whole IDPR with expecting for better performance.

From the results shown in Figure 6 and Figure 7, it is clear that the proposed method can achieve much more improvement of iris recognition accuracy in both EER and d' than [4], [2]. By using IDPR-motion, the EER in second experiment drops 60 percents, which is 3 times more than the method in [4]. Especially, the whole IDPR achieves better performance on DB-database, as the PSF can be initialized more effectively.

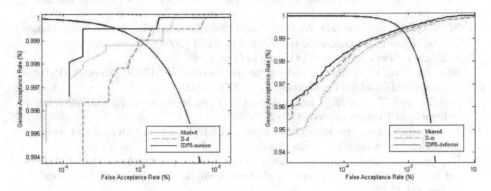

Fig. 7. ROC curves on real-world images: MC/MB-dataset (left), ICE'2005 [7] (right)

5   Conclusions

In this paper, a novel method named IDPR has been proposed to enhance the quality of general blurred iris images, which makes the recognition systems more tolerant to blurred images. IDPR can be used for a wide range of applications, since it requires no extra information and hardwares. IDPR adopts an advanced structure consisting of PSF initialization and PSF refinement, which makes full use of the characteristics of iris images. To the best of our knowledge, IDPR is the first iris image deblurring method incorporating PSF parameters estimation and blind deconvolution. In the future work, we plan to develop a more efficient way to refine the PSF including a better method for deconvolution. In addition, a large-scale database for research and evaluation of iris image deblurring methods will be constructed.

Acknowledgement. This work is funded by the National Basic Research Program of China (Grant No. 2012CB316300) and International S&T Cooperation Program of China (Grant No.2010DFB14110).

References

1. Fergus, R., Singh, B., Hertzmann, A., Roweis, S., Freeman, W.: Removing camera shake from a single photograph. ACM Trans. on Graphics 25, 787–794 (2006)
2. Kang, B., Park, K.: Real-time image restoration for iris recognition systems. IEEE Trans. on Systems, Man, and Cybernetics, Part B: Cybernetics 37, 1555–1566 (2007)
3. Huang, X., Ren, L., Yang, R.: Image deblurring for less intrusive iris capture. In: IEEE Conf. on Computer Vision and Pattern Recognition, pp. 1558–1565. IEEE (2009)
4. Kang, B., Park, K.: Restoration of motion-blurred iris images on mobile iris recognition devices. Optical Engineering 47, 117202 (2008)
5. Cho, S., Lee, S.: Fast motion deblurring. In: ACM Trans. on Graphics, vol. 28, p. 145 (2009)
6. Shan, Q., Jia, J., Agarwala, A.: High-quality motion deblurring from a single image. In: ACM Trans. on Graphics, vol. 27, p. 73. ACM (2008)
7. ICE, http://www.nist.gov/itl/iad/ig/ice.cfm
8. Sun, Z., Tan, T.: Ordinal measures for iris recognition. IEEE Trans. on Pattern Analysis and Machine Intelligence, 2211–2226 (2009)
9. Wei, Z., Tan, T., Sun, Z., Cui, J.: Robust and fast assessment of iris image quality. Advances in Biometrics, 464–471 (2005)
10. Daugman, J.: How iris recognition works. IEEE Trans. on Circuits and Systems for Video Technology 14, 21–30 (2004)
11. Daugman, J.: High confidence visual recognition of persons by a test of statistical independence. IEEE Trans. on Pattern Analysis and Machine Intelligence 15, 1148–1161 (1993)
12. He, Z., Tan, T., Sun, Z., Qiu, X.: Toward accurate and fast iris segmentation for iris biometrics. IEEE Trans. on Pattern Analysis and Machine Intelligence 31, 1670–1684 (2009)
13. Levin, A., Weiss, Y., Durand, F., Freeman, W.: Understanding and evaluating blind deconvolution algorithms. In: IEEE Conf. on Computer Vision and Pattern Recognition, pp. 1964–1971. IEEE (2009)
14. Xu, L., Jia, J.: Two-Phase Kernel Estimation for Robust Motion Deblurring. In: Daniilidis, K., Maragos, P., Paragios, N. (eds.) ECCV 2010, Part I. LNCS, vol. 6311, pp. 157–170. Springer, Heidelberg (2010)
15. Krishnan, D., Tay, T., Fergus, R.: Blind deconvolution using a normalized sparsity measure. In: IEEE Conf. on Computer Vision and Pattern Recognition, pp. 233–240. IEEE (2011)

Super Resolution Reconstruction and Recognition for Iris Image Sequence

Huiying Ren, Yuqing He, Jing Pan, and Li Li

Key Laboratory of Photoelectronic Imaging Technology and System, Ministry of Education of China, School of Optoelectronics, Beijing Institute of Technology, Beijing, China
orangerhy@sina.com, yuqinghe@bit.edu.cn

Abstract. As a non-invasive and stable biometric identification method, iris recognition is widely used in safety certification. In large scenes or long-distance conditions, the iris images acquired may has low resolution. Lack of information in these images or videos affects the performance of the iris recognition greatly. In this paper, we proposed a scheme of super resolution to reconstruct high-resolution images from low-resolution iris image sequences. The proposed scheme applies an improved iterated back projection algorithm to reconstruct high-resolution images and does not have a restriction on the numbers of base images. We simulated our method and conducted experiments on a public database. The results show that the reconstructed high-resolution iris image provides enough pixels which contain sufficient texture information for recognition. Lower Equal Error Rate is achieved after the robust super resolution iris image reconstruction.

Keywords: super resolution, reconstruction, iris recognition, image sequence.

1 Introduction

Iris recognition is an anti-deceptive, stable, unique and non-invasive technique among many kinds of biometric recognition methods [1]. It is superior to other biometrics due to its highest recognition rate. Generally, current iris recognition system needs the cooperation of the user to obtain clear and high-resolution iris images for feature extraction and recognition. According to the ISO standard for biometric data interchange formats, the acceptable quality of iris images expects a diameter of 150 pixels or more for iris recognition [2]. However, in large scenes or long-distance conditions, the pixel number of iris in captured images may below this level, which will lead to deterioration of the recognition performance. Quality evaluation of input images is done before recognition to select appropriate images and do the following recognition in some cases. Most of the quality evaluation methods may discard these low resolution images. But the spatio-temporal activity in low-resolution iris image sequence provides more information than a single image. We can use these image sequences to improve the robustness of the recognition. Super resolution method is introduced to fuse this information and we can reconstruct high-resolution image from low-resolution iris image sequence.

W.-S. Zheng et al. (Eds.): CCBR 2012, LNCS 7701, pp. 193–201, 2012.

There emerge some researches on super resolution of iris images in recent years. Kwang et al. proposed a method of iris image super resolution based on multiple Multi-Layer Perceptrons (MLPs) [3]. The output pixels of trained multiple MLPs and bilinear interpolation is used to reconstruct the high-resolution iris image. The accuracy of recognition is improved through this way. They used a single low-resolution image to reconstruct a learning-based high-resolution image. Gamal Fahmy presented a technique of a cross correlation model for the registration of iris images from a 3-feet away digital camera [4]. 4 low-resolution iris images are reconstructed to high-resolution images with 4 times and 16 times resolution of the original ones. The registration process is executed on the whole eye image so that it takes much time with parts only containing iris regions. Raghavender Jillela and Arun Ross combined Principal Components Transform (PCT) with image averaging to 6 original low-resolution images and achieve high-resolution iris images which show respectively low EER [5]. Kien Nguyen et al. used a focus-score weighed super-resolution method and a feature domain Bayesian maximum a posteriori probability estimate obtaining high resolution features from 6 blurred low-resolution iris images for reconstructing a high-resolution image[6].They also optimized the image averaging algorithm for image fusion[7]of several low-resolution images to get a robust mean super resolution method[8]. Huang et al proposed an algorithm that learned the prior probability relation between the information of different frequency bands of iris features and then restored an iris image [9]. All the above researches got high-resolution images, but most of them didn't take various numbers of low-resolution images into consideration.

In this paper we proposed a super resolution image reconstruction scheme for low-resolution iris images sequences. In our scheme, image number may not be fixed and the resolution rises. In the proposed method, the distinct and proper low resolution iris images from the video are selected firstly. Then iris is located and segmented from the whole low-resolution images. The segmented iris parts are normalized to low-resolution polar images, from which a robust super resolution algorithm is used to reconstruct the high-resolution images. After the feature of high-resolution normalized iris images are extracted and encoding, the performance of our method is evaluated and compared against the robust mean averaging super resolution. Experimental results show that our method can achieve higher performance.

The remaining part of the paper is organized as follows: Section 2 describes the detailed procedure of our whole super resolution scheme. We conduct the experiments and give the results in section 3. Section 4 gives the conclusions.

2   Methodology: Iris Image Super Resolution Reconstruction

The overall scheme of our proposed super resolution method with low-resolution iris images is shown in Fig. 1. We first select several distinct low-resolution iris images, locate the iris and normalize the segmented iris part into polar coordinate images. To insure that we get correct data of the original signal, image registration is essential to the reconstruction of several images with different shifts and rotations. After the normalized low-resolution images are registered, the super resolution method is used to reconstruct a high-resolution image. The reconstruction contains two steps: (i) interpolating to the first input image to get a high-resolution reference image, (ii) then iterating the reference image with the calculated total square error.

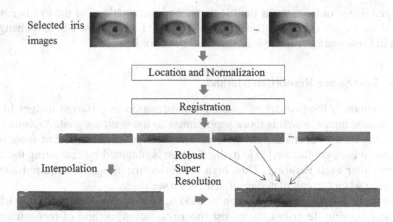

Selected iris images

Location and Normalizaion

Registration

Interpolation

Robust Super Resolution

Fig. 1. Super resolution reconstruction method of iris image sequence

2.1   Image Selection and Normalization

Several well-focused low-resolution iris images without significant occlusion are selected from iris video. Normalization is the process of normalizing the iris region segmented from the whole image to polar coordinates. Before this, the iris must be located accurately, which can be achieved by both Daugman and Wildes' methods [1] [12]. The inner and outer boundary separated the iris region from the image are defined based on a voting mechanism described by Hough Transform. Then the separated region is normalized to polar coordinates. When transforming the iris region into polar image, Interpolation needs to be done in the Cartesian coordinates to fill in the pixels in polar coordinates that have no corresponding grids to the Cartesian grids. Then we get a (r,θ) image only contains iris texture for recognition.

2.2   Image Registration

The image registration process is actually the process of looking for mapping relation between two images, which means finding the corresponding points.

Image registration can be conducted in spatial or frequency domain. In our study, we apply the method proposed by Vandewalle et al. [10] to estimate the shifts and rotations between the images.

As we all know, a shift in spatial domain corresponds to a linear phase shift in the Fourier domain. We transform the image to Fourier domain and calculate the slope of the phase difference. Then the shift parameter in image domain is obtained.

The rotation angle can be computed as the value when the Fourier transform of the reference image and the rotated input image has the maximum correlation. A one-dimensional correlation is computed during this process.

In our experiment, we chose one low-resolution iris image randomly and interpolate it to a high-resolution reference image. The shifts between the input images and the chosen low-resolution image are calculated continuously. Although the pupil nystagmus may occur during the image acquisition, it can't affect the iris image since the normalized image only contains the iris parts. And the rotations of the eye is not considered since we use the normalized images to do the registration, where it change the rotation in Cartesian coordinate into shift in Polar coordinates.

2.3   Robust Super Resolution Method

Super resolution is the process of fusing the information in different images to get a high-resolution image which is more approximate to the source signal. A. Zomet et al. proposed the robust super resolution algorithm which is similar with but more robust than repeated back projection [11].Gradient image is obtained by correcting the calculated error after each iteration. Thus high-resolution iris image is acquired after the last iteration when the calculated error achieves a set value.

We took the robust super resolution method to reconstruct high resolution iris images. The following describes the robust super resolution method of reconstructing a high resolution image from several low resolution images. The number of the original images may not be fixed in this method. Firstly, we construct a high-resolution image with nearest interpolation of the first input low-resolution image. Then the total square error between the reference image and the continuous input images is calculated. Iterations are done with the sum of the images and the gradient of the total square error. The algorithm can be described as follows:

Given n input images $I_1,...I_n$, the total square error S can be defined as:

$$S\left(\overrightarrow{X}\right)=\frac{1}{2}\sum_{k=1}^{n}\left\|\overrightarrow{I_k}-A_k\overrightarrow{X}\right\|_2^2 .$$

(1)

Where X is the high resolution image. I_k is the k-th input low resolution image. A_k represents the degradation matrix which is the product of decimation matrix, blurring matrix and geometric warp matrix . X, I_k and A_k are all reordered in vectors.

Let B_k be an integrated factor as:

$$\overrightarrow{B_k}=A_k^T A_k .$$

(2)

Then the gradient of S can be calculated by the sum of the gradient over the input images:

$$\nabla S\left(\overrightarrow{X}\right)=\sum_{k=1}^{n}\overrightarrow{B_k} .$$

(3)

In order to improve the robustness of the algorithm, we use the median of $\{B_k(x,y)\}_{k=1}^n$ to accurately approximate the mean in case of distant outliers. This approximation is more robust than the mean when the outliers are non-symmetrically with respect to the mean.

The iterations are done according to the following formula:

$$\overrightarrow{X}^{n+1}=\overrightarrow{X}^{n}+\lambda\nabla S(\overrightarrow{X}) .$$

(4)

Where λ is a scale factor determining the step of S.

In every iteration, the estimated high-resolution is down-sampled to the lattice of the input low-resolution images. The projection into high-resolution lattice is made by the difference between the down-sampled image and the input image.

The total square error S is computed after every iteration. When S achieves a threshold value, iterations will end. The final high-resolution image is obtained by the Equation (4).

2.4   Feature Extraction and Matching

Gabor filters work effectively in description of spatial frequency, spatial location and selectivity of direction information in an image [13] [14]. We apply Gabor filters with different frequencies and different direction to extract the feature information in the normalized iris image. The extracted features are encoded and saved to represent the iris, with which the recognition is done.. When matching the iris images, the Hamming distance between the input image and the gallery image is computed. Recognition decision is made according to the Hamming distance and the threshold.

3   Experiments and Results

To evaluate the effect of the super resolution algorithm for iris image sequence, we conducted experiments on a public database and simulate the low resolution image.

3.1   Database

Super resolution is conducted on sequence of low-resolution iris images. We build our experimental database based on the CASIA3.0 database. From the database, we randomly selected the image sets which contain 100-class iris images with 12 images in every class. We down-sampled the original 640×480 pixel resolution iris images to 50% (with a resolution of 320×240) and 25 %(with a resolution of 160×120)size of the original images, referred the three resolution images as Set S1, Set S2 and Set S3 respectively. The resolutions of normalized iris images are 512×64, 256×32 and 128×16 corresponding to Set S1, S2, and S3. The reconstructed images from Set S2 and S3 also have a resolution of 512×64.

3.2   Comparison of Various Image Numbers Used in Reconstruction

Several normalized images from Set S2 are reconstructed to a single high-resolution image. Super resolution images are reconstructed with different image numbers of 2, 4 and 6 respectively. The result of reconstructed high-resolution normalized iris images is shown in Fig.2. From it we can see high-resolution images with more information are obtained.

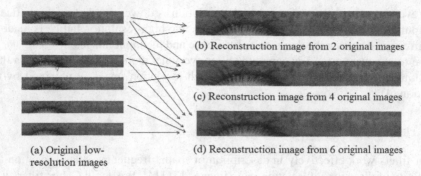

(a) Original low-resolution images

(b) Reconstruction image from 2 original images

(c) Reconstruction image from 4 original images

(d) Reconstruction image from 6 original images

Fig. 2. A sample of reconstructed normalized iris images. From the images shown in (a), we reconstructed the images shown in (b) (c) and (d). Images have been scaled to fit the document.

We establish twenty Gabor filters in five different frequencies and four different directions. The imaginary part of each filter is returned as the Gabor coefficient. The convolution of different Gabor coefficient and image blocks divided by Gabor size is the feature information, thus we get the feature code vector as the extracted iris texture feature.

The performance of our robust super resolution algorithm with different numbers of iris images is shown in Fig.3. Hamming distance between the input image and all the gallery images in the same Set are calculated. We tested 2, 4 and 6 images to calculate the Receiver Operating Characteristic (ROC) curves. From it we see that EER drops when image number rises. But with the increase of the image numbers, the appropriate time consumption will also increase. The EER of reconstruction with 6 original images is lowest but its time consumption is huge. At the same time, the EER of reconstruction result with 6 original images doesn't improve greatly comparing with 4 images. So we choose 4 original low-resolution images to do super resolution with different methods to compare our method with others.

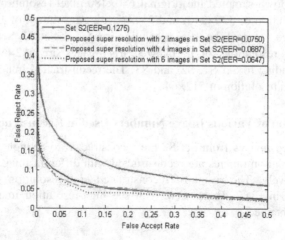

Fig. 3. ROC curves of proposed super resolution with various number of iris images

3.3   Comparison with Different Resolution Image

We did super resolution with 4 low-resolution images in each set and evaluate the performance of the three sets to assess the effect by the resolution level of the input images in the super resolution scheme. Fig.4 gives the ROC curves of the original three image sets S1, S2 and S3 which have not been reconstructed.

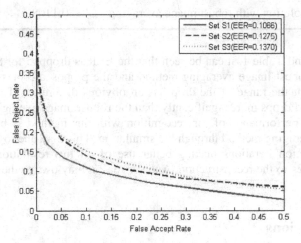

Fig. 4. ROC curves in different resolution data set

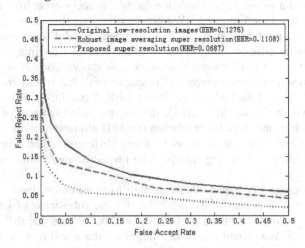

Fig. 5. ROC curves obtained before and after two super resolution methods for Set S2

Experimental results show that EER has risen for Set S2 and Set S3.The increase for Set S3 is more significant than that for Set S2. We used the above method to do super resolution for the down-sampled Set S2 and Set S3. The performance of reconstructed Set S2 is shown in Fig.5. To compare with other iris super resolution method, performance of super resolution using robust mean averaging method by Kien Nguyen et al [8] is also evaluated and demonstrated in Fig.5. The EER is shown in Table 1.

Table 1. Comparison of EER with various methods and various resolutions

Method	Set S2	Set S3
Low-resolution images without reconstruction	0.1275	0.1370
Super resolution with proposed method	0.0687	0.0869
Super resolution with robust image averaging	0.1108	0.1173

From Fig.5 and Table 1, it can be seen that the EER is dropped for Set S2 and S3 with both the robust image averaging method and the proposed robust super resolution method. But the range of the drop has an obvious difference. The EER of the proposed method drops more significantly than the robust image averaging method. It proves that the performance of iris recognition with our method is better than the robust mean averaging method through the simulation. This may due to the factor that the back projection iterations making better use of all low-resolution information which contributes to the reconstruction. Another reason may owe to the robustness of our algorithm.

4   Conclusions

This paper applied a robust super resolution method to reconstruct high resolution iris image from low-resolution sequence. We conduct the experiment on the dataset constructed based on a public database. In the experiment, we did super resolution image reconstruction with different number and different resolution images. Experiment results with drops of EER after super resolution have shown that this algorithm works well with low-resolution iris sequence. Compared with the robust mean averaging algorithm, the proposed method can get lower EER. Combining all the experiments and results shown above, we can conclude that our proposed scheme for super resolution of iris sequence improved the resolution level. The image number for reconstruction is not fixed while various numbers performs differently. The proposed method outperforms the images averaging algorithm by providing more information accurate with the source signal.

In future work, we will expand the algorithm to more constrained conditions and videos to exert the advantage of the algorithm for the robustness of iris recognition system. We may also study fusion of multiple-method or combine different domains of super resolution. We should extend to a larger database and make efforts on accurately location and registering. The performance of our super resolution reconstruction system can also be promoted by optimizing the recognition algorithm.

Acknowledgement. This project is supported by National Science Foundation of China (No. 60905012, 60572058) and Open Fund of Beijing Institute of Technology. We would like to thank Institute of Automation, Chinese Academy of Sciences for allowing us to use the CASIA database in this research.

References

1. Daugman, J.: How Iris Recognition Works. IEEE Transactions on Circuits and Systems for Video Technology 14(1), 21–30 (2004)
2. ISO/IEC 19794-6:2011, Information technology — Biometric data interchange formats, Part 6:iris image data
3. Shin, K.Y., Park, K.R., Kang, B.J., Park, S.J.: Super-Resolution Method Based on Multiple Multi-Layer Perceptrons for Iris Recognition. In: Proceedings of the 4th International Conference on Ubiquitous Information Technologies & Applications, pp. 1–5. IEEE Press, Fukuoka (2009)
4. Fahmy, G.: Super-resolution Construction of Iris Images from a Visual Low Resolution Face Video. In: National Radio Science Conference, pp. 1–6. IEEE Press, Cairo (2007)
5. Jillela, R., Ross, A., Flynn, P.J.: Information Fusion in Low-resolution Iris Videos Using Principal Components Transform. In: 2011 IEEE Workshop on Applications of Computer Vision (WACV), pp. 262–269. IEEE Press, New York (2011)
6. Nguyen, K., Fookes, C., Sridharan, S., Denman, S.: Focus-score Weighted Super-resolution for Uncooperative Iris Recognition at a Distance and on The Move. In: 2010 25th International Conference of Image and Vision Computing New Zealand (IVCNZ), pp. 1–8. IEEE Press, Queenstown (2010)
7. Hollingsworth, K.P., Bowyer, K.W., Flynn, P.J.: Image Averaging for Improved Iris Recognition. In: Tistarelli, M., Nixon, M.S. (eds.) ICB 2009. LNCS, vol. 5558, pp. 1112–1121. Springer, Heidelberg (2009)
8. Nguyen, K., Fookes, C., Sridharan, S.: Robust Mean Super-resolution for Less Cooperative NIR Iris Recognition at a Distance and on the Move. In: Proceedings of the 2010 Symposium on Information and Communication Technology, pp. 122–127. ACM Press, New York (2010)
9. Huang, T.T.J., Ma, L., Wang, Y.: Learning based resolution enhancement of iris images. In: Proceedings of the British Machine Conference, pp. 16:1–16:10. BMVA Press, Norwich (2003)
10. Vandewalle, P., Susstrunk, S., Vetterli, M.: A Frequency Domain Approach to Registration of Aliased Images With Application to Super-resolution. EURASIP Journal on Applied Signal Processing (01), 233–233 (2006)
11. Zomet, A., Rav-Acha, A., Peleg, S.: Robust super-resolution. In: Proceedings of the 2001 IEEE Computer Society Conference on Computer Vision and Pattern Recognition, CVPR 2001, pp. 645–650. IEEE Press, Hawaii (2001)
12. Wildes, R.E.: Iris Recognition: An Emerging Biometric Technology. Proceeding of the IEEE 85, 1348–1363 (1997)
13. Clausi, D.A., Jernigan, M.E.: Designing Gabor Filters for Optimal Texture Separability. Pattern Recognition 33(11), 1835–1849 (2000)
14. Ma, L., Wang, Y., Tan, T.: Iris Recognition Based on Multichannel Gabor Filtering. In: Asian Conference on Computer Vision, pp. 279–283. ACCV Press, Melbourne (2002)

Fusion of Iris and Periocular Biometrics for Cross-Sensor Identification

Lihu Xiao, Zhenan Sun, and Tieniu Tan

National Laboratory of Pattern Recognition, Institute of Automation,
Chinese Academy of Sciences, Beijing 100190, China
{lhxiao,znsun,tnt}@nlpr.ia.ac.cn

Abstract. As a reliable personal identification method, iris recognition has been widely used for a large number of applications. Since a variety of iris devices produced by different vendors may be used for some large-scale applications, it is necessary to match heterogeneous iris images against the variations of sensors, illuminators, imaging distance and imaging conditions. This paper aims to improve cross-sensor iris recognition performance using a novel multi-biometrics strategy. The novelty of our solution is that both iris and periocular biometrics in heterogeneous iris images are combined through score-level information fusion for approaching the problem of iris sensor interoperability. Then the improved feature extraction method, namely Multi-Directions Ordinal Measures, is applied to encode both iris and periocular images to describe the distinctive features. The experimental results on images captured from three iris devices, including two close-range iris devices and one long-range iris device, demonstrate the effectiveness of the proposed method.

Keywords: Iris Recognition, Periocular Recognition, Ordinal Measures, Cross-Sensor.

1 Introduction

Iris recognition has attracted great research effort for twenty years and a number of iris devices have been developed for real world applications. Although iris texture pattern is an ideal identifier, the large intra-class variations of iris images determine that it is a nontrivial task to match iris images captured from the same subject. There are three main factors jointly determining the variations of iris images, i.e. sensor, subject and environment. Most research work in iris recognition only considers the subject issues such as pose, gaze, iris texture deformation, eyelids and eyelashes or environmental issues such as illumination changes. However, the cross-sensor iris recognition problem is less addressed. With the wide deployments of iris recognition systems for mission-critical applications such as border crossing, banking, etc., the interoperability of iris recognition systems provided by different vendors has become a real problem. There are significant differences between various iris devices in terms of wavelength of illuminators,

W.-S. Zheng et al. (Eds.): CCBR 2012, LNCS 7701, pp. 202–209, 2012.

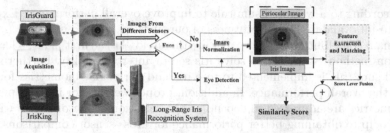

Fig. 1. Flowchart of the proposed method for cross-sensor comparison

optics, CCD or CMOS, etc. The accuracy of iris recognition degrades dramatically when cross-sensor iris images were used for identity authentication, as reported in [1].

The interoperability of cross-sensor biometric recognition systems has been discussed in the literature. Ross et al. investigated this problem on fingerprint [2]. Fernandez et al. used two different tablet computers to evaluate the sensor fusion and sensor interoperability for signature verification [3]. Philips et al. pointed out that face verification algorithms are sensitive to camera types [4]. Gonzalez et al. explored the interoperability among different hand biometric systems [5]. Recently, Bowyer et al. discussed the problem of iris sensor interoperability, and conducted some experiments to evaluate the impacts of cross-sensor iris images to iris recognition performance [6,7]. The conclusion is that both the selection of sensor and algorithm should be taken into consideration to construct a successful biometric system. The current research for cross-sensor iris recognition only considers iris biometrics and other soft biometrics in iris images such as periocular biometrics have not been considered for improving the identification accuracy.

The objective of this paper is to provide an improved solution to the interoperability problem between different iris sensors. We propose to combine multibiometric features defined as ocular biometrics in our method in cross-sensor iris images. Ocular region contains both iris and periocular biometrics. Then an improved feature representation method named Multi-Directions Ordinal Measures (abbreviated as Multi-OM) is proposed based on our previous work [8]. Ordinal Measures (abbreviated as OM) can represent the distinctive and robust features of iris patterns, and achieve state-of-the-art performance for single-sensor iris recognition. However, the information of the original version of horizontal OM is not enough to obtain good recognition performance for cross-sensor iris recognition problem. This motivates us to extend the original version of horizontal OM to multiple directions, which is more discriminative for representing features of both iris and periocular biometrics.

Fig. 1 illustrates the flowchart of the proposed method. We use three different iris imaging devices to capture iris images, which usually contain both iris texture pattern and periocular pattern. The features of both iris and periocular regions are extracted by Multi-OM. The only difference is that iris texture and periocular biometrics are encoded into binary strings and statistical distribution of ordinal codes, respectively. Then, these two ocular biometrics modalities are fused according to a weighted sum rule to improve overall performance. Experimental results validate the effectiveness of our method.

The main contributions of this paper are threefold. At the first place, a feature extraction method is applied to solve iris sensor interoperability. Furthermore, weighted sum rule is implemented to fuse iris and periocular biometrics for improving the overall performance. In addition, proper weights for iris and periocular biometrics are addressed to depend on the selection of sensors. This will be of great help to obtaining better performance for cross-sensor comparisons.

The rest of this paper is organized as follows. Section 2 details the procedure of the proposed method. Experimental results are discussed in Section 3. The concluding remarks are drawn in Section 4.

2   Proposed Method

Due to various imaging conditions, both iris and periocular images should be preprocessed. Images from different database should have different preprocessing procedure. Based on our previous work [9], we used three different iris acquisition systems to capture iris and periocular images. The first sensor is IrisGuard H100 (Abbreviated as IG) which is a monocular handheld iris capture system with the capture distance of approximately 12 to 30 centimeters [10]. The second sensor is IKEMB-110 (Abbreviated as IK) [11] from Irisking Tech.co.. It is also a monocular iris imaging sensor with the capture distance of approximately 22 to 40 centimeters. We also use the long-range iris recognition system [9] to capture image at 3 to 5 meters away(Abbreviated as LRI). This imaging system mainly consists of two wide-range web cameras, a narrow-range high resolution NIR (near-infra-red) camera, a pan-tilt-zoom (PTZ) unit and NIR light source. These three iris capture systems can represent the mainstream of iris capture systems which have been applied in the market. IG and IK share the same procedure, but LRI should add eye detection so as to speed up the iris recognition process besides the procedure. For iris image preprocessing, the critical step is iris localization. Iris localization is to find iris pupillary and limbic boundaries. Here, we employ the localization method of Daugman [12], which is well-known as integral-differential operator to perform iris localization. We adopt the rubber sheet model and linear normalization to obtain normalized iris images. For periocular image preprocessing, we predefine a normalized iris radius R_0. Given an input periocular image and its iris radius R_1, the image will be resized by multiplying R_0/R_1. Finally, the normalized periocular image centered with iris will be cropped at a fixed size from the input image.

2.1   Feature Extraction and Matching

The problem of iris sensor interoperability is addressed by weighted fusion of information from multiple directions of OM [8].

The possible rotation differences, pupil dilation and sensor intrinsic characteristics are considered in the proposed method. Consequently, multiple directions of

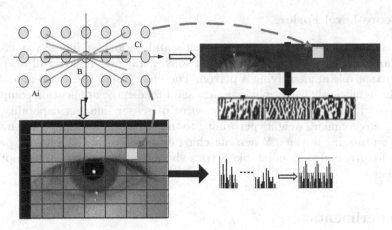

Fig. 2. This figure describes the proposed feature extraction method. Multi-OM is utilized to extract features of iris and periocular biometrics. Center point B is set by weighted fusion of codes generated from ordinal measures of multiple directions, the width of sampling line shows the weight in generating the final code of center point B.

ordinal measures should be utilized and fused to seek for more robust features for iris recognition in various environments. Weight for direction closer to horizontal one should be set larger because of its robustness. As can be seen in Fig. 2, the binary code of the sampling pixel B in the center can be calculated as follows:

$$\text{IrisCode} = F\left(\sum_{i=0}^{N} w_i F(A_i + C_i - 2B)\right), \qquad \sum_{i=0}^{N} w_i = 1, \qquad (1)$$

where $F(.)$ is a sign function, N is the number of sampling directions, and w_i is weight for the direction. Point A_i and C_i are used to compare with center point B to generate sub-binary codes, for the gray values of A_i and C_i which are not in the center of pixels can be estimated by bilinear interpolation. $F(x)$ is 1 if $x \geq 0$ and 0 otherwise. All the sub-binary codes will be fused with different weights to generate the final binary code of point B. The Hamming-distance is used as a measure of dis-similarity between two iris images.

To encode the normalized periocular images, we change the specific strategy. After generating sub-binary codes, the pattern of the sampling pixel B in the center of the following Fig. 2 can be given in decimal form by

$$\text{PerioCode} = \sum_{i=0}^{N} 2^{N-i} F(A_i + C_i - 2B). \qquad (2)$$

The normalized periocular image is divided into blocks. In each block, the frequency of patterns are concatenated into a histogram by their number of occurrences. Then the final descriptor of the image is computed by concatenating all the histograms. The Chi-square method is adopted to measure the similarity of periocular images.

2.2   Score Level Fusion

Given captured ocular images, both the iris and periocular biometrics can be used. Particularly in cross-sensor comparisons, periocular region will also play an important role in identifying a person. Therefore fusing these two modalities will yield significantly better performance and broaden the application compared with single modality. Due to the differences of sensor imaging capability and changing environment, weights pertaining to the two modalities may vary, mainly depend on imaging sensors. When matching cross-sensor ocular images, proper weights for iris and periocular biometrics should be set to guarantee optimal performance.

3   Experiments

3.1   Experimental Datasets

Three databases are collected by different high resolution camera, IG, IK, LRI. There are 3000 iris images from 600 eyes of 300 people for each database. Image resolution from IG and IK is 640×480. Image resolution from LRI is 2352×1728. Images from these three databases can be seen in Fig. 1.

3.2   Experiment Settings

Experiments are conducted to demonstrate the robustness of the proposed method. Left and right eyes from the same individual are considered separately. Then we can simply employ weighted sum rule to obtain a higher performance. The raw images are preprocessed to obtain the normalized periocular images (resolution 480×320) and iris images (resolution 540×66). To investigate cross-sensor iris image comparisons, we compared Multi-OM with OM [8], the parameters are set similarly, tri-lobe ordinal filters are adopted for better representing iris texture, each lobe in the filter is a Gaussian filter with $\sigma = 1.2$ and size 7×7, and the interval between adjacent lobes is 10 pixels. We randomly choose the sampling directions close to the horizontal one,here we select the directions of $0, \pm 5, \pm 10$ degrees. For periocular image comparisons, Multi-OM is also adopted to extract features of periocular images, and is compared with original LBP [13] which has been widely applied in representing periocular images. The periocular images are divided to 10×10 patches, and the degrees of Multi-OM are set uniformly between 0 to 90 degrees, here, we select the directions of $0, \pm 25, \pm 50, \pm 75$ degrees.

3.3   Results and Discussions

We make a comparison of periocular and iris recognition. Experiment results show the effectiveness of the proposed Multi-OM method. Then scores from iris and periocular image comparisons are fused using different weights to improve the overall performance.

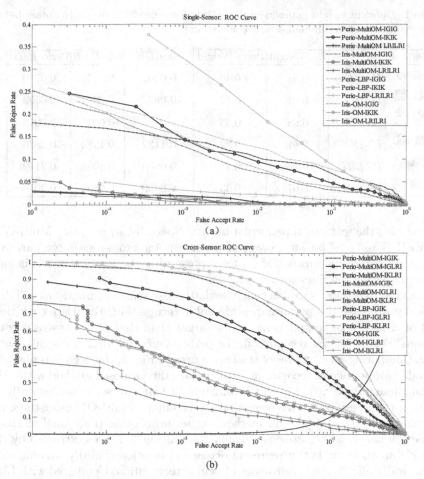

Fig. 3. (a). Experiments on ocular images from same sensors. (b). Experiments on ocular images from different sensors.

Receiver Operating Characteristic (ROC) curves are illustrated in Fig. 3 to show the performances of single and cross-sensor comparisons, the blue lines are equal error rate lines which refer to the point in receiver operating characteristic (ROC) when FAR (False Accept Ratio) is equal to FRR (False Reject Ratio). In the label, "Perio" denotes experiments on periocular images, "MultiOM","LBP" and "OM" denote feature extraction method adopted in the experiments, "IGIK" and other similar labels denote comparisons between corresponding sensors. Black and cyan lines denote ROC curves from experiments on periocular images with different feature extraction methods. Red and green lines denote ROC curves from experiments on iris images.

As shown in Fig. 3, the performance of cross-sensor comparisons decrease dramatically compared with that of single-sensor comparisons. In both figures, comparing black lines with cyan ones, Multi-OM outperforms LBP [13] for

Table 1. Different weight experimentally setting for score level fusion to obtain better performance between different sensor comparisons

Method		Iris-Weight	Perio-Weight	FusionEER	Iris-EER	Perio-EER
	(IG-IG)	0.51	0.49	0.0307	0.0436	0.0760
	(IK-IK)	0.81	0.19	0.0022	0.0041	0.0592
	(LRI-LRI)	0.65	0.35	0	0.0041	0.0073
	(IG-IK)	0.61	0.39	0.1132	0.1383	0.2826
	(IG-LRI)	0.55	0.45	0.0808	0.1088	0.2172
	(IK-LRI)	0.67	0.33	0.0409	0.0600	0.2018

representing the features of periocular images. Specially, by adopting Multi-OM, the EER is reduced by an average of 5 percent for cross-sensor comparisons. Multi-OM also outperforms OM [8] for representing the features of iris images when comparing red lines with green ones.

From the ROC curves we can conclude that: cross-sensor comparisons will dramatically decrease the performance of ocular recognition. For iris recognition, EER of cross-sensor comparisons will be larger than that of single-sensor comparisons. For periocular recognition, the performance will decrease significantly more. Comparing ROC curves of the two figures in Fig. 3, the decline is obvious. Secondly, for periocular recognition, we compare the proposed method with LBP (Local Binary Patterns) [13], the parameters of LBP are set experimentally to obtain optimal results. For iris recognition, we compare Multi-OM using the same lobe distance with OM [8]. Our method outperforms other traditional methods on the comparisons of cross-sensor ocular recognition. Features extracted by the proposed method can better represent ocular information. Thirdly, missing data dramatically affects the performance of ocular recognition. Compared with LRI, a binocular acquisition system which can obtain lager periocular region, IG and IK capture partial periocular images at close range, leading to the dramatically declining performance. Fourth, weights are determined by sensor characteristics for iris and periocular matching scores. Table 1 shows the different weights for cross-sensor comparisons. "IGIK" denotes the comparison between images captured from IG and IK, "Iris-Weight" and "Periocular-Weight" denote weights for iris and periocular biometrics. Therefore, sensor selection will affect weights for both biometric models.

4   Conclusions

This work focuses on the problem of iris sensor interoperability, demonstrates the fusion of iris and periocular biometrics for cross-sensor human identification. An improved feature extraction method (Multi-OM) is applied to representing the discriminative features. Features of iris and periocular images are extracted and encoded by Multi-OM and different encoding strategies. Iris and periocular biometrics are fused for cross-sensor comparisons. Experiments demonstrate the robustness of the proposed method. Although performance of cross-sensor ocular recognition is disappointing to some extent, ongoing research will encourage the development of more robust feature extraction methods and matching algorithms for cross-sensor biometrics, leading to wider application of iris biometrics.

Acknowledgements. This work is funded by National Natural Science Foundation of China (Grant No. 61075024), and International S&T Cooperation Program of China (Grant No.2010DFB14110).

References

1. IBG-Report:
   http://www.ibgweb.com/sites/default/files/IBG%20Fact%20Sheet.pdf
2. Ross, A., Nadgir, R.: A calibration model for fingerprint sensor interoperability. In: Spie Conference on Biometric Technology For Human Identification Iii (2006)
3. Alonso-Fernandez, F., Fierrez-Aguilar, J., Ortega-Garcia, J.: Sensor Interoperability and Fusion in Signature Verification: A Case Study Using Tablet PC. In: Li, S.Z., Sun, Z., Tan, T., Pankanti, S., Chollet, G., Zhang, D. (eds.) IWBRS 2005. LNCS, vol. 3781, pp. 180–187. Springer, Heidelberg (2005)
4. Phillips, P.J., Martin, A., Wilson, C.L., Przybocki, M.: An introduction to evaluating biometric systems. Computer 33(2), 56–63 (2000)
5. Gonzalez, E., Morales, A., Ferrer, M.A., Travieso, C.M.: Looking for hand biometrics interoperability. In: International Conference on Hand-Based Biometrics (ICHB), pp. 1–6 (November 2011)
6. Connaughton, R., Sgroi, A., Bowyer, K., Flynn, P.: A cross-sensor evaluation of three commercial iris cameras for iris biometrics. In: IEEE Computer Society Conference on Computer Vision and Pattern Recognition Workshops (CVPRW), pp. 90–97 (June 2011)
7. Connaughton, R., Sgroi, A., Bowyer, K., Flynn, P.J.: A multialgorithm analysis of three iris biometric sensors. IEEE Transactions on Information Forensics and Security 7(3), 919–931 (2012)
8. Sun, Z., Tan, T.: Ordinal measures for iris recognition. IEEE Transactions on Pattern Analysis and Machine Intelligence 31(12), 2211–2226 (2009)
9. Dong, W., Sun, Z., Tan, T.: A design of iris recognition system at a distance. In: Chinese Conference on Pattern Recognition, CCPR 2009, pp. 1–5 (November 2009)
10. IrisGuardH100:
    http://www.irisguard.com/pages.php?menu_id=29&local_type=0
11. IKEMB110: http://irisking.diytrade.com
12. Daugman, J.: How iris recognition works. IEEE Transactions on Circuits and Systems for Video Technology 14(1), 21–30 (2004)
13. Ojala, T., Pietikinen, M., Menp, T.: Multiresolution gray-scale and rotation invariant texture classification with local binary patterns. IEEE Transactions on Pattern Analysis and Machine Intelligence (2002)

A Review of Advances in Iris Image Acquisition System

Yong Liu, Yuqing He, Chunquan Gan, Jiadan Zhu, and Li Li

Key Laboratory of Photoelectronic Imaging Technology and System,
Ministry of Education of China, School of Optoelectronics,
Beijing Institute of Technology, Beijing 100081, China
yuqinghe@bit.edu.cn

Abstract. Iris recognition is a high-precision biometric identification technology with the advantages of uniqueness, stability, non-invasive. Iris image's quality affect the performance of the recognition algorithms. The ease of use and robustness of the recognition system is also affected by the image acquisition method, so iris image acquisition plays an important role in the whole system. Based on the basic principles of iris image acquisition, this paper gives the current advances of the iris recognition system. Describes and analyzes the typical commercial products of iris image acquisition system, including the operating range, capture volume, illumination mode, etc.. According to the bottleneck of the current iris image acquisition and recognition system, major research issues in the area of iris image acquisition are presented and analyzed, such as the stand-off system, variety of illumination mode, etc. At last, gives the development trend and future work of the iris image acquisition system.

Keywords: iris recognition, image acquisition, stand-off, illumination mode.

1   Introduction

The iris has distinct textures and details in automated biometric identification systems [1]. With the advantages of non-invasiveness, uniqueness, stability and low false recognition rate, the iris is a highly accurate biometric identifier. The dramatic growth in practical applications for iris biometrics has been accompanied by relevant developments in the underlying algorithms and techniques.

A typical iris recognition system [2,3] includes image acquisition, image pre-processing, feature extraction and template creation, feature matching and decision making. The diameter of iris is about 11mm. The iris has a very complex composition, including a variety of structural texture and a variety of pigment texture. The color of iris is different between different races. ISO iris image format standard noted that the accepted iris diameter is 150 pixels or more [4]. With these physiological characteristics and the image acquisition requirement, it is not easy to capture iris images in practice. The iris image's quality will greatly affect the performance of the recognition algorithms, so iris image acquisition is a key step and plays an important role in the iris recognition.

In 1991, Johnson first reported to realize an iris recognition system [5]. Subsequently, the prototype iris recognition systems including the basic iris image

W.-S. Zheng et al. (Eds.): CCBR 2012, LNCS 7701, pp. 210–218, 2012.
© Springer-Verlag Berlin Heidelberg 2012

acquisition part was documented by Daugman and Wildes [6,7]. Both of the systems require the operator to self-position his eye region in front of the cameras. There are lots of commercial iris image acquisition platforms later. Some of these based on PC and others are based on embedded system. Some of them need the user's fully self-position to help to acquire iris image. Most of these systems have iris positioning technology which can conduct the user's self-position. However, these systems work in a short distance and still need the user's cooperation.

Base on analyzing the basic principles of iris image acquisition, the paper compares the performance of typical commercial iris imaging systems. Major research works in iris image acquisition methods are presented and analyzed. The research trends of the iris imaging techniques are listed at last.

2   Principles of Iris Image Acquisition

The basic structure of a typical iris imaging system consists optical lens, illuminator, image sensor and electronic control unit.

Optical lens abides to the lens imaging geometry, the iris image focused on the image sensor through the lens. The depth of field, field of view and focal length are critical to design a suitable lens for iris recognition system. The focal length of lens determines the magnification of the image [8]. Some commercial iris acquisition products use fix focus lens to imaging iris [25, 26], but they have a small depth of field. Some iris recognition systems use a fully automated lens to complete iris acquisition in a short time [9,29,36].

The illumination is another important factor. Most of commercial products use near-infrared (NIR) LED as illuminator. It should noted that the intensity should not exceed the safety limit of illumination - defined at about 10 mw/cm^2[10]. There also emerges a variety of illumination mode in recent works. We will see different structure texture under different wavelength [11]. Incandescent, fluorescent, and arc lamps have been used in some laboratory experiments, but these have not been used in any commercial products[12].

The commonly used image sensor is CCD or CMOS image sensor[13,14]. To image the iris in proper size, combining with the optical lens and the working distance, the resolution and sensitivity of the image sensor are important parameters.

The signal processor plays a role of platform for processing the image data and running the iris recognition algorithms. Wang [15] proposed an embedded iris recognition system based on ARM. Liu-Jimenez et al. [16] and Rakvic et al. [17] describe the implementation of iris biometric algorithms on FPGAs. Zhao and Xie [18] describe an iris biometric system based on DSP. Jang et al. [19] designed a system with an "ultra-mobile personal computer", Kang and Park [20] describe an iris biometrics system implemented to operate on a mobile phone. Petr Gajdos et al. [21] proposed method has been implemented on graphic processor unit.

Iris recognition systems need users to cooperate with machines and move to the proper imaging position. Some iris positioning technologies[15] were used to help users to move to the specific area rapidly. Yoon et al.[22] use light stripe projection to provide the position of user and an auto focus lens to complete iris acquisition.

3   Typical Commercial Iris Imaging Systems

Many commercial recognition systems have been developed by some companies such as Panasonic[23], OKI, LG[24], Sarnoff[25][26], Aoptix[9], etc.. Most of the products are non-contacting products and can acquire iris images at a distance. These systems have different camera type and capture volume. We compare their performance as shown in Table 1. The operating range of typical commercial iris acquisition systems are under 3 meters, most of them are less than 1 meter. IOM PassPort™ has the largest capture range. Most of the Iris cameras with the capture range beyond 1 meter use auto-focus lens. Embedded system is the main type of the signal processor.   From the operating range, we can see that most of them have small depth of field.   All of them capture iris with NIR illumination.

Table 1. Performance comparison of typical commercial iris image cameras

System type	Capture volume (cm^3)	Operating Range (m)	Illumination	Iris camera	Processing Type
IrisAccess 3000	\	0.08-0.25	2 NIR LED	auto-focus	PC
IrisAccess 4000	\	0.26-0.36	2 NIR LED	auto-focus, two cameras	Embedded system
IrisAccess 7000	\	0.31-0.35	2 NIR LED	auto-focus, two cameras	Embedded system
BM-ET300	\	0.30-0.40	NIR LED	fix-focus, two cameras	Embedded system
BM-ET200	\	0.30-0.40	NIR LED	fix-focus, two cameras	Embedded system
IOM PassPort™	50×50×20	3	NIR LED	Fix-focus, four cameras	PC
IOM RapID-Cam™ II	\	0.30-0.45	NIR LED	\	wireless Embedded system
IOM N-Glance™	13×10×28	0.53-0.80	NIR LED	\	Embedded system
InSight™ SD	100×75 at2m	1.5-2.5	850nm LED	auto-focus	PC
InSight® Duo	100×75 at 2m	1.5-2.5	850nm LED	auto-focus, two cameras	PC
IKEMB-100	\	0.22-0.4	NIR LED	Fix-focus, two cameras	Embedded system

4   Current Research Work for Iris Image Acquisition

To improve the image acquisition system's performance, major research focuses on increasing the working distance, reducing the user's cooperation, changing the illumination mode, extending the depth of field and etc. This section describes some major researches in iris image acquisition in recent years.

4.1   "Stand off"Iris Imaging

Extending the working distance can improve the convenience of the iris recognition system. A typical "stand off " iris recognition system such as Eagle-Eyes is illustrated by Bashir et al[27]. The system uses three cameras to acquire multiple biometrics. The scene camera is used for detect and track the human; a narrower FOV camera, termed the face camera is used to acquire higher resolution imagery of the subject's face; the iris camera uses a proprietary dual sensor camera(VGA) design to acquire iris images. The face camera, iris camera and NIR laser illumination source are setup together on a pan-tilt to target the subject's face and irises. The system can complete dual-eye iris recognition at a large stand-off distance (3-6 meters) and within a large capture volume ($3\times2\times3$ m^3).

From 2008, researchers began to develop long operating range iris imaging system. Wheeler et al. [28] describe a prototype "stand-off" iris recognition system designed to work at sensor-to-subject distances of up to 1.5 m. The system uses two wide-field-of-view cameras to determine the location of their face in 3D and a iris camera on a pan-tilt platform to toward the subject. Ho Gi Jung et al.[29] developed a coaxial optical structure iris acquisition system, the working distance can up to 1.5m. Dong et al. [30] discuss the design of a system to image the iris at a distance of 3 meters, the system can work in auto-focus mode. Venugopalan et al. [31] designed a iris acquisition system uses Canon 5D Mark II camera with 21.1 megapixel Full-frame CMOS sensor that can capturing images of the iris up to distances of 8 meters with a resolution of 200 pixels across the diameter; if the resolution requirement is decreased to 150 pixels, the "stand off" distances can reached 12 meters. De Villar et al. [32] introduces the Irisat-a-Distance (IAAD) system. The IAAD system is a prototype that illustrates the feasibility of iris recognition at a distance of 30 meters. The narrow field of view (NFOV) iris image acquisition camera is attached to the telescope eyepiece and is used to capture iris image. A laser range finder is mounted on the telescope body along its boresight to determine subject distance for focus information.

Table 2 gives the comparison of different "stand off" iris recognition systems. Although these works successfully suggested that iris recognition at larger distances was feasible, but still there is no product for iris acquisition working beyond 3 meters. The IAAD system has a long working distance, but it has a lower speed compared to other systems. Venugopalan's system has a number of 'burst' images. Till now, these systems can not be applied in practice.

Table 2. Comparison of stand off iris imaging systems

Author	Operating distance(m)	Iris sensor's resolution	Number of camera	Illumination	Focal length(mm)
Wheeler etc[28]	1.5	1394×1024	3	LED(810nm)	160
Dong etc[30]	3	4-mega pixels	2	\	300
Bashir etc.[27]	6	640×480	3	NIR laser	\
Venugopalan etc[31]	12	21.1megapixel	1	LED(850nm)	800
De Villar etc[32]	30	2592×1944	2	\	\

4.2   Variety of Illumination Imaging

The typical commercial iris recognition system uses 850nm NIR illumination. Long distance image acquisition needs higher intensity light sources and this may be harm to people's health. Differences in iris texture across spectral bands are considerable, this can be exploited to enhance iris recognition performance. Nowadays, there emerges different iris illumination mode to improve the iris image's textures.

It is possible to image different iris structure with different wavelength illumination, raising the possibility of multi-spectral matching as a means to increased recognition accuracy [33,34]. Ngo et al. [35] describe an multispectral iris acquisition system. The iris camera is a Si-based camera (AVT Guppy F503) with a resolution of 640×480 and a spectral response in the range of 400-1000 nm. Twelve illuminators used in this work have peak wavelengths at 405 nm, 505 nm, 590 nm, 700 nm, 810 nm,910 nm, 970nm, 1070 nm, 1200 nm, 1300 nm, 1450 nm, and1550 nm, each illuminator consists of 60-LED. Each illuminator is turned on, an image is snapped and saved to disk, the illuminator is turned off and the program moves on to the next illuminator. Gong et al. [36] present a high-speed multispectral iris capture system. A complete capture cycle (including 700nm, 780nm, 800nm) can be completed within 2 or 3 s. It uses a Sony CCD camera and an automatic focusing lens as the capture unit, and the working distance is about 300 mm. The camera with the Sony ICX205 HAD CCD sensor (640×480) which has a spectral response from 400nm to 1000nm wavelengths. Chou et al.[14] developed a dual-CCD camera to acquire four-spectral iris images, they utilizes the enriched iris boundary information contained in a four-spectral iris image to reduce the off-axis iris distortion.

Ross et al. [37] images the iris with short infrared illumination in the 950nm to 1650nm range using InGaAs detectors. Initial experiments suggest the possibility of cross-spectral matching in the 900 to 1400nm range.

Grabowski et al. [38] describe a new side illumination approach regarding human iris image acquisition. Image captured in this system can be used in order to extract information about depth of iris structure. They placed small, high luminance LED around of the eye as near as possible in order to eliminate cornea reflections problems. Front-side illuminator is used to search for the best position, when the best focus position is achieved, the front-side illumination (Visible light) is turned off and the side illuminators are turned on, the system begin to acquire subsequent images. The iris diameter was around 800 pixels.

Proenca[39] using visible wavelength images captured under high heterogeneous lighting conditions with subjects at-a-distance (between 4 and 8 meters) and on-the-move to do some experiments to give some results about the amount of information.

We compare the different illumination mode above as shown in Table 3. Visible light was used to improve the recognition accuracy and working distance. Most of these systems illuminated both with visible light and NIR. Different with the CCD or CMOS, short infrared cameras are used. Ngo et al. used a Si camera,   Ross et al. used a camera based on InGaAs. The aim of these systems is to increase the iris image's quality and extend the working distance. Experiments show that the performance of these systems is good.

Table 3. Comparison of variety of illumination for iris acquisition

Author	Method of illumination	Wavelengths(nm)	Image Sensor
Gong et al.[36]	NIR and Visible light	700-800	CCD sensor 640×480
Chou et al[14]	NIR and Visible light	R,G,B,NIR	Dual-CCD camera
Ngo et al.[35]	NIR and Visible light	400 -1550	Si camera 640×480
Ross et al.[37]	NIR	950-1700	InGaAs 320×256
Grabowski et al.[38]	Visible light, side-illumination	/	2268×1512
Proenca[39]	Visible light	/	Canon EOS 5D

4.3   Wavefront-Coded Iris Imaging

Typical commercial systems have a small depth of field about tens of centimeters and require user cooperation. The traditional solution to increased depth of field is to increase the f number of the lens, this hurting the signal-to-noise ratio(SNR). It is show that wavefront coded system can greatly extend the depth of field of iris imaging without significantly decreasing the SNR[40]. Narayanswamy et al.[41] modified a standard Nikon 210mm F/3.3 lens by adding the wavefront coded phase element at the diaphragm of the lens. They experimentally demonstrated a 40cm depth of field with the wavefront Coded system, while a comparable traditional imaging system has 16.5cm of depth-of-field. Boddeti and Kumar [42] investigate the use of wavefront-coded imagery for iris recognition. They use a larger data set and present experiments to evaluate how different parts of the recognition pipeline are affected by wavefront coding. They conclude that wavefront coding could help increase the depth of field of an iris recognition system by a factor of four.

5   Development Trends and Future Work

Great progress has been made since the automated iris imaging devices and products was proposed. However, much more remains to be done on iris image acquisition to further improve the performance of iris recognition systems

- **Multi-biometric system**. Multimodal systems have been used for the increased robustness of biometric recognition tasks. Combining iris with other biometric has become the research trend.
- **Non-cooperative iris image acquisition**. Current iris acquisition systems need user to cooperate in a certain extent, this has limit the deployment of iris recognition. Different with active authentication, passive authentication may not want to be identified by the recognition system, and may even take the boycott strategy. The non-cooperative working mode may result in a more robust iris recognition.
- **Increasing the depth of field**. Existing imaging systems have small depth of field,   so some iris positioning techniques were developed to help user to find the correct position. Extending the depth of field can reduce these constraints and help realizing iris acquisition more friendly.

- **High quality imaging under special illumination mode.** All the successfully deployed iris recognition systems use NIR active light sources to acquire images at very limited distances. Other method of illumination, such as the different illumination wavebands, natural light and etc, should be considered to increase the iris image quality in long working distance.
- **Mobile iris image acquisition.** Due to the rapid development of mobile phone hardware, mobile iris recognition systems have emerged[20][43]. It's a safe method to determine the online transactions or recognizing the proper user through iris recognition. Using the mobile sensor to realize high quality image deserves further research.

6   Conclusions

Iris image acquisition has received increasing attention from both research community and industry. Significant progress has been made in the last decade and important practical applications are found in areas. This paper analyzed the key points and difficulties of iris image acquisition. We analyzed the parameters and compared the performance of the typical commercial system. Based on the bottleneck of the existing iris recognition systems, this paper described the major research interests of iris imaging technique in recent years.

Acknowledgement. This work is supported by National Science Foundation of China (No. 60905012, 60572058) and International Fund of Beijing Institute of Technology.

References

1. Mansfield, T.: Kelly, et al.: Biometric Product Testing Final Report. CESG Contract X92A/4009309, Centre for Mathematics & Scientific Computing, National Physical Laboratory, Queen's Road, Teddington, Middlesex TW11 0LW
2. Tan, T., Ma, L.: Iris Recognition: Recent Progress and Remaining Challenges. In: Proceedings of SPIE - The International Society for Optical Engineering, vol. 5404, pp. 183–194 (2004)
3. Daugman, J.: The Importance of Being Random: Statistical Principles of Iris Recognition. Pattern Recognition 36, 279–291 (2003)
4. http://www.biometrics.gov/Documents/irisrec.pdf
5. Johnson, R.G.: Can iris patterns be used to identify people? In: Chemical and Laser Sciences Division LA-12331-PR, Los Alamos National Laboratory, Los Alamos, Calif. (1991)
6. Daugman, J.: High Confidence Visual Recognition of Persons by a Test of Statistical Independence. IEEE 15, 1148–1161 (1993)
7. Wildes, R., et al.: Machine-vision System for Iris Recognition. Machine Vision and Applications 9, 1–8 (1996)
8. Yuqing, H.: Key Techniques and Methods for Imaging Iris in Focus. In: International Conference on Pattern Recognition, vol. 4, pp. 557–561 (2006)
9. http://www.aoptix.com/index.php

10. Hugo, P.: On the Feasibility of the Visible Wavelength, At-A-Distance and On-The-Move Iris Recognition. In: IEEE Workshop on Computational Intelligence in Biometrics, p. 7 (2009)
11. Vatsa, M., Singh, R., Ross, A., Noore, A.: Quality-based fusion for multichannel iris recognition. In: ICPR 2010, pp. 1314–1317 (2010)
12. James, R., et al.: Iris Recognition – Beyond One Meter. Part II (2009)
13. He, Y., Wang, Y., Tan, T.: Iris Image Capture System Design for Personal Identification. In: Li, S.Z., Lai, J.-H., Tan, T., Feng, G.-C., Wang, Y. (eds.) SINOBIOMETRICS 2004. LNCS, vol. 3338, pp. 539–545. Springer, Heidelberg (2004)
14. Chou, C.T., et al.: Non-Orthogonal View Iris Recognition System. IEEE Transactions on Circuits and Systems for Video Technology 20, 417–430 (2010)
15. Yuanbo, W., et al.: Design method of ARM based embedded iris recognition system. In: The International Society for Optical Engineering, September 26, vol. 6625, pp. 66251G-1-9 (2007)
16. Liu-Jimenez, J.R., et al.: Iris Biometrics for Embedded Systems. IEEE Transactions on Very Large Scale Integration Systems 19, 274–282 (2011)
17. Rakvic, R.N., et al.: Parallelizing Iris Recognition. IEEE Transactions on Information Forensics and Security 4, 812–823 (2009)
18. Xin, Z., Mei, X.: A Practical Design of Iris Recognition System Based on DSP. In: IHMSC 2009, vol. 1, pp. 66–70 (2009)
19. Jang, Y., et al.: A Novel Portable Iris Recognition System and Usability Evaluation. International Journal of Control, Automation, and Systems 8, 91–98 (2010)
20. Kang, et al.: A new multi-unit iris authentication based on quality assessment and score level fusion for mobile phones. Machine Vision and Applications 21, 541–553 (2010)
21. Petr, G., Jan, P., Pavel, M.: Iris Recognition on GPU with the Usage of Non-Negative Matrix Factorization. In: Proceedings 10th International Conference on Intelligent Systems Design and Applications (ISDA 2010), pp. 894–899 (2010)
22. Sowon, Y., et al.: Non-intrusive Iris Image Capturing System Using Light Stripe Projection and Pan-Tilt-Zoom Camera. In: CVPR 2007, pp. 2994–3000 (2007)
23. http://catalog2.panasonic.com/webapp/wcs/stores/servlet/
24. http://www.irisid.com/
25. http://www.sri.com
26. Matey, J.R., Hanna, K., et al.: Iris on the move: Acquisition of Images for Iris Recognition in Less Constrained Environments. Proceedings of the IEEE Col. 94(11), 1936–1947 (2006)
27. Faisal, B., Pablo, C.: Eagle-EyesTM: a system for iris recognition at a distance. In: THS 2008, pp. 426–431 (2008)
28. Wheeler, F.W., et al.: Stand-off Iris Recognition System. In: 2008 IEEE Second International Conference on Biometrics: Theory, Applications and Systems, p. 7 (2008)
29. Jung, H.G., Jo, H.S., Park, K.R., Kim, J.: Coaxial optical structure for iris recognition from a distance. Optical Engineering 50, 053201 (2011)
30. Wenbo, D., Zhenan, S.T.: A design of iris recognition system at a distance. In: CJKPR, pp. 553–557 (2009)
31. Shreyas, V., Unni, P.: Long Range Iris Acquisition System for Stationary and Mobile Subjects. In: 2011 International Joint Conference on Biometrics, IJCB (2011)
32. De Villar, J.A., et al.: Design and Implementation of a Long Range Iris Recognition System. In: Conference Record - Asilomar Conference on Signals, Systems and Computers, pp. 1770–1773 (2010)

33. Imai, F.H.: Preliminary Experiment for Spectral Reflectance Estimation of Human Iris using a Digital Camera. Munsell Color Science Laboratory Technical Report (2000)
34. Boyce, et al.: Multispectral Iris Analysis: A Preliminary Study. In: IEEE Computer Society Workshop on Biometrics at the Computer Vision and Pattern Recognition Conference (2006)
35. Ngo, H.T., Ives, R.W., et al.: Design and Implementation of a Multispectral IrisCapture System. In: 2009 Conference Record of the Forty-Third Asilomar Conference on Signals, Systems and Computers, pp. 380–384 (2009)
36. Yazhuo, G., David, Z., Pengfei, S., Jingqi, Y.: High-Speed Multispectral Iris Capture System Design. IEEE (2012)
37. Ross, R., et al.: Exploring multispectral iris recognition beyond 900nm. In: IEEE 3rd International Conference on Biometrics: Theory, Applications, and Systems (2009)
38. Grabowski, K., et al.: Iris Structure Acquisition Method. In: 16th International Conference of Integrated Circuit and Systems (MIXDES 2009), pp. 640–643, 25–27 (2009)
39. Hugo, P.: On the Feasibility of the Visible Wavelength, At-A-Distance and On-The-Move. Iris Recognition. In: 2009 IEEE Workshop on Computational Intelligence in Biometrics: Theory, Algorithms, and Applications (2009)
40. Kelly, N., Smith, V., et al.: Extended Evaluation of Simulated Wavefront Coding Technology in Iris Recognition. In: BTAS 2007, pp. 316–322 (2007)
41. Narayanswamy, et al: Iris Recognition at a Distance with Expanded Imaging. In: The International Society for Optical Engineering, vol. 6202, pp. 62020G-1-12, 17 (2006)
42. Boddeti, V.N.: Extended-Depth-of-Field Iris Recognition Using Unrestored Wavefront-Coded Imagery. IEEE Transactions on Systems, Man and Cybernetics, Part A (Systems and Humans) 40, 495–508 (2010)
43. Kang, J.-S.: Mobile iris recognition systems: An emerging biometric technology. International Journal of Imaging Systems and Technology 19, 323–331 (2009)

3D Pure Ear Extraction and Recognition

Jiangwei Wu, Zhichun Mu, and Kai Wang

School of Automation and Electrical Engineering,
University of Science and Techonology Beijing, Beijing, China

Abstract. In this paper, we present a complete ear recognition system. A new edge-based approach is proposed to extract the pure ear automatically, using both the edge information form the intensity images and depth images. Once the pure ear is extracted, the well-known ICP algorithm is applied for recognition. We achieve a Rank-1 recognition rate of 98.8% for an identification scenario and an equal error rate of 2.1% for a verification scenario on a database of 415 subjects.

Keywords: 3D Pure ear extraction, Canny edge detector, ICP Algorithm, Ear recognition.

1   Introduction

In recent years, ear biometrics is becoming more and more popular in dealing with the recognition of individuals due to its advantages over other biometrics such as face and fingerprint. For instance, the ear is rich in features and it has a stable structure which does not change much with age[1]; its size, which is not too big as face is or too small as fingerprint is, makes it capable of being captured from a distance without interruption. Moreover, because the ear has no expressions, there is no necessity to cope with the difficulty face biometrics encounters.

At the beginning, the studies were based on the 2D intensity images, for example, [2,3]. From these work, researchers concluded that the performances of the methods based on 2D intensity images are greatly affected by the pose variation and imaging conditions such as lighting and shadow [4]. So, when cameras with range sensor are capable of imaging the ear in 3D, researchers, such as Hui Chen and Ping Yan, turn to rang image which is relatively insensitive to illuminations and has been combined with many algorithms to form intact ear recognition systems.

Although the methods used in these systems may be different, the main steps are: 1)extract ear from the rang image which contains the profile of a subject; 2) get the initial translation to align the ear; 3) choose approaches for recognition.

In the previous work, the ears extracted by the researches are mostly the ear region which contains many non-ear patches rather the pure ear. There is no experiment done to justify whether these non-ear patches have positive or negative impact on the performance; in other words, the influence of the non-ear patches is uncertain. Thus, in this paper we proposed a new method to crop the pure ear region rather than regions that contain data out of the ear. This method is based on the experimental

W.-S. Zheng et al. (Eds.): CCBR 2012, LNCS 7701, pp. 219–226, 2012.
© Springer-Verlag Berlin Heidelberg 2012

evidence that relates to the distribution of the edges in the intensity images and in the depth image. We designed a method to get the outer brim of the ear and when it is extracted, the two endpoints are pinpointed and connected to get a closed region that includes the pure ear. The initial translation is calculated from the centroids of the pure ears. As long as the pure ear is extracted and the initial translation is calculated, a modified ICP algorithm is used in the recognition step.

The paper is organized as follows: A review of the related work is given in the second section. Section 3 shows the details of the automatic pure ear extraction approach. In section 4, the ICP algorithm is modified. Finally, in section five, the experiment material and the several results are showed and analyzed.

2   Related Work

There are many methods presented by researches to extract the ear, however the ear extracted by most of the methods contains many non-ear patches whose impact on the recognition system is unjustified, for example, Ping Yan and Kevin W.Bowyer used ear templates and manually selected landmarks to extract the ear region in [5,6]; Hui Chen, Bir Bhanu used manually extracted ear region in [7] and later in [4] they use a automatic method to extract the ear region. However none of the ear regions extracted above is pure ear.

The most similar work in extracting the pure ear is find in [8, 9], where Ping Yan and Kevin W.Bowyer developed a method to extract the ear named "Active Contour Algorithm". To crop the ear, there are several steps to do. Firstly, they should find the ear pit. To find the ear pit, the position of the nose tip should be located first, when the nose tip is located, they will generate a sector spanning +/- 30 degrees perpendicular to the face line with a radius of 15cm and with the nose tip as the center. Skin region detection is used to eliminate the region of the hair and clothes, and finally, they use surface segmentation and classification using surface curvature to locate the ear pit. When the ear pit is found, an ellipse with the ear pit as the center is generated and is served as the initial contour, based on which the active contour grows until it finds the ear edge. It is worth to mention that they concluded from their experiments that the performance by using both the color image and the depth image in the active contour is better than that of using just one of them. This support the view in our paper that the color image and the depth image should combined together to achieve better performance in extraction the pure ear. The ear pit location got from the previous step is used to calculate the initial translation. The main weakness of this method is that the procedure is so complicated that it takes much time to crop the ear.

3   Pure Ear Extraction

Before we show the details of the method to crop the pure ear, we'd like to introduce the materials, the intensity images and depth images, we used in this paper. Actually, the images we used are derived from the result of [10], in which the rough ear region is extracted using the Adaboost algorithm. As is showed in figure 1, the cropped ear region extracted from the profile image, though has eliminated much data that doesn't belong to the ear, still contains a lot of non-ear data. This will have a precarious effect on the performance of the later algorithms applied for ear recognition. For example, the hair in the non-ear region, whose distribution and shape will change from one image to another even the images belongs to the same subject, will lead to a bad performance of the ICP-based algorithms in recognition. Moreover, redundant data means that the ICP algorithm needs to deal with more data which, as a result, requires more time. Thus, it is better if the pure ears can be cropped.

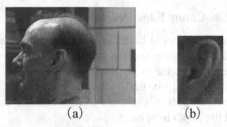

(a)   (b)

Fig. 1. Example of the profile image of one subject(a), and the correspondent extracted ear region by Adaboost algorithm(b)

3.1 Experimental Facts

Depth images are not affected by the illumination and they have sharp change between the ear region and the non-ear region. Thus, a Canny edge detector would perform well in finding the fringe of the ear. However, though the fringe of the lower parts of the ear is exactly found, the fringe of the upper part of the ear is missing because the upper parts of the ear, whose surface is much close to the skin of the face and sometimes will be affected by the existence of the hair or earring, do not have the sharp change. As showed in figure 2.

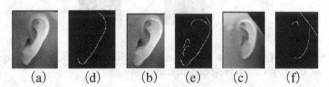

(a)   (d)   (b)   (e)   (c)   (f)

Fig. 2. Examples of cases that adopt the Canny edge detector in depth images. The first line is examples of the depth images and the second line is the images of the correspondent edge images of the depth images.

The distribution of the edges found in the intensity images is just the opposite compared with the distribution of edges found in the depth images, that is, in intensity images, the fringe of the upper ear can be found exactly while the fringe of the lower parts of the ear is sometimes undistinguishable. The reason is that, in the intensity images, the upper parts of the ear can be easily distinguished from the background which is mainly comprised of hair; while the fringe of the lower parts of the ear cannot be differentiate from the skin of the face because the skin on this part of the ear has the same color as the skin of the face.

Because of this difference of the distribution of edges between these two kinds of images, the whole outer brim of the ear is able to be found when they are combined together. Then, the outer brim of the ear is extracted using a method we will present later in section. When the brim is extracted, we are able to get the pure ear region. Thus, the whole method consists of three parts: 1): Find edges using Canny edge detector in both the intensity images and the depth images; 2): Combine these edges and get rid of the mussy edges, extract the whole outer brim of the ear; 3): Find the endpoints of the brim and connect them to get the region of the pure ear.

3.2   Find Edges Use Canny Edge Detector

The first step is to get the edges in both the intensity images and the depth images. In this step, a Canny edge detector is used to find the edges in both two kinds of images. Before the Canny edge detector is applied in the intensity images, the histogram equalization method is used to make the edges in the intensity images more distinguishable. The thresholds of the Canny edge detector are 0.5 and 2 both in the intensity images and the depth images.

3.3   Extract the Outer Brim of the Ear

Once the edges in both the two kinds of images are found, we are able to combine these edges, eliminate the edges that are not the outer brim of the ear and, finally, the whole outer brim of the ear will be extracted. The main idea in extracting the outer brim of the ear is that it should be the longest edge in the image. However, the edges detected by the Canny are mussy and it is hard to find the longest. Therefore, the mussy edges must be ruled out. In fact, there are two steps in this procedure.

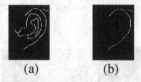

(a)   (b)

Fig. 3. An example of ruling out the edges in the inner ear. (a) is the edge images of an intensity image and (b) is the correspondent output image.

The first step is taken before the combination. This is intended to rule out the mussy edges especially the edges in the inner ear, separately, both in the edges images derived from the intensity images and depth images. Because the inner ear is always located in the middle of the image, a specific region in the middle of the ear is selected and a curve tracing method is applied to remove the edge points in this region and edge points that connected to the curves in this region. The tracing continues until it comes across a point that is the juncture of two curves. By doing so, the edges in the inner ear are eliminated without destroying the edges of the outer brim of the ear. Then the longest edge in the image is supposed to be the outer brim of the ear. In fact, we finally choose the longest two edges as the result of this step to ensure the outer brim of the ear is selected. This is illustrated in figure 3.

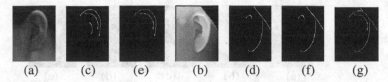

(a)   (c)   (e)   (b)   (d)   (f)   (g)

Fig. 4. An example of the extracting of the outer brim of the ear. (a)is the intensity image and (b) is the depth image; (c)and (d)are the edge image of (a)and(b); (e)and (f)are the result of the first step; (g)is the final result.

The second step is during the process of combination. After the two output images get from the first step is combined and a new image is generated, curve tracing is used and the edge points in the output image of the intensity image get from the first step are selected as the start point. It helps to eliminate some edges that are not the outer brim of the ear. Figure 4 is an example of the total process.

3.4 Get the Region of the Pure Ear

Once the outer brim of the ear is extracted, the two endpoints can be located, then the endpoints are connected to get a closed region that is the pure ear. The endpoints are easy to be found because the previous steps have eliminated the edge points that will lead to the wrong selection of the endpoints. In fact, all the endpoints of the curves is detected and the two points that locate in the left part of the image and have a significant distance are selected. The region of the pure ear is represented as a mask. Figure 5 is an example of this process.

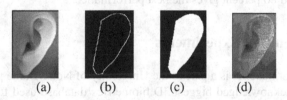

(a)   (b)   (c)   (d)

Fig. 5. One example of the process to get the pure ear. (a) is the original depth image, (b)is the final extracted region of the pure ear, (c) is the correspondent mask image of(b), (d)is the image that applies the mask to the depth image.

3.5 Extraction Result

This method is able to extract the pure ear in most of the cases; however it fails when the outer brim of the ear in the intensity image doesn't accord with that in the depth image. As showed in figure 6. This result from the innate problem of the UND data set because when the range image was taken by the Minolta Vivid 910, it takes 8 seconds during which time the subjects moved. Some differences between intensity image and the depth image are even bigger than the difference in figure 6.

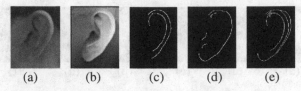

(a)   (b)   (c)   (d)   (e)

Fig. 6. An example of the problem described in section3.3. (a)and(b)is the intensity image and the depth image; (c)and(d) is the corresponding edge images; (e)is the combined image.

4   Ear Recognition

Before the ICP algorithm is applied, the ears should be aligned. To align the extracted ears, the centroids of the pure ears are calculated and are used to give the initial translation. The 3D data is first gridded and then the 3D surface is smoothed using the code in [11] called Gridfit.

When the ears are aligned, a well-known algorithm to accomplish the range image registration task named the iterative closest point algorithm(ICP) is applied. Some measures are taken to improve the performance of the original ICP algorithm. Firstly, in the process of selecting the correspondent closest point pairs to calculate the rigid translation, the pairs whose distance is larger than a specific threshold is abandoned. The threshold used in this paper is the sum of 2*R and the mean distance between the two views, where R is the resolution of the probe view. The second is in the procedure of calculating the distance of these two views, actually, the distance values of the closest point pairs are sorted and only the lower 80 percent of the pairs are selected to compute the final mean distance. Other thresholds (95, 90, 85, 75, 70) were tested and 80 percent gives the best performance.

5   Recognition Experiments

The experiment material is a part of the University of Notre Dame public data set[12] which is the acknowledged biggest 3D biometrics database used for ear recognition. The images used in this paper are from the collection J2. 415 subjects are selected and each subject has two intensity images and two corresponding depth images. One of the two is severed as the probe and the other is served as the model. The whole algorithm is implemented in Matlab 2012(a) and run on work station with two quadri-processor 2.53GHz Intel(R) Xeon(R).

5.1   Performance of the Pure Ear

In this experiment, the modified ICP algorithm is applied on the images of the pure ears extracted in this paper. The prove ears are all sub sampled by every 2 points. The performance is shown in Figure 7. The Rank-one recognition rate we obtain is 98.8% with the EER(Equal Error Rate) 2.1%. The recognition rate is higher than that in [8](97.8%) and that in[4](96.36%). The EER is better than [4] which obtain 3.2% and 2.3% for two different method; however, it is a little worse than [8](1.2%).

In these subjects, there are 24 subjects whose ears have the earring and 35 subjects whose ears are slightly covered by the hair. We make a statistics of the performance of these subjects. 23 subjects out of the 24 subjects with earring are correctly recognized and 34 out of the 35 subjects with hair covering are correctly recognized. In fact the ear that is incorrectly recognized in these two situation is the same ear.

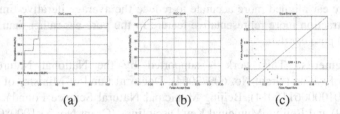

(a)   (b)   (c)

Fig. 7. Performance of the Pure Ear. (a) CMC curve. (b) Roc curve. (c) EER.

5.2   Performances Comparison between the Ear Region and the Pure Ear

In this experiment, the modified ICP algorithm is applied both on the images of the ear region derived from the Adaboost algorithm and images of the pure ears extracted in this paper. The prove ears are all sub sampled by every 2 points. The performances are listed in table 1.

According to table 1, the Rank-1 recognition rate of the pure ear is far better than that of the ear region, improved to 98.8% from 83.1%. Moreover, it takes less iterative times in pure ear recognition and less time is needed. The recognition rate is also higher than that in [8](97.8%) and that in[4](96.36%).

Table 1. Comparison of the result of the ear region and the pure ear

Image types	Recognition rate (Rank-1)	Average time (s)	Average iterative times
Images of ear region	83.1%	0.78	31
Images of the pure ear	98.8%	0.16	22

5.3   Performance of Different Sub-sample Methods

Different sub sample methods are applied in the probe ears and the model ears, the results are listed in the table 2. In the table P(n) means that the probe ears are sub sampled every n points.

Table 2. Results of different sub sample methods

Sub-sample Methods	Recognition Rate (Rank-1)	Average time (s)	Average iterative times
No Sub-Sample	97.4%	0.34	23.7
P(2)	98.8%	0.16	22
P(3)	96.4%	0.12	22

6   Conclusion

In combining the edges found in the intensity image and the depth image using the canny edge detector, we can find the whole outer brim of the ear and it can be extracted to generate the pure ear for recognition. Performance using pure ear is better than that using ear region and that in [4] and [8]. In the future work, we intend to do have the pure ear aligned more accurate to reduce the average iterative times and we intend to extraction more representative feature in the pure ear rather than the whole set of the 3D pure ear data.

Acknowledgments. This work is supported by the National Nature Science Foundation of China (Grant No. 60973064), Doctoral Fund of Ministry of Education of China (20100006110014), Beijing Municipal Natural Science Foundation (Grant No. 4102039) and Beijing Municipal Key Disciplines (Grant No. Xk100080537). The authors would like to thank the computer vision research laboratory at University of Notre Dame for providing the biometrics datasets.

References

1. Iannarelli, A.: Ear Identification. Paramont Publishing (1989)
2. Burge, M., Burger, W.: Ear Biometrics in Computer Vision. In: Proc. Int'l Conf. J. Pattern Recognition, vol. 2, pp. 822–826 (2000)
3. Hurley, D., Nixon, M., Carter, J.: Force Field Feature Extraction for Ear Biometrics. Computer Vision and Image Understanding 98(3), 491–512 (2005)
4. Chen, H., Bhanu, B.: Human Ear Recognition in 3D. IEEE Trans. on PAMI. 29(4), 718–737 (2007)
5. Yan, P., Bowyer, K.W.: Ear Biometrics Using 2D and 3D Images. In: IEEE Computer Society Conference on Computer Vision and Pattern Recognition, vol. (3), p. 121 (2005)
6. Yan, P., Bowyer, K.W.: ICP-Based Approaches for 3D Ear Recognition. In: Proc. SPIE Conf. Biometric Technology for Human Identification, pp. 282–291 (2005)
7. Chen, H., Bhanu, B., Wang, R.: Performance Evaluation and Prediction for 3D Ear Recognition. In: Proc. Conf. Audio and Video-Based Biometric Person Authentication, pp.748–757 (2005)
8. Yan, P., Bowyer, K.W.: Biometric Recognition Using 3D Ear Shape. IEEE Transactions on Pattern Analysis and Machine Intelligence 29(8), 1297–1308 (2007)
9. Yan, P., Bowyer, K.W.: An automatic 3d ear recognition system. In: Proceedings of the Third International Symposium on 3D Data Processing, Visualization and Transmission University of North Carolina, Chapel Hill (2006)
10. He, Z.: Research of 3D Ear Recognition Based on Model Matching. University of Science and Technology Beijing (2010)
11. Errico, J.D.: Surface Fitting using gridfit (OL/CP), http://www.mathworks.com/matlabcentral
12. The Computer Vision Research Laboratory at the University of Notre Dame. University of Notre Dame Biometrics Database Distribution (DB/OL)

Multimodal Ear Recognition
Based on 2D+3D Feature Fusion

Mingduo Guo, Zhichun Mu, and Li Yuan

School of Automation and Electronic Engineering,
University of Sience and Technology Beijing, Beijing, China
mu@ies.ustb.edu.cn

Abstract. According to the limitation of 2D or 3D ear recognition and the complementarity between two recognition strategies, a multimodal ear recognition method based on 2D and 3D ear feature-level fusion is presented in this paper. Firstly, LGBP algorithm is used to describe textural feature of 2D ear and depth feature of 3D ear respectively. Then two feature vectors are concatenated to form a high dimensional fused feature. Finally, the KPCA+ReliefF method is proposed to eliminate the correlation between 2D and 3D ear images and remove the redundancy data. Experimental results show that the multimodal ear recognition outperforms either using 2D or 3D alone, especially under illumination variation, partial occlusion and posture change.

Keywords: Ear recognition, Feature fusion, 2D intensity images, 3D depth images.

1 Introduction

As a non-intrusive recognition method, ear recognition has attracted extensive attentions recently. For ear is a common biological characteristic of human being and it has significant properties for biometric identification such as uniqueness and stability, ear recognition has become an identification technology even as important as face or iris. For 2D ear recognition, all the methods in [1-5] achieved satisfactory results in high-quality images without big posture change and illumination variation. Influenced by shooting environment ear images may have shadow or anamorphose that lead to an undesirable recognition accuracy and robustness.

Recently, many researchers have focused on 3D domain. A fast algorithm for ICP-based was proposed in [6], and LSP (Local Surface Description) is also an effective way to represent 3D ear [7]. Paper [8] combined local and holistic 3D ear features and got an outstanding performance. It is evident that 3D data can represent shape information explicitly and compensate for the lack of depth information in 2D [9]. 3D depth information is invariant under the color and lighting change. In addition, ear posture can be corrected easier in 3D image. On the other hand, it's worth noting that the variety of 2D images (gray-level information) gives more detailed texture information than 3D. For reasons above, integrating 2D and 3D ear information by a simple way will bring an improvement in systems originally relying only on single 2D or 3D data. Paper [10] indicated that there are four possible fusion levels in biometric

W.-S. Zheng et al. (Eds.): CCBR 2012, LNCS 7701, pp. 227–234, 2012.
© Springer-Verlag Berlin Heidelberg 2012

recognition information fusion (sensor level, feature level, matching score level and decision level). In paper [10], the fusion rules work at the matching score level and multi-modal with 2D PCA and 3D ICP gives the highest performance (87.7% rank-one recognition in the 302-person dataset of UND). Feature level fusion is in the forepart of the recognition system. Abundant information contributing to the final recognition will be reserved. So in our study, 2D and 3D ear information will be mixed in feature level.

LBP (Local Binary Patterns), a grayscale-invariance texture description algorithm, is capable of representing the image edge and corner-point that are crucial to distinguish different ears. Since original LBP algorithm extracts texture feature in only one orientation and scale, and it's also sensitive to the noise. Multi-orientation and multi-scale Gabor filters are introduced to solve these problems. Combining local intensity distribution with the spatial information, LGBP (Local Gabor Binary Patterns) is robust to noise and local image transformations due to variations of lighting occlusion and pose [11]. Considering the compatibility between two different feature modals, LGBP will be used to represent both 2D intensity images and 3D depth images. Then two LGBP feature histogram sequences will be combined in series.

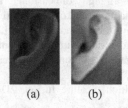

(a)   (b)

Fig. 1. Ear images. (a) is a 2D ear image and (b) is a 3D ear depth-intensity image.

Two ears in Fig.1 are from one person. It is obvious that they have similar texture information on the ear outline and the similarity means a strong correlation between 2D and 3D ear data. This kind of correlation will bring information redundancy that would reduce recognition efficiency. In this paper, feature selection and dimensionality reduction is realized by KPCA+ReliefF method. KPCA (kernel Principal Component Analysis) is used to eliminate redundant information to reduce feature dimension. ReliefF algorithm is weak in removing redundancy, however it is fast and efficient for feature selection and assigning weight for every feature component. Experimental results illustrate that, compared with the recognition based on single type of sensory data (2D or 3D), the feature-fusion (2D+3D) ear recognition achieves higher recognition accuracy and better robustness under illumination variation, occlusion and pose change.

2   Ear Detection and 3D Ear Pose Correction

All the images used in this paper were acquired at the University of Note Dame between October 7, 2003 and March 19, 2004 [10]. Images that disqualified to application such as serious occlusion and blurring are abandoned. An improved AdaBoost algorithm is used to detect and locate ear area automatically in 2D ear dataset [12]. The information of ear location is helpful to segment ear area from the corresponding 3D cloud point data. Fig.2 shows the detection result in a 2D image. The red rectangle in (b) is the detected ear area.

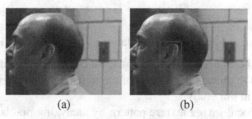

(a)   (b)

Fig. 2. Ear detection result: (a) A left-side face image (b) The detected ear area

There are total of 1708 pairs of 2D and 3D ear images from 372 persons used in this work. Among these 372 people, there are 40 with occlusion, 24 with obvious pose change and 55 with obvious illumination variation. These three situations are shown in fig.3.

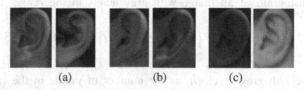

(a)   (b)   (c)

Fig. 3. Ear images under following three situations: (a) Occlusion (b) Pose change (c) Illumination variation

Recognition accuracy will be influenced by ear pose change in 2D ear recognition. While the pose can be corrected through a common-use depth registration algorithm, ICP (Iterative Closest Point) method. We perform the fist 2D image of each person as the reference model ear. Ear poses of the rest images of the same person will be corrected according to the model one (an example in Fig.4). Test results in Part 5 demonstrate that the corrected ears obtain a better performance.

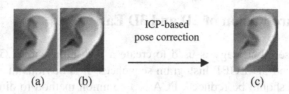

ICP-based
pose correction

(a)   (b)   (c)

Fig. 4. 3D ear pose correction: (a) Modal ear (b) An ear to be corrected (c) Corrected ear

3   LBGP Ear Representation Method

LGBP is a representation approach that multi-scale and multi-orientation Gabor filters are used for the decomposition of an ear image, followed by the LBP encoding. The

Gabor filters used in this paper are referenced the definition in [13]. Let $I(z) = I(x, y)$ be the ear image, its convolution with a Gabor filter $\psi_{u,v}(z)$ is defined as follows

$$G(z, u, v) = I(z) * \psi_{u,v}(z) \tag{1}$$

Five scales $v \in \{0, ..., 4\}$ and eight orientations $u \in \{0, ..., 7\}$ Gabor filters are used.

After convolving the image with each of the 40 Gabor filters can generate the Gabor features. Because the phase information of the transform is time-varying [14], only its magnitude is used in our study.

LBP describes local image texture pattern by analyzing pixels intensity changes in local windows, and represents global image feature after statistic computing (See [15] for the detailed principle). Encoding the Gabor magnitude with LBP, we get LGBP operator as follows

$$LGBP = \sum_{p=0}^{7} S(G_p(z, u, v) - G_c(z, u, v)) 2^p \tag{2}$$

The LGBP histogram of an image with gray levels in the range [0,255] could be defined as

$$h_{u,v}(i) = \sum_z F\{LGBP(z, u, v) = i\} \quad i = 0, 1, ..., 255 \tag{3}$$

where i is the i-th gray level, h_i is the number of pixels in the image with gray level i and $F\{A\} = \begin{cases} 1, & A \text{ is ture} \\ 0, & A \text{ is false} \end{cases}$. So the histogram sequence of each LGBP is obtained as $H_{u,v} = \{h_{u,v}(i) \mid i = 0, 1, ..., 255\}$, where $u \in \{0, ..., 7\}$, $v \in \{0, ..., 4\}$.

Finally, all the histogram pieces from the 40 Gabor maps are concatenated to a histogram sequence $\Re$, as the final ear representation

$$\Re = (H_{0,0}, ..., H_{0,4}, ..., H_{7,4}) \tag{4}$$

4   Feature Fusion of 2D and 3D Ear

In our work, serial strategy is used to create a high-dimension LGBP feature vector fused by 2D and 3D LGBP histogram sequences. It is obvious that the dimension of fusion feature should be reduced. PCA is a common method to dimension reduction, for it is good at deleting correlated coefficients. But only linear correlations can be eliminated by PCA. Instead of ignoring to the non-liner correlations between 2D and 3D feature, KPCA can transform linear non-separable feature into a high-dimensional feature space to obtain the linear separability. For a more efficient recognition, RelifF algorithm is used after KPCA, which could assign a weight to each selected feature component.

4.1   Serial Feature Combination

Actually all features should be normalized before fusion to achieve the same performance in recognition. $Z-score$ method is adopted in our study. $\Re_{2D}$ and $\Re_{3D}$ represent the LGBP feature vector of 2D and 3D ear image. The normalized features are

$$\begin{cases} \Re_{nor\_2D} = (\Re_{2D} - \mu_{2D}) / \sigma_{2D} \\ \Re_{nor\_3D} = (\Re_{3D} - \mu_{3D}) / \sigma_{3D} \end{cases} \tag{5}$$

where μ_{2D} and μ_{3D} are the mean vector of 2D and 3D LGBP feature vector. σ_{2D} and σ_{3D} are the mean standard deviation vectors on each feature component. Then we get the normalized feature vectors with zero mean and variance 1. Finally feature of 2D intensity image will be serial combined with feature from 3D depth image as follows

$$\Re_{Fusion} = (\Re_{nor\_2D}, \Re_{nor\_3D}) \ . \tag{6}$$

4.2   Feature Selection Based on KPCA+ReliefF

Following are the detailed steps of feature selection using KPCA+ReliefF. Input the training dataset X , iterations n , number of near neighbor instances k and target dimension of KPCA d . *Step1*. Reduce the dimension of training set by KPCA to get a new dataset X' . *Step2*. Suppose the initial weight value of each feature component in dataset X' is zero, namely $W(i)=0, i=1,2,...,d$. *Step3*. Randomly select a instance x'. Then find k -near instances in the congener samples of x', which would be recorded as $P_j (j=1,2,...,k)$, and find k -near instances in the rest samples, which are recorded as $M_j (j=1,2,...,k)$. *Step4*. Update feature component weight $W(i)$ in accordance with

$$W(i) = W(i) - \frac{1}{nk} \sum_{j=1}^{k} d(i,x',P_j) + \frac{1}{nk} \sum_{c \neq c(x')} [\frac{p(c)}{1-p(c(x'))} \sum_{j=1}^{k} d(i,x',M_j)] \tag{7}$$

where c is class label, $c(x')$ represents the class of x', $d(i,x,y)$ is the distance between x and y on the i –th feature component, and $p(c)$ represents the probability of class c . *Step5*. Repeat the process of step3 to step4 n times. Output W and delete the feature component with negative weight.

5   Experiments and Analysis

We design two experiments in the following sections for the evaluations of the proposed approach. Our experimental environment is listed as follows. *Operating system*: Microsoft Windows XP SP3. *Processor*: Intel Pentium(R) Core(TM)2 Duo CPU 2.2GHz 2.19GHz. *System memory*: 2.0G. *Running environment*: Matlab R2011a.

We select one pair of images (a 2D image and its corresponding 3D image) from each person randomly to create a testing set. Training set is composed of the rest images. So the training set includes 1336*2 images and the testing set includes 372.

The weighted χ^2 distance $\chi^2_\omega = \sum_{j,i} \omega_j \left(\dfrac{\left| g(j,i) - h(j,i) \right|^2}{g(j,i) + h(j,i)} / 2 \right)$ is used to measure

histogram similarity, where ω_j gets weight value from ReliefF. The dimension of fusion feature is reduced to 200 according to repeated tests. In addition, the nearest neighbor classifier is used in final recognition. Recognition rates in the following test results are all rank-one.

5.1   Test1

This experiment is designed to confirm both the superiority of LGBP method and the advantage of ICP-based pose correction on 3D recognition. Firstly, we use PCA, global LBP, block LBP and LGBP to represent 2D and 3D ear images, where global LBP feature is the representation of the whole image while block LBP divides an image into 16 blocks and concatenates 16 LBP features into a vector. Experimental results are illustrated in Table 1 as follows.

Table 1. The recognition rates and average recognition times

Methods	2D recognition rate	3D recognition rate	Pose Correction (3D)	Average time of 2D ear (s)
PCA	47.5%	54.5%	57.6%	0.14
Global LBP	34.4%	56.6%	59.6%	0.33
Block LBP	77.8%	84.9%	87.9.%	0.98
LGBP	84.9%	88.9%	91.9%	1.42

From table 1, it is obvious that 3D ear recognition generally performed better than 2D. After analyzing classification results, we find that 3D LGBP could correctly classify 46 instances in 55 with illumination variation while 2D recognition could only recognize 22. In addition, introducing ICP-based pose correction enhances the number of correctly classified instances with pose change from 7 to 19. All results from above prove the superiority of 3D ear recognition under illumination and pose change.

Nevertheless, it is should be emphasized that the performance of 3D recognition is not simply improves on 2D's basis. That is to say some ears can be labeled with right classes in 2D recognition but wrongly classified in 3D, which shows the outperformance of the richer texture information in 2D images over 3D. For these reasons, fusion of 2D and 3D is a promising strategy.

It also clearly indicates that LGBP achieves a highest recognition accurate over other methods. However, it's worth noting that the running time of LGBP is increased by the high dimension of feature vector, which will affect recognition efficiency seriously. Thus it can be seen dimension reduction is necessary.

5.2   Test2

The purpose of this experiment is to evaluate the performance of the method proposed in this paper and to show the superiority of KPCA+ReliefF. In this test, LDA and PCA serve as comparisons with KPCA+ReliefF. Detailed results are listed in Table 2 in where column3 to column5 are the number of successfully recognized instances under corresponding situations.

Table 2. Multimodal ear recognition based on 2D+3D feature fusion

Recognition method	Recognition rate	Illumination variation (55)	Pose change (24)	Occlusion (40)	Average time per ear(s)
2D LBGP	84.9%	22	7	16	1.42
3D LBGP	91.9%	46	19	33	1.10
Simple serial combination	95.5 %	52	21	36	1.98
LDA	91.7%	47	17	34	0.42
PCA	94.9%	52	29	36	0.44
KPCA	95.5 %	53	21	36	0.41
PCA+ReliefF	96.1%	53	21	37	0.38

From Table 2, it is easy to see that PCA+ReliefF method achieves the highest recognition rate and the shortest recognition time. Compared with the ear recognition only rely on single type of dataset, the multimodal ear recognition based on 2D and 3D feature-level fusion is more robust to illumination variation, pose change and occlusion especially under occlusion.

6   Conclusion

A novel ear recognition strategy based on 2D+3D feature fusion is proposed in this paper. We combine 2D intensity LGBP feature with 3D depth LGBP feature and reduce the dimension of fusion feature through KPCA+ReliefF. Then the selected fusion feature components are used for final recognition.

By analyzing results of certain samples, the complementarity between 2D and 3D ear images is proved. Test2 evidently illustrates the effectiveness and robustness of the fusion method proposed in this paper. When there is illumination variation, pose change or occlusion in ear images, fusion recognition performs more outstanding than single 2D or 3D recognition. With a finite amount of time, we haven't found the most optimal algorithm for single 2D or 3D feature representation, which might affect final recognition rate. However, 2D and 3D feature fusion will be a promising approach to find the breakthrough to get an improvement in .

Acknowledgements. This work is supported by the National Nature Science Foundation of China (Grant No. 60973064), Doctoral Fund of Ministry of Education of China (20100006110014), Beijing Municipal Natural Science Foundation (Grant No. 4102039) and Beijing Municipal Key Disciplines (Grant No. Xk100080537).

References

1. Burge, M., Burger, W.: Ear biometrics in computer vision. In: 15th International Conference on Pattern Recognition, vol. 2, pp. 181–184. IEEE Press, Barcelona (2000)
2. Hurley, D.J., Nixon, M.S., Carter, J.N.: Force field energy functionals for image feature extraction. In: Image and Vision Computing, vol. 20, pp. 311–317. Elsevier (2002)
3. Liu, J.M., Wang, L.: Ear Recognition Based on the Edge Information of the Auricle Contour. Journal of Computer—Aided Design & Computer Graphics 20(3), 337–342 (2008)
4. Yuan, L., Mu, Z.C., Liu, L.M.: Ear recognition based on kernel principal component analysis and Support vector machine. Journal of University of Science and Technology Beijing 28(9), 890–895 (2006)
5. Wang, Z.L., Mu, Z.C., Wang, X.Y., et al.: Ear recognition based on Moment Invariants. Pattern Recognition and Artificial Intelligence 17(4), 502–505 (2004)
6. Yan, P., Bowyer, K.W.: A fast algorithm for ICP-based 3D shape biometrics. Computer Vision and Image Understanding 107, 195–202 (2007)
7. Chen, H., Bhanu, B.: Human Ear Recognition in 3D. IEEE Trans. on Pattern Analysis and Machine Intelligence. 29, 718–737 (2007)
8. Zhou, J.D., Cadavid, S., Abdel- Mottaleb, M.: An Efficient 3-D Ear Recognition System Employing Local and Holistic Features. IEEE Trans. on Information Forensics and Security. 7, 978–991 (2012)
9. Wang, Y.J., Chua, C.S., Ho, Y.K.: Facial feature detection and face recognition from 2D and 3D images. Pattern Recognition Letters 23, 1191–1202 (2002)
10. Yan, P., Bowyer, K.W.: Multi-biometrics 2D and 3D Ear Recognition. In: Kanade, T., Jain, A., Ratha, N.K. (eds.) AVBPA 2005. LNCS, vol. 3546, pp. 503–512. Springer, Heidelberg (2005)
11. Zhang, W.C., Shan, S.G., Gao, W., et al.: Local Gabor binary pattern histogram sequence (LGBPHS): a novel non-statistical model for face representation and recognition. In: 10th IEEE International Conference on Computer Vision, vol. 1, pp. 786–791. IEEE Press (2005)
12. Zhang, W., Mu, Z.C., Li, Y.: Fast Ear Detection and Tracking Based on Improved AdaBoost Algorithm. Journal of Image and Grafhics 12(2), 222–227 (2007)
13. Lades, M., Vorbruggen, J.C., Buhmann, J., Lange, J., Malsburg, C., Wurtz, R.P., Konen, W.: Distortion invariant object recognition in the dynamic link architecture. IEEE Trans. on Computers 42(3), 300–311 (1993)
14. Wiskott, L., Fellous, J.M., Kruger, N., Malsburg, C.: Face recognition by elastic bunch graph matching. IEEE Trans. on Pattern Analysis and Machine Intelligence 19(7), 775–779 (1997)
15. Ojala, T., Pietikainen, M., Harwood, D.: A comparative study of texture measures with classification based on feature distributions. Pattern Recognition 29(1), 51–59 (1996)

Toward Emotional Speaker Recognition: Framework and Preliminary Results

Yingchun Yang and Li Chen

College of Computer Science & Technology, Zhejiang University, Hangzhou, China
{yyc,stchenli}@zju.edu.cn

Abstract. Besides channel and environment noises, emotion variability in speech signals has been found to be another important factor that degenerates drastically the performance of most speaker recognition systems proposed in the literature. How to make current GMM-UBM system adaptive to emotion variability is one consideration. We thus propose a framework named Deformation Compensation (DC) for emotional speaker recognition, which viewing emotion variability as deformation (some sort of distribution distortion in the feature space) and trying to take deformation compensation by making dynamic modification on the feature, model and score level. This paper reports the preliminary results which have been gained so far, including our proposed Deformation Compensation framework together with the preliminary case study on GMM-UBM.

Keywords: emotional speaker recognition, deformation compensation framework, human machine gap.

1   Introduction

Current GMM-UBM (Gaussian Mixture Model-Universal Background Model) speaker recognition system can achieve excellent performance in constrained situations. However, this system still encounters difficulties in dealing with large number of variations due to extrinsic and intrinsic variability. Most of the research work focused on coping with the former, like channel mismatch and background noises. Nowadays, intrinsic variation, especially emotion variability, has attracted more and more attentions. The mismatch of the speaker's emotion states between training and testing causes unacceptably high error rates in automatic speaker recognition (ASR) systems.

Mitigating extrinsic variability is the mainstream of the research field. The NIST Speaker Recognition Evaluation (SRE) mostly focused on combating technical error sources, most notably those of training/test channel mismatch. There are also many other factors that influence the speaker recognition performance. We should also address human related error sources, such as the effects of emotions, vocal organ illness, aging, and level of attention [1]. The NIST SRE 2010 has added vocal effort data [2].

To investigate the long running performance of GMM speaker recognition system, a speech check-in system was launched in our CCNT Lab from 2005. It's found that

W.-S. Zheng et al. (Eds.): CCBR 2012, LNCS 7701, pp. 235–242, 2012.

the system performance is related to speaker's mood more than cold, which did sur-
prise us a lot.   To further verify this phenomenon, an emotional speech corpus
named MASC (Mandarin Affective Speech Corpus) was collected by our lab and later
submitted to LDC [122]. Supported by a five-year Chinese High-tech Research &
Development (863) Program entitled "Processing Technology for Emotion Compensation based Speaker Recognition" initiated in 2006, some research have been made
to address the problem of emotional speaker recognition, i.e. speaker recognition
under emotion variability [4,9,11,16]. This paper gives a brief summary for our
project result: Emotion variability is an important challenge for real world application
of speaker recognition. We give a systematic Deformation Compensation (DC)
framework to cope with emotion variability.

The rest of the paper is organized as follows. Section 2 shows the effect of emotion
variability on speaker recognition, related work, and our observation and hypothesis.
Section 3 presents our Deformation Compensation (DC) framework for emotional
speaker recognition. Section 4 gives one Deformation Generation case of our DC
framework and experimental results. Finally, the conclusion is drawn in Section 5.

2   Emotion Variability

2.1   Baseline Performance

Mandarin Affective Speech Corpus (MASC) [12], an emotional speech database, is
used in our experiments. The corpus contains recordings of 68 Chinese speakers (23
female and 45 male). All speech is expressed in five kinds of emotion: neutral, anger,
elation, panic and sadness. 20 utterances are spoken for three times under each emotional state, and 2 extra paragraphs for neutral. Utterance is short and the length is
between 5s and 10s, while paragraph is longer relatively, lasting about 40s. All speech
is recorded with the same microphone.

13 Mel Frequency Cepstral Coefficients (MFCC) with 32ms window length and
16ms frame rate is utilized. 5 GMMs(neutral, anger, elation, panic and sadness) for
each speaker are trained with first 5 utterances (three times each) under the speaker's
corresponding emotion by EM(Expectation Maximization). The rest 15 utterances
(three times each)   under each emotion state are used as testing data.

Table 1 shows the Identification Rate (IR) when training and testing speech are in
different emotional states. The row represents the state under training while the
column indicates the emotional state under testing. Obviously, when the emotional
state of training is consistent with that of testing, the IR is relatively higher. When the
emotional state of the test speaker is different from that of his/her training data, the
performance of the speaker recognition system will decline dramatically. Therefore,
emotion variability is a major factor on the performance degradation of speaker
recognition system.

Table 1. Identification Rate with GMM under different emotional states of training and testing

Test / Train	Neutral	Anger	Panic	Elation	Sadness
Neutral	**89.28%**	28.27%	31.67%	26.90%	49.74%
Anger	21.34%	**75.95%**	31.99%	27.91%	17.39%
Panic	25.00%	18.14%	**70.59%**	19.84%	27.65%
Elation	28.30%	17.94%	27.52%	**67.78%**	28.82%
Sadness	43.01%	23.99%	21.99%	23.86%	**89.15%**

2.2 Related Work

Emotional speaker recognition(ESR) refers to speaker recognition faced with the issue of emotional variability, i.e. the inconsistency of the speaker's emotion states between the training and testing phases, which often results in unacceptably high error rate in ASR(Automatic Speaker Recognition) systems. Up till now, there are two main approaches to cope with emotional variability for speaker recognition. One is "structured training", which trains the speaker model on a variety of styles to improve performance [3], and the other is "channel treatment" , which treats emotional variability as the problem of channel variability[5,6]. While enhancing the speaker recognition performance to some degree, the two approaches has their own drawbacks individually. For " structured training" , it's the most effective, however, it's difficult, even impossible to collect utterances to cover all possible variations, even for the same emotion of the same speaker. As to "channel treatment" , the emotion variability is different from the channel variability in two ways. Firstly, the effect on speaker recognition is static and speaker-independent under the same channel, while it varies with speakers under the same emotion. Secondly, emotional data is more difficult to gather compared with channel data, therefore sparse compared with the latter. Compared with channel variability, emotion variability has its own characteristics. Therefore, special measures should be taken for emotional speaker recognition.

2.3 Our Observation

Different emotion states will affect speech production mechanism of a speaker in different ways [3]. As was concluded in [10], emotions will influence more than 20 types of speech features, such as pitch, intensity, formants, speech rate, energy and duration. Inspired by these precedent studies, we further inference that the intra-speaker vocal variability induced by emotion can lead to deformation in acoustic feature distribution, therefore cause model mismatch and aggravate the recognition system performance.

To test our deformation hypothesis in emotional speech, an experiment is launched to visualize the speech features under different emotions by manifold analysis. From MASC Corpus, six people (3 males and 3 females) are selected according to three level(high, medium and low)) of recognition performance (IR: Identification Rate).

Here, we choose female1 with 68.3%, female 2 with 41.7%, female 3 with 20%, male 1 with 63.3%, male 2 with 41.7%, and male 3 with 21.7%. Elation and neutral utterances from the 6 people are chosen and segmented into each phoneme through HTK with the scripts. 13 dimension MFCC of these segments are generated and those of 'a', 'o', 'e' are selected for further manifold analysis. ISOMAP (Isometric mapping) is used to explore the intrinsic dimension of the manifold and map the original high dimension 13 into a low dimension 3. We apply ISOMAP with k=6 neighbors to build the NN-graph. The manifold result is shown in Fig. 1, and the data of vowel 'a' under neutral is revealed in red, while under elation is in black; the data of vowel 'o' under neutral is revealed in blue, while under elation is in magenta; the data of vowel 'e' under neutral is revealed in green, while under elation is in cyan.

From Fig.1, it's evident that different level of recognition performance is related to different manifold morpholog change, i.e. the higher the IR, the higher the volume overlap between the neutral and elation data. The volume overlap can be regarded as an indicator of deformation of MFCC feature distribution. The lower the volume overlap, the higher the deformation and the more serious the recognition performance deterioration. Therefore, we can conclude here that emotion variability can be assumed to lead to some sort of deformation of speech feature distribution space, which results in the decrease of speaker recognition performance.

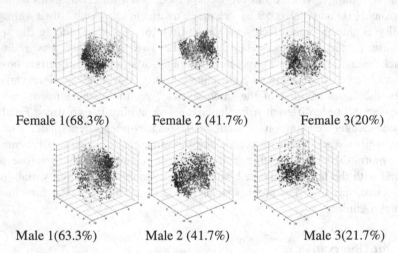

Female 1(68.3%)   Female 2 (41.7%)   Female 3(20%)

Male 1(63.3%)   Male 2 (41.7%)   Male 3(21.7%)

Fig. 1. Three-Dimensional Isomap embedding of utterances of the vowel of 'a', 'o', 'e' of 6 people (Number in comma refers to IR for each person, data number of female1, female2, female3, male1, male2 and male3 is 1304, 1571, 1870, 1918, 1684, 1999 respectively.)

3   DC Framework

Inspired by the above analysis, we propose our Deformation Compensation (DC) framework as in Fig. 2. Our assumption is to regard emotion variability as some sort of deformation of feature distribution space and compensates for the deformation by adaptively regulating the corresponding features, models or scores. The main difference from the traditional speaker recognition is the addition of the Deformation Compensation module, which is denoted by a larger dotted square. The speech variability is regarded as some sort of distribution space deformation. Thus, DC module is to take dynamic modification to make speaker features and models adaptive to intra-speaker variability.

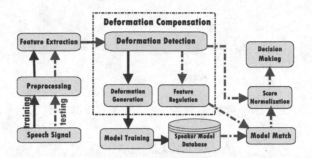

Fig. 2. Deformation Compensation based Speaker Recognition

Deformation Detection (D-D) module estimates the feature distribution of training and testing, computes the difference between the two by some metrics, i.e. DF (Deformation Factor). As a result, D-D marks those segments of feature as distorted part for subsequent compensation if the difference measure is larger than a certain threshold.

Compensation can be made on the feature, model and score level, i.e. Feature Regulation, Deformation and Score Normalization.

Feature Regulation is to reduce the variation in the input feature distribution between testing and training, which consists of Deformation Reversion and Deformation Elimination. Deformation Reversion is to tries to recover the distorted feature by shifting its distribution along the reverse direction of the detected distortion, while Deformation Elimination is to simply discard the distorted part of the feature.

Deformation Generalization extends the idea of "structure learning" by adding real or synthesized emotional speech to make the model contain as many sorts of variation as possible, thus making the system familiar with the emotional variations of the user's voice.

Score Normalization module is to utilize some sort of transformation to normalize the decision scores according to the Deformation Factor.

4   Case Study

One specific case is illustrated to explain how the DC framework works.

4.1   Shifting Frequency

Deformation Generalization method is to enrich the neutral model by utilizing real or synthetic emotional speech data to train the speaker model, hoping that all sorts of emotion variability could be captured by the model.

Fig. 3 shows the spectrum of certain feature vector extracted from anger and neutral utterance (vowel 'e'). It gave us the hint that the anger speech can be shifted from neutral spectrum to change the formants. Hence, the emotion spectrum can be converted from the neutral spectrum by shifting its spectrum, though it is not precise.

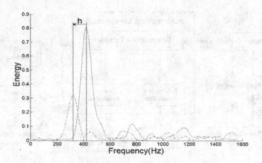

Fig. 3. The spectrum of anger and neutral vowel 'e'. (The dashed and solid line represents the anger and neutral spectrum individually)[4].

To solve the bottleneck problem of obtaining real emotional speech, we proposed a method named Shifting Frequency (SF)[4], aimed to synthesize quasi-emotional speech from neutral one by changing its spectrum, through shifting the spectrum of neutral speech frame to change the distribution of energy in the frequency band. And the resulting synthesized quasi-emotional speech differed from the neutral in pitch, formants and energy distribution, which are the main differences between neutral and emotional speech.

Thus, for each neutral speech feature, we will generate its quasi-emotional counterpart by shifting spectrum. These quasi-emotional speech can be utilized to train its quasi-emotional models, thus enriching the original neutral model to contain emotion variability possibly met in later tests.

4.2   Experimental Results

Mandarin Affective Speech Corpus (MASC) [12] is also used in our experiments. The development dataset is composed of all paragraphs and utterances of the first 18 speakers. 13 Mel Frequency Cepstral Coefficients (MFCC) with 32ms window length and 16ms frame rate is utilized. For GMM-UBM (Gaussian Mixture Models-Universal Background Model), the gender-independent 512 UBM is trained by using the first 18 speakers' neutral utterances and paragraphs. Target GMMs are adapted from the UBM with the speaker's neutral paragraph by maximum a posterior (MAP) adaptation. Only the means of the Gaussian components are adapted, and no score normalization is used. As to EFA (Emotional Factor Analysis), state-of-the-art algorithm for channel compensation, please refer to [9] for details.

For our SF (Shifting Frequency), the speech is first segmented into frames by a 20-ms window progressing at a 10-ms frame rate. Secondly, FFT of the size 512 is used to transform the speech frames into frequency domain. Then, spectrogram shifting method is applied to obtain synthesized spectrums. The length unit of shifting is

8000/512=15.625Hz. And in the experiment, the shifting length h is ±1, ±2, ±3 ±4, ±5 unit. Thus, 10 phrases are created from one neutral phrase. Finally, reverse FFT transforms them into time domain to get quasi-emotion utterance [4], which will generate its quasi-emotion models. Thus, one's neutral GMM model(ϕ_0) generates a set of GMM models($\phi_1, \phi_2, ..., \phi_L$), which will applied into the speaker recognition. The posterior probability of speech given feature vector X with respect to speaker S is as

$$p(s \mid X) = \max p(X \mid S, \Phi_l) \qquad (1)$$

Table 2. Comparison of IR between different methods on MASC Corpus

Emotion	GMM-UBM	EFA	SF
Neutral	96.23%	93.07%	91.15%
Anger	31.50%	50.13%	46.9%
Elation	33.57%	51.33%	50.2%
Panic	35.00%	45.97%	49.9%
Sadness	61.43%	65.20%	68.6%
Average	51.55%	61.64%	61.35%

It can be seen from Table 2 that IR of EFA and SF algorithm increases by 10% or so compared with the baseline GMM-UBM, however, our SF algorithm needs less space/ time costs compared with EFA. It's interesting to compare the case between neutral and sadness. For the baseline GMM-UBM, the recognition performances of the two are relatively better compared with other three emotions including anger, panic and elation. After applying variability compensation with EFA and SF, the IR increases are relatively higher under anger, panic and elation, while relatively smaller under sadness, even negative under neutral. We assumed that there remains similarity between neutral and sad speech feature distribution, while the distribution resemble more to each other among other three emotions. Furthermore, there are many other indices prove that the five emotion types can be categorized into two groups: high deviation from neutral (HD) including panic, anger and elation, and low deviation from neutral (LD) including neutral and sadness [11].

5   Conclusion

Emotion variability is found to be an an important challenge for real world application of speaker recognition. Motivated by visualization of speech data, we give a systematic solution Deformation Compensation (DC) framework for emotional speaker recognition. Our SF(Shifting Frequency) obtained comparable performance improvement with state-of-the-art channel compensation algorithm EFA.

Acknowldgement. This work is supported by 863 project (2006AA01Z136) and NSFC (60970080). Thanks a lot for Dr. Ke Chen and Mingjie Zhao for their valuable discussion.

References

1. Kinnunen, T., Li, H.: An overview of text-independent speaker recognition: From features to supervectors. Speech Communication 52(1), 12–40 (2010)
2. National Institute of Standards and Technology. The NIST year 2010 speaker recognition evaluation plan (2010),
   http://www.itl.nist.gov/iad/mig/tests/sre/2010/index.html
3. Scherer, K., Johnstone, T., Bänziger, T.: Automatic verification of emotionally stressed speakers: The problem of individual differences. In: Proc. SPECOM (1998)
4. Yang, Y., Shan, Z., Wu, Z.: Frequency Shifting for Emotional Speaker Recognition, Pattern Recognition. In: Yin, P.-Y. (ed.) Pattern Recognition, pp. 305–318. InTech (October 2009)
5. Wu, W., Zheng, T.F., Xu, M.X., Bao, H.J.: Study on Speaker Verification on Emotional Speech. In: Proceedings of ICSLP 2006, pp. 2102–2105 (2006)
6. Bao, H.J., Xu, M.X., Zheng, T.F.: Emotion Attribute Projection for Speaker Recognition on Emotional Speech. In: InterSpeech 2007, pp. 758–761 (2007)
7. Shriberg, E., Kajarekar, S., Scheffer, N.: Does Session Variability Compensation in Speaker Recognition Model Intrinsic Variation Under Mismatched Conditions? In: Interspeech 2009, Brighton, United Kingdom, pp. 1551–1554 (2009)
8. Kenny, P., Boulianne, G., Ouellet, P., Dumouchel, P.: Speaker and session variability in GMM-based speaker verification. IEEE Transactions on Audio, Speech and Language Processing 15(4), 1448–1460 (2007)
9. Chen, L., Yang, Y.: Applying Emotional Factor Analysis and I-Vector to Emotional Speaker Recognition. In: Sun, Z., Lai, J., Chen, X., Tan, T. (eds.) CCBR 2011. LNCS, vol. 7098, pp. 174–179. Springer, Heidelberg (2011)
10. Louis, T.B.: Emotions, speech and the ASR framework. Speech Communication 40, 213–225 (2003)
11. Huang, T., Yang, Y.: Applying pitch-dependent difference detection and modification to emotional speaker recognition. In: Interspeech 2011 (2011)
12. Wu, T., Yang, Y., Wu, Z., Li, D.: MASC: A Speech Corpus in Mandarin for Emotion Analysis and Affective Speaker Recognition. In: ODYSSEY 2006, pp. 1–5 (June 2006)
13. Read, D., Craik, F.I.M.: Earwitness identification: some influences on voice recognition. Journal of Experimental Psychology: Applied 1, 6–18
14. Rosenberg, A.E.: Listener performance in speaker verification tasks. IEEE Transactions on Audio and Eletroacoustics AU-21, 221–225
15. Hautamaki, V., Kinnunen, T., Nosratighods, M., Lee, K.-A., Ma, B., Li, H.: Approaching human listener accuracy with modern speaker verification. In: Interspeech 2010, pp. 1473–1476 (2010)
16. Yang, Y., Chen, L., Wang, W.: Emotional Speaker Identification by Humans and Machines. In: Sun, Z., Lai, J., Chen, X., Tan, T. (eds.) CCBR 2011. LNCS, vol. 7098, pp. 167–173. Springer, Heidelberg (2011)

Orthogonal Subspace Combination
Based on the Joint Factor Analysis
for Text-Independent Speaker Recognition

Liang He and Jia Liu

Tsinghua National Laboratory for Information Science and Technology,
Department of Electronic Engineering, Tsinghua University, Beijing 100084, China
{heliang,liuj}@mail.tsinghua.edu.cn

Abstract. To apply a joint factor analysis (JFA) in a multiple channel circumstance, this paper proposes an orthogonal subspace combination method for a text-independent speaker recognition system. On the condition of multiple channels, the subspace loading matrix estimated by a mixed data corpus suffers from the data masking effects. And the subspace loading matrix estimated by a simple combination method has a drawback of subspace overlapping. To overcome these problems, this paper presents an orthogonal subspace combination method. The proposed method is based on a proper approximation of the core computation of the JFA and makes use of the Gram-Schmidt orthogonalization. On the NIST SRE 2008 core tasks corpus, the proposed method has a better performance.

Keywords: Gaussian mixture models, joint factor analysis, subspace combination, text-independent speaker recognition.

1 Introduction

The joint factor analysis (JFA) is an excellent solution to solve the text-independent speaker recognition problem [1],[2]. A basic assumption of the JFA is

$$m_{s,h} = m_u + V y_s + U x_h + D \tag{1}$$

where m_u is the mean supervector of the UBM. It can be seen as an offset. V ($CF \times R_v$, R_v is the dimension of this subspace) is the eigenvoice subspace loading matrix. y_s is the loading factor. U ($CF \times R_u$, R_u is the dimension of this subspace) is the eigenchennel subspace loading matrix. x_h is the loading factor. D is the residual subspace and has little impact. s denotes speaker and h denotes channel. C is the component number. F is the feature dimension.

For a simple channel case, the JFA works well. When the channel is complicated, the configuration is a challenging job. For example, there are three different types of utterances in the NIST SRE08 [3]. They are interview (int), microphone (mic) and telephone (tel) utterances. In the JFA framework, it can

W.-S. Zheng et al. (Eds.): CCBR 2012, LNCS 7701, pp. 243–250, 2012.

handle with utterances from a single channel but not from multiple channels. To solve it, there are two methods. The first is to train the subspace loading matrix using a mixed data. If the data from different sources are not balanced, the trained subspace will capture more information of one source but less information of the other one. We take this phenomena as the data masking effects. Another method is the simple combination. It simply combines the subspace loading matrix from different sources together [4]. However, the subspace loading matrix trained by this method has not only captures individual information of each source but also common information. The common part will be computed more than once in the subsequent procedures. This will degrease the system performance.

In this paper, we present a novel method termed orthogonal subspace combination for the JFA. The proposed method combines the subspace load matrix (either eigenchannel or eigenvoice) from different channels by a Gram-Schmidt orthogonalization. The proposed method is based on the appropriate simplification of the JFA algorithm. The combined subspace loading matrix can handle with the unbalanced data and avoid subspace overlapping.

The remainder is as follows. Section 2 formulates the derivation of JFA. In section 3, an orthogonal subspace combination method is presented. Section 4 compares our proposed methods with related works. Detail experiments were carried out on the NIST SRE08 data corpus. Finally, we summarize this paper in section 5.

2   Joint Factor Analysis

The excellent performance of the JFA in the text-independent speaker recognition has drawn lots of research. Lots of variations based on the JFA are proposed and thoroughly studied. These variations differs in the estimation sequence, joint estimation or separate estimation and the test method. Although these variations have their cons and pros, the core algorithm is the same and their performances are similar. According to related research, we select the sequence estimation method to train the subspace, Gauss-Seidel alike method to build the target speaker model and integral method for test [5],[6].

2.1   Sequence Estimation of Eigenchannel and Eigenvoice Subspace Loading Matrix

We estimate the eigenchannel subspace loading matrix U first. The eigenvoice subspace loading matrix V is estimated subsequently based on the estimated U.

Estimation of U. Since the V is unknown, we have to rewrite equation 2 to estimate U.

$$m_{s,h} - m_u - \triangle y_s = U x_{s,h} \tag{2}$$

where $\triangle y$ is a supervector which is irrelevant to channel subspace. The estimation procedure is based on the variational bayesian theory and carried out in an iterative manner.After the initialization of the U (random initialization is fine), the iterative procedure contains four steps.

1. Collect the zero, first and second order statistics.

$$N_{s,h,c} = \sum_t \gamma_{c,t}$$

$$F_{s,h,c} = \sum_t \gamma_{c,t} \left(o_t - m_{u,c}\right) \tag{3}$$

$$S_{s,h,c} = \text{diag}\left(\sum_t \gamma_{c,t} \left(o_t - m_{u,c}\right) \left(o_t - m_{u,c}\right)^{\mathrm{T}} \right)$$

where, t is the time index. $\gamma_{c,t}$ is the occupancy of o_t on the c-th component. $\text{diag}(\cdot)$ is an operation which turn a vector into a diagonal matrix.

2. Collect the first and second order statistics of loading factors. $F_{s,h,c}$ and $S_{s,h,c}$ are stacked to form supervectors $F_{s,h}$ and $S_{s,h}$. The first and second order statistics of loading factors are computed as follows

$$L_{s,h} = I + U^{\mathrm{T}} \Sigma^{-1} N_{s,h} U$$

$$E[\boldsymbol{x}_{s,h,c}] = L_{s,h}^{-1} U^{\mathrm{T}} \Sigma^{-1} F_{s,h,c} \tag{4}$$

$$E[\boldsymbol{x}_{s,h,c} \boldsymbol{x}_{s,h,c}^{\mathrm{T}}] = E[\boldsymbol{x}_{s,h,c}] E[\boldsymbol{x}_{s,h,c}^{\mathrm{T}}] + L_{s,h}^{-1}$$

where, $L_{s,h}$ is temporal variable and Σ is the covariance matrix of UBM.

3. Estimate $\triangle y$. For c-th component, the $\triangle y_{s,c}$ is calculated as follows

$$\triangle y_{s,c} = \frac{1}{N_{s,c} + \tau} \left[\sum_{h=1}^{H_s} F_{s,h,c} - \sum_{h=1}^{H_s} N_{s,h,c} U_c E[\boldsymbol{x}_{s,h,c}] \right] \tag{5}$$

4. Update U. The update equation for the c-th component is

$$\sum_s \sum_{h=1}^{H_s} N_{s,h} U_c E[\boldsymbol{x}_{s,h,c} \boldsymbol{x}_{s,h,c}^{\mathrm{T}}] = \sum_s \sum_{h=1}^{H_s} [F_{s,h,c} - N_{s,h,c} \triangle y_{s,c}] E[\boldsymbol{x}_{s,h,c}^{\mathrm{T}}] \tag{6}$$

After several iterations, U is converged.

Estimation of V. The procedure to estimate V is similar to the above procedure. We rewrite the equation (2)

$$\boldsymbol{m}_{s,h} - \boldsymbol{m}_u - U\boldsymbol{x}_{s,h} = V\boldsymbol{y}_s \tag{7}$$

After the initialization of the V (random initialization is fine), the iterative procedure contains three steps.

1. Collect the zero, first and second order statistics.

$$N_{s,c} = \sum_t \sum_h^{H_s} \gamma_{c,t}$$

$$F_{s,c} = \sum_t \sum_h^{H_s} \gamma_{c,t} \left(o_t - m_{u,c} - U_c x_{s,h} \right) \tag{8}$$

$$S_{s,c} = \mathrm{diag}\left(\sum_t \sum_h^{H_s} \gamma_{c,t} \left(o_t - m_{u,c} - U_c x_{s,h} \right) \left(o_t - m_{u,c} - U_c x_{s,h} \right)^{\mathrm{T}} \right)$$

2. Collect the first and second order statistics of loading factors.

$$L_s = I + V^{\mathrm{T}} \Sigma^{-1} N_s V$$

$$E[y_{s,c}] = L_s^{-1} V^{\mathrm{T}} \Sigma^{-1} F_{s,c} \tag{9}$$

$$E[y_{s,c} y_{s,c}^{\mathrm{T}}] = E[y_{s,c}] E[y_{s,c}^{\mathrm{T}}] + L_s^{-1}$$

3. Update V and Σ.

$$\sum_s N_{s,h} V_c E[y_{s,c} y_{s,c}^{\mathrm{T}}] = \sum_s F_{s,c} E[y_{s,c}^{\mathrm{T}}] \tag{10}$$

$$\Sigma_c = \left[\sum_s N_{s,c} \right]^{-1} \left\{ \sum_s S_{s,c} - \mathrm{diag}\left(\left(\sum_s F_{s,c} E[y_{s,c}^{\mathrm{T}}] \right) V^{\mathrm{T}} \right) \right\} \tag{11}$$

After several iterations, V and Σ are converged.

Since the importance of residual space is far less than the eigenchannel and eigenvoice subspace, we make no further discussion about it.

2.2   Enrollment of a Target Speaker

The target speaker model is

$$m_s = m_u + V y_s + D z_s \tag{12}$$

The enrollment procedure of a target speaker can be accomplished by estimating $x_{s,h}$, y_s and z_s. The $x_{s,h}$ and y_s estimation procedure is given by the equation 3, 4, 8 and 9.

2.3   Integral Method for Test

Once the target speaker model is build, the integral method can be used to test an unknown utterance. The integral is try to remove the channel effects. More explanation can be found in the reference [2] and we just state final result.

$$\sum_{c=1}^C N_c \frac{1}{(2\pi)^{\frac{F}{2}} |\Sigma_c|^{\frac{1}{2}}} - \frac{1}{2} \mathrm{tr}\{\Sigma^{-1} S_s''\} - \frac{1}{2} \log |L| + \frac{1}{2} \|L^{-\frac{1}{2}} U^{\mathrm{T}} \Sigma^{-1} F_s''\|^2 \tag{13}$$

where

$$N_{s,c} = \sum_t \gamma_{c,t}$$

$$F''_{s,c} = \sum_t \gamma_{c,t} (o_t - m_s)$$

$$S''_{s,c} = \mathrm{diag}\left(\sum_t \gamma_{c,t} (o_t - m_{s,c})(o_t - m_{s,c})^{\mathrm{T}} \right)$$

$$L = I + U^{\mathrm{T}} \Sigma^{-1} N_s U$$

(14)

Note that, only the second and fourth items in the equation 13 take effect. The first and third items are eliminated during the process of computing log-likelihood ratio.

3   Orthogonal Subspace Combination

In the above section, we review the JFA. By comparing equation 3, 4, 8, 9, 14 and 13, we find that the core computation of each procedure is the same and the difference is the statistics. In this section, we further demonstrate that the core computation can be approximated by an oblique projection and propose the orthogonal subspace combination based on the approximation.

The core computation is

$$UE[\boldsymbol{x}_{s,h}] = U\left[I + U^{\mathrm{T}}\Sigma^{-1}N_{s,h}U\right]^{-1} U^{\mathrm{T}}\Sigma^{-1}F_{s,h}$$

$$\approx \Sigma^{\frac{1}{2}} Q\left[Q^{\mathrm{T}}Q\right]^{-1} Q^{\mathrm{T}} \left[\Sigma^{-\frac{1}{2}} m_{s,h}\right]$$

(15)

where $Q = \Sigma^{-\frac{1}{2}}U$. The above approximation is to take the identity matrix off. Because the diagonal value of $U^{\mathrm{T}}\Sigma^{-1}N_{s,h}U$ is much larger than 1, and the impact of identity matrix is little. After the remove of identity matrix, we see that the coere computation is an oblique projection. The projection operator is

$$P = Q\left[Q^{\mathrm{T}}Q\right]^{-1} Q^{\mathrm{T}}$$

(16)

Note that, we use U and $\boldsymbol{x}_{s,h}$ in the above discussion. The derivation is also suitable for V, $\boldsymbol{y}_s$ and the integral test.

To further illustrate the space overlapping, we assume two eigenchannel loading matrix U_{tel} and U_{mic}. The simple combination loading matrix is $U_{com} = [U_{tel}, U_{mic}]$. So we have

$$U_{com}E[\boldsymbol{x}_{com,s,h}]$$
$$= [U_{tel}, U_{mic}] [E[\boldsymbol{x}_{tel,s,h}], E[\boldsymbol{x}_{mic,s,h}]]$$
$$= \Sigma^{\frac{1}{2}} [Q_{tel}, Q_{mic}] \left[Q_{com}^{\mathrm{T}} Q_{com}\right]^{-1} Q_{com}^{\mathrm{T}} \Sigma^{-\frac{1}{2}} m_{s,h}$$

(17)

where

$$\left[Q_{com}^{\mathrm{T}} Q_{com}\right]^{-1} =$$
$$\left[\begin{matrix} \left(A_{tt} - A_{mt}A_{mm}^{-1}A_{tm}\right)^{-1} & -\left(A_{tt} - A_{mt}A_{mm}^{-1}A_{tm}\right)^{-1} A_{mt}A_{mm}^{-1} \\ -\left(A_{mm} - A_{tm}A_{tt}^{-1}A_{mt}\right)^{-1} A_{tm}A_{tt}^{-1} & \left(A_{mm} - A_{tm}A_{tt}^{-1}A_{mt}\right)^{-1} \end{matrix}\right] \tag{18}$$

and

$$A_{tt} = Q_{tel}^{\mathrm{T}}Q_{tel}, \quad A_{tm} = Q_{tel}^{\mathrm{T}}Q_{mic}$$
$$A_{mt} = Q_{mic}^{\mathrm{T}}Q_{tel}, \quad A_{mm} = Q_{mic}^{\mathrm{T}}Q_{mic} \tag{19}$$

Since

$$A_{tm} \neq 0, \quad A_{mt} \neq 0 \tag{20}$$

which means the U_{mic} and U_{tel} influence each other. To overcome it, we hope that $A_{tm} = 0$ and $A_{mt} = 0$. That means the common space shared by the different channel loading matrix are reserved once. Based on this ideas, we propose orthogonal subspace combination method by the Gram-Schmidt algorithm. Suppose the matrix to be combined is $U_0, U_1, U_2, \cdots, U_K$. The combination procedure is as follows

1. Initialization. Compute $Q_0, Q_1, Q_2, \cdots, Q_K$ (K is the number of combined subspace loading matrix) and let $Q_{com} = Q_0$
2. Orthogonal combination. For $i = 1, 2, \cdots, K$
   (a) Calculate a standard orthogonal basis $\{\eta_{com,1}, \eta_{com,2}, \cdots, \eta_{com,R_{u,com}}\}$ of Q_{com}.
   (b) For the Q_i to be combined, remove the part of Q_i lying in the span of $\{\eta_{com,1}, \eta_{com,2}, \cdots, \eta_{com,R_{u,com}}\}$ by the Gram-Schmidt orthogonalization and get Q_i'.
   (c) Combination. The new Q_{com} is $[Q_{com}, Q_i']$.

4   Experiments

Experiments were carried out on the SRE08 core task (male). We use SWB+SRE04 data to train the UBM and V, SRE05+SRE06+SRE08 Followup data to train the U.

A speech/silence segmentation was performed by a G.723.1 VAD detector. A 13-dimension MFCC was extracted. Delta and acceleration coefficients were appended. 39-dimension vectors were subjected to feature warping. UBMs with 1024 Gaussian components were gender-dependent.

First, we present the correlation matrix of the combined subspace, see the Fig 1. From the figure, we can see that the orthogonal subspace combination remove overlapping parts.

The experimental results on the SRE08 were given in the Table 1. From the this table, we find that the both of the combination methods are better than the mix data method. That's because the combination can also be seen as a fusion of statistical models. The combination method not only works for the cross channel

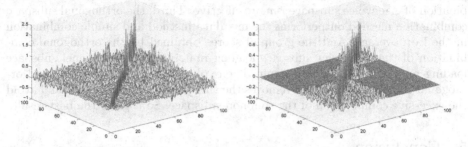

Fig. 1. The correlation matrix of the simple combination and orthogonal subspace combination

Table 1. Experimental results for the SRE08

Male	c1	c2	c3	c4	c5	c6	c7	c8
				U mix, *V* mix				
EER(%)	1.16	0.31	1.20	5.71	6.40	6.13	3.75	3.29
MDCF	0.0420	0.0121	0.0422	0.2999	*0.2511*	0.2737	0.1583	0.1341
				U mix, *V* simple				
EER(%)	1.31	0.31	1.38	5.86	*5.61*	*5.98*	3.39	3.07
MDCF	0.0510	0.0040	0.0526	*0.2149*	0.2831	0.2789	0.1529	*0.1207*
				U mix, *V* orth				
EER(%)	0.95	*0.00*	0.99	*5.27*	5.99	6.11	3.47	3.00
MDCF	0.0321	*0.0000*	0.0330	0.2405	0.2583	*0.2733*	0.1571	0.1297
				U simple, *V* mix				
EER(%)	1.55	0.41	1.61	6.12	*5.79*	*5.98*	3.6	3.5
MDCF	0.0789	0.0245	0.0817	0.2646	0.2762	0.2798	*0.1485*	0.1259
				U orth, *V* mix				
EER(%)	1.22	0.31	1.28	7.26	6.43	6.33	3.9	3.77
MDCF	0.0570	0.0040	0.0588	0.3220	0.2719	0.2830	0.1544	0.1308
				U orth, *V* orth				
EER(%)	*0.86*	*0.00*	*0.91*	5.47	5.88	6.07	*3.32*	*2.98*
MDCF	*0.0307*	*0.0000*	*0.0317*	0.2278	0.2563	0.2742	0.1571	0.1297

situation but also improves the system robustness. That's the reason why the combination method performs well even in the same channel trial. Second, the combination (both the simple combination and the orthogonal combination) of eigenvoice subspace loading matrix is more effective than the eigenchannel subspace loading matrix. A reasonable explanation is that the rank of eigenvoice subspace is low and the rank of eigenchannel subspace is a little high. So the combination of eigenvoice subspace is more effective. Third, the orthogonal subspace combination method outperforms the mix data method and simple combination method on average. And the group of scores obtained by the orthogonal combination of the eigenvoice subspace loading matrix and eigenchannel subspace loading matrix gives the best result. The explanation is that the proposed orthogonal combination method removes the subspace overlapping part and avoid the excessive computation of the common subspace. So it gives the best result.

5   Conclusion

JFA is one of the state-of-art system for the text-independent speaker recognition. The application of JFA in a multiple channel circumstance is studied in this paper. We analyze each procedure in the JFA system, make a reasonable approximation and find that the core computation is an oblique projection. Based on the findings, an orthogonal subspace combination is proposed to avoid excessive computation. Experimental results on the NIST SRE08 core task demonstrated the effectiveness of the presented method.

Acknowledgments. This work was supported by the China Postdoctoral Science Foundation under Grant No. 2012M510448, and in part by the National Natural Science Foundation of China under Grant No. 61005019, 61105017 and 90920302, and in part by the National High Technology Research and Development Program of China (863 Program) under Grant No. 2008AA040201.

References

1. Kenny, P., Ouellet, P., Dehak, N., Gupta, V., Dumouchel, P.: A Study of Inter-speaker Variability in Speaker Verification. IEEE Transactions on Audio, Speech, and Language Processing 16, 980–988 (2008)
2. Kenny, P., Boulianne, G., Ouellet, P., Dumouchel, P.: Joint Factor Analysis Versus Eigenchannels in Speaker Recognition. IEEE Transactions on Audio, Speech, and Language Processing 15, 1435–1447 (2007)
3. National Institute of Standards and Technology. NIST speaker recognition evaluation, http://www.itl.nist.gov/iad/mig/tests/spk/2008/index.html
4. Guo, W., Li, Y.J., Dai, L.R., Wang, R.H.: Factor Analysis and Space Assembling in Speaker Recognition. Acta Automatica Sinica 35(9), 1193–1198 (2009)
5. Vogt, R., Sridharan, S.: Experiments in Session Variability Modelling for Speaker Verification Acoustics. In: IEEE International Conference on Acoustics, Speech, and Signal Processing, pp. 897–900. IEEE Press, New York (2006)
6. Glembek, O., Burget, L., Dehak, N., Brummer, N., Kenny, P.: Comparison of scoring methods used in speaker recognition with Joint Factor Analysis. In: IEEE International Conference on Acoustics, Speech, and Signal Processing, pp. 4057–4060. IEEE Press, New York (2009)

Exploration of Phase and Vocal Excitation Modulation Features for Speaker Recognition

Ning Wang, P.C. Ching, and Tan Lee

Department of Electronic Engineering, The Chinese University of Hong Kong,
Hong Kong, P. R. China
{nwang,pcching,tanlee}@ee.cuhk.edu.hk

Abstract. Mel-frequency cepstral coefficients (MFCCs) are found closely related to the linguistic content of speech. Besides cepstral features, there are resources in speech, e.g, the phase and excitation source, are believed to contain useful properties for speaker discrimination. Moreover, the magnitude-based features are insufficient to provide satisfactory and robust speaker recognition accuracy in real-world applications when large variations exist between the development and application scenarios. AM-FM signal modeling technique offers an effective approach to characterize and analyze speech properties. This work is therefore motivated to capture the relevant phase and vocal excitation related modulation features in complementing with MFCCs. In the context of multi-band demodulation analysis, we present a novel parameterization of speech and vocal excitation signal. A pertinent representation for most dominant primary frequencies present in the speech signal is first built. It is then applied to frames of the speech signal to derive effective speaker-discriminative features. The source-related amplitude and phase quantities are also parameterized into feature vectors. The application of the features is assessed in the context of a standard speaker identification and verification system. Complementary correlation between MFCCs and the modulation features is revealed by system fusion on score level.

Keywords: Speaker recognition, phase information, excitation modulation features.

1 Introduction

Cepstral coefficients such as MFCCs are widely used in recognizing phonemes and discriminating speakers. However, it is found that they have bias towards the content of the speech unit [1], and are sensitive to the environmental variations. This motivates the exploration of new features that can offer assistances to the conventional cepstral coefficients in practical applications.

Auditory experiments show insensitivity of human ears to phase information in perceiving phonetic content of speech signal. However, the discarded phase information may provide useful acoustic cue for identifying individual speaker, this is especially useful for speaker recognition systems operated with degraded magnitude in adverse conditions. Short-time Fourier analysis provides important magnitude characteristics for speech, however, since it cannot effectively

W.-S. Zheng et al. (Eds.): CCBR 2012, LNCS 7701, pp. 251–259, 2012.
© Springer-Verlag Berlin Heidelberg 2012

capture the phase variation in speech, it is hard to quantify the phase spectrum and distinguish useful components contained therein. Previous studies on speech synthesis and coding have employed the multi-band demodulation framework to analyze and quantify speech components in terms of instantaneous amplitude and frequency [2], [3]. The modulation property of the vocal tract system has been involved in discriminating individual speakers. For example, the spectral centroids that depends on the frequency modulation component of signals by Paliwal *et al.* in [4], average of instantaneous frequencies weighted by amplitudes by Dimitriadis *et al.* in [5], etc. Estimation of the primary formants also involved the multi-band decomposition of speech signal in the frequency domain [6]. These researches inspire the exploration of proper representation for phase information in speech signals.

Significant observations was made on the amplitude and frequency modulations present in speech formants through speech signal analysis. Besides, in applications like speech analysis, synthesis, transformation, etc, the excitation signal waveform has been represented as a sum of sine waves [2]. Harmonic plus Noise Model (HNM), moreover, assumes that a speech signal is composed of a harmonic part and a noise part. The harmonic part, which accounts for the periodic structure of the voiced speech signal in HNM, is formulated by a sum of harmonically related sinusoidal components with discrete time-varying amplitude and phase quantities. These methods are primarily employed for pitch tracking [7], and are used in excitation coding technique. However, most of the modulation properties of the excitation source are excluded from speaker discrimination studies.

In this paper, we attempt to explore the speaker-relevant characteristics of the modulation phenomena in speech. Unlike the synthesis and coding systems, whose focus are speech intelligibility, waveform matching or transmission load, our method concentrates on characterizing the slow temporal (envelope and frequency) modulations in the speech signal, by using multi-band analysis and the nonlinear signal processing method. LP residues are taken as representatives of vocal source to provide excitation-related vocal characteristics in speech. We propose phase-related parameters, which are estimated from the multi-band AM-FM model of the speech signal, namely, Averaged Instantaneous Frequency of Speech (SAIF); as well as excitation modulation features from the residual signal notedly as Averaged Instantaneous Envelope of Residues (RAIE) and Averaged Instantaneous Frequency of Residues (RAIF), respectively. In a multi-stream speaker recognition system, these features are to be evaluated independently and used as the complementary speech features to MFCCs.

2   Derivation of Modulation Features

2.1   Representing Excitation Signal in AM-FM Model

Conventional studies on extracting vocal source-related characteristics for speaker recognition purposes, were largely connected with either pitch-periodicity, or the relevant harmonic structure properties, but consider less about the inter-correlation among the multi-components existing in an excitation signal. Excitation waveform modeling approaches, on the other hand, consider more about the components contained in an excitation signal. A common approach of getting these inclusive components are through nonlinear signal decomposition.

A *monocomponent* AM-FM signal is described by Equation 1 [8],

$$x(n) = A(n)cos[\Theta(n)], \tag{1}$$

where $A(n)$ denotes the instantaneous amplitude of the monocomponent signal and $\Theta(n)$ denotes its instantaneous phase.

In practice, *multicomponent* AM-FM signals are present everywhere in natural sounds, including human speech. Like that in the sinusoidal and harmonic plus noise models, the excitation signal in the AM-FM representation is interpreted as a multicomponent AM-FM signal.

2.2 Identifying Primary Frequencies in Speech

In the source-filter speech production model, a periodic impulse sequence is filtered with a glottal filter to produce the periodic part of the excitation signal, while the non-periodicity and the turbulent content are obtained by adding an additional white noise source. The resulting signal excites the vocal tract system, which is characterized by its formant structure. O'Shaughnessy pointed out that the spectral formant and harmonic structure models only spectral behavior of these speech properties [9]. The spectro-temporal characteristics of the primary speech elements therefore should also be addressed.

A typical formant in the vocal tract system is formulated to be a monocomponent AM-FM term $A(n)cos[\Theta(n)]$, as shown in Equation 1. Besides principal formants, the formant structure possesses a number of other components, for instance, the spread of spectral envelope and transitions between formants, etc. A pitch harmonic can also be interpreted as an AM-FM component. However, besides the formants, the pitch and its principal harmonics, there are other primary components that result from the interferences among all different harmonics and from the interactions within the vocal tract. Speaker-discriminative properties of a speech signal is therefore being possessed by these components. A speech signal can thus be written as a linear combination of amplitude and frequency modulated components which we called the primary components,

$$s(n) = \sum_{k=1}^{K} A_k(n)cos[\Theta_k(n)] + \eta(n) \tag{2}$$

$$= \sum_{k=1}^{K} A_k(n)cos\left\{\left[\Omega_c(k)n + \sum_{r=1}^{n} q_k(r)\right]\right\} + \eta(n),$$

where $A_k(n)$ denotes the instantaneous amplitude of the kth primary component and $\Theta_k(n)$ denotes its instantaneous phase. With the backward difference

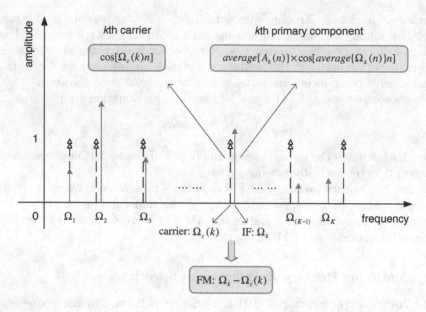

Fig. 1. A pictorial illustration for primary speech components under AM-FM framework

between $\Theta_k(n)$ and $\Theta_k(n-1)$, the instantaneous frequency (IF) sequence is defined as $\Omega_k(n) = \Omega_c(k) + q_k(n) = \frac{2\pi}{f_s} f_c(k) + q_k(n)$, where f_s is the sampling frequency, $q_k(n)$ is the frequency modulation (FM) component. $\eta(n)$ takes into account additive noise and errors of modeling, especially errors due to the finite summation. This model has also been described as the elementary waveform speech model [2].

Depending on the application, the number of primary components required for processing may vary. For coding purposes, synthesis-by-analysis coders based on the sinusoidal representation use a fairly large number of primary components, even for unvoiced sounds. But in the representation of vocal properties of speaker, the relevant components are usually identified with the formants and pitch harmonics.

In Figure 1, the primary AM-FM components extracted from multi-bands of a speech segment as well as the corresponding carriers are illustrated. For a clear presentation, the carriers are displayed in dash, and the identified AM-FM components are in real line. Each arrow in the plane expresses an AM-FM element, where its length stands for the mean value of segmental amplitude and the horizontal distance from origin indicates the averaged frequency quantity. The carriers are of unit amplitude for all frequency bands, while their frequencies are delivered by $\Omega_c(k)$, $k = 1, 2, \ldots, K$. When taking the kth subband for a close inspection, a space is discerned between the carrier and the detected center, it is therein noted as the FM component that measures the deviation of dominant frequency from carrier.

2.3   Modulation Feature Extraction

The process of computing the SAIF, RAIE and RAIF features is summarized as follows:

1. *Voicing decision*: The features are extracted from voiced speech $s(n)$ only. The voicing status is detected using Talkin's Robust Algorithm for Pitch Tracking [10].
2. *LP filter estimation*: To obtain the prediction filter coefficients $\{a_i\}, i = 1, 2, \ldots, p$, for yielding the LP residual signal.
3. *LP inverse filtering*: The residual signal $e(n)$ is obtained for each frame by taking LP inverse filtering. A voiced segment is divided into overlapping frames with 30 msec duration and 10 msec frame shift. To diminish intra-speaker variation, the amplitude of the residual segment is normalized to the range of $[-1, 1]$.
4. *Filter bank filtering*: Applying a bank of K Gamma-tone filters on both voiced speech segment $s(n)$ and the residual signal $e(n)$ to produce the sub-band signals. The center frequency $f_c(k)$ ranges from 4 kHz to 80Hz with k increase from 1 to K.
5. *Multi-band demodulation*: Teager's energy separation algorithm is employed in obtaining the instantaneous envelope (IE) sequence $|A(n)|$ and the instantaneous angular frequency $\Omega(n)$ (IF) on a frame-by-frame basis for each subband signal.
6. *Smoothing of the IE and IF sequence*: A 21-point median filter is applied to remove the abrupt impulses in the frames of IE and IF sequence.
7. *Frame averaging of the smoothed IE and IF*: An averaging operation is conducted on the smoothed IE and IF frames in each subband frame by frame. In this step, we remove the fluctuations of the IE and IF sequences, and track the most dominant amplitude and frequency components.

3   Performance Evaluation of Modulation Features

3.1   Speech Database: CU2C

CU2C is a dual-condition Cantonese speech database developed for speaker recognition research at the Chinese University of Hong Kong [11] in 2005 (http://dsp.ee.cuhk.edu.hk/html/cuothers.html). It contains parallel data collected under two different acoustic conditions: the wideband desktop microphone and public fixed-line telephone channel. In the recording process, each speaker was asked to read the same materials twice under the two recording conditions, one after the other immediately. These two kinds of data can be used separately to develop different applications. Thus, it provides a proper platform for the study of channel effects in speaker recognition systems. We use part of CU2C, which contains the speech data from 50 male speakers. Each speaker has 18 sessions of recordings which were made over a time span of 4-9 months. There are 6 utterances in each session, with each utterance contains a sequence of 14 randomly generated digits. The utterance length is about 5 to 6 seconds. The original sampling frequency of the microphone data was 16 kHz, and they were down-sampled to 8 kHz for use in this work.

3.2   Experimental Set-Up

For all speakers, 6 out of the 18 sessions are used to train the speaker models, and the remaining data are used for performance evaluation. The standard approach for UBM-GMM training is adopted. Separate systems are built based on the MFCCs, SAIF, RAIE and RAIF, respectively. The features SAIF, RAIE and RAIF are used as complementary counterparts of the MFCCs, respectively, in the three sets of experiments. The score-level fusion technique is used to combine the contributions of the systems by MFCCs and one of the modulation parameter sets. The final decision is determined by the overall combined score. In the identification tasks, the log-likelihood score of each test is a linear combination of the log-likelihood scores from the cepstral coefficients MFCCs and the modulation parameters SAIF/RAIE/RAIF, with weighting parameters w_C and w_M (i.e., $L = w_C L_C + w_M L_M$). Meanwhile, in the verification tasks, the fusion is performed on the log-likelihood ratio scores, that is, $\lambda = w_C \lambda_C + w_M \lambda_M$. In both tasks, w_C and w_M are related by $w_C + w_M = 1$. The weighing strategy is described as follows: initially, let $w_C = 0$, and $w_M = 1$. Next, we empirically increase w_C by a step of $\frac{1}{50}$, and repeat this for 50 times, with $w_M = 1 - w_C$ satisfied. Finally, we identify the optimum parameter set $[w_C, w_M]$ with the best recognition results.

For SID and SV tasks, the identification error rate (IDER) and equal error rate (EER) are used as the primary performance indicators, respectively.

3.3   Speaker Recognition Experimental Results

In Table 1 and Table 2, evaluation performance of the proposed modulation parameter sets SAIF, RAIE and RAIF in various SID/SV tasks are recorded. The standard MFCCs features we used contain 39 components: the log energy, 12 static coefficients, and their dynamic and acceleration coefficients.

3.4   Observations and Analysis

♦ **Recognition Performance**

It is found that the SAIF features perform well in both SID and SV tests. The best performed SAIF_40 parameter set is of comparable dimension with MFCCs, while it provides phase characteristics for individual speaker that are independent to the magnitude information carried by MFCCs. With a simple linear combination method, 25.00% and 23.68% relative reductions over that of MFCCs in IDER and EER have been achieved, respectively.

Table 1. Evaluation on excitation modulation features: IDER & EER (*in %*)

Feature configuration		IDER (%)	EER (%)
Baseline	MFCC	2.44	1.52
Effects of feature dimension	RAIE_20	40.72	13.17
	RAIF_20	35.11	10.42
	RAIE_40	27.28	9.46
	RAIF_40	19.67	8.01
Combination with MFCC	MFCC+RAIE_20	2.39	1.49
	MFCC+RAIF_20	2.28	1.24
	MFCC+RAIE_40	2.44	1.44
	MFCC+RAIF_40	**2.06**	**1.27**

Table 2. Evaluation on phase-related parameters: IDER & EER (*in %*)

Feature configuration		IDER (%)	EER (%)
Baseline	MFCC	2.44	1.52
Effects of feature dimension	SAIF_20	6.33	3.72
	SAIF_40	**4.78**	**2.70**
Supplementing cepstral features	MFCC+SAIF_40	**1.83**	**1.16**
Combining with source features	RAIE_40+SAIF_40	5.33	2.69
	RAIF_40+SAIF_40	4.61	2.65

◆ **Effects of Feature Dimension**

The modulation feature vectors derived under the multi-band demodulation framework are containing K parameters each. Considering there is no strict derivation to determine an optimal subband number K, and the frequency resolution by the 20-channel Gammatone filterbank can separate the harmonically related frequency components for the data we used, we initially determined the K to be 20, and then increase it to 40. When looking through either feature SAIF, RAIE or RAIF in terms of their individual performance, it is found that all of these parameters have attained improved results after their dimension was doubled.

◆ **Complementary Effects in Fusion**

Figure 2 gives a comparison on performance of the three sets of modulation parameters RAIE, RAIF and SAIF when working individually or together with MFCCs, respectively. It is shown that the performance of speaker recognition system is considerably improved when integrating the discriminative power of phase-related SAIF parameters and magnitude-specific MFCCs features.

Besides, Table 2 reveals the intriguing results of employing only modulation features in speaker recognition tasks. It is noted that the SAIF-RAIF fusion can

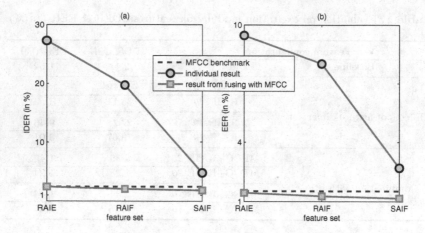

Fig. 2. Results of SAIF, RAIE and RAIF features when employed individually and combining with MFCC for : (a) SID experiments; (b). SV experiments

offer some assistance to improve the SAIF-only results, but the support received herein is much smaller than that from fusing with the MFCCs. While, fusing SAIF-RAIE is revealed ineffective in this case.

♦ **SAIF** *vs.* **RAIF**

When inspecting the effectiveness of the AIF parameter set derived from the residual signal or speech signal, i.e., the RAIF and SAIF features, it is found that the SAIF outperforms the other part, as indicated by Figure 2 vividly. Although under quite similar flow path in generation, the phase-related parameter set capturing primary frequencies present in speech signals apparently show higher discriminative power in discriminating different speakers. Taking them individually first, it is possible that a part of harmonics that conveyed by the RAIF set is also captured by the SAIF vectors, where the latter then take advantage of both vocal excitation- and formant-related information and win. Regarding the complementary employment with MFCCs, the SAIF features are obviously of greater predominance than RAIF. Finally, the usefulness of effectively extracted phase characteristics of speech is confirmed.

4   Conclusion

Magnitude feature-oriented front-ends provide significant information for understanding the speech content, but neglect the potential of using phase information and vocal excitation characteristics as speaker representatives. In alleviating the deficiency of spectral features in providing sufficient and reliable recognition performance under various application scenarios. This paper made efforts to explore distinctive and effective speaker-specific phase and excitation-related properties to complement with conventional magnitude-based features. A novel formulation for representing the speech and vocal excitation signal in terms of their primary amplitude and frequency components in the multi-band decomposition framework is first built. The most dominant frequencies present in the speech signal as well as the primary amplitude-frequency components in the excitation signal are then parameterized into phase- and excitation-related feature vectors, respectively. Through simulation tests under standard speaker recognition protocol, it is revealed that the modulation features are capable of: (1). capturing the phase and vocal differences among speakers; (2). offering consistent complementary assistance in recognizing speakers to spectral features; and (3). leading to new perspective in exploiting alternative and comprehensive speech representatives for speaker discrimination purposes.

References

1. Chan, W.N., Zheng, N., Lee, T.: Discrimination power of vocal source and vocal tract related features for speaker segmentation. IEEE Trans. Audio, Speech, and Language Processing 15(6), 1884–1892 (2007)
2. Mcaulay, R.J., Quatieri, T.F.: Speech analysis/synthesis based on a sinusoidal representation. IEEE Trans. Acoustics, Speech, and Signal Processing 34(4), 744–754 (1986)
3. Stylianou, Y.: Harmonic plus noise models for speech, combined with statistical methods, for speech and speaker modification. PhD Thesis, Ecole Nationale Supérieure des Télécommunications (1996)
4. Chen, J., Huang, Y., Li, Q., Paliwal, K.K.: Recognition of noisy speech using dynamic spectral subband centroids. IEEE Signal Processing Letters 11(2), 258–261 (2004)
5. Dimitriadis, D.V., Maragos, P., Potamianos, A.: Robust AM-FM features for speech recognition. IEEE Signal Processing Letters 12(9), 621–624 (2005)
6. Potamianos, A., Maragos, P.: Speech formant frequency and bandwidth tracking using multiband energy demodulation. J. Acoustical Society of America 99(6), 3795–3806 (1996)
7. Mcaulay, R.J., Quatieri, T.F.: Pitch estimation and voicing detection based on a sinusoidal speech model. In: Proc. IEEE, pp. 249–252 (1990)
8. Maragos, P., Kaiser, J.F., Quatieri, T.F.: Energy separation in signal modulations with application to speech analysis. IEEE Trans. Signal Processing 41(10), 3024–3051 (1993)
9. O'Shaughnessy, D.: Speech communication: human and machine. Addison-Wesley Publishing Co., Reading (1987)
10. Talkin, D.: A robust algorithm for pitch tracking. In: Kleijn, W.B., Paliwal, K.K. (eds.) Speech Coding and Synthesis. Elsevier (1995)
11. Zheng, N., Qin, C., Lee, T., Ching, P.C.: CU2C: A dual-condition Cantonese speech database for speaker recognition applications. In: Proc. Oriental-COCOSDA, pp. 67–72 (2005)

Cross-View Action Recognition Based on Statistical Machine Translation

Jing Wang and Huicheng Zheng

School of Information Science and Technology, Sun Yat-sen University
135 West Xingang Road, 510275 Guangzhou, China
wangj63@mail2.sysu.edu.cn, zhenghch@mail.sysu.edu.cn

Abstract. In this paper, we propose an approach for human action recognition from different views in a knowledge transfer framework. Each frame in an action is considered as a sentence in an article. We believe that, though the appearance for the same action is quite different in different views, there exists some translation relationship between them. To abstract the relationship, we use the IBM Model 1 in statistical machine translation and the translation probabilities for vocabularies in the source view to those in the target view can be obtained from the training data. Consequently, we can translate an action based on the maximum a posteriori criterion. We validated our method on the public multi-view IXMAS dataset and obtained promising results compared to the state-of-the-art knowledge transfer based methods.

Keywords: action recognition, cross view, knowledge transfer, IBM Model 1.

1 Introduction

Human action recognition has drawn much attention in computer vision over the past several decades. It has a wide spectrum of potential applications, such as activities monitoring in surveillance scenarios, content-based video retrieval, athletic performance analysis, advanced man-machine interface, and so on [4].

In general, actions are often observed in arbitrary viewpoints due to varying relative positions of cameras and actors in practical applications. View robust human action recognition from video becomes a core unsolved computer vision problem. First, the appearance of human actions changes dramatically with viewpoints. Second, activities involve information across time and across the body, different actors appear to have different somatotypes and speed of behavior. Third, it is difficult to transduce the configuration of body, and it is hard to obtain a good description of activity across views [3].

There are several possible solutions. The most brutal approach is to train a separate classifier for each view. However, it is costly to get sufficient labeled samples for each view. Another one is based on the geometric property of actors and cameras which infers three-dimensional scene structure and derives view-adaptive action descriptors while suffers from the problem of computational cost [9,12]. Recently, two new categories of methods have been proposed. One is to find the

W.-S. Zheng et al. (Eds.): CCBR 2012, LNCS 7701, pp. 260–267, 2012.

view-independent features such as temporal self-similarities of action sequence and the view stability is demonstrated empirically [5,6]. One is based on the concept of knowledge transfer by adapting features in the source view to a target view where the task of recognition will be performed and exhibits promising performance [3,7].

In this paper, we transfer the view knowledge by a different approach that significantly relaxes the requirement of preset parameters and the global temporal information of the action will be taken into consideration in our work. Different from the work in [7], though we also consider action models in different views as articles written in different languages, we treat articles as collections of sentences as opposed to bags of words.

In order to abstract the transfer relationship between two views, we use the method used in statistical machine translation (SMT). Specifically, we choose the IBM Model 1 [1,10] to model the translation probabilities for vocabularies in the source view to those in the target view. The probabilities can be obtained by EM algorithm collecting fractional counts from the training data and update them iteratively. Given the translation probabilities and training data, the translation can be carried out based on maximum a posteriori criterion.

The remaining parts of this paper are organized as follows. Section 2 introduces the knowledge transfer model and the theory of the IBM Model 1. Section 3 applies the IBM Model 1 in action translation and proposes the translation method. Experimental results of the proposed method and comparison to other state-of-the-art methods are presented in Section 4. Finally, this paper is concluded by Section 5.

2   Knowledge Transfer Model

The idea behind statistical machine translation comes from information theory. IBM models are seminal and form the basis for many complex SMT models [10]. Consider the task of translating a French sentence into English. The model can be represented as a noisy-channel model:

$$e^* = \arg\max_{e \in E} p(e)p(f|e). \tag{1}$$

There are two components [10]:

1. The *language model* $p(e)$ which determines the probability for any sentence e in English.
2. The *translation model* $p(f|e)$ which assigns a conditional probability to any French/English pair of sentences.

Given the two components of the model, the translation result can be determined by (1). And the task of translation becomes to find the *language model* $p(e)$ and the *translation model* $p(f|e)$. Note that the priori probability $p(e)$ can be estimated from the training corpus. The remainder of the note will focus on the following question: how can we define the translation model $p(f|e)$.

2.1   IBM Model 1

We now turn to the problem of modeling the conditional probability $p(f|e)$ for any pair of French/English sentences, denoted as f and e, respectively. Given an English sentence e with the length of l, the translation model involves a two-step choice: first, choose the length m of the French sentence; second, choose the words $f_1, f_2, \cdots, f_m$ composing the French sentence. Thus we have

$$p(f|e) = \epsilon(m|l)p(f_1, f_2, \cdots, f_m|e_1, e_2, \cdots, e_l, m). \tag{2}$$

$\epsilon(m|l)$ can be regarded as a variable following some distribution.

It is difficult to find the value of $p(f_1, f_2, \cdots, f_m|e_1, e_2, \cdots, e_l, m)$ directly. So a set of alignment variables $a_1, a_2, \cdots, a_m$ are introduced. Each alignment variable a_j corresponds to a French word in the sentence and can take any value in $\{0,1,2,\cdots,l\}$. These alignment variables specify the alignment of each French word to the word in the English sentence. With the help of alignment variables, we have

$$p(f|e, m) = \sum_{a_1=0}^{l} \cdots \sum_{a_m=0}^{l} p(f, a_1, a_2, \cdots, a_m|e, m). \tag{3}$$

Following the definition of IBM Model 2 in [1,10], (3) can be further expressed as

$$p(f|e, m) = \prod_{i=1}^{m} \sum_{j=0}^{l} a(j|i, l, m)t(f_i|e_j), \tag{4}$$

where $a(j|i, l, m)$ is the conditional probability of the alignment for the i-th word in the French sentence to the j-th word in the English sentence, $t(f_i|e_j)$ can be interpreted as the conditional probability of generating French word f_i from English word e_j. Note that $j \in \{0,1,2,\cdots l\}$ and e_0 is defined as a special NULL word. See [1,10] for more details about the IBM models.

In IBM Model 1, the $a(j|i, l, m)$ in IBM Model 2 is considered as a uniform distribution and then we have $a(j|i, l, m) = (1 + l)^{-1}$. As we can see from (2) and (4),

Algorithm 1. The procedure of action recognition with IBM Model 1.

Objective: Given a set of parallel frames $\{f^{(k)}, e^{(k)}\}_{k=1}^{K}$ of unlabeled shared activities, the set of training actions $\{a_m^s\}_{m=1}^{M}$ and the orphan action a^t, recognize a^t.

---

1. Estimate the translation probabilities $t(f|e)$ for vocabularies in the source view to those in the target view with $\{f^{(k)}, e^{(k)}\}_{k=1}^{K}$ by the IBM Model 1 introduced in Section 2.
2. For each training action a_m^s, calculate the conditional probability $p(a^t|a_m^s)$ based on (8).
3. Choose the class of a_m^s according to (7) as the class of a^t.

finding out the best translation model $t(f|e)$ is a chicken-and-egg problem. So the EM algorithm is employed to solve this problem. The objective function to be optimized is the log-likelihood function of the observed parallel corpus $\{f^{(k)}, e^{(k)}\}_{k=1}^{n}$, it is a function of the translation model $t(f|e)$.

$$L(t) = \log(\prod_{k=1}^{n} p(f^{(k)}|e^{(k)}, m_k; t)) = \sum_{k=1}^{n} \log p(f^{(k)}|e^{(k)}, m_k; t). \quad (5)$$

As discussed in [10], $L(t)$ is convex and the algorithm can converge to the global optimum of the function.

3   Action Model Transfer

In this section, we will introduce how to apply the IBM Model to translate actions across views. Just like [3,7], we consider two types of activities: the shared activities observed in both *source* and *target* view, and the orphan activities that are only observed in the *source* view. We treat the shared activities as the parallel corpus mentioned above. Note that we do not need any label information about the parallel corpus.

In order to represent actions as corpus, we extract descriptors in each frame and each frame of the action is represented as a histogram of visual words. The frame in source view and the corresponding one in target view compose a pair of sentences. By collecting the frame-based pairs of sentences for all shared actions, we get a large set of parallel corpus and the translation probabilities can be estimated by IBM Model 1 introduced in section 2.

3.1   Action Translation

Once the translation model for the source and target view is obtained, the action translation can be carried out based on (1). Specifically, we regard each frame as one sentence, and the action sequence can be considered as an article composed by several sentences. Consider two actions $a^s = (s_1^s, s_2^s, \cdots, s_v^s)$ and $a^t = (s_1^t, s_2^t, \cdots, s_u^t)$ in source and target view, respectively. (1) can be rewritten as

$$\max_{a^s} p(a^s|a^t) = \max_{a^s} p(a^t|a^s)p(a^s). \quad (6)$$

Given the parallel shared activities, $p(a^s)$ can be considered as uniform distribution. And (6) becomes

$$\max_{a^s} p(a^s|a^t) = \max_{a^s} p(a^t|a^s). \quad (7)$$

The conditional probability of two actions is

$$p(a^t|a^s) = \sum_b p(a^t, b|a^s) = \epsilon(u|v) \prod_{i=1}^{u} \sum_{j=1}^{v} p(j|i, u, v)p(s_i^t|s_j^s), \quad (8)$$

where $b = (b_1, b_2, \cdots b_u)$ is a set of alignment variables for the frames in the v-frame source view action to those in the u-frame target view action. $\epsilon(u|v)$ is the probability of the target view action of length u conditioned on the source view action of length v. s_j^s, s_i^t are the j-th frame and i-th frame in the source view action and the target view action, respectively. Consider the relative position of the mapped pair of sentences in two articles, a sentence at the beginning of the source language article has a very high probability to be translated into a sentence also at the beginning of the target language article, and vice versa. Based on this fact, we can assume that $p(j|i, u, v)$ follows a Gaussian distribution. The conditional probability of two sentences $p(s_i^t|s_j^s)$ can be calculated based on (4).

Given an orphan action a^t to be recognized, we just search an action a^s in the training samples according to (7) as the result. The procedure of action recognition is summarized in Algorithm 1.

| cam0 | cam1 | cam2 | cam3 | cam4 |

Fig. 1. Exemplar frames from IXMAS data set. Each column corresponds to one view and each row shows changes across views.

4   Experiments

To validate the performance of our transfer model, we test the model on the IXMAS multi-view action data set [13]. There are 11 actions performed 3 times by 12 actors and recorded in 5 views simultaneously. The action sequences are time aligned, and silhouette information of the actors is also provided. Figure 1 shows some examples of the actions in the data set.

In order to demonstrate the performance of our approach versus the state-of-the-art knowledge transfer methods, we compare our approach to the work in [3,7] and follow the same *leave-one-action-out* strategy for choosing the orphan action. The results are averaged over all action classes. We test our model on the descriptors used in [3] and [7], respectively.

4.1   Comparison to [3]

The descriptor used in [3] is a histogram of the silhouette and of the optical flow. Given the bounding box of the actors, the optical flow is computed using Lucas-Kanade algorithm [8]. The feature consists of three channels: horizontal optical flow, vertical optical flow, and silhouette. The feature extraction window is divided into 2×2 sub-windows, and each sub-window is further divided into 18 pie slices each covering 20 degrees. The feature values are integrated over the domain of every slice. The descriptors are computed by PCA on the concatenate features of the three channels. In order to capture the temporal information, the features of the previous and next frame windows are stacked together with those of current frame window. These descriptors are also quantized into visual words. See [11] for more details.

Table 1. Performance comparison of our method to the approach in [3]. The rows and columns correspond to source and target views, respectively.

%	Camera 0		Camera 1		Camera 2		Camera 3		Camera 4	
	ours	[3]	ours	[3]	ours	[3]	ours	[3]	ours	[3]
Cam0	-	-	**86**	72	**68**	61	**72**	62	**53**	30
Cam1	**81**	69	-	-	**69**	64	65	**68**	**53**	41
Cam2	**65**	62	67	67	-	-	**75**	67	**66**	43
Cam3	**67**	63	67	**72**	**78**	68	-	-	**48**	44
Cam4	**58**	51	54	**55**	**64**	51	44	**53**	-	-

In the comparison experiment, we choose a different number of visual words. 500 clusters are chosen for k-means clustering. The results are shown in Table 1. Our approach gets relatively large improvement in 15 out of 20 pairs of views and achieves an average increase of 6.8% on the recognition accuracy of all pairs of views. There are two reasons for this improvement at least. First, the split-based descriptor in [3] is based on the assumption that the split of clusters in the target view has the same cell structure as that in the source view. The descriptors of the corresponding frames in the source view and target view lie on the same side of the corresponding hyperplanes in the two views, respectively. This strict constraint leads to less accurate estimation of relationship between vocabularies in the two views. In contrast, our method models the relationship in a looser manner and the relationship is based on the co-occurrence of visual words in the two views. Second, actions are represented as codeword-based descriptors in [3] that ignore the global temporal information of actions, which is considered in our method.

4.2 Comparison to [7]

The descriptor used in [7] is the gradient-based descriptor for spatio-temporal volumes around the interest points. This descriptor is first proposed in [2]. Specifically, the gradient-based descriptor is represented by the flatted gradient of the volumes around the spatio-temporal interest points. The local interest point detector consists of two components: a 2D spatial Gaussian filter followed by a 1D temporal Gabor filter. The interest points are detected at the local maximum responses. Then the spatio-temporal volumes around the points are extracted and gradient-based descriptors are computed and the dimension is reduced by PCA. These descriptors are further quantized to visual words by k-means clustering. Afterwards, each frame can be represented as a histogram of visual words which is regarded as a sentence in IBM Model.

Table 2. Performance comparison of our method to the approach in [7]. The rows and columns correspond to source and target views, respectively.

%	Camera 0		Camera 1		Camera 2		Camera 3		Camera 4	
	ours	[7]	ours	[7]	ours	[7]	ours	[7]	ours	[7]
Cam0	-	-	**90.7**	75.5	**69.3**	64.4	65.9	**67.7**	60.1	**66.0**
Cam1	**92.0**	75.7	-	-	**72.1**	64.2	58.5	**68.1**	**61.0**	56.0
Cam2	**73.9**	70.3	**76.6**	66.3	-	-	**80.3**	71.3	**79.7**	62.4
Cam3	70.6	**73.7**	63.1	**65.6**	**83.0**	71.3	-	-	49.7	**58.0**
Cam4	**71.7**	71.3	**69.4**	66.3	**78.5**	70.9	55.7	**63.6**	-	-

The parameters we choose in the experiment are the same as those in [7]. Specifically, 100-dimensional descriptors are learned using PCA, all descriptors are quantized into 1000 visual words by k-means clustering. $\epsilon(m|l)$ and $\epsilon(u|v)$ are assumed to follow uniform distributions in (2) and (8), respectively. $p(j|i,u,v)$ is a Gaussian distribution and we set $\mu = i\frac{v}{u}$, $\sigma = 1$. The results are shown in Table 2. Our approach gets promising results in most of the pairs of views and achieves an average increase of 3.7% on the recognition accuracy of all pairs of views. Compared with the method in [7], our method relaxes the requirement of preset parameters while the results in [7] have a close dependence on the parameter preset for calculating the affinity matrix. The bag-of-words model used in [7] also ignores the global temporal information of the actions. For example, consider the actions *scratch head* and *wave*. Both of the two actions are composed of the sub-actions *raise hand* and *put down hand*. Given one frame of either of the two sub-actions, it is difficult to distinguish which sub-action the frame belongs to ignoring the relationship with neighboring frames. Since the bag-of-words-based descriptor is a histogram of frame-based visual words, the descriptors of *scratch head* and *wave* may be similar to that of *cross arm* which only contains *raise hand* of the two sub-actions. This is the reason why our method achieves better results at 61% and 59% on average for the actions *scratch head* and *wave* respectively even when ours only considers the interest point feature compared to the fusion features in [7].

5   Conclusion

In this paper, we propose an approach for cross-view action recognition, in which the relationship between two views is modeled by statistical machine translation model. The IBM Model 1 is employed to estimate the translation probabilities of vocabularies in the source view to those in the target view. The recognition of actions is based on the maximum a posteriori criterion. Experiments on the IXMAS dataset verified the superior performance of the proposed method compared to the state-of-the-art knowledge transfer based methods.

Acknowledgements. This work was supported by National Natural Science Foundation of China (61172141), Specialized Research Fund for the Doctoral

Program of Higher Education (20080558-1005), and Fundamental Research Funds for the Central Universities (09lgpy52).

References

1. Brown, P.F., Pietra, V.J., Pietra, S.A.D., Mercer, R.L.: The mathematics of statistical machine translation: parameter estimation. Computational Linguistics 19, 263–311 (1993)
2. Dollar, P., Rabaud, V., Cottrell, G., Belongie, S.: Behavior recognition via sparse spatio-temporal features. In: IEEE International Workshop on VS-PETS (2005)
3. Farhadi, A., Tabrizi, M.K.: Learning to Recognize Activities from the Wrong View Point. In: Forsyth, D., Torr, P., Zisserman, A. (eds.) ECCV 2008, Part I. LNCS, vol. 5302, pp. 154–166. Springer, Heidelberg (2008)
4. Ji, X., Liu, H.: Advances in view-invariant human motion analysis: a review. IEEE Transactions on System, Man, and Cybernetics, Part C: Applications and Reviews 40(1), 13–24 (2010)
5. Junejo, I.N., Dexter, E., Laptev, I., Pérez, P.: Cross-View Action Recognition from Temporal Self-similarities. In: Forsyth, D., Torr, P., Zisserman, A. (eds.) ECCV 2008, Part II. LNCS, vol. 5303, pp. 293–306. Springer, Heidelberg (2008)
6. Junejo, I.N., Dexter, E., Laptev, I., Pérez, P.: View-independent action recognition from temporal self-similarities. IEEE Transactions on Pattern Analysis and Machine Intelligence 33(1), 172–185 (2011)
7. Liu, J., Shah, M., Kuipers, B., Savarese, S.: Cross-view action recognition via view knowledge transfer. In: IEEE Conference on Computer Vision and Pattern Recognition (2011)
8. Lucas, B., Kanade, T.: An iterative image registration technique with an application to stereo vision. In: International Joint Conference on Artificial Intelligence, vol. 2, pp. 674–679 (1981)
9. Lv, F., Nevatia, R.: Single view human action recognition using key pose matching and Viterbi path searching. In: IEEE Conference on Computer Vision and Pattern Recognition (2007)
10. Collins, M.: Statistical machine translation: IBM models 1 and 2, http://www.cs.columbia.edu/~cs4705/notes/ibm12.pdf
11. Tran, D., Sorokin, A.: Human Activity Recognition with Metric Learning. In: Forsyth, D., Torr, P., Zisserman, A. (eds.) ECCV 2008, Part I. LNCS, vol. 5302, pp. 548–561. Springer, Heidelberg (2008)
12. Weinland, D., Boyer, E., Ronfard, R.: Action recognition from arbitrary views using 3D exemplars. In: IEEE International Conference on Computer Vision (2007)
13. Weinland, D., Ronfard, R., Boyer, E.: Free viewpoint action recognition using motion history volumes. In: Computer Vision and Image Understanding, vol. 104, pp. 249–257 (2006)

A Comparative Study of Several Feature Extraction Methods for Person Re-identification

Zhao Yang, Lianwen Jin, and Dapeng Tao

College of Electronic and Information,
South China University of Technology, China
yangdxng100@126.com,
{lianwen.jin,dapeng.tao}@gmail.com

Abstract. Extracting meaningful features from images is essential for many computer vision tasks. In this paper, we propose color histogram based on locality-constrained linear coding (LLC) feature representation for person re-identification. We compare the performance of five features with five metric learning methods for person re-identification. Extensive experiments on two publically available benchmarking datasets are carried out to compare the performance of various features. There are two contributions in this study. First, we present a new feature extraction technique which integrates the LLC and color histogram for person re-identification. Second, we conduct quantitative and comparative experiments of various feature extractions in the context of person re-identification and some useful conclusions are made.

Keywords: Person re-identification, Feature extraction, SIFT, PHOG, LBP, HSV histogram, Lab histogram.

1 Introduction

Person re-identification means to match observations of the same person across different time and possibly different cameras. There are two steps for person re-identification. First, visual appearance features are computed from train and test images. Second, the distance between each pair of potential matches is measured, which is then used to for ranking [1]. It is fundamentally challenging because of the large visual appearance changes such as variations of illumination conditions, poses and occlusions. To address these challenges, most previous approaches aim to model and seek optimal metric learning algorithms [14], [10]. However, there are few reports on the feature extraction methods for person re-identification.

In this paper, we focus on the first step of person re-identification, namely, extracting distinctive and reliable visual features. Also we make comparison between several features widely used in the field of computer vision. Among them, SIFT feature is extracted for its excellent performance shown in many computer vision tasks. To capture texture information we extract PHOG [8] and LBP [9] features, and we introduce LLC coding [6] into HSV and Lab histograms to describe color cues. At

W.-S. Zheng et al. (Eds.): CCBR 2012, LNCS 7701, pp. 268–277, 2012.

last all the features are concatenated to a discriminative and comprehensive feature representation for person re-identification.

For conducting a fair comparison of different features, five metrics are used in the experiments. Metric calculation is very troublesome if the dimensionality of the input data is high. Thus the principal component analysis (PCA) is used to reduce the dimensionality.

Extensive and comparative experiments using these features with different metric learning algorithms are conducted on two publically available large person re-identification datasets, including the VIPeR [2] and ETHZ [3] datasets. During the experiments, the similar and dissimilar pairs (see Fig. 1) in the train set are used to learning a Mahalanobis metric, which is used for metric ranking in the test sets. The cumulative matching characteristic (CMC) curve is used for evaluate the performance of different features. Some assessments of comparative results are reported at last.

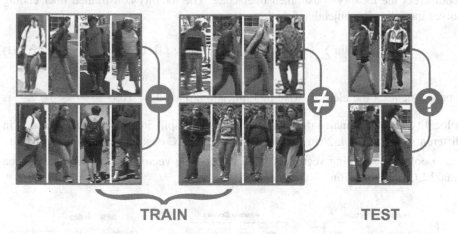

Fig. 1. Examples of similar and dissimilar pairs in VIPeR dataset. These similar and dissimilar pairs constitute the train set, and the rest are test set.

The remainder of the paper is organized as follows. Section 2 describes the feature extraction methods used for comparison. Section 3 describes several widely used metric learning algorithms. Section 4 provides comparative experiments of the proposed feature extraction methods on the two datasets. Section 5 concludes the paper.

2   Feature Extraction

Before describing the feature extraction, we first have a simple overview on feature representation and introduce an impressive feature representation method with excellent performance.

For many computer vision tasks, features extracted from the images (low level features) are not used directly. In general there is a feature representation process for better performance. Several feature representation methods are proposed in the recent literatures, such as SPM [4], ScSPM [5] and LLC [6]. Compared to SPM and ScSPM, LLC has achieved superior performance in many fields [6]. So we adopt LLC feature representation for SIFT and color histogram features in this paper. To explicate the process of feature extraction in person re-identification, we give in the following a short description of the LLC representation.

A typical step of the LLC approach is illustrated in Fig. 2. First, the input image is partitioned into many patches in regular girds and low level feature (such as SIFT and color histogram) is extracted from each patch. Let $\mathbf{X} = [\mathbf{x}_1, \mathbf{x}_2, ..., \mathbf{x}_N] \in \mathbb{R}^{D \times N}$ stands for dense feature descriptors from an image. All the low level features are used to compute a codebook ($\mathbf{B} = [\mathbf{b}_1, \mathbf{b}_2, ..., \mathbf{b}_K] \in \mathbb{R}^{D \times K}$) using K-means or some other methods [6]. In this paper, we just use K-means to train the codebook for simplicity. Second, for each feature of the patches, K nearest neighbors ($\mathbf{B}$) of it are used to reconstruct the locality-constrained liner code. The locality-constrained liner coding solves the following objection function.

$$\min_{\mathbf{C}} \sum_{i=1}^{N} \left\| \mathbf{x}_i - \mathbf{Bc}_i \right\|^2 + \lambda \left\| \mathbf{d}_i \odot \mathbf{c}_i \right\|^2, \, s.t. \, \mathbf{1}^T \mathbf{c}_i = 1, \, \forall i \tag{1}$$

where $\odot$ denotes the element-wise multiplication, and $\mathbf{d}_i = \exp(\dfrac{dist(\mathbf{x}_i, \mathbf{B})}{\sigma}) \in \mathbb{R}^K$ is a locality adaptor. Finally the image of patches is split into $2^l \times 2^l$ sub-regions in different scale $l = 0, 1, 2$ in a pyramid style, and LLC descriptors in a sub-region are max pooled to a pooling vector. Then all the pooling vectors are concatenated as the final LLC representation for the image.

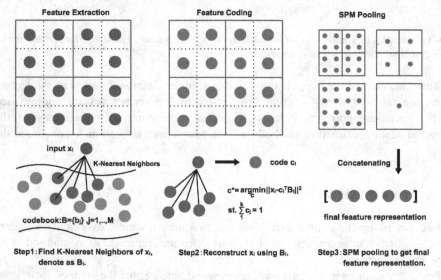

Fig. 2. A Flowchart of LLC Coding

2.1   SIFT Feature

SIFT [7] is a feature which has been widely used in many methods of computer vision tasks. So we try to test the performance of this feature for person re-identification. To get better performance, LLC feature representation is used.

2.2   PHOG and LBP Features

We capture texture information by PHOG [8] and LBP [9]. PHOG was originally proposed by Bosch [8] and gets widely application in general object classification. It extracts HOG features in a pyramid style and represents the local shape and the relationship of the shape of an image. LBP extracts features by subdividing an image into small regions (patches), and then creating a histogram for each patch by analyzing pixel to pixel intensity changes within each other. In essence, LBP extract the unique textural features of an image.

2.3   Color Histogram Features

Histogram is a widely used method in computer vision because of it robust and effectiveness. However there are two main drawbacks for the histogram approach: lack of spatial information and the tradeoff between high quantization errors with coarse binning and sparseness with fine binning. To solve this problem, we introduce LLC coding into histogram.

For person re-identification, we compute HSV and Lab histograms to describe color features. First, an input image is transformed into HSV color space and Lab color space separately and portioned into regular small patches. Second HSV histogram and Lab histogram are calculated over each path with 8 color bins for each channel, and three channels are connected to a 24 dimensional vector respectively. Last, LLC coding is used to get the final HSV histogram and Lab histogram feature descriptors.

3   Mahalanobis Metric Learning

The person re-identification experiment is essentially the metric calculations of different persons. The results may differ greatly with different metrics even if using the same features. Therefore, to make a fair comparison of different features, we should use multiple metrics.

In the field of person re-identification, metric learning is well-studied [1], [10]. Although Euclidean distance provides a simple and mathematically convenient metric, there is no reason to assume that it is optimal for the task. Therefore, there has been a great deal of research devoted to the design of algorithm for learning an optimal metric [10], [11], [12]. A typical class of distance functions that show good generalization performance for many machine learning problems is Mahalanobis metric learning. In general, a Mahalanobis distance metric measures the squared distance between the data points x_i and x_j :

$$d_M^2(\mathbf{x}_i, \mathbf{x}_j) = (\mathbf{x}_i - \mathbf{x}_j)^T \mathbf{M}(\mathbf{x}_i - \mathbf{x}_j), \tag{2}$$

where $\mathbf{M} \geq 0$ is a positive semi definite matrix and $\mathbf{x}_i, \mathbf{x}_j \in \mathbb{R}^d$ is a pair of samples (i, j). There are many metric learning algorithms to learn the $\mathbf{M}$ matrix. These include Large Margin Nearest Neighbor Learning (LMNN) [11], Information Theoretic Metric Learning (ITML) [12] and Keep it Simple and Straightforward (KISS) [10]. In this paper, we choose Euclidean distance, Mahalanobis metric (In this it means the $\mathbf{M}$ matrix which is calculated as the inverse of the covariance matrix of sample, and it is abbreviated to MAHAL in the experiments), LMNN, ITML and KISS for comparative experiments.

4   Experiments

In this section we conduct quantitative and comparative experiments of different features with five metric learning algorithms. The main goal is to find which feature is more discriminative for person re-identification.

For LLC coding, we extract low level feature of 8×8 pixel patches over a grid with 4 pixels throughout the experiments, and the pyramid level is $L = 2$. We perform K-means clustering of all patches from the whole dataset to form a codebook (dictionary), and the vocabulary size of the codebook is $M = 1024$. The length of the final LLC representation is $(1 + 4 + 16) \times 1024 = 21504$. For the efficiency of metric calculation we perform dimensionality reduction by PCA to a 34 dimensional subspace. Because the influence of the dimensionality is not too critical, the reduced dimensionality is 34 throughout the experiments for a fair comparison.

Two challenging datasets are used for comparative evaluation. We do our comparative experiments follow the evaluation protocol defined in [13]. First, we split the image pairs into two equivalent parts. One is to set up the training and the other is used for test. The training set is composed of relevant pairs and irrelevant pairs. A pair of images of each person form a relevant pair and one image of him/her and one another person in the train set form an irrelevant pair. The test set is composed of a gallery set and a probe set. The gallery set consists of one image of each person, and the rest images are used for probe set.

For evaluation of the performance of various features, we use the average Cumulative Match Characteristic (CMC) curves with five metrics to show the rank matching rates. A rank r matching rate indicates the percentage of the probe images with correct matches found in the top r ranks against the gallery image. To get reasonable statistical significances, each trial is repeated ten times.

4.1   Experiments on VIPeR Dataset

We first compare the features performance on VIPeR dataset, which is presented by Gray *et al.* [2]. The VIPeR dataset is a person re-identification dataset consisting of 632 pedestrian image pairs taken from two camera views with normalized size at

64×128 pixels. The low-resolution images exhibit significant variations in pose, viewpoint and also considerable changes in illumination. Most of the matched image pairs contain a viewpoint change of about 90 or 180 degrees, making person re-identification very challenging. Some examples are given in Fig. 1.

In the following part, we give CMC results for each feature descriptor.

SIFT. All images are transformed into gray scale and resized to be no larger than 300×300 pixels with preserved ratio. For each patch the sift descriptor is extracted with a dimensionality of 128, and then LLC coding is used to get the final sift descriptor (called dense sift) of an image. Last the LLC dense sift features are projected into a 34 dimensional subspace by PCA. The matching experiment is done for ten times. In Fig. 3 we report the average CMC curves using various metric learning algorithms.

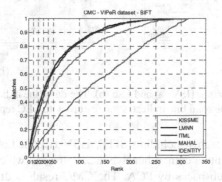

Fig. 3. Average CMC curves for SIFT feature using five metric, in which IDENTIY means the M matrix in Mahalanobis metric is identity matrix

PHOG and LBP. The average CMC curves for PHOG feature and LBP feature using five metric learning algorithms are reported in Fig. 4.

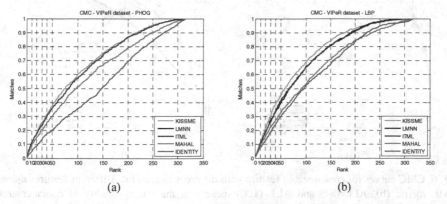

(a)   (b)

Fig. 4. CMC curves for feature PHOG (a) and LBP (b)

Color Histogram. To demonstrate the effectiveness of LLC feature representation, comparative experimental results for color histogram feature with and without representation are shown in Fig. 5. The dash line indicates the feature without representation and the solid line indicates the feature with representation. By comparison the dash line and solid line, we can clearly find that LLC representation has significant performance.

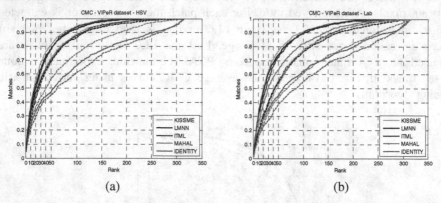

(a)   (b)

Fig. 5. CMC curves for feature HSV (a) and Lab (b). The dash line indicates the feature without LLC representation and the solid line indicates the feature with LLC representation.

ALL Feature. Five features including SITF, HSV (LLC), Lab (LLC), PHOG and LBP are concatenated into a comprehensive descriptor and which is projected to a 34 and 100 dimensional subspaces by PCA. The CMC result is displayed in Fig. 6 (a). The comparative experimental results with different features using ITML metric are showed in Fig. 6 (b). (In our experiment we find that ITML metric is a relatively stable metric, so we choose it for comparative experiments.)

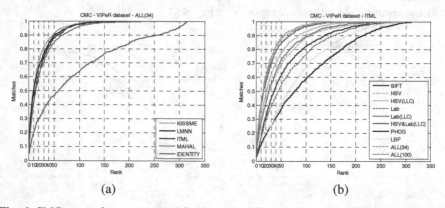

(a)   (b)

Fig. 6. CMC curves for concatenated feature with different metrics (a). Different features using ITML metric (b). ALL (34) and ALL (100) mean that the dimensionality of concatenated features is reduced to 34 and 100 by PCA respectively.

From Fig. 3 ~ Fig. 5, we can find that KISS, LMNN and ITML deliver similar performance and are much better than MAHAL and IDENTITY. By comparison the CMC curves in Fig. 6 (b), it can be seen that HSV (LLC) and Lab (LLC) outperform the other three features, SITF (LLC), LBP and PHOG.

4.2 Experiments on ETHZ Dataset

In addition to VIPeR, we also evaluate the feature performance on ETHZ dataset [3]. The ETHZ dataset was originally designed for person detection and tracking in four video sequences. Schwartz and Davis [14] converted it into a person re-identification dataset with 146 persons by extracting images from the video sequence. We randomly select two images of one person to form a person re-identification dataset. Each of the images has been scaled to a uniform size with 64×128 pixels. The challenge of the dataset is the diversified resolution and occlusions on people's appearance. A few example image pairs are shown in Fig. 7 (a).

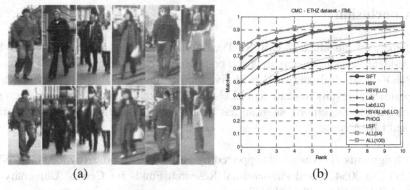

(a)   (b)

Fig. 7. Some examples are from ETHZ dataset. Each column is a same-person pair (a). CMC curves for different feature using ITML metric (b).

Similar to VIPeR, to evaluate the performance of different features, comparative experiments are done using ITML metric (see Fig. 7 (b)). Table 1 shows the matching rates with different rank. As we can see, the color features (HSV & Lab (LLC) means the concatenation of HSV (LLC) and Lab (LLC)) have superior performance than texture features (PHOG and LBP) in our experiments.

Table 1. Person re-identification matching rates on the ETHZ dataset with different rank

Features	r = 1	r = 5	r = 10	r = 20	r = 30	r = 40	r = 50
PHOG	43.15	65.07	73.97	83.56	90.41	94.52	97.94
LBP	38.36	69.18	83.56	93.83	96.58	97.26	99.31
Lab(LLC)	54.11	79.45	85.62	93.15	96.58	98.63	100
SIFT	62.33	85.62	91.78	95.89	98.63	100	100
HSV(LLC)	67.12	87.67	94.52	97.26	97.95	98.63	98.63
HSV & Lab(LLC)	68.49	88.36	93.15	96.58	97.95	98.63	100
ALL	74.66	91.78	95.89	97.26	98.63	100	100

4.3   Experimental Analysis

From above CMC figures, several conclusions can be drawn as follows:

1) First, LLC representation after low level feature extraction improves the matching performance significantly.
2) Second, the color histogram features, HSV and Lab, are more useful features compared to PHOG and LBP for person re-identification. As we can see, the same person pairs in both VIPeR and ETHZ datasets are in same clothes, so the color information is an important factor for person matching.
3) Finally, although SIFT feature have been shown excellent performance in many computer vision tasks, it does not perform very well for person re-identification in our experiments. This is because the images are transformed into gray scale during the preprocessing of feature extraction and some useful information is lost.

5   Conclusion

In this paper, we introduce LLC to SIFT and color histogram features extraction for person re-identification. Quantitative and comparative experiments with five features, SIFT, PHOG, LBP, Lab and HSV, with five metric algorithms have been conducted. Our experimental results indicate that LLC representation is very useful for person re-identification and the color histogram has better discriminant ability compared with PHOG and LBP.

Acknowledgments. This work is supported by NSFC (Grant no. 61075021), GDNSF (no. S2011020000541), and Fundamental Research Funds for Central University of China (no. 2012ZP0002, 2012M0022).

References

1. Zheng, W.S., Gong, S., Xiang, T.: Re-identification by Relative Distance Comparison. IEEE Transactions on Pattern Analysis and Machine Intelligence (2012), http://doi.ieeecomputersociety.org/10.1109/TPAMI.2012.138
2. Gray, D., Brennan, S., Tao, H.: Evaluating Appearance Models for Recognition, Reacquisition, and Tracking. In: IEEE International Workshop on Performance Evaluation of Tracking and Surveillance (2007)
3. Ess, A., Leibe, B., Van Gool, L.: Depth and Appearance for Mobile Scene Analysis. In: IEEE International Conference on Computer Vision, pp. 1–8. IEEE Press, New York (2007)
4. Lazebnik, S., Schmid, C., Ponce, J.: Beyond Bags of Features: Spatial Pyramid Matching for Recognize Natural Scene Categories. In: IEEE Conference on Computer Vision and Pattern Recognition, pp. 2169–2178. IEEE Press, New York (2006)
5. Yang, J., Yu, K., Gong, Y., Huang, T.: Linear Spatial Pyramid Matching Using Sparse Coding for Image Classification. In: IEEE Conference on Computer Vision and Pattern Recognition, pp. 1794–1801. IEEE Press, New York (2009)

6. Wang, J., Yang, J., Yu, K., Lv, F., Huang, T., Guo, Y.: Locality-constrained Linear Coding for Image Classification. In: IEEE Conference on Computer Vision and Pattern Recognition, pp. 3360–3367. IEEE Press, New York (2010)
7. Lowe, D.G.: Distinctive Image Features from Scale-Invariant Keypoints. International Journal of Computer Vision 60(2), 91–110 (2004)
8. Bosch, A., Zisserman, A., Munoz, X.: Representing shape with s spatial pyramid kernel. In: Proceedings of the 6th ACM International Conference on Image and Video Retrieval, pp. 401–408. ACM Press, New York (2007)
9. Ojala, T., Pietikainen, M., Maenpaa, T.: Multiresolution Gray-Scale and Rotation Invariant Texture Classification with Local Binary Patterns. IEEE Transactions on Pattern Analysis and Machine Intelligence 24(7), 971–987 (2002)
10. Kostinger, M., Hirzer, M., Wohlhart, P., Roht, P.M., Bischof, H.: Large Scale Metric Learning from Equivalence Constraints. In: IEEE Conference on Computer Vision and Pattern Recognition, pp. 2288–2295. IEEE Press, New York (2012)
11. Weinberger, K.Q., Blitzer, J., Saul, L.K.: Distance Metric Learning for Large Margin Nearest Neighbor Classification. In: Neural Information Processing Systems, pp. 1475–1482. MIT Press, Massachusetts (2006)
12. Davis, J.V., Kulis, B., Jain, P., Sra, S., Dhillon, I.S.: Information-Theoretic Metric Learning. In: Proceedings of the 24th International Conference on Machine Learning, pp. 209–216. ACM Press, New York (2007)
13. Bazzani, L., Perina, A., Murino, V., Cristani, M.: Person Re-identification by Symmetry-Driven Accumulation of Local Features. In: IEEE Conference on Computer Vision and Pattern Recognition, pp. 2360–2367. IEEE Press, New York (2010)
14. Schwartz, W.R., Davis, L.S.: Learning Discriminative Appearance-based Models Using Partial Least Squares. In: Brazilian Symposium on Computer Graphics and Image Processing (SIBGGRAPI), pp. 322–329 (2009)

Improving Biometric Verification Systems by Fusing Z-norm and F-norm

Messaoud Bengherabi[1], Farid Harizi[1], Norman Poh[2], Elhocine Boutellaa[1],
Abderrazek Guessoum[3], and Mohamed Cheriet[4]

[1] Centre de Développement des Technologies Avancées, Division ASM, Algeria
[2] University of Surrey, Guildford, GU2 7XH, Surrey, UK
[3] Université Saad Dahleb de Blida, Route De Soumaa, Blida BP 270, Algeria
[4] École de Technologies Supérieure Montréal, Québec, Canada
{mbengherabi,fharizi,hboutellaa}@cdta.dz, n.poh@surrey.ac.uk,
aguessouma@hotmail.com, Mohamed.Cheriet@etsmtl.ca

Abstract. User-specific score normalization which is related to biometric menagerie has received a lot of attention in the last decade. It is a one-to-one mapping function such that after its application, only a global threshold is needed. In this paper we propose a novel user-specific score normalization framework based on the fusion of Z-norm and F-norm. In this framework, firstly one post-processes the biometric system scores with Z-norm and F-norm procedures. Then, one feeds the resulting two dimensional normalized score vector to a fusion classifier to obtain a final normalized score. Using logistic regression as a fusion classifier, experiments carried out on 13 face and speech systems of the XM2VTS database show that the proposed strategy is likely to improve over the original separate score normalization schemes (F-norm or Z-norm). Furthermore, this novel strategy turns out to be the best strategy for applications requiring low false acceptance rate.

Keywords: User-specific normalization, Biometric Menagerie, Z-norm, F-norm, score level fusion.

1   Introduction and Motivation

There is rising evidence that the performance of a biometric system will vary from one user to another. While some users are harder to recognize, other users can be easily impersonated, hence, giving raise to different false rejection and false acceptance rates. This phenomenon is called the **Biometric Menagerie**. It is a collection of user categories describing a subject's matching tendencies and characterizing the ways in which users can be recognized easily or with difficulties by a biometric system [1],[2]. The issue of performance variability among different users in biometric systems was first addressed by Campbell [3] in his tutorial on speaker recognition. Later, Doddington *et al.* [4] classified speakers into different groups based on their propensity to contribute to the False Reject and False Accept Rates (FRR and FAR). It should be noted that FAR here results from   zero-effort impostors.

W.-S. Zheng et al. (Eds.): CCBR 2012, LNCS 7701, pp. 278–287, 2012.

By zero-effort impostor, we understand that the non-match attempts are due to different users/subjects and not due to dedicated spoofing attacks. In the context of zero-effort assessment, Doddington *et al* introduced a classification scheme of users, known as "Doddington's Zoo". This scheme assigned users into several categories labeled as Sheep, Lambs, Goats and Wolves which analogously reflects their behavior.

Assuming similarity scores throughout this paper: Sheep are characterized by high matching scores whereas goats are characterized by low matching scores. Lambs are defined as a symmetry of goats, i.e., having high non-match scores. Finally, wolves are persons who can consistently give high non-match similarity scores when matched against all the enrolled models in the biometric gallery. While Goats, Lambs and Wolves represent only a minority in the biometric database, their contribution in terms of the overall error rate of the biometric system may be large. A recent study on speaker recognition shows that 50% of the false rejection and false alarm errors are caused by only 15-25% of the speakers [5]. Users in these categories are therefore referred to as *"weak, troublesome or problematic users"* due to their negative impact on the error rate of the system.

A potential weakness of the classifications proposed by Doddington *et al* is their reliance only on the matching scores for goats and only on the non-match scores for lambs and wolves. Starting from the fact that the *recognizability* of each client in a biometric system depends on both genuine (match or positive class) and impostor score characteristics (non-match or negative class), new four additional classes have been proposed by Yager and Dunstone [6]: worms (low match, high non-match), Chameleons(high match, high non-match), Phantoms (low match, low non-match) and Doves (high match, low non-match).

There is an important body of research literature showing that user-specific processing can greatly bolster the performance of a biometric system. User-specific processing is done either by user-specific normalization [7],[8], user-specific threshold setting [9], user-specific fusion [10],[8] and user-specific template update [11].

Despite the open debate about the existence of doddington zoo [12], the previous user-specific processing has demonstrated its effectivness especially in score normalization which is the subject of our study. For more details the reader can refer to the previous works of Fierrez *et al* [13] and Poh and Kittler [7].

User-specific normalization refers to the operation that transforms the score distribution of each user to a standard domain. The aim is to facilitate the application of a global threshold after minimizing the score variations induced by the biometric menagerie. Examples of these normalization procedures are the popular Z-norm and F-norm. Recently, Poh and Tistarelli [14] improve these procedures by introducing *discriminative* versions of F-norm and Z-norm – **dF-norm** and **dZ-norm** respectively; and a *discriminative parametric* version – **dp-norm**. In the discriminative versions, the weights of the linear constituent terms of Z-norm or F-norm are obtained by learning a logistic regression coefficients and in the *discriminative parametric* versions, additional client-specific parameters are incorporated as covariates. Indeed the two proposed frameworks can be seen as creating a new evidence space for a linear logistic regression by stacking raw scores with covariates that are a good predictor of score (quality measures).

This paper explores a novel strategy of user-specific score normalization based on the fusion of the popular and simple Z-norm and F-norm . The motivation is to exploit the strength of each of them. Z-norm attempts to normalize the non-match score distributions to zero-mean unit-variance. It is applied principally to reduce false alarm rate resulting from wolves' access requests. However, the match score distributions are not aligned. On the other hand, F-norm is designed to simultaneously align the first order moments of the match and non-match user-specific scores. However, its main weakness is that the non-match score distributions have no longer unit-variance as in Z-norm. This deficiency will result in a user-dependent variance. This weakness can be accentuated if the user belongs to the problematic worm category (a user with low match scores and high non-match scores). The contributions of this paper are summarized as follow: a) proposing a novel user-specific score normalization based on the fusion of two well known score normalization techniques, hence, opening the door for researchers to investigate the complementarities between different user-specific normalization techniques, b) providing experimental evidence illustrating the merit of our proposal for voice and face modalities.

This paper is organized as follow: Section 2 reviews Z-norm and F-norm as well as presents our proposed normalization framework. Section 3 describes our experimental investigation. This is followed by a conclusion in Section 4.

2   The Proposed Normalization Strategy

2.1   Overview of Z-norm and F-norm

Let y be a matching score. Furthermore, let μ_j^k and σ_j^k be respectively the client-specific mean score and standard deviation for class $k \in \{C, I\}$ which can be a match (genuine) or a non-match (impostor) comparison. Z-norm is an impostor-centric normalization relying only on user-specific non-match score statistics μ_j^I and σ_j^I;

$$y_j^Z = \frac{y - \mu_j^I}{\sigma_j^I} \tag{1}$$

F-norm is a client-impostor centric normalization defined as:

$$y_j^F = \frac{y - \mu_j^I}{\mu_j^{C\,MAP} - \mu_j^I} \tag{2}$$

where $\mu_j^{C\,MAP}$ is a maximum *a posteriori*-adapted client-specific mean score. It is obtained by interpolating between a client-specific mean of match scores μ_j^C and the global mean μ^C from the entire match scores [15].

$$\mu_j^{C\,MAP} = \gamma \mu_j^C + (1 - \gamma)\mu^C$$

The parameter $\gamma \in [0\ 1]$ weighs the contribution between the client-specific genuine mean score and the client-independent one. The authors in [7] recommend $\gamma = 0.5$ when there is only one or few samples. This recommendation is followed in our experiments.

F-norm has the following effect: the expected genuine scores will be near one and the expected impostor scores will be zero, i.e., across all models. F-norm relies only on the first order moment hence providing some robustness to the scarcity of the client match scores, which is a critical problem in any user-specific processing. However, this desirable alignment of user-specific first order moments is achieved at the price of scaling the second order moments. It is straightforward from equation (2) that the variance of y_j^F is inversely proportional to the term $(\mu_j^{C\ MAP} - \mu_j^I)^2$. This term is user-dependent. Furthermore, for a small value of this term, for instance, in the case of a user belonging to the worm category, the application of F-norm alone will yield degraded performance.

2.2   The Fusion of Z-norm and F-norm

The block diagram of the proposed normalization framework based on the fusion of Z-norm and F-norm is depicted in Figure.1.

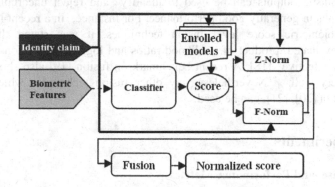

Fig. 1. The general block diagram of the proposed normalization scheme

In this framework, we first post-process the scores with Z-norm and F-norm procedures. Then, then we combine the resultant output using a conventional user-independent common classifier f:

$$f : y_j^Z, y_j^F \rightarrow y_{norm} \tag{3}$$

where y_j^Z, y_j^F are respectively, the result of Z-norm and F-norm score normalization procedures specific to the claimed identity j.

The Logistic Regression (LR) discriminative classifier yielding to a simple linear decision hyperplane is adopted in this work. The output of logistic regression approximates the posterior probability of being match score. LR is defined as:

$$y_{norm} = \frac{1}{1+\exp(-g(y))} \qquad \text{where} \qquad g(y) = \sum_{i=1}^{2}\beta_i y_i + \beta_0 \tag{4}$$

$g(y)$ can be obtained by applying the *logit* function to y_{norm}. The function *logit* is actually an inverse of a sigmoid (or logistic) function. The *logit* function transform the sigmoid function to linear regression.

y_i's are the element of the two dimensional vector **y** resulting from F-norm and Z-norm. The weight parameters β_i are optimized using gradient ascent to maximize the likelihood of the training data on the development set [16].

It can be easily demonstrated that the decision hyperplance obtained by using Bayesian decision rule is the following [17]:

$$\sum_{i=1}^{2} \beta_i y_i + \beta_0 > \Delta \tag{5}$$

Where Δ is an application dependent decision threshold, trading off false acceptance rate for false rejection rate. We chose to use logistic regression for at least three reasons. First, its iterative optimization procedure of the maximum likelihood estimator is well understood; it converges to a global maximum, meaning that there is a unique solution. Second, its output can be interpreted as a probability and so presenting this information to the user is more meaningful than just the raw score. This probabilistic outputs can be used to identify and reject uncertain decisions. Third, it results in generally good performance. For instance, in a recent NIST report evaluating biometric score level fusion techniques, it was stated that "of the techniques evaluated, product of likelihood ratios and logistic regression were found to be highly effective" [18]. A recent benchmark on fusion [19] also shows that LR performs very well. Nevertheless, any other fusion techniques which are well documented in [20], [21] can be used.

3   Experiments

3.1   Dataset and Performance Metrics

In our experiments, we have used the publicly available XM2VTS Multimodal Biometric Score Benchmark database [22], which is downloadable from:http://personal.ee.surrey.ac.uk/Personal/Norman.Poh/web/fusion. The original database contains 295 subjects, roughly balanced between genders [23]. For the voice modality, Each speaker was recorded saying all ten digits four times in four different sessions in a *quiet* environment, and for the face modality the recording sessions were distributed evenly over a period of approximately five months and at each session the external conditions were controlled. All images were taken against a more or less uniform background, that good illumination conditions were present during the recording, and that only small tilts and in-plane rotations were allowed. This controlled acquisition conditions make of the XM2VTS database very suited to our study. The 295 subjects of the database are divided into a set of 200 clients and 95 impostors. Impostors are divided in two sets: an evaluation or validation set (25 impostors) and a test set (70 impostors). Two different partitioning approaches of the training and evaluation sets exist. They are called Lausanne Protocol I and II. There are 8 samples per subject. In protocol I, 3 samples (per subject) are used for training, 3 for evaluation, and 2 for testing whereas for protocol II, these 3 partitions contain 4,

2 and 2 samples respectively. The score datasets for the two protocols are illustrated in Table 1. The database scores correspond to 8 baseline systems (5 faces and 3 speakers verification systems). Each system is a combination of a type of feature extraction and a classifier used to generate the client model. Three types of feature extraction are used for face: FH (Face Histogram), DCTs and DCTb (Discrete Cosine Transform, s and b stand for the size of the DCT blocks). For speech three categories of feature extraction are used: LFCC (Linear Filter-bank Cepstral Coefficient), PAC (Phase Auto Correlation MFCC) and SSC (Spectral Sub-band Centroid). The scores are calculated by using two classifiers: Multi Layer Perceptrons (MLPs) and Gaussian Mixture Models. In addition to the controlled acquisition scenario of both modalities and using central limit theorem, the Gaussian density is a natural candidate for a GMM based systems due to the fact that their score is the average log likelihood ratio of the target speaker model to the universal background model [24]. This score is obtained by summing many random variables representing the log-likelihood ratio score at each frame in speech and each block in face. This Gaussian density is a desirable condition of Z-norm and F-norm. The multi-layer perceptron MLP classifier results in scores peaked around 1 and -1, resulting in scores distributions far from the Gaussian assumption. In this case, it is recommended that before applying user-specific normalization, we first apply the inverse tangent hyperbolic transformation $\tanh^{-1}$ to the raw scores [25].

Table 1. Description of the Lausanne Protocols PI and PII

Dataset	LAUSANNE PROTOCOLS	
	PI	PII
Evaluation Client Accesses	600 (3×200)	800 (4×200)
Evaluation Impostor Accesses	40.000 (25 impostor × 8shots × 200 client subjects)	
Test Client Accesses	400 (2 shots × 200 client subjects)	
Test Impostor Accesses	112.000 (70 ×8×200)	

Regarding performance metrics: the first measure used in our work is the *a posteriori* equal error rate EER obtained when FAR equal FRR on the test set. The second performance metric is the pooled Expected Performance Curve EPC [26]. Rather than just calculating EER on the test set, hence implicitly optimizing the decision threshold on the test data, EPC attempts to optimize a criterion that determines the decision threshold. For this purpose, Weighted Error Rate (*WER*) is used in EPC; it is given by:

$$WER(\alpha, \Delta) = \alpha FAR(\Delta) + (1 - \alpha) FRR(\Delta) \qquad (6)$$

where $\alpha \in [0, 1]$ balances between FAR and FRR and Δ is the threshold. An EPC is constructed as follows: for various values of α between 0 and 1, select the optimal threshold Δ^* minimizing WER on a development(training) set, apply the decision threshold on the test set, and finally, compute the Half Total Error Rate (*HTER*) so obtained which is given by:

$$HTER(\Delta_\alpha^*) = \frac{FAR(\Delta_\alpha^*) + FRR(\Delta_\alpha^*)}{2} \qquad (7)$$

EPC is simply a plot of HTER versus α. The lower the curve, the better the generalization performance. Pooled EPC curve is used to summarize an ensemble of experiments [26]. The third performance measure is the conventional Detection Error Trade-off (DET) curve [27].

3.2   Results

To compare the performance of the proposed normalization strategy to Z-norm and F-norm, we have used the same experimental settings as those specified in [7] . The results in terms of *a posteriori* EER are shown in Table.2. In this table, the third column represent the classifiers. For instance, the system "PI:1(F)", which means that it is taken from Protocol I of system 1and it is a face modality. The last row labeled "top" measures the number of times a method attains the lowest *a posteriori* EER. As can be observed, the proposed norm outperforms Z-norm and F-norm in the majority of experiments (9/13) and it is ranked first or second best normalization strategy in all experiments. More insight about the generalization performance of the three normalization techniques under different applications scenarios (costs and prior probabilities) can be obtained from the pooled EPC curves illustrated in Figure.2. This figure shows that the proposed normalization gives the best performance for $\alpha \in$ [0.2, 1] and the gain in performance is more pronounced for α greater than 0.5. The figure suggests that our proposal is superior for applications requiring low false alarm rate. To confirm this, we plot the DET curves of the first and last classifiers whose performance in terms of *a posteriori* EER outperform the proposed normalization. These DET curves are illustrated in Figure.3.

Table 2. Comparison of Z-norm, F-norm and the proposed-norm in terms of *a posteriori* EER (%),,iMLP *systems are* MLP systems post-processed by the $\tanh^{-1}$ transformation [7]

P	no.	system (modality, feature,classifier)	*a posteriori* EER(%)		
			Z-norm	F-norm	Proposed-norm
PI	1	(F,DCTs,GMM)	4.04	*3.57	3.91
	2	(F,DCTb,GMM)	1.92	*1.43	1.52
	3	(S,LFCC,GMM)	1.34	0.68	*0.40
	4	(S,PAC,GMM)	4.96	4.63	*4.53
	5	(S,SSC,GMM)	2.57	2.33	*1.99
	6	(F,DCTs,MLP)	3.28	3.14	*2.95
	7	(F,DCTs,iMLP)	3.18	3.19	*2.95
	8	(F,DCTb,MLP)	*6.32	6.53	6.45
	9	(F,DCTb,iMLP)	6.35	6.84	*6.20
PII	10	(F,DCTb,GMM)	0.97	0.79 (0.790)	*0.79 (0.787)
	11	(S,LFCC,GMM)	0.99	0.58	*0.46
	12	(S,PAC,GMM)	4.65	5.28	*4.55
	13	(S,SSC,GMM)	*2.20	2.60	2.44
	Top		2	2	9

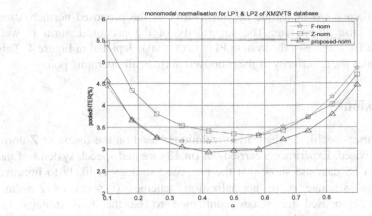

Fig. 2. Comparison of the pooled EPC curves of Z-norm, F-norm and the proposed-norm

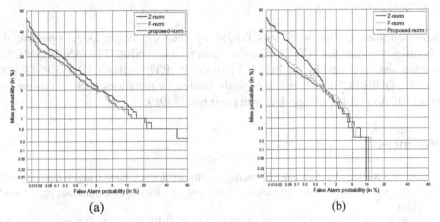

(a)   (b)

Fig. 3. Comparison of the DET curves of Z-norm, F-norm and the proposed-norm, (a) for the PI(F,DCTs,GMM) system and (b) for the PII(S,SSC,GMM)

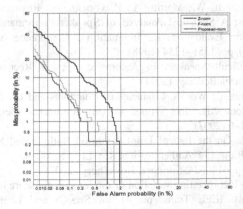

Fig. 4. DET curve of Z-norm, F-norm and the proposed-norm for the PI (S,LFCC,GMM) system

The two DET curves demonstrate the superiority of the proposed normalization strategy at low false alarm rate. The superiority of the proposed norm is well illustrated by the DET curve of the system PI (S,LFCC,GMM) depicted in Figure.4. This figure demonstrates the superiority of the proposed norm at all operating points.

4   Conclusion

In this paper, a user-specific normalization technique based on the fusion of Z-norm and F-norm is devised. Experiments carried out on 13 face and speech systems of the controlled XM2VTS database show that the proposed strategy is likely to improve over the original separate score normalization schemes (F-norm or Z-norm). Furthermore, the proposed techniques confirmed to be the best strategy for applications requiring low false acceptance rate. An ongoing research work is on studying the impact of the proposed normalization technique on the fusion of biometric systems.

Acknowledgments. This work was funded by the "Centre de Développement des Technologies Avancées"-CDTA-Algeria, under the FNR/CDTA/ASM/BSM/25.E. Boutellaa was supported by the PURAQ project "PARTENARIAT UNIVERSITAIRE ALGERO-QUEBECOIS". N.Poh was partly funded by the Biometrics Evaluation and Testing (BEAT), an EU FP7 project with grant no. 284989.

References

1. Poh, N., Kittler, J.: A biometric menagerie index for characterizing template/model-specific variation. In: 3rd International Conference on Biometrics, Sardinia, pp. 816–827 (2009)
2. Yager, N., Dunstone, T.: The Biometric Menagerie. IEEE Trans. on Pattern Analysis and Machine Intelligence 32 (2010)
3. Campbell, J.P.: Speaker recognition: A tutorial. IEEE 85, 1437–1462 (1997)
4. Doddington, G., Liggett, W., Martin, A., Przybocki, M., Reynolds, D.: Sheep, Goats, Lambs and Wolves: A Statistical Analysis of Speaker Performance in the NIST 1998 Speaker Recognition Evaluation. In: International Conference on Spoken Language Processing (ICSLP), pp. 1351–1354 (1998)
5. Stoll: Finding Difficult Speakers in Automatic Speaker Recognition. Ph.D. thesis, University of California Berkeley (2011)
6. Yager, N., Dunstone, T.: Worms, Chameleons, Phantoms and Doves: New Additions to the Biometric Menagerie. In: Workshop on Automatic Identification Advanced Technologies, pp. 1–6 (2007)
7. Poh, N., Kittler, J.: On the Use of Log-Likelihood Ratio Based Model-Specific Score Normalisation in Biometric Authentication. In: Lee, S.-W., Li, S.Z. (eds.) ICB 2007. LNCS, vol. 4642, pp. 614–624. Springer, Heidelberg (2007)
8. Poh, N., Kittler, J.: Incorporating variation of model specific score distribution in speaker verification systems. IEEE Trans. on Audio, Speech and Language Processing 16, 594–606 (2008)

9. Chen, K.: Towards Better Making a Decision in Speaker Verification. Pattern Recognition 36, 329–346 (2003)
10. Fierrez, J., Ortega-Garcia, J.: Fusion, User-Specific. Encyclopedia of Biometrics. In: Li, S.Z. (ed.), pp. 621–624. Springer (2009)
11. Rattani, A., Marcialis, G.L., Roli, F.: An Experimental Analysis of the Relationship between Biometric Template Update and the Doddington's Zoo in Face Verification. In: 14th International Conference on Image Analysis and Processing, Italy (2009)
12. Teli, M.N., Beveridge, J.R., Phillips, P.J., Givens, G.H., Bolme, D.S., Draper, B.A.: Biometric Zoos: Theory and Experimental Evidence. In: IEEE International Joint Conference on Biometrics, Washington DC (2011)
13. Fiérrez-Aguilar, J., Ortega-Garcia, J., Gonzalez-Rodriguez, J.: Target Dependent Score Normalization Techniques and Their Application to Signature Verification. In: Zhang, D., Jain, A.K. (eds.) ICBA 2004. LNCS, vol. 3072, pp. 498–504. Springer, Heidelberg (2004)
14. Poh, N., Tistarelli, M.: Customizing biometric authentication systems via discriminative score calibration. In: CVPR, pp. 2681–2686 (2012)
15. Gauvain, J., Lee, C.H.: Maximum a Posteriori Estimation for Multivariate Gaussian Mixture Observations of Markov Chains. IEEE Trans. Speech Audio Processing 2, 290–298 (1994)
16. Dobson, A.J.: An Introduction to Generalized Linear Models. CRC Press (1990)
17. Duda, R.O., Hart, P.E., Stork, D.G.: Pattern Classification and Scene Analysis. John Wiley and Sons, New York (2001)
18. Ulery, B., Fellner, W., Hallinan, P., Hicklin, A., Watson, C.: Evaluation of Selected Biometric Fusion Techniques. Technical Report, NIST (2006)
19. Poh, N., Bourlai, T., Kittler, J., Allano, L., Alonso-Fernandez, F., Ambekar, O., Baker, J., Dorizzi, B., Fatukasi, O., Fierrez, J., Ganster, H., Ortega-Garcia, J., Maurer, D., Salah, A.A., Scheidat, T., Vielhauer, C.: Benchmarking Quality-dependent and Cost-sensitive Multimodal Biometric Fusion Algorithms. IEEE Trans. on Information Forensics and Security 4, 849–866 (2009)
20. Ross, A., Nandakumar, K., Jain, A.: Handbook of Multibiometrics. Springer (2006)
21. Scheirer, W., Rocha, A., Michaels, R., Boult, T.E.: Meta-Recognition: The Theory and Practice of Recognition Score Analysis. IEEE Trans. on Pattern Analysis and Machine Intelligence 33, 1689–1695 (2011)
22. Poh, N., Bengio, S.: Database, Protocol and Tools for Evaluating Score-Level Fusion Algorithms in Biometric Authentication. J. Pattern Recognition 39, 223–233 (2006)
23. Messer, K., Matas, J., Kittler, J., Luettin, J., Maitre, G.: XM2VTSDB: the extended M2VTS database. In: Proceedings of the 2nd International Conference on Audio- and Video-Based Person Authentication, Washington DC, pp. 72–77 (1999)
24. Reynolds, D.A., Quatieri, T.F., Dunn, R.B.: Speaker verification using adapted Gaussian mixture models. Digital Signal Processing 10, 19–41 (2000)
25. Poh, N.: Multi-system Biometric Authentication: Optimal Fusion and User-Specific Information. Ph.D. thesis, Swiss Federal Institute of Technology in Lausanne (Ecole Polytechnique Fédérale de Lausanne) (2006)
26. Bengio, S., Marithoz, J.: The Expected Performance Curve: a New Assessment Measure for Person Authentication. In: The Speaker and Language Recognition Workshop (Odyssey), Toledo, pp. 279–284 (2004)
27. Martin, A., Doddington, G., Kamm, T., Ordowsk, M., Przybocki, M.: The DET Curve in Assessment of Detection Task Performance. In: Eurospeech, Rhodes, pp. 1895–1898 (1997)

Biometric Identification System's Performance Enhancement by Improving Registration Progress

Shilei Liu, Beining Huang, Yuankai Yu, and Wenxin Li

School of Electronics Engineering and Computer Science, Peking University, Beijing, China
cs_lsl@pku.edu.cn

Abstract. Recently, biometric recognition techniques have become more and more important in security defense industry, among which stands out finger-vein identification technique, with distinctive advantages on accuracy, convenience, sanitation, safety, etc. Encouraged by its great features, we develop a series of finger-vein identification algorithms and apply them in a practical application system – the Peking University Exercise Attendance System (PUEAS), which is based on finger-vein recognition technique. The system has been running for more than three years till now, accumulating more than 20,000 registered users, 900,000 finger-vein templates and 1,400,000 matching records. However, when we focus on how to make further improvement on the system, we find that the quality of the registration process plays a key role in determining the performance of the whole system. After discussing on some essential issues of the registration process, we conduct corresponding improvement measures to eliminate their influence. The experiment results well demonstrate enhancement of performance of the whole PUEAS.

Keywords: finger-vein recognition, biometric system, registration quality, PUEAS.

1   Introduction

Nowadays, several biometric recognition techniques using finger features are becoming highly focused. Among them finger-vein recognition12 is a newly-risen technique, with distinct advantages such as successfully eliminating influence of abrasion and sanitation of all the contact recognition methods, convenience of usage, hard to get stolen or faked, small size of acquisition device, no need for assisting test on object's living status, etc.

However, finger-vein recognition technology hasn't been perfect yet and has plenty of room for further improvement. This technique belongs to non-contact recognition methods, thus having problems on locating when collecting images. Due to the fact that different people have different fingers, fingers are of different size and shape, making it impossible for acquisition device to strictly locate every user's finger when collecting images. Hence, postures and positions of fingers could be easily changed during the course of acquiring images.

In the year 2009, our group developed a series of finger-vein recognition algorithms and applied them into a practical system – the Peking University Exercise Attendance

W.-S. Zheng et al. (Eds.): CCBR 2012, LNCS 7701, pp. 288–299, 2012.

System (PUEAS), which is based on finger-vein recognition technique. The system has been running for more than three years till now, accumulating more than 20,000 registered users, 900,000 finger-vein templates and 1,400,000 matching records. Like other traditional biometric recognition systems, the PUEAS involves two parts: (a) registration part, including collecting and enrolling user's finger-vein information; (b) identification part, including using the stored finger-vein information to identify the current user.

When we focus on make further improvement on the system's performance (in this paper we mainly concern on identification rate between user's newly-acquired samples and existing templates), we find that the fluctuation of finger's postures and shapes can easily influence the quality of registered templates, thus making an evident impact on the whole system's performance.

In this paper, we mainly concern on discussing how user's behavior can influence registration's quality, and how to improve registration's quality accordingly. We've used more than two years on improving registration's quality and observing how the whole system's performance improves accordingly. The experimental result has been a firm support for our guess that improvement on registration progress can effectively improve the entire system's performance.

2   Structure Analysis of PUEAS

Traditional biometric recognition systems have two working patterns: identification and verification (Fig. 1).

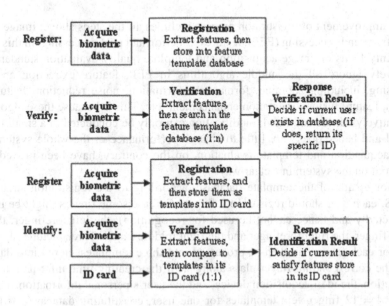

Fig. 1. A biometric recognition system

Considering of the large quantity of users and the subsequent large database, the PUEAS use Identification mode (referring to the down half part of Fig. 1), combining with user's ID card, to reduce system's reacting time for every single recognition task.

In this system, the registration procedure is to treat the original image (Fig. 2) acquired from the device by a series of processing, and finally to generate feature template.

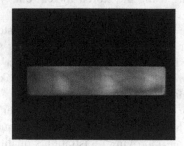

Fig. 2. Original Image

Basic process of registration is shown in Fig.3.

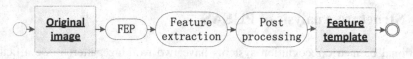

Fig. 3. Registration Process

The improvement of registration process includes all the steps above: image acquisition, front-end processing (FEP), feature extraction and post processing. In this paper, we mainly focus on image acquisition and template quality evaluation standard, and selectively ignore all the middle algorithms in FEP, feature extraction and post processing, including zooming, format transformation, noise reduction, feature extraction, feature fusion, orientation enhancement, etc. This is because these algorithms are relatively mature and fixed; modification can only be conducted in a small limited interval and hence does very little to change performance of the whole system. The image acquisition and template evaluation, on the contrary, have been proved to be influential on the system in a clear way.

As for details of the template database, according to the registration strategy of PUEAS, each user should register four fingers (in case some fingers might be injured unexpectedly and hence cannot be used for recognition): the left forefinger, the left middle finger, the right forefinger and the right middle finger. Three pictures should be taken for each finger and then be processed into three templates, stored into database under the corresponding finger class along with the creating time information, place information, the id of acquisition device, and the user's personal information. Thus we have 3*4 = 12 finger-vein templates for one user, constituting database for further verification or identification process.

3   Related Works

Currently, when it comes to how to improve performance of biometric recognition system, most of the biometric recognition researches usually focus on better algorithms on feature extraction, feature enhancement, feature fusion, multi-feature introduction, etc. During the researching years, it is common for researchers to accept the fact that system's performances are related to registration process, but few has ever conducted serious research on how much the quality of registration could influence the system's performance.

Hence it is still fresh work to explore the influence of registration process on system performance.

4   Registration-Based Enhancement

4.1   Influential Factors Analysis on Registration Quality

There are large amounts of influential factors on registration quality, which can be category into roughly four main aspects:

1) Acquisition Devices
Taking cost and convenience into consideration, it is common to use near-infrared imaging method (wavelength usually from 760-850nm) to acquire finger-vein images. The principle is that oxygenated hemoglobin in venous blood owns a much higher absorption rate on the near-infrared light of specific band than other human organs, hence forming dark areas 3 in the image when under near-infrared light irradiation. Compared to other common vein imaging methods45 in the medical field, the near-infrared imaging has advantages of low hardware cost, smallness of device bulk, high imaging speed, convenience for usage, harmless to health, etc. We apply this method in the PUEAS, and use the reflection-type (Fig.4b) instead of the perspectivity-type (Fig.4a) due to higher performance on imaging.

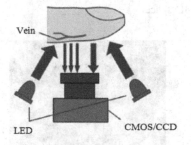   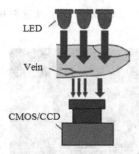

Fig. 4(a). Perspectivity-type acquisition device   **Fig. 4(b).** Reflection-type acquisition device

In the finger-vein image acquisition frame based on near-infrared imaging method mentioned above, there are mainly two ways to improve quality of acquired images:

- Use component of higher performance, mainly image transducer and camera lens. This solution is somehow effective, but will cause obvious increase on hardware cost and possibly device bulk. In this paper we won't focus on this method.
- Adjust intensity of illumination. This solution can also improve images' quality with a much lower cost, and can meanwhile improve device's adaptability on environment variations and different users' fingers. Hence we would like a further discussion of this method hereinafter.

When trying to improve registration quality considering acquisition device aspect, the only practical direction is to develop better illumination adjustment algorithm, and examine each image's illumination distribution status when carrying on registration task.

2) User Behavior
During registration progress, untrained user could possibly behave unpredictably and may cause troubles for collecting effective finger-vein information. Several possible problems can be listed here:

- Wearing hands defend. We observe lots of acquired images of PUEAS, and are astonished to find that some users wear all kinds of hands defend that might affect finger-vein registration such as gloves, rings, etc.
- Using different finger postures. With non-contact acquiring strategy, the finger can freely shift along or rotate around x, y, z axis. (Shown in Fig.5)

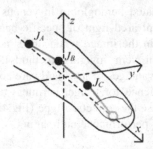

Fig. 5. Finger in 3D space

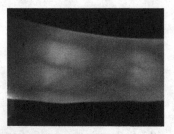
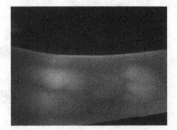

Fig. 6(a). Same finger in 2009-7-8 17:43:48   **Fig. 6(b).** Same finger in 2009-7-9 18:41:53

- Making unstable finger location. The device cannot strictly locate users' finger, so the finger can easily lean to the left or to the right (Show in Fig.6).
- Abnormal fingers or wrong fingers registered. The users may register fingers which are under abnormal status, such as with bruise or under postoperative situation. And also may wrongly change fingers when the same finger templates acquiring still goes on (decrease the similarity of the same finger), or do not change fingers in time when registration of the last finger has been successfully done (increase the similarity of different fingers).

Analysis of user behavior indicates that it can greatly affect registration quality, and several potential improving solution can be tried based on the analysis above, which we will discuss in detail in part B.

3) Templates Extraction Algorithms

The basic idea of identification method we use is to take the size and shape of vein in finger-vein images as feature for matching. Hence the purpose of extraction method is to highlight the vascular in finger-vein images as much as possible. And there are many classic algorithms in the extraction method like Niblack 67 method for binaryzation, line feature extraction method8 by Laura Liu, David Zhang and Jane You, feature fusion method9 for dark feature and line feature extraction, using direction information for image enhancement method1011, etc. We use these classic methods for reference, with several adjustments, to build up our own extraction method for PUEAS. During the system's running, we find it does little on systems performance when conducting change on extraction algorithm. Therefore, it will not be discussed in this paper.

4) Templates Evaluation Algorithms

As is mentioned in part 2, each user register four fingers, and three templates are re-quired for each finger. The similarity of templates from same finger and divergence of templates from different fingers describes the quality of one user's registration process. With the logic that knowing how well one is registered will help improve one's regis-tration process, it is reasonable to assume that developing a fine mechanism of deciding how well a user's templates are registered will be able to improve registration quality. Further details of solution will be discussed hereinafter.

4.2   Solutions on Relative Factors

After previous discussion on these factors influence on registration quality and evaluate how practical corresponding solutions can be, we choose more relative factors to dis-cuss their solutions and consequent results. We mainly focus on issues including light-dimming, real-time man-machine interaction, registration templates evaluation mechanisms.

The PUEAS has been running since Mar. 2009, and in Sept. 2009, we applied these improving solutions on it. The following part is how these solutions work.

1)   Light-Dimming Strategy

Image transducer is a device that accumulates exposed light energy during exposure time and then transforms it into electrical signal, finally quantifies into pictures with 8-bit gray scale for each pixel. The transformation equation is showed here:

$$\text{Gray Level} = \begin{cases} 0, & E \le E_{min} \\ 255, & E \ge E_{max} \\ GL(E), & \text{others} \end{cases}$$

(1)

In it $GL(x)$ is a monotonically increasing function, and E is accumulated luminous intensity during exposure time.

The transmitting of infrared light in finger is described in formula (2), which is called Beer-Lambert Formula 12.

$$\ln \frac{I_o}{I_i} = AC \cdot d + G$$

(2)

Here I_i stands for luminous intensity, AC stands for absorbing ratio, d stands for optical path length (depending on reflection ratio, reflection function and distance to image transducer), and G is an unknown geometry-related parameter.

Due to the difference between vein's absorbing & reflecting ratio and other human organs', under near-infrared with the same intensity, luminous intensity will become lower than other nearby organs, and appear smaller gray scale in images. In this way we can locate finger-vein in images.

The complexity of finger structure makes it impossible to measure absorbing ratio AC, reflecting ratio SC and optical path length d in reality. However we managed to find an approximate rule to describe luminous intensity of every area of finger, as is shown in formula (3).

$$G(x) = \alpha(x)I + I_{min}$$

(3)

Here x stands for each area's location coordinate, α is a location-related parameter, depending on that very location's absorbing ratio AC, reflection ratio SC and optical path length d, etc. I and I_{min} are based on G and the settlement of image transducer.

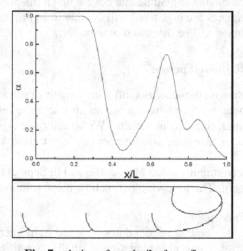

Fig. 7. relation of α and x/L of one finger

This is a real example of finger, and Fig.7 shows the corresponding relationship of α and x/L (L stands for finger length). It can be inferred that each parts of human finger has quite different transparency ratios.

Referring to formula   (2), now that we know d is depending on absorbing ratio AC and reflecting SC, so these two parameters can be treated as fixed for on the same finger; the exposure time of each image frame can also be treated as fixed. Therefore the definition of finger-vein area in image is depending on incident light I.

Therefore, to acquire high quality images, the illumination should satisfy the following requirements:

- Referring to formula (1), E should be controlled between E_{max} and E_{min}, and over range situation would lead to information loss.
- Assuming regardless of the tiny dynamic change of human body, as discussed above on formula (2), the higher I is, the higher contrast of final image would be.

As for AC and DC, different parts of finger are of different thickness, and finger structure (existing knuckles, nails) will also lead to uneven transparency-ratio of each parts of finger. Hence it is necessary to use uneven illuminate intensity to acquire images of high quality.

In this case, we use automatic-control method based on control feedback strategy to acquire finger-vein image, the main steps are:

Step 1: According to current parameters, set illuminate intensity distribution of the light source;

Step 2: Acquire an image into PC;

Step 3: Judge if the image is qualified, and output it if yes, then exit;

Step 4: Calculate illuminate parameters of next imaging frame acquisition, turn to step 1;

Step 1, 2 can be achieved by hardware design, and step 3, 4 mainly by software.

In step 3, we need to judge if one image is qualified, i.e. if each parts of finger image satisfy illumination requirements. For this part, we need to divide finger into several sections, and for each section using standards discussed on table 1, i.e. neither too bright nor too dim, and as much bright as possible within permitted interval.

Step 4 is the key of this self-adjust dimming method. The parameters that need to be adjusted are mainly luminous intensity distribution parameters for the next imaging frame acquisition.

As is shown in Fig.8, assuming there are n light sources (we denote n by 8 in the figure). Current illuminate intensity parameter is $L = \langle L_1, L_1, ..., L_n \rangle$, and parameter for next acquisition is $L' = \langle L'_1, L'_2, ..., L'_n \rangle$. The finger is divided into n parts referring to the corresponding location of the light source. Each part has its average gray scale $G = \langle G_1, G_2, ..., G_n \rangle$, and its corresponding transparency-ratio $\alpha = \langle \alpha_1, \alpha_2, ..., \alpha_n \rangle$. The illuminate intensity for n parts is $I = \langle I_1, I_2, ..., I_n \rangle$.

Use linear model to similarly describe relationship of L, I, α, G, as is shown in formula (4).

$$\begin{cases} I = B \cdot L \\ G = \alpha \cdot I \end{cases} \qquad (4)$$

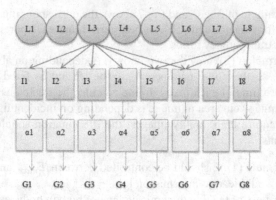

Fig. 8. Light adjustment model

Here B is an n*n matrix, indicating each light source's contribution to each part's intensity. We should calculate B and α, then calculate L, when we start each frame's acquisition.

For further discussion, given the fact that formula (4) is an approximate formula, and B and α are not strictly accurate, we can use certain strategies to calculate L' for the next frame such as dichotomy, greedy method, etc. In this paper we won't discuss more details here.

2)   Real-Time Man-Machine Interaction
The real-time man-machine interaction intends to watch the quality of acquired templates and to give user real-time clues for better registration; therefore it can help to stop the appearance of low quality registered templates. There are several situations where low quality templates appear: too bright or too dim templates, finger in motion, finger lean to left or right side, etc. The light adjustment issue has been discussed previously, hence in this part we focus to solve the other problems using real-time man-machine interaction.

- Finger in motion. Fig.9 is an example that motion leads to blur in the finger-vein's image. Our solution is easy and effective: conducting a difference between current frame and the previous frame; meanwhile examine the contour of finger to see if it changes.

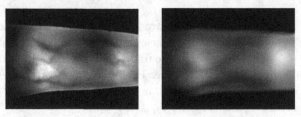

Fig. 9. Normal finger image and finger in motion

- Finger lean to one side. We calculate finger's upper and lower contour to get a main direction of the finger, and decide if the main direction is parallel to the edge of the image.

3) Registration Templates Evaluation Mechanism

There two aspects to evaluate how well one is registered: both divergence of templates from one's different fingers and similarity of templates from one's same fingers indicate high registration quality. However, it is hard to fully evaluate between-class divergence, so we turn to other way, and build up templates quality evaluation mechanism based on the similarity of in-class templates.

Therefore, the new registration process can be described as follows:

Step 1: Acquire an image;

Step 2: Match it with all the previous templates from the same finger, see if we can find the other two templates that any two-two match among these three templates can reach required threshold. If yes, choose these three templates as official templates for this finger, then exit;

Step 3: If none is found, add current template into previous templates collection, then turn to step 1.

However, taking the practical situation into consideration, the system is facing pressure from the large number of users and high requirements of interacting speed, we finally take a compromising strategy: set the maximum number of templates for one finger to 6, and if it cannot choose qualified three templates after taking the sixth templates, we choose three templates that has the highest average two-two match similarity rate.

5   Experimental Results

5.1   Experimental Data

The PUEAS has been running since Mar. 2009. We use it as the source of experimental data, and apply these mentioned improving methods in the system. Since all of the mentioned improving solutions were conducted in Sept.2009 and in March 2010, we pick data from three semesters that cover these changes. The experimental database has 17,847 users, 372,330 templates, and 750,685 matching records, with time-span for one and a half year.

5.2   Experiments and Results

We use the passing rate as the ultimate comparison standard. The final experiment result is shown in Table 1.

Table 1. Experimental result of three semesters

	2009 spring	2009 autumn	2010 spring
Average mark	0.4061	0.4064	0.3821
Threshold	0.4	0.4	0.3
Passing rate	51.27%	54.76%	75.70%

In Sept. 2009, we introduced registered templates evaluation mechanism, and the passing rate increased by more than 3%. In Mar. 2010, we introduced light-dimming method and real-time man-machine interaction strategy, and the passing rate increased greatly by 20.94%.

Meanwhile, I'd like to mention that the extraction method and matching method were exactly the same during this time-span, and the hardware was stable too. Therefore, the inspiring experiment result is authentic, which is able to reflect the real enhancement of the whole system's performance by improving quality of registration process.

To be noticed, the low passing rate (around 50%) is because this system runs in a real open circumstance, and owns a large group of users, most of which are untrained and inexperienced. This system performs much greater in laboratory circumstance.

6   Conclusion and Discussion

In this paper, we introduce the Peking University Exercise Attendance System (PUEAS) based on finger-vein recognition technique. By observing its running status, we analysis several key issues that might influence the whole system's performance. Based on these issues which occur during registration process, we propose the thought that we can enhance the whole system's performance by improving registration process. We then analysis influential factors on registration quality and discuss how practical the corresponding solution method could be, followed by detailed descriptions of the focused improving strategies. The experiments show complete supportive results on how improvement of registration process can greatly enhance the whole system's performance. Moreover, all the improving solutions do not lead to any increase on system's economic or time cost.

Encouraged by the inspiring experiment result, we conclude that in finger-vein recognition system, improvement of registration can greatly enhance the whole system's performance, without excluding the possibility of being further applied to relative biometric techniques.

References

1. Miura, N., Nagasaka, A., Miyatake, T.: Feature extraction of finger-vein patterns based on repeated line tracking and its application to personal recognition. Machine Vision and Applications 15, 194–203 (2004)
2. Miura, N., Nagasaka, A., Miyatake, T.: Extraction of finger-vein patterns using maximum curvature points in image profiles. IEICE Transactions on Information and Systems 90, 1185–1194 (2007)
3. Kono, M., Ueki, H., Umemura, S.: A new method for the identification of individuals by using of vein pattern matching of a finger, pp. 9–12 (2000)
4. Nanda, S.K., Hatchell, D.L., Tiedeman, J.S., Dutton, J.J., Hatchell, M.C., McAdoo, T.: A new method for vascular occlusion: photochemical initiation of thrombosis. Archives of Ophthalmology 105, 1121 (1987)
5. Nishimura, D.G., Macovski, A., Pauly, J.M., Conolly, S.M.: MR angiography by selective inversion recovery. Magnetic Resonance in Medicine 4, 193–202 (1987)

6. Sauvola, I., Seppanen, T., Haapakoski, R., Pietikainen, M.: Adaptive Document Binarization. In: International Conference on Document Analysis and Recognition, vol. 1, pp. 147–152 (1997)
7. Niblack, W.: An Introduction to Digital Image Processing, pp. 115–116. Prentice-Hall, Englewood Cliffs (1986)
8. Liu, L., Zhang, D., You, J.: Detecting Wide Lines Using Isotropic Nonlinear Filtering. IEEE PAMI 16(6) (June 2007)
9. Toet, A.: Hierarchical image fusion. Machine Vision and Applications. Springer (1990)
10. Hong, L., Wan, Y., Jain, A.: Fingerprint image enhancement: algorithm and performance evaluation. IEEE Transactions on Pattern Analysis and Machine Intelligence 20(8), 777–789 (1998)
11. Hong, L., Jain, A.K., Pankanti, S., Bolle, R.: Fingerprint enhancement. In: Proceedings of the IEEE Workshop on Applications of Computer Vision, Sarasota, FI, pp. 202–207 (1996)
12. Delpy, D., Cope, M., Zee, P., Arridge, S., Wray, S., Wyatt, J.: Estimation of optical pathlength through tissue from direct time of flight measurement. Physics in Medicine and Biology 33, 1433 (1988)

Ethnicity Classification Based
on a Hierarchical Fusion

De Zhang, Yunhong Wang, and Zhaoxiang Zhang

Laboratory of Intelligent Recognition and Image Processing,
Beijing Key Laboratory of Digital Media,
School of Computer Science and Engineering,
Beihang University, Beijing 100191, China

Abstract. In this paper, we propose a cascaded multimodal biometrics system involving a fusion of frontal face and lateral gait, for the specific problem of ethnicity classification. This system performs human ethnicity classification first from the cues of gait recorded by a long-distance camera and requires next classification using facial images captured by a short-distance camera only when gait based ethnicity identification fails. For gait, we use Gait Energy Image (GEI), a spatio-temporal compact representation of gait in video, to characterize human walking properties. For face, we extract the well-known Gabor feature to render the effective facial appearance information. Experimental results obtained from a database of 22 subjects containing 12 East-Asian and 10 South-American shows that this cascaded system is capable of providing competitive discriminative power on ethnicity with a correct classification rate over 95%.

Keywords: Ethnicity, Face, Gait, Fusion.

1   Introduction

Ethnicity is an important demographic attribute for a person. It doesn't change during one's whole lifetime. In many social activities, people usually show manifold behaviors due to the differences caused by ethnicity. Therefore, human ethnicity classification is a significant requirement for lots of tasks including access control, vital statistics and commercial analysis etc. There already have been some studies on distinguishing ethnic categories from facial images in the computer vision literature [1, 2, 3].

In recent years, more and more techniques have been proposed which integrate face and gait with the aim of investigating whether such a combination will improve upon the performance of methods which exclusively employ only one of these biometrics. Particularly, there are some specific reasons for considering the integration of face and gait biometrics. Face is a short-range biometric. That is to say, only when a person is close enough to the camera for sufficient details of his/her facial features to be captured, the face image can be used effectively for identification. In contrast, gait is a medium to long-range biometric, which can be extracted reliably even from low-resolution imagery and is more invariant to

W.-S. Zheng et al. (Eds.): CCBR 2012, LNCS 7701, pp. 300–307, 2012.

slight changes in viewpoint. Hence, combining these two biometric traits would be more robust to variations in distance between a subject and the camera.

Shakhnarovich et al. compute an image based visual hull from a set of monocular views [4]. Then the visual hull is used to render virtual canonical views for tracking and gait recognition. Also, this method is used to render frontal face images. Their work needs 4 monocular cameras to get both the side view of gait and the frontal view of face simultaneously. Later, Kale et al. present a fusion system consisting of gait recognition and face recognition algorithm based on sequential importance sampling [5]. They consider the single camera case only. In [6], Zhou and Bhanu propose an approach for the fusion of the side view of both gait and face from non cooperating subjects. In their approach, PCA and MDA are used to extract gait and face features and the combination of gait and face is carried out at the score level.

In this paper, we are interested in the study of recognizing human ethnicity by combining face and gait cues. Our first work is to build a database consisting of gait data and face data captured in the same walking sequence of each subject. These subjects come from East Asia and South America respectively. Secondly, we design a hierarchical fusion system in which gait works at the first level as the long-distance biometric and face is employed at the second level as the short-distance biometric. Only the subjects classified incorrectly at gait level enter the face based ethnicity classification stage.

The remainder of this paper is organized as follows. Section 2 describes the video based fusion system, utilizing and integrating information from long-distance gait and short-distance face. GEI construction and Gabor feature extraction are introduced in this section. In Section 3, the collection of multiple ethnicities database is detailed and the experimental results are compared and discussed. Section 4 concludes the paper.

2   Technical Approach

The overall technical approach is shown in Fig. 1. The whole cascaded fusion system is composed of two levels involving gait-based ethnicity classification (the first level) and face-based ethnicity classification (the second level). At the first stage, we construct Gait Energy Image (GEI) as the gait template from video sequences. Then, PCA is used to project GEI into a lower dimensional feature space and Support Vector Machine (SVM) is trained to classify ethnicity. If a person's ethnicity was classified to a wrong category at the first level, he/she would be classified once more at the second stage. Gabor wavelet transformation is applied to extract features from facial images at this stage. The algorithm of Real Adaboost is then used to find the final results.

2.1   Gait Energy Image Construction

It is known from the biomechanics literature that a given person will perform his or her walking pattern in a fairly repeatable way [8]. Therefore, it is possible to divide the entire gait sequence into cycles.

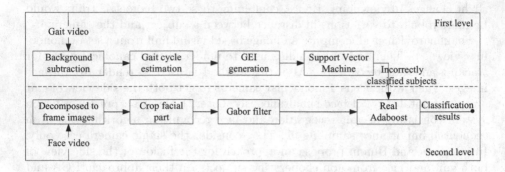

Fig. 1. Our approach for a hierarchical fusion system of face and gait

The necessary preprocessing includes background subtraction with output of binary silhouette image sequences. Then, the extracted silhouettes are centered and normalized to the same size. In a preprocessed silhouette sequence, the time serials signal of foreground pixels in the lower half silhouette is of period. Let N_{gait} denote the number of frames included in one gait cycle. We count the number of foreground pixels $N_{f(t)}$ in the lower half of the silhouette in each frame over time as described in [7]. This number will reach a maximum when the two legs are farthest apart and drop to a minimum when the legs overlap. For a body height H, the estimation of the vertical position of waist was set by study of anatomical data to be $0.53H$ [9]. We choose the part of the silhouette below waist to calculate $N_{f(t)}$ in each sequence. An example of variation of $N_{f(t)}$ is shown in Fig. 2. According to the periodicity of $N_{f(t)}$, N_{gait} can be easily obtained.

Given the preprocessed binary gait silhouette image $B_t(x, y)$ at time t in a sequence, the gray-level gait energy image (GEI) is defined as following [10]:

$$G(x,y) = \frac{1}{N_{gait}} \sum_{t=1}^{N_{gait}} B_t(x,y) \tag{1}$$

Fig. 3 shows the sample silhouette images of one stride in a gait cycle and the rightmost image is the corresponding GEI. It can be seen that GEI implicitly captures the shapes of silhouettes and their changes over a gait cycle. The time spent at each stance shows up indirectly as intensity in GEI representation.

2.2 Gabor Feature Extraction from Facial Image

The Gabor wavelets (filters) have been found to be particularly suitable for image decomposition and representation with the aim of obtaining local and discriminating features. Donato et al. have experimentally shown that the Gabor filter representation gave better performance for classifying facial actions [11].

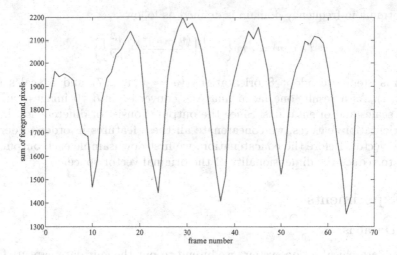

Fig. 2. Variation of the number of foreground pixels from below-waist part of the silhouette in one sequence

Fig. 3. Examples of normalized silhouette images from one stride. The rightmost image is the GEI of the corresponding whole gait cycle.

A family of complex Gabor filters can be defined as follows:

$$\varphi_{u,v}(x) = \frac{\|k_{u,v}\|^2}{\sigma^2} exp\Big(\frac{-\|k_{u,v}\|^2\|x\|^2}{2\sigma^2}\Big)\Big[exp(ik_{u,v} \cdot x) - exp\Big(-\frac{\sigma^2}{2}\Big)\Big] \quad (2)$$

where u and v define the orientation and scale of the Gabor filters, and the wave vector $k_{u,v}$ is defined as:

$$k_{(u,v)} = k_v exp(i\phi_u) \quad (3)$$

where $k_v = \frac{k_{max}}{f^v}$ and $\phi_u = \frac{u\pi}{8}$. k_{max} is the maximum frequency and f is the spacing factor between kernels in the frequency domain. In most face applications, $\sigma = 2\pi$, $k_{max} = \frac{\pi}{2}$, $f = \sqrt{2}$, $v \in \{0, ..., 4\}$, $u \in \{0, ..., 7\}$.

A two dimensional form of Gabor wavelet consists of a planer sinusoid multiplied by a two dimensional Gaussian [12]. Local features of an image can be extracted effectively using the 2D Gabor wavelet and the advantage is the high tolerance of changes in location, shape, scale and light. The formula of Gabor wavelet in space domain is expressed as:

$$g(x,y) = \Big(\frac{1}{2\pi\sigma_x\sigma_y}\Big)exp\Big[-\frac{1}{2}\Big(\frac{x^2}{\sigma_x^2} + \frac{y^2}{\sigma_y^2}\Big) + j2\pi\omega x\Big] \quad (4)$$

The formula in frequency domain is defined as follows:

$$G(u,v) = exp\Big\{-\frac{1}{2}\Big[\frac{(u-\omega)^2}{\sigma_u^2} + \frac{v^2}{\sigma_v^2}\Big]\Big\} \qquad (5)$$

In our system, we adopt 8 orientations ($u = 0, 1, ..., 7$) and 5 scales ($v = 0, 1, ..., 4$). As a result, one facial image is converted into 40 images with different scales and orientations. Since the outputs consist of different local, scale and orientation features, we concatenate all these features in order to derive a feature vector. Before the concatenation, we first downsample each output by a factor to reduce the dimensionality of the original vector space.

3   Experiments

3.1   Database

In this hierarchical fusion system, we intend to put the gait data captured from a long distance on the first stage and utilize the face data obtained from a short distance at the second stage. Two cameras are placed in an indoor laboratory scenario and the cameras setup can be described in Fig. 4. The walking start is labeled by the left black point S. The right black point denotes camera C_1 that is used to capture face images and camera C_2 at lower point is used to record gait data. During the collecting process, each person was asked to walk along the line between point S and camera C_1 naturally.

Camera C_2 recorded his/her movements during the whole walking and C_1 began to capture face images only when the distance between the person and itself is short enough. In our case, this distance is less than 2.0 meters. 26 of the subjects in our database are students from East Asia and the remaining 10 are from South America. As a result, we obtained a small database including 36 subjects, each of which consists of five gait and face video sequences. According to our initial consideration in Section 1, the gait data were captured by a long-range camera C_2 with a distance more than 6.5 meters to the object and the face data were obtained from a short-range camera C_1 in our case, as shown in Fig. 4.

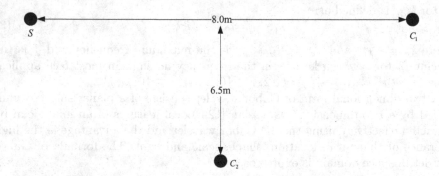

Fig. 4. Cameras setup for data collection

3.2 Experiments and Comparisons

For ethnicity recognition from gaits, there have been no related studies so far as we know mainly because all the shared gait databases are not collected for the specific consideration. Based on our database, we first make an evaluation on the performance of gait based ethnicity classification. The two gait representations which have been used for gender classification in [7, 13] are introduced to carry out the task of ethnicity classification in our experiments. One representation is GEI that is described in Section 2. The details of the other representation that is to fit ellipses on different regions of human body can be found in [13].

The experimental results show that the ethnicity classification performance based on gait is not optimistic. Table 1 lists the correct ethnicity classification rates. We trained and tested SVM to implement ethnicity classifications.

Table 1. Results of gait based ethnicity classification

Classifier	Correct Classification Rate	
	GEI representation	Ellipse representation
SVM(linear)	77.3%	72.7%
SVM(poly)	67.8%	62.5%
SVM(RBF)	63.5%	60.2%

Due to the higher recognition rates of GEI representation, we choose to construct GEI as gait features at the first level in our cascaded fusion system. For face based ethnicity classification at the second level, we applied Gabor filter to facial images as [1] and adopt Real Adaboost to classify ethnicity as shown in [3]. In our database, each subject corresponds to 5 facial image sequences and we select 6 images from every sequence for our experiments. Under random-person test, our experiment results are better than the results derived from the methods in [1, 3] when running on the same database, as listed in Table 2.

The integration of gait and face cues is cascaded. Because the system of ethnicity classification based on gait performs worse than the one based on face, we put gait modality at the first level. 8 of 36 persons are classified into incorrect ethnicity at the first stage and this error rate seems a little unacceptable for a robust recognition system. Then, we further distinguish these 8 persons' ethnicity at the second face-based stage. The final output says that only one person is labeled in error. In other words, the correct classification rate reaches 95.5% which is higher than the best classification rate in [3] based on face in large databases. Table 3 gives our fusion results. The encouraging recognition rate of the final output provides a powerful support to our hierarchical fusion system theoretically. The integration of long-range and short-range biometrics, such as combining gait and face, will receive more and more attentions in the computer vision research community.

Table 2. Results of face based ethnicity classification

Methods	Authors	Database	Correct Classification Rate
Gabor+SVM	Hosoi S. et al.	446 Asian, African and European images	88.3%
LBP+Real Adaboost	Yang Z. et al.	11680 Asian images and 1016 non-Asian images	93.2%
Gabor+Real Adaboost	This paper	780 Asian images and 300 South-American images	86.2%
Hosoi S. et al.	This paper	the same as above	81.8%
Yang Z. et al.	This paper	the same as above	82.8%

Table 3. Results of ethnicity classification in our cascade system

Modality	Correct Classification Rate
Gait only	77.3%
Face only	86.2%
Fusion of face and gait	95.5%

4   Conclusions and Future Work

In this paper, we have presented an effective hierarchical fusion system for ethnicity recognition. Based on the investigation of ethnicity discriminability of both gait and face features firstly, we use gait data at the first level and put face data at the second level. Although the output of gait based ethnicity classification is not satisfying, the face classifier at the second stage plays a complementary and improving role. Such a fusion system can find its applications in surveillance and security environment easily because one of its big characteristics is to integrate the long-range biometrics and short-range biometrics.

In the future, there is still much work to do. For gait, we will utilize more dynamics information that is intrinsic for the style of human walking to increase the recognition accuracy. For face, we need to find a faster algorithm than Gabor filter to meet a real-time requirement. In addition, the database is too small to give more reliable results. Hence, to enlarge the database and design more complex fusion systems is also an important and pressing task.

References

1. Hosoi, S., Katikawa, E., Kawade, M.: Ethnicity estimation with facial images. In: Proc. of International Conference on Automatic Face and Gesture Recognition, pp. 195–200 (2004)
2. Lao, S., Kawade, M.: Vision-based face understanding technologies and their application. In: Proc. of International Conference on Biometric Recognition, pp. 339–348 (2004)

3. Yang, Z., Ai, H.: Demographic classification with local binary patterns. In: Proc. of International Conference on Biometrics, pp. 464–473 (2007)
4. Shakhnarovich, G., Lee, L., Darrell, T.: Integrated face and gait recognition from multiple views. In: Proc. of IEEE International Conference on Computer Vision and Pattern Recognition, vol. 1, pp. 439–446 (2001)
5. Kale, A., Roychowdhury, A., Chellappa, R.: Fusion of gait and face for human identification. In: Proc. of International Conference on Acoustics, Speech, and Signal Processing, vol. 5, pp. 901–904 (2004)
6. Zhou, X., Bhanu, B.: Integrating face and gait for human recognition. In: Proc. of IEEE Workshop on Computer Vision and Pattern Recognition, pp. 55–62 (2006)
7. Sarka, S., Phillips, P.J., Liu, Z., Vega, I.R., Grother, P., Bowyer, K.W.: The HumanID Gait Challenge Problem: Data Sets, Performance, and Analysis. IEEE Transactions on Pattern Analysis and Machine Intelligence 27(2), 162–177 (2007)
8. Winter, D.: The biomechanics and motor control of human gait, 2nd edn. Waterloo Biomechanics, Ottawa (1996)
9. Dempster, W.T., Gaughran, G.R.L.: Properties of body segments based on size and weight. American Journal of Anatomy 120, 33–54 (1967)
10. Han, J., Bhanu, B.: Individual recognition using gait energy image. IEEE Transactions on Pattern Analysis and Machine Intelligence 28(2), 316–322 (2006)
11. Donato, G., Bartlett, M.S., Hager, J.C., Ekman, P., Sejnowski, T.J.: Classifying facial actions. IEEE Transactions on Pattern Analysis and Machine Intelligence 21, 974–989 (1999)
12. Lyons, M., Budynek, J., Plante, A., Akamastus, S.: Classifying facial attributes using a 2D gabor wavelet representation and discriminant analysis. In: Proc. of International Conference on Automatic Face and Gesture Recognition, pp. 202–207 (2000)
13. Grimson, W., Lee, L.: Gait analysis for recognition and classification. In: Proc. of International Conference on Automatic Face and Gesture Recognition, pp. 148–155 (2002)

An Algorithm for Retina Features Extraction
Based on Position of the Blood Vessel Bifurcation

Radek Drozd, Josef Hájek, and Martin Drahanský

Faculty of Information Technology, Brno University of Technology,
Božetěchova 2, 61266 Brno, Czech Republic
xdrozd07@stud.fit.vutbr.cz,
{ihajek,drahan}@fit.vutbr.cz

Abstract. This paper deals with a proposal of the algorithm for features extraction from the blood vessels on the back of eyeball. Automated extraction is based on the bifurcations (points where a single vessel splits into two vessels) in retina. Each particular bifurcation is subsequently specified by its own position given by the coordinate system derived from the mutual position of the optic disc and fovea. The complete algorithm has been developed in C++ language and uses OpenCV library for image processing. This proposed method was evaluated on available images of the STARE and DRIVE databases.

Keywords: retina, biometrics, fundus camera, blood vessel, matched filtering, digital signal processor, filtering, optic disc, macula, bifurcation point.

1   Introduction

Human recognition which uses pattern of blood vessels on the back of the eyeball is very specific branch of biometrics. Although retina based technique of identification is often perceived as very secure biometric approach, this method is not widely used due to a few major disadvantages.

One of them is related to security. Retina is located inside on the back of the eye and it is technically difficult to acquire the retinal image as well as inconvenient. Retina is not a visible part of human body, in comparison to iris or face, which allows being captured even from longer distances. In this case, it is necessary to have appropriate optical system which is able to focus the whole eye through the pupil and take a picture of the retinal part. On the other hand, it is very hard to counterfeit such recognition because the attacker would have to obtain retinal image from the relevant individual and simulate an optical system of the eye.

Retina is very suitable for biometric purposes. Blood vessel pattern consists of up to 400 unique features and is stable for the whole life of an individual [1].

Vascular network, optic disc (part of the retina where the optic nerve comes into the eye) and macula (part of the retina with greatest number of receptors) are three major elements of the human retina. In fig. 1, optic disc can be seen as the brightest area of the image, containing pixels of yellow hue. Macula's distance from optic disc center is approximately double of the optic disc's diameter. It can be classified as the

W.-S. Zheng et al. (Eds.): CCBR 2012, LNCS 7701, pp. 308–315, 2012.

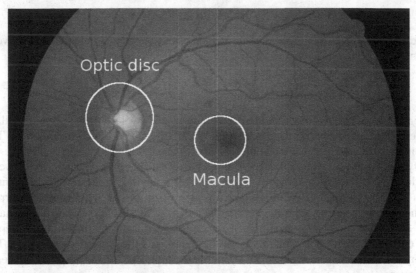

Fig. 1. Retina image (source: Gold standard database for Evaluation of Fundus Image Segmentation Algorithms[1])

darkest area of the image. Blood vessels are contrasting with the background, mostly in green channel of the image.

The algorithm described below uses these aspects for features extraction. In this case, vascular system is represented by vessels bifurcation points and each particular feature is represented by position of this point. The coordinate system is given by mutual position of the optic disc and fovea (center of macula). That means each particular bifurcation point has own exact position in the image.

2   Methodology

Application by itself deals with extraction of blood vessels bifurcations. These are determined by its position. We use the same approach as in [2] – polar coordinate system. Point p is determined by its distance from the coordinate system's origin and by the angle of ray towards it and positive x axis (1).

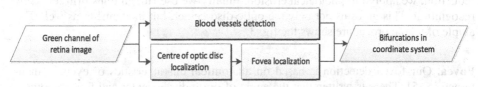

Fig. 2. Overview of the proposed approach

---
[1] Available at http://www5.informatik.uni-erlangen.de/research/data/fundus-images

$$p_1 = [d, \varphi] \tag{1}$$

The distance d is defined as Euclidean distance and angle φ is calculated by inverse trigonometric function *arctan*.

2.1   Coordinate System Definition

Important issue is how to define the coordinate system, where the bifurcation will be located (In order to get information about position of each particular bifurcation). This system must be invariant to rotation, translation and scaling of an input image. To satisfy this demand, the coordinate system is based on anatomical structures of eye. In [2], there is the coordinate system determined by optic disc's center and the position of its closest bifurcation. We think that this approach may be predisposed to errors, because there are plenty of bifurcations located in optic disc area, and their distance from optic disc center is very similar. Consequently, during the measurement repetition, each time a different bifurcation can be marked as the closest to optic disc. This is why we determine the coordinate system by mutual position of optic disc center and fovea.

2.2   Fovea and Optic Disc Localization

Accurate localization of optic disc center and fovea is crucial for coordinate system determination. In the case of wrongly determined coordinate system, the whole measurement will be incorrect.

Centre of Optic Disc. Several papers deal with optic disc localization. For example, [3] uses methods called *Principal component analysis* and *Gradient Vector Flow Snakes* for optic disc borders recognition. Nevertheless, the position of optic disc borders is not essential for us, because we only need to find the center of this area. Another approach is mentioned in [5]. It is based on the assumption, that an optic disc roughly takes up to 5% of the area of the brightest pixels. Our algorithm uses the approach mentioned in [4]. This is based on low-pass filter application. The brightest area is considered as the center of region of interest.

In the next step, we only deal with this area. First, we apply morphological dilatation and Gaussian blur. It removes blood vessels from the area. Then we use Sobel edge detector and convert an image to a binary form, using thresholding. For noise reduction, we apply morphological erosion. Finally we use Hough transform for circle recognition. This gives us not only the optic disc center, but its diameter as well. Example of whole procedure shows the fig. 3.

Fovea. Our fovea detection is based on anatomical characteristics of eyeball, mentioned in [5]. There is written that the angle of optic disc's center and fovea's joint is between -6 and +3 degrees from the horizontal line. Their distance roughly corresponds to double of the optic disc's diameter. This defined sector is used and the rest of the image is marked by white color. In the next step we try again to localize the area containing pixels with lowest intensity, using the low-pass filter.

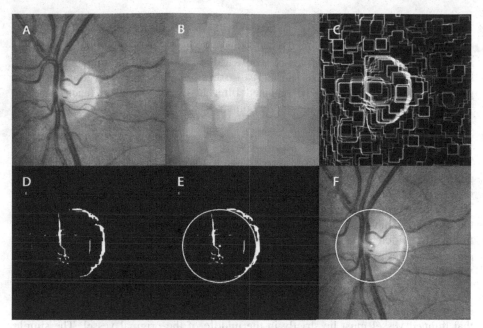

Fig. 3. Optic disc localization: A) Region of interest; B) removed blood vessels; C) Sobel edge detector; D) eroded binary image; E) Hough circle; F) circle in the original image

2.3   Bifurcation Search

Precondition to a bifurcation search is blood vessels detection. Several papers deal with these approaches. They can be divided into two groups. Papers in the first group are based on morphological operation. For example [3] uses *stop-hat* operation. Our approach is based on the other group of papers. *Match filtering* is used for blood vessels detection in those approaches. All following operations are applied on the green channel of the given image, because the blood vessels have the highest contrast on it.

Automatic Contrast Adjustment. Despite the use of green channel, blood vessels may have low contrast in some images, due to poor quality of these images. In this case, it is necessary to adjust contrast. Commonly used methods, such as Histogram Equalization, are not very suitable for our case. Manual contrast adjustment has mostly the best results, but unfortunately it cannot be applied. According to [3], the method called *Fast Gray Level Grouping* gives satisfying results. The principle and implementation details are described in [6] and [7]. The main advantage of this method is the fact that the new histogram will have nearly the uniform distribution.

Matched Filter. The most important part of blood vessels detection process is the vessels segmentation from the image background. We use 2D filter response, which is defined by (2).

$$\mathbf{K}(x,y) = -e^{\left(\frac{x^2}{2\sigma^2}\right)} for \ y \le \left|\frac{L}{2}\right| \tag{2}$$

L stands for minimal length of vessel, where it does not change its orientation and σ is standard deviation in Gaussian (normal) distribution. The exact procedure of filter generation is based on [8]. The obtained filter is 12 times rotated (each time for 15degrees). All twelve filters are applied on an image, and their responses are added with weighting.

Thresholding. It is desirable to convert an image into a binary form, for a subsequent processing. This is made by thresholding. The threshold is computed for every input image. We proceed with the assumption that blood vessels take up approximately 3-10% of retina image (according to a specific type of fundus camera).Another way is the use of adaptable thresholding. Main disadvantage of this method are small white fragments, which are misclassified as vessels. We apply morphological operation *close* after thresholding. This removes small holes and increases the connectivity of vessels.

Thinning. Last step, preceding the bifurcation localization, is thinning. It is essential, that thinned vessel must lie strictly in the middle of the original vessel. The simple algorithm is overtaken from [9]. The thinning is executed from four directions, to ensure position of thinned vessel in the middle of the original one.

Bifurcation Localization. Now, we can finally localize bifurcations. This is made by checking 8-neighbor of every positive pixel. When there are three vessels, coming out from one point, they are marked as a bifurcation. The only problem is caused by short pieces at ends of vessels. These were created as a side effect of thinning. This problem is solved by the definition of minimal length of whole 3 vessels coming out from the point.

3   Experimental Results

The application was primarily tested on *Gold Standard Database for Evaluation of Fundus Image Segmentation Algorithms*[2]. This database consists of 48 images, with resolution about 8MPix.Those images are divided into three groups. The first one are images of healthy eyes, second one contains eyes afflicted by glaucoma and the last one are eyes afflicted by diabetic retinopathy. The database contains manually segmented blood vessels.

These tests were supplemented by tests on DRIVE[3]and STARE[4] databases. Results of these two tests are rather for illustration, because our algorithm is optimized for pictures with higher resolution.

---

[2] Available at http://www5.informatik.uni-erlangen.de/research/data/fundus-images

[3]Available at http://www.isi.uu.nl/Research/Databases/DRIVE

Last database, which we used for testing, is set of images taken in STRaDe (Security Technology Research and Development – research group at Faculty of Information Technology, Brno University of Technology in Czech Republic, which is focused on security in IT and biometric systems) laboratory. Database contains more than 300 images in 10MPix resolution. Unfortunately, significant part of this set consists of very low quality pictures. There are many reflections in these images. Some pictures are also very dark close to borders. That is why we made a selection of 148 finest images, which we used for testing. Manually segmented vessels, corresponding to these images, do not exist, so we used them only for optic disc center and fovea localization testing.

Blood Vessel Segmentation. The testing of blood vessels segmentation was driven in the way of comparing the corresponding pixels of manually segmented vessels and algorithm output after the closing operation. We used a mask to compare only foreground pixels, not the background ones. See fig. 4 for details.

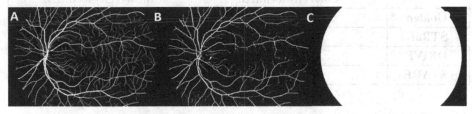

Fig. 4. Example of blood vessels segmentation: A) Manually segmented vessels; B) output from our algorithm; C) used mask

The final score was computed as the ratio of the same value pixels count to the count of all foreground pixels. The results can be seen in table 1.

Table 1. Results of blood vessels segmentation

	Healthy	Glaucoma	Diabetic retinopathy
Golden	95,78 ± 1,01%	95,00 ± 0,98%	94,12 ± 1,77%
DRIVE	92,90 ± 2,27%		
STARE	79,62 ± 7,03%		

Optic Disc Localization. The correct application behavior is that the optic disc center is successfully recognized or the application is terminated with an error message. The case, when the application misclassifies optic disc center and continues in running is considered as incorrect. The results are shown in table 2.Our application has troubles with locating the optic disc in images of eyes which are highly afflicted by diabetic retinopathy.

---

[4]Available at http://www.parl.clemson.edu/stare

Table 2. Results of optic disc recognition

	Correctly localized	Not localized	Incorrectly localized
Golden	89,58%	8,33%	2,08%
STRaDe	70,95%	28,38%	0,68%
DRIVE	85%	5%	10%
STARE	64,26%	21,43%	14,29%

Fovea Localization. The essential precondition for fovea localization is the successful optic disc's center localization. The results in table 3 consider only the situations, when the precondition has been met.

Table 3. Results of fovea localization

	Correctly localized	Incorrectly localized
Golden	95,35%	4,65%
STRaDe	90,48%	9,52%
DRIVE	70,59%	29,41%
STARE	55,56%	44,44%

4   Conclusion

This paper describes a potential part of biometric system which can be used in a real device for human beings recognition. The presented input samples for the algorithm have been taken from fundus cameras under almost ideal conditions and it is supposed that the real pictures from camera for recognition purposes will be in lower quality in comparison with those from medical device.

In the future we would like to develop our own optical system and adjust this algorithm for our own recognition device.

Acknowledgement. This work is partially supported by the research plan "Security-Oriented Research in Information Technology", MSM0021630528 (CZ), by the grant "Advanced secured, reliable and adaptive IT", FIT-S-11-1 (CZ), by the grant "Information Technology in Biomedical Engineering", GD102/09/H083 (CZ) and by the project "The IT4Innovations Centre of Excellence", ED1.1.00/02.0070 (CZ).

References

1. Das, R.: Retina recognition: Biometric technology in practice. Journal of Documents: A Bimonthly Magazine about Developments in the Security Industry (22), 11–14 (2011)
2. Chowdhary, B., Latif, S.: Pattern Matching Algorithm using Polar Spectrum in Retina Recognition for Human Identification System. Australian Journal of Basic and Applied Sciences/International Network for Scientific Information; INSInet (5), 1385–1392 (2011)

3. Saradhi, G.V., Balasubramanian, S., Chandrasekaran, V.: Performance Enhancement of Optic Disc Boundary Detection using Active Contours via Improved Homogenization of Optic Disc Region. In: International Conference on Information and Automation, ICIA, pp. 264–269 (2006)
4. Aquino, A., Gegúndez, M.E., Marín, D.: Automated Optic Disc Detection in Retinal Images of Patients with Diabetic Retinopathy and Risk of Macular Edema. World Academy of Science, Engineering and Technology (60), 87–92 (2009)
5. Siddalingaswamy, P.C., Prabhu, G.K.: Automated Detection of Anatomical Structures in Retinal Images. In: International Conference on Computational Intelligence and Multimedia Applications, vol. 3(10), pp. 164–168 (2007)
6. Chen, Z., Abidi, B.R., Page, D.L., Abidi, M.A.: Gray-Level Grouping (GLG): An Automatic Method for Optimized Image Contrast Enhancement—Part I: The Basic Method. IEEE Transactions on Image Processing: A Publication of the IEEE Signal Processing Society (8), 2290–2302 (2006)
7. Chen, Z., Abidi, B.R., Page, D.L., Abidi, M.A.: Gray-Level Grouping (GLG): An Automatic Method for Optimized Image Contrast Enhancement—Part II: The Variations. IEEE Transactions on Image Processing: A Publication of the IEEE Signal Processing Society (8), 2303–2314 (2006)
8. Chaudhuri, S., Chatterjee, S., Katz, N., Nelson, M., Goldbaum, M.: Detection of blood vessels in retinal images using two-dimensional matched filters. IEEE Transactions on Medical Imaging (3), 263–269 (1989)
9. Parker, J.: Algorithms for image processing and computer vision. John Wiley & Sons (1996) ISBN 0471140562

Recognition of Petechia Tongue Based on LoG and Gabor Feature with Spatial Information

Yangyang Zhao, Xiaoqiang Li, and Zhicheng Fu

School of Computer Engineering and Science, Shanghai University
xqli@shu.edu.cn

Abstract. Recognition of petechia tongue is still a challenging problem due to different color, morphology and texture in tongue image. This paper presents a new method to automatically recognition of petechia tongue based on LoG and Gabor feature with spatial information. The proposed approach begins with a normalized LoG filter to locate the suspected petechia areas in tongue image. In the subsequent step, the spatial position feature and Gabor feature were extracted as a feature descriptor of these regions. Support vector machine is used as a classifier to classify these suspected petechia areas into petechia and non-petechia areas. Finally, the proposed method judge whether the tongue image have petechia according to the proportion of petechia regions to all suspected petechia regions. Experimental results on two hundred tongue images indicate the better performance of our method, the accuracy achieves to 84.91%.

Keywords: tongue petechia detection, Laplace of Gaussian (LoG), Gabor filter, spatial feature, support vector machine.

1   Introduction

Tongue diagnosis [1-2] is one of the most important and valuable diagnostic methods in traditional Chinese medicine (TCM) and has been widely applied to clinical analyses and applications for thousands of years. The theory of TCM holds that the feature of tongue reflects the condition of organs, and is a remarkable evidence for diagnosis. Whenever there is a complex disorder full of contradictions, examination of the tongue can instantly clarify the main pathological processes. However, the subjectivity of traditional Chinese tongue diagnosis is too strong, which lack of quantitative basis. In the recent years, with AI widely applied in the development of medicine, it is inevitable for us to blaze new ways in the field of tongue diagnosis instead of some traditional artificial means of diagnosis, which relies on the magnificent process capability of computer [3-11]. For instance, extracting tongue cracks using the wide line detector by Liu [5-6], Pang's researches on the tongue diagnosis for appendicitis with computer technology [7], robust lip segmentation method based on level set [8], feature extraction method for recognition of petechia tongue by some researcher [9-11], and so on.

Recognition of petechia tongue is an important feature and manifestation of certain diseases for tongue diagnosis in TCM. And combined it with other tongue

W.-S. Zheng et al. (Eds.): CCBR 2012, LNCS 7701, pp. 316–323, 2012.

pathological features also provides an important basis for the diagnosis of disease [9]. It is generally used to carry out the judgment for the TCM practitioners according to the contrast of petechia area with its surrounding local area, spatial position and darker color. Several methods have been presented to recognize the tongue with petechia. Wang and Zong [9] proposed a recognition method based on Bayesian networks and elliptical or circle shape feature of petechia. However, the elliptical or circle edge extraction is a very difficult program in tongue image with complicated background such as different texture and color. Li and et al [10,11] presented a feature extraction method for recognition of petechia dot in tongue image employing graylevel-height based thresholding, Top-hat high-pass filtering, and Gaussian histogram specification. Graylevel contrast-stretch and morphological filters are designed as preprocessing method to make petechia dot more apparent. Finally, algorithm erasing falsely selected pixel is presented to avoid misjudgment with help of region growing and Hit-or-Miss transform. This scheme is time-consuming and the robustness of which is low for its heuristic design. In addition, the scheme assumes that there is generally one petechia in tongue.

In the theory of TCM, the petechia is a darker region compared with its surround pixels, whereas not all the darker region is really petechia. So the theory of TCM claims that tongue with a number of petechia regions is defined as a petechia tongue. However, this number is an undeterminate quantity and varies with different tongue. Based on the prior knowledge above, this paper proposes a promising method recognizing petechia tongue. Firstly, the suspected petechia regions in tongue image are located by LoG filter. Then, the spatial feature and Gabor texture feature of these suspected regions are extracted and used to train SVM classifier to classify suspected petechia region into petechia and non-petechia region. Finally, the tongue is recognized as petechia tongue if the proportion of the petechia regions to all the suspected ones is larger than the threshold originated from statistical results.

The remainder of this paper is organized as follows. In section 2, the suspected petechia regions are detected based on the normalized LoG filter. Extracting the spatial feature and Gabor texture feature of these regions in tongue image is shown in section 3, then the feature of petechia is used to train SVM classifier and petechia tongue recognition method is introduced. In section 4, the proposed approach is tested on two hundred tongue images. The conclusions and future work are given in the end.

2   Detection of Suspected Petechia Regions

Through the observation and analysis of a large number of petechia and non-petechia areas in tongue images, the petechia regions present the following characteristics: 1) prominent contrast to the local neighbored area; 2) circle region with almost the same radius; 3) the color tend to black or dark; 4) majority distribute in the marginal; 5) fine-grained local texture. In this section, we use the frontal four properties to locate the suspected petechia.

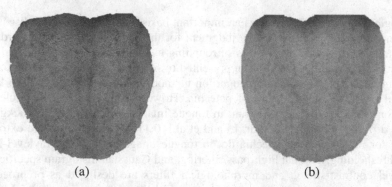

(a)   (b)

Fig. 1. Petechia tongue and non-petechia tongue. (a) petechia tongue; (b) non-petechia tongue.

Figure 1 shows two typical tongues, one is petechia tongue the other is non-petechia tongue. The important feature of petechia is that its brightness is lower than the surrounding pixels. There are other phenomena such as crack, red prickles, taste buds and so on. The difference between the petechia and other phenomena exist at the two aspects. One is the contrast or color, the phenomena as red prickles is brighter and redder than its surrounding region. Another different is the shape, the phenomena as crack is line or curve.

So we decided to identify petechia region based on contrast and spatial position. According to the prominent contrast of petechia area and its surrounding local area, we can locate darker salient regions in tongue image as suspected petechia areas. However, there are also some non-petechia regions in these suspected petechia regions due to the influence of crack, shadow, or other factors like noise. We will deal with this problem in the next section.

The suspected petechia regions are located by the convolution of tongue image with Laplace of Guassian operator. Here, we used a normalized Laplace of Guassian which can be written as

$$\nabla^2_{norm}g = -\frac{1}{\pi\sigma^4}\left[1 - \frac{x^2+y^2}{2\sigma^2}\right]e^{-\frac{x^2+y^2}{2\sigma^2}} \qquad (1)$$

By finding the extreme point of $\nabla^2_{norm}g$, that is when scale $\sigma = \sqrt{(x^2+y^2)/2}$, $\nabla^2_{norm}g$ reach the maximum response. So, we can detect suspected petechia regions of different size by changing the value of σ.

In order to convert the convolution of template into box filter operation, we need to simplify the Gaussian Laplace template and make the simplified template composed of several rectangular areas of each was filled with the same value. Because the luminance of petechia region tends to be darker compared with peripheral region, the value of inner black area is set to be -1, outer white area is 1, middle gray area is 0, as shown in Figure 2. In this paper, Laplace of Guassian operator is simplified and normalized into the template of 15×15 as shown in formula (2). Using this kind of template can detect the region whose luminance is lower than its surrounding.

Fig. 2. Template of LoG and simplification. (a) $\nabla^2_{norm} g$. (b) simplification of $\nabla^2_{norm} g$

$$\text{kernel}(i, j) = \begin{cases} \dfrac{1}{104} & \begin{array}{l} 1 \leq i \leq 2, \ 14 \leq i \leq 15 \text{ and } 1 \leq j \leq 15 \\[4pt] \text{or } 1 \leq j \leq 2, \ 14 \leq j \leq 15 \text{ and } 3 \leq j \leq 13 \end{array} \\[12pt] -\dfrac{1}{9} & 7 \leq i \leq 9 \text{ and } 7 \leq j \leq 9 \\[8pt] 0 & \text{others} \end{cases} \tag{2}$$

After locating the suspected petechia by LoG filter (shown as Figure. 3(a)), we also need to execute two post-processing. Because the strong response of convolution template to the edge of tongue, it is inevitable that there are some regions on the edge of tongue are falsely considered as suspected petechia region. According to the theory of TCM, these strong response regions cannot be petechia region, so we had better rule them out. In addition, some regions will produce several strong responses to the convolution template with variational size, and are maybe marked as suspected pete-chia for several times. These repeat markers (circle) are also need to be removed and reserve only one. The final suspected petechia regions can be located after these two steps post-processing as shown in Figure 3.

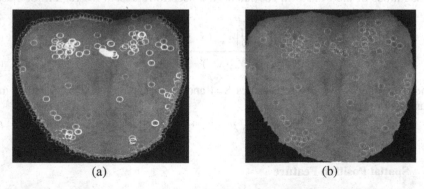

Fig. 3. The location process of suspected petechia. (a) The initial suspected petechia areas marked by white circles. (b) The suspected petechia after post-processing by remove edge circle and repeat circle.

3   Recognition of Petechia Tongue

Through the observation and analysis of petechia regions and non-petechia regions, we find that the texture in the petechia region tends to be more fine-grained, contrarily the texture around the non-petechia region tends to be more coarse-grained. However, these two kinds of regions are all possible detected and considered as suspected petechia, because they have the same property that the luminance is lower than surrounding. So, we need to use this prominent texture difference between petechia and non-petechia region to analyze suspected petechia region. In this section, we extract the texture feature of suspected petechia region based on Gabor filtering to distinguish them. Moreover, spatial position feature is another important feature for petechia region, according to the statistical results of TCM. Based on the above analysis, we extract these two aspect features to recognize the petechia tongue.

3.1   Gabor Texture Feature

Gabor features have been used and proven effective in several image analysis including texture classification and segmentation, image recognition and motion tracking [12]. The Gabor representation has advantage to be optimal in the sense of minimizing the joint two-dimensional uncertainty in space and frequency. These filters can be considered as orientation and scale tunable edge and line detectors, and the statistics of these micro-features in a given region are often used to characterize the underlying texture information.

In this section, we use a simple and effective texture representation based on Gabor features [12].

Given an image $I(x, y)$, its Gabor wavelet transform is then defined to be

$$W_{mn}(x, y) = \int I(x_1, y_1) g_{mn}*(x - x_1, y - y_1) dx_1 dy_1 \tag{3}$$

Where * indicates the complex conjugate. It is assumed that the local texture regions are spatially homogeneous, and the mean μ_{mn} and the standard deviation σ_{mn} of the magnitude of the transform coeffcients are used to represent the region for classification purpose:

$$\mu_{mn}(x, y) = \iint |W_{mn}(x, y)| dx dy \tag{4}$$

$$\sigma_{mn}(x, y) = \sqrt{\iint (|W_{mn}(x, y)| - \mu_{mn})^2 dx dy} \tag{5}$$

In the experiments, we use four scales S=4 and six orientations K=6, resulting in a texture feature vector

$$\overline{f} = [\mu_{00} \ \sigma_{00} \ \mu_{01} \ \sigma_{01} \cdots \mu_{35} \ \sigma_{35}] \tag{6}$$

3.2   Spatial Position Feature

The position of suspected petechia is also important information for TCM practitioner to recognize the petechia tongue, while the size of different tongue is differ in thousands ways. In addition, to increase the robustness of proposed method, we also need to quantify the coordinate space to N×N to reduce the influence of petechia's position. In other words, we extract the quantitative coordinates of each petechia region in the tongue image instead of precise position coordinates. To extract the same spatial feature of suspected petechia of different tongue with the same offset position in respective tongue, the proposed method construct a normalization and quantization space for different tongue images. First, Tongue image with different size is normalized into the same size S×S. Then, normalized tongue image is quantized rectangular region shown as Figure 4. Spatial feature of each petechia region is extracted at last. In practice, we use S = 512and N=4.

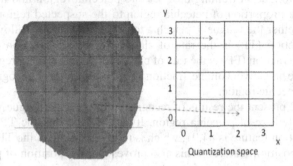

Fig. 4. Normalization and Quantization space

3.3   Recognition Method

Thus, the feature vector of a suspected petechia region is a fifty dimensions vector compose of texture feature and spatial position feature, and is described as formula (7), where x and y is horizontal and vertical axis quantitative coordinates respectively in normalized tongue image.

$$\bar{\bar{f}} = [x, y, \mu_{00}\ \sigma_{00}\ \mu_{01}\ \sigma_{01} \cdots \mu_{35}\ \sigma_{35}] \tag{7}$$

The first step of recognition is to classify the suspected petechia region. Many fifty dimension feature vector of petechia region or non-petechia region from training data set is used to train SVM classifier. The petechia region is considered as positive sample, the non-petechia region negative sample. The classifier is then used to classify the suspected petechia into each tongue into petechia or non-petechia region.

The second step of recognition is to classify tongue image. For each tongue image, it is recognized as petechia tongue or non-petechia tongue based on the proportion of petechia region to the all suspected region. In the proposed method, if this proportion is larger than 20%, the tongue is recognized as petechia tongue. Otherwise, is as non-petechia tongue.

4   Experimental Results

Two hundred tongue images are used in our experiments to verify effectiveness of the proposed algorithm. The images come from shanghai DaoSheng medical technology co ltd. Each tongue image showed in this paper is obtained by segmentation from face image including tongue captured by special acquisition device. There are one hundred images is petechia tongue, the other one hundred images is non-petechia tongue. At the beginning, training set of tongue images are randomly taken from half of the petechia and non-petechia images respectively, the rest are used as testing images. And ten-fold cross validation is used to avoid stochastic good results. The proposed algorithm was written by VC++ and OpenCV library. The experiment was completed on the Dell OptiPlex 780.

In experiment, selected petechia and non-petechia region are firstly used to train SVM classifier. Then, the SVM classifier is used to classify the suspected petechia region for each tongue in training data set into petechia region and non-petechia region. At last, the proportion of petechia region to the suspected region is established to recognize whether the tongue is petechia tongue or not. In the following, true positive volume fraction (TP) is the rate of classifying petechia region correctly, false positive volume fraction (FP) is the rate of classifying non-petechia region as petechia region, and false negative volume fraction (FN) is the rate of recognizing petechia region as non-petechia region.

Table 1 and 2 present the results of recognition of petechia tongue with or without spatial position feature of petechia region. It can be seen that the TP of recognition with spatial position feature is 84.91, which is more precise than the TP of recognition without spatial position feature. This also proves that the position of petechia region is important information to recognize petechia tongue.

Table 1. Results of recognition of petechia tongue with spatial position feature

Samples \ Result	Petechia Tongue	Non-Petechia Tongue	FN (%)	FP (%)	TP (%)
Petechia Tongue	45	5	9.43	15.09	84.91
Non-PetechiaTongue	8	42			

Table 2. Results of recognition of petechia tongue without spatial position feature

Samples \ Result	Petechia Tongue	Non-Petechia Tongue	FN (%)	FP (%)	TP (%)
PetechiaTongue	42	8	14.28	25.00	75.00
Non-PetechiaTongue	14	36			

In addition, we also use linear classifier, Bayes classifier, and decision tree instead of SVM to train the classifier on the same data sets. The FN, FP and TP of three different classifiers are shown in Table 3, respectively. The SVM classifier performs much better than the other classifier.

Table 3. Comparison of different classification algorithm

Algorithm	FN%	FP%	TP%
Linear classifier	11.32	16.87	78.42
Bayes classifier	10.09	16.13	79.23
Decision Tree	9.82	15.95	83.54
SVM	9.43	15.09	84.91

5   Conclusions

In this paper, we presented a recognition method of petechia tongue based on LoG and Gabor texture feature with spatial information. The proposed method includes two steps. Firstly, to classified suspected petechia region into petechia region or non-petechia region. Second, to recognize petechia tongue based on the proportion of petechia region to non-petechia region. Comparative study with three classifier methods has been done, which also proved the proposed method is more effective.

One further work is to give experimental comparison with other algorithm list in reference on a large database of tongue image. Another future work is to verify that whether more prior knowledge and/or more complicated machine learning method help to improve recognition accuracy.

Acknowledgments. This work is supported by Shanghai Natural Science Foundation under Grant No. 10ZR1411700.

References

1. Chiu, C.C.: A novel approach based on computerized image analysis for traditional Chinese medical diagnosis of the tongue. Computer Methods and Programs in Biomedicine 61, 77–89 (2000)
2. Wang, K., Zhang, D., Li, N., Pang, B.: Tongue Diagnosis Based on Biometric Pattern Recognition Technology. In: Pal, S.K., Pal, A. (eds.) Pattern Recognition from Classical to Modern Approaches, 1st edn., pp. 575–598. World Scientific, Singapore (2001)
3. Zhang, D., Pang, B., Li, N.M., Wang, K.Q., Zhang, H.Z.: Computerized Diagnosis from Tongue Appearance Using Quantitative Feature Classification. The American Journal of Chinese Medicine 33(6), 859–866 (2005)
4. Pang, B., Zhang, D., Wang, K.Q.: Computerized Tongue Diagnosis Based on Bayesian Networks. IEEE Transactions on Biomedical Engineering 51(10), 1803–1810 (2004)
5. Liu, L.L., Zhang, D., et al.: Detecting Wide Lines Using Isotropic Nonlinear Filtering. IEEE Transactions on Image Processing 16(6), 1584–1595 (2007)
6. Liu, L.L., Zhang, D., et al.: Tongue line extraction. Pattern Recognition. In: Proc. of ICPR, pp. 1–4 (2008)
7. Pang, B., Zhang, D., Wang, K.Q.: Tongue image analysis for appendicitis diagnosis. Information Science 175(3), 160–176 (2005)
8. Yan, X.-p., Li, X.-q., Zheng, L.-l., Li, F.-f.: Robust Lip Segmentation Method Based on Level Set Model. In: Qiu, G., Lam, K.M., Kiya, H., Xue, X.-Y., Kuo, C.-C.J., Lew, M.S. (eds.) PCM 2010, Part I. LNCS, vol. 6297, pp. 731–739. Springer, Heidelberg (2010)
9. Wang, H.Y., Zong, X.J.: A New Computerized Method for Tongue Classification. In: Proc. of Int. Conf. on Intelligent Systems Design and Applications (ISDA) (October 2006)
10. Li, J.F., Wang, K.Q., et al.: A Feature Extraction Method for Recognition of Petechia Dot in Tongue Image. In: Proc. of Int. Conf. on Information Science and Engineering (ICISE), pp. 3560–3563 (December 2009)
11. Li, J.F., Zhang, H.Z., et al.: An automated feature extraction method for recognition of Petechia Spot in Tongue Diagnosis. In: Proc. Int. Conf. on Future Bio-Medical Information Engineering (FBIE), pp. 69–72 (December 2009)
12. Manjunath, B.S., Ma, W.Y.: Texture Features for Browsing and Retrieval of Image Data. IEEE Tran. on PAMI 18(8), 837–842 (1996)

Human Age Estimation Using Ranking SVM

Dong Cao[1], Zhen Lei[2], Zhiwei Zhang[2], Jun Feng[1], and Stan Z. Li[2,3]

[1] HoHai University
[2] Center for Biometrics and Security Research & National Laboratory of Pattern Recognition, Institute of Automation, Chinese Academy of Sciences
[3] China Research and Development Center for Internet of Thing
{dcao,zlei,zwzhang,szli}@cbsr.ia.ac.cn, fengjun@hhu.edu.cn

Abstract. This paper proposes a human age estimation method using Ranking SVM method. Given a face image, most previous methods estimate the human age directly. However, the face images from the same age vary so much that it's really a difficult problem to estimate the human age accurately. In this work, we adopt an alternative way to estimate the human age. First, the rank relationship of the ages is learned from various face images. Then, the human age is estimated based on the rank relationship and the age information of a reference set. There are two advantages of the proposed method. (i) The rank relationship rather than the absolute human age is learned so that the absolute age estimation problem can be simplified. (ii) The human age is determined based on the rank relationship and the known human age of the reference set so that the face image variations from the same age group can be considered. Experimental results on MORPH and Multi-PIE databases validate the superiority of the rank based human age estimation over some state-of-the-art methods.

Keywords: age estimation, Ranking SVM, rank relationship.

1 Introduction

Recently, there has been growing interest in human age estimation due to its potential applications such as human-computer interaction and electronic customer relationship management (ECRM). The task of human age estimation is to estimate a person's exact age or age-group based on face images.

There has been a number of human estimation methods proposed in recent years. Guo et al. [1] used SVM to learn the relationship between feature and age, which treated the age estimation as a multi-class classification problem. In [2], researcher adopted SVR to estimate human age and used SVM for local adjustment. In [3], Guo et al. investigated the gender classification and age estimation problem, indicating that the gender information is helpful for age estimation. There were also works using manifold learning based methods to solve the age estimation problem [4–6]. Guo et al. [7] defined a framework for automatic age estimation in which different manifold learning methods were used for gender classification and age estimation respectively. Geng et al. [8] proposed AGES for

W.-S. Zheng et al. (Eds.): CCBR 2012, LNCS 7701, pp. 324–331, 2012.

age estimation, and each aging pattern was composed of images from the same person. However, AGES achieved good result on the supposition that test image was similar with one of the training subjects and it was difficult to correctly predict the testing instance without corresponding training data.

Observing that the ranking age relationship is more easily to be determined, some researchers proposed to use ranking model for age estimation which is supposed to be more effective to estimate the age accurately. So far, several ranking methods have been proposed. Yang et al. [9] employed Ranking Boost with Haar features to estimate the human age. However, they only considered the ranking information among images from the same person, and the relationship from different persons were ignored. Chang et al. [10] proposed Ordinal Hyperplanes Ranker for age estimation which aggregated K-1 binary classifiers. In age estimation phase, there were K-1 age estimation operators which was somewhat computationally expensive in real applications. All the previous ranking models just used the pairs composed of images from different ages, which could only reflect the order information indicating who is younger or older. The consistent information from the pairs was ignored. For a robust algorithm, it should not only calculate the image's age correctly, but also ensure images with the same ages getting consistent age estimation values.

In this paper, we propose a Ranking SVM [11] based human age estimation approach. The framework of our algorithm is shown in Figure 1. In the training phase, the ranking information of images is exploited by applying a Ranking SVM method. In the testing phase, with a reference set including true age information prepared in advance, the ranking relationship between the test image and images in the reference set is determined by the learned Ranking SVM model. The age of the test image is finally obtained based on the ranking relationship and the true age of the images in the reference set. Different from the previous methods, not only the pairs composed of different age images (defined as Ordinal Pairs), but also those from the same age (defined as Consistent Pairs) are considered in the rank learning phase. Moreover, the adaptive regularized coefficient is also used in the Ranking SVM to improve the age estimation accuracy. To our best knowledge, the Ranking SVM has not been explored before in age estimation problem.

2   Proposed Method

2.1   Feature Extraction and Data Organization

In this paper, Gabor feature with five scales and eight orientations in [12] is employed, then 3000 dimensions selected by Adaboost learning for face recognition are used for face representation [13]. Since the feature extraction is beyond the scope of this paper, we simply use the feature representation for face recognition. The assumption is that the features used for face recognition are also suitable for age estimation.

The organization of pairs for the Ranking SVM is an important step. Previous methods constructed data only using ordinal pairs, however, the consistent pairs

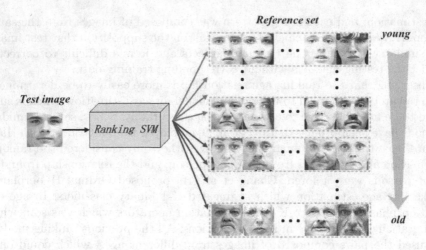

Fig. 1. After getting the ranking value, the image is compared to the reference set which is organized with the same age in each row. The age grows gradually row by row along the direction of the arrow located right.

which contain consistent information were ignored. In our experiments, we build pairwise instances (x_i, x_j) in both types for ranking:

$$O = \{(x_i, x_j) | age(x_i) > age(x_j)\} \qquad (1)$$

$$I = \{(x_i, x_j) | age(x_i) = age(x_j)\} \qquad (2)$$

where $age(.)$ is a function obtaining images' true age. For set O, the age of x_i is larger than x_j; for set I, their ages equal to each other.

2.2 Ranking SVM

Herbrich et al. [11] proposed Ranking SVM to classify the order of pairs of objects. Suppose that there are numbers of objects with various grades, the purpose of Ranking SVM is to obtain the weight vector w corresponding to the function $f(x) = <w, x>$ and project images with w to get the ranking value. Specific to the age estimation problem, we hope to calculate a weight vector w which can project older person with higher ranking value than the younger one. Traditional Ranking SVM only used the ordinal pairs which could not ensure getting consistent ranking values in the same grade. Parikh et al. [14] proposed a novel form of Ranking SVM to predict the relative strength of each attribute in test images, which utilized both ordinal and consistent pairs. Experimentally, we find that although Ranking SVM without consistent pairs can get correct order, the gap inside each grade is also significant which can be ameliorated by the ranking model utilizing both pairs. Inspired by this work, in our Ranking SVM, we consider couple constraints, one ensuring the order among different age correct, another guaranteeing the values calculated in the same age consistent. The formula we utilize in our paper is defined as follows:

$$min\{\frac{1}{2}\|w^T\|_2^2 + (\sum C_{ij}^o \xi_{ij}^2 + \sum C_{ij}^s \gamma_{ij}^2)\} \tag{3}$$

$$s.t. \quad w^T(x_i - x_j) \geq 1 - \xi_{ij}; \quad \forall(i,j) \in O \tag{4}$$

$$|w^T(x_i - x_j)| \leq \gamma_{ij}; \quad \forall(i,j) \in I \tag{5}$$

where C_{ij}^o and C_{ij}^s are the adaptive regulative coefficients of ordinal and consistent pairs, ξ_{ij} and γ_{ij} denote the corresponding slack variables respectively. We solve the above problem using Newton's method mentioned in [15]. In the Ranking SVM, the adaptive regulative coefficient should differ according to the cost of misclassification. For example, when the difference of the true ages in the pair are small, the cost of misclassification will also be small, so we set a small regulative coefficient, and vice versa. In this paper, We defined C_{ij}^o as

$$C_{ij}^o = \frac{age(x_i) - age(x_j)}{max(age) - min(age)} \tag{6}$$

where $max(age)$ and $min(age)$ are the training data's maximum and minimum age. The C_{ij}^s value is stationary for all the consistent pairs.

2.3   Age Estimation

The research in [16] has shown that human's age processing follows the common development trend: when puberty, craniofacial structure grows rapidly; when adulthood, the skin texture changes great. However, different people have different rates of aging process. In the previous works, most methods ignored the personalized information. For example, when applying SVM [1], all the images of 20 years old have the same certain label 20 supposing that the 20 years old persons have the same aging process. In our algorithm, we construct a reference set in which each age group has a number of persons with different ranking values which contain two properties: the difference among the values reflects the personalized property, meanwhile, most of the values located in some range reflect the common trend. In prediction phase, when the number of images in one age group, whose ranking value is smaller than the test image, is larger than a predefined threshold, we think the age of the test image is larger. The proposed algorithm is summarized as follows:

1. Images are organized into two models: ordinal pairs set O and consistent pairs set I.
2. Ranking SVM is employed to get the ranking function $f(x)$
3. A reference set is constructed according to their true ages. The ranking values of images in the set are calculated by $f(x)$.

4. For a test image x, the ranking value is firstly calculated by $f(x)$ and then compared with the reference set to obtain the estimation age. If the value is larger than some proportion of the images from one age in the set, we define x's age is larger than that age. Experimentally, the proportion is set to 0.5. Inspired by [10], the final age is calculated as

$$age(x) = 1 + \sum_{k=1}^{K} G(\sum_{j}^{J} G(f(x) > f(x_j)) > \frac{J}{2}) \tag{7}$$

where K is the number of age grades and J is the number of images in each age k in the set. Function $G(.)$ is 1 if the inner condition is true and 0 otherwise.

To summarize, the proposed algorithm employs Ranking SVM as classifier which reflects the nature of age relationship. Both ordinal and consistent pairs are used in our experiment to improve the accuracy and consistence simultaneously. We also set adaptive regularized coefficients according to the age's gap in each ordinal pair.

3 Experiments

3.1 Databases

We performed age estimation experiments on two databases: MORPH Album 2 [17] and Multi-PIE [18]. MORPH Album 2 contains about 55,000 face images with several races and its age ranges from 16 to 77 years old. We randomly select a subset about 8000 images in our experiment. For training set, each age contains over 20 images. The reference set is constructed with the same strategy, and the rest are used for testing. The Multi-PIE database consists 4 sessions about more than 755,000 images, which come from 337 different persons with 15 different poses and 20 illuminations. In our experiment, we use session 1 containing 249 persons. To reduce the influence from pose and illumination changes, we employ frontal images with illumination 6-8.

3.2 Experimental Results

The images are cropped and resized to 128×128. In our experiments, we compare the proposed method with standard age estimation SVM [1], SVR [2], Sparse [19] and Partial Least Squares (PLS) [20, 21]. In SVM and SVR learning, the non-linear RBF kernel which has shown its effectiveness in previous age estimation algorithm is used for estimation and the associated parameters such as C and γ are selected by five-fold cross validation. The number of hidden variables in PLS is 30. Experimentally, we define the image is older than some age if the estimation value is larger than a certain percentage of the images from that age in the reference set. Figure 2 shows the mean age error (MAE) with different

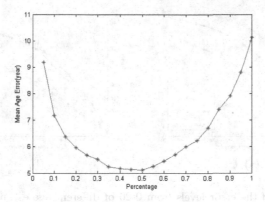

Fig. 2. The MAE under different percentage when comparing with reference set

Table 1. MAEs of the compared age estimation methods on the MORPH and Multi-PIE databases

Train	Test	MAE(year)						
		SVM	SVR	PLS	SPARSE	RSWARC	RSWCP	Ours
MORPH	MORPH	11.87	8.63	5.41	7.60	5.25	5.37	5.12
MORPH	Multi-PIE	14.42	10.61	8.68	8.31	6.95	7.02	6.92

percentage configuration and indicates that the algorithm gets the best result under the percentages of 50%. To demonstrate the importance of the consistent pairs and the adaptive regularized coefficient, we also compare our method with Ranking SVM Without Consistent Pairs (RSWCP) and Ranking SVM Without Adaptive Regularized Coefficient (RSWARC). The performance of age estimation are evaluated by the mean absolute error (MAE) and cumulative score (CS) [1, 2] in our experiments.

Table 1 shows the MAE results of different methods derived on the MORPH and Multi-PIE database. The experimental results on the MORPH demonstrate that our Ranking SVM method ($MAE = 5.12$) using ranking relationship between images instead of absolute age value achieves the best result. For all the algorithms, SVM ($MAE = 11.87$) gives the worst result, indicating that treating age just as category labels is not optimal. Compared with RSWARC ($MAE = 5.25$), RSWCP ($MAE = 5.37$) is worse which indicates that the consistent pairs is useful to improve the performance of age estimation. Figure 3 shows the CS curves for different error levels. Almost in all the error levels, the Ranking SVM has the highest accuracy which validates its effectiveness for age estimation problem.

To examine the generalization of our algorithm, we further design a cross-database experiment. Images from MORPH are also used for training data and reference set and the facial images from Multi-PIE are used for testing. Table 1

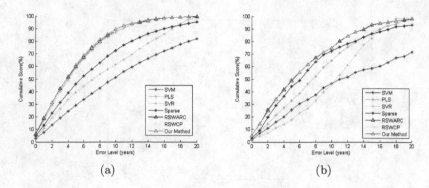

Fig. 3. CS curves of the error levels from 0-20 of different age estimation algorithms on (a) MORPH and (b) Multi-PIE databases

and Figure 3 show the MAE and CS results. We can find that for cross-database age estimation, the performance of other methods decline more remarkably compared to the proposed method whose MAE is still small. For example, although the PLS has an MAE of 5.41 years on the MORPH database, which is similar to our proposed method, its performance ($MAE = 8.68$) years is much worse than ours ($MAE = 6.97$) on Multi-PIE database, indicating that the proposed method has good generalization performance and is practical in real application.

4   Conclusion

In this paper, we propose Ranking SVM based algorithm for age estimation in which the age estimation problem is divided into two steps. The first ranking step uses Ranking SVM to get the ranking value and the final age is estimated by being compared with the reference set. Ordinal and consistent pairs are employed to make the result correct and consistent. The adaptive regularized coefficients are introduced to Ranking SVM learning to further improve the performance. Experimental results show that the proposed Ranking SVM algorithm outperforms some existing methods.

Acknowledgments. This work is supported by the Chinese National Natural Science Foundation Project #61070146, #61105023, #61103156, #61105037, #61203267, National IoT R&D Project #2150510, Chinese Academy of Sciences Project No. KGZD-EW-102-2, European Union FP7 Project #257289 (TABULA RASA http://www.tabularasa-euproject.org), and AuthenMetric R&D Funds.

References

1. Guo, G., Mu, G., Fu, Y., Huang, T.S.: Human age estimation using bio-inspired features. In: CVPR, pp. 112–119 (2009)

2. Guo, G., Fu, Y., Dyer, C.R., Huang, T.S.: Image-based human age estimation by manifold learning and locally adjusted robust regression. IEEE Transactions on Image Processing 17(7), 1178–1188 (2008)
3. Guo, G., Fu, Y., Dyer, C.R., Huang, T.S.: Human age estimation what is the influence across race and gender. In: AMFG (2010)
4. Fu, Y., Huang, T.S.: Human age estimation with regression on discriminative aging manifold. IEEE Transactions on Multimedia 10(4), 578–584 (2008)
5. Fu, Y., Xu, Y., Huang, T.S.: Estimating human age by manifold analysis of face pictures and regression on aging features. In: ICME, pp. 1383–1386 (2007)
6. Scherbaum, K., Sunkel, M., Seidel, H.P., Blanz, V.: Prediction of individual non-linear aging trajectories of faces. Comput. Graph. Forum 26(3), 285–294 (2007)
7. Guo, G., Mu, G., Fu, Y., Dyer, C.R., Huang, T.S.: A study on automatic age estimation using a large database. In: ICCV, pp. 1986–1991 (2009)
8. Geng, X., Zhou, Z.H., Smith-Miles, K.: Correction to "automatic age estimation based on facial aging patterns". IEEE Trans. Pattern Anal. Mach. Intell. 30(2), 368 (2008)
9. Yang, P., Zhong, L., Metaxas, D.N.: Ranking model for facial age estimation. In: ICPR, pp. 3404–3407 (2010)
10. Chang, K.Y., Chen, C.S., Hung, Y.P.: Ordinal hyperplanes ranker with cost sensitivities for age estimation. In: CVPR, pp. 585–592 (2011)
11. Herbrich, R., Graepel, T., Obermayer, K.: Large margin rank boundaries for ordinal regression. In: NIPS (1999)
12. Liu, C., Wechsler, H.: Gabor feature based classification using the enhanced fisher linear discriminant model for face recognition. IEEE Transactions on Image Processing 11(4), 467–476 (2002)
13. Yang, P., Shan, S., Gao, W., Li, S.Z., Zhang, D.: Face recognition using ada-boosted gabor features. In: FGR, pp. 356–361 (2004)
14. Parikh, D., Grauman, K.: Relative attributes. In: ICCV, pp. 503–510 (2011)
15. Chapelle, O.: Training a support vector machine in the primal. Neural Computation (2007)
16. Fu, Y., Guo, G., Huang, T.S.: Age synthesis and estimation via faces: A survey. IEEE Trans. Pattern Anal. Mach. Intell. 32(11), 1955–1976 (2010)
17. Ricanek Jr., K., Tesafaye, T.: Morph: A longitudinal image database of normal adult age-progression. In: FG, pp. 341–345 (2006)
18. Gross, R., Matthews, I., Cohn, J.F., Kanade, T., Baker, S.: Multipie. Image Vision Comput. 28(5), 807–813 (2010)
19. Yang, M., Zhang, L., Feng, X., Zhang, D.: Fisher discrimination dictionary learning for sparse representation. In: ICCV, pp. 543–550 (2011)
20. Di, L., Xiong, Z., Yang, X.: Nonlinear process modeling and optimization based on multiway kernel partial least squares model. In: Winter Simulation Conference, pp. 1645–1651 (2008)
21. Rosipal, R., Krämer, N.C.: Overview and Recent Advances in Partial Least Squares. In: Saunders, C., Grobelnik, M., Gunn, S., Shawe-Taylor, J. (eds.) SLSFS 2005. LNCS, vol. 3940, pp. 34–51. Springer, Heidelberg (2006)

Distance Entropy as an Information Measure for Binary Biometric Representation

Yi Cheng Feng, Pong Chi Yuen, and Meng-Hui Lim

Department of Computer Science,
Hong Kong Baptist University, Hong Kong
{ycfeng,pcyuen,mhlim}@comp.hkbu.edu.hk
http://www.comp.hkbu.edu.hk

Abstract. To uphold the security of individuals, analyzing the amount of information in binary biometric representation is highly essential. While Shannon entropy is a measure to quantify the expected value of information in the binary representation, it does not account the extent to which every binary representation could distinctively identify a person in a population. Hence, it does not appropriately quantify the hardness of obtaining a close approximation of the user's biometric template if one maliciously leverages the population distribution. To resolve this, relative entropy has been used to measure information of user distribution with reference to the population distribution. However, existing relative-entropy estimation techniques that are based on statistical methods in the Euclidean space cannot be directly extended to the Hamming space. Therefore, we put forward a new entropy measure known as distance entropy and its estimation technique to quantify the information in binary biometric representation more effectively with respect to the discrimination power of the binary representation.

Keywords: Binary biometric representation, security, distance entropy.

1 Introduction

Binary biometric representation has been widely adopted in many existing biometric recognition systems due to several advantages: (1) quick matching; (2) light storage; and (3) suitability for most template protection schemes. Typically, the binary representation of a user is generated either through binarizing the extracted features [5, 6, 15, 17, 20]; or extracting binary features directly from the raw biometric image (e.g., iris code [8] and palmprint competitive code [22]).

Quantification of information in a binary biometric representation has become more and more essential, ever since security issues started to raise public concerns. Shannon entropy [7, 18] has been regarded as a standard measure for quantifying the expected value of information in binary biometric representation [12–14]. This measure can alternatively be perceived as a measure of unpredictability associated with a random variable (a specific target binary representation in our context). For instance, a 128-bit binary string that is *randomly*

W.-S. Zheng et al. (Eds.): CCBR 2012, LNCS 7701, pp. 332–339, 2012.
© Springer-Verlag Berlin Heidelberg 2012

generated has 128 bits of entropy and it would take 2^{128-1} guesses on average to break by brute force. A well-known entropy-estimation algorithm for binary biometric representation is known as the degree of freedom (DOF)[8].

Nevertheless, when it comes to measuring information in binary biometric representation, Shannon entropy is lacking in a few aspects:

1. Due to intra-user variance, an adversary does not need to guess the exact binary biometric template to impersonate the target user. In fact, an adversary is considered making a right guess if he is able to fabricate a "close" approximation of the enrolled binary template (within the range of intra-user variance). Evidently, the Shannon entropy is not appropriate to be employed as an information measure, since the corresponding brute force attack is aiming to find the exact binary template.
2. Instead of guessing naively by brute force, the adversary could opt to estimate the population distribution of the binary biometric representation from his collected set of multiple users' biometric images (so-called local dataset); and guess the enrolled binary template based on such distribution. In this case, an appropriate entropy measure should vary in accordance with the discrimination power of binary biometric representation. (e.g., highly discriminative representation contains large amount of information/uncertainty and vice versa).

Alder et al. [1–3] and Yagiz et al. [19] suggested to measure the biometric information using the *relative entropy* [7, 11], which is a measure of the distance between two probability distributions (the user distribution and population distribution). However, their entropy estimation techniques are limited to real-valued biometric information and cannot be extended to the Hamming space. This stems from the fact that their constructed statistical models are only applicable in the Euclidean space.

In view of this limitation, we put forward an entropy measure known as "distance entropy" to quantify the information of binary biometric representation. Our proposed distance entropy indicates the average information in binary biometric representation with respect to the discrimination power of the binary representation. Different from Shannon entropy which only corresponds to naive guessing by brute force, this measure is more appropriate for use when the adversary has the ability to estimate the population distribution and conduct our proposed error-correcting attack (ECA) to guess a binary string variant of a target user.

The remainder of this paper is organized as follows. Section 2 describes our proposed technique for estimating the distance entropy. The experimental results are given in Section 3. Section 4 concludes the paper.

2   Distance-Entropy Estimation

The discrimination power or relative information of a binary string of a user with respect to that of another user can be quantified by the number of disagreeing bits (Hamming distance) between them and the intra-user variances of both users. Generally, the larger the hamming distance is and the smaller the intra-variances are, the more discriminative the relative information would be.

Suppose that each Alice and Bob has a query binary string ($\mathbf{b}_A$ and $\mathbf{b}_B$, respectively) and that both query strings are matched against Alice's binary template $\mathbf{b}'_A$, yielding distances d_G and d_I, respectively. The case where $d_I \leq d_G$ implies that $\mathbf{b}_B$ falls within the intra-user variance of the binary representation of Alice, allowing Bob to be misrecognized as Alice. Hence, $d_I - d_G$ can be utilized for (relative) information measurement.

Let the probability mass function (pmf) of the genuine score distribution be denoted by $P_G(\cdot)$, and the pmf of the imposter score distribution be denoted by $P_I(\cdot)$, Statistically, both distributions can be expressed by:

$$P_G(x) = \begin{cases} 0 & \text{iff } x < 0 \\ \frac{n_G(x)}{N_G} & \text{iff } 0 \leq x \leq k \\ 0 & \text{iff } x > k \end{cases} \quad (x \in \mathbb{Z}) \qquad (1)$$

$$P_I(x) = \begin{cases} 0 & \text{iff } x < 0 \\ \frac{n_I(x)}{N_I} & \text{iff } 0 \leq x \leq k \\ 0 & \text{iff } x > k \end{cases} \quad (x \in \mathbb{Z}) \qquad (2)$$

where k denotes the length of the binary representation, N_G and N_I denote the total number of samples in P_G and P_I, respectively; and $n_G(x)$ and $n_I(x)$ denote the number of samples that has Hamming distance x in P_G and P_I, respectively. Since d_I and d_G are dependent on the distributions of P_I and P_G, correspondingly, we can calculate the distribution of $d_D = d_I - d_G$ by

$$P_D(x) = \sum_{y=-\infty}^{\infty} P_G(y)P_I(x+y) \qquad (3)$$

The mean m_d of distribution P_D indicates the average difference between d_I and d_G, which can contribute to the measure of relative information (e.g., Figure 1(a) has a larger value of m_d than Figure 1(b)). However, using m_d alone as an information/discrimination measure is insufficient: the spread (variance) of the genuine and imposter distributions should also be taken into account. Taking comparison between distributions in Figure 1(a) and Figure 1(c) as an instance, Figure 1(c) has the same distance between genuine and imposter mean as that in Figure 1(a). However, the variance of distributions in Figure 1(c) tends to be larger, leading to degradation in discrimination power and thus achieving lower relative information of binary representation of genuine user with respect to the imposter distribution.

To measure the information of a binary representation relative to the population distribution in an appropriate manner, we first evaluate the adversarial probability of making a "correct" guess that enables the adversary to be misrecognized as the genuine user via our proposed error correcting attack (ECA).

Error Correcting Attack (ECA). Suppose that an adversary wishes to guess a binary-string variant of the target user. With the availability of a local

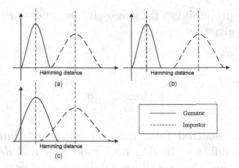

Fig. 1. The relation between the discriminative information content and the genuine and imposter distributions

dataset where the samples are assumed to follow the population distribution, the guessing strategy can be carried out as follows:

1. generates binary representation of all images in the local dataset and generates the genuine and imposter score distributions;
2. randomly picks the binary representation of a raw image from the local dataset;
3. guesses a number of bit errors between the binary representation of the chosen image and the (unknown) target binary template based on the genuine and imposter score distributions; and
4. outputs the resultant binary string upon error subtraction.

The relative information of binary templates can be reflected by the success probability of ECA. A smaller inter-user variance usually leads to an easier guess. With a lower number of distinguishable candidates, any output binary guess $\mathbf{b}_R$ could be a lot similar to the binary template $\mathbf{b}_I$, yielding a higher success probability of the ECA. Generally, the ECA takes no more than $\binom{k}{d_I}$ attempts to guess the exact binary template when altering $d_D = d_I$ bits is needed. For instance, the case where d_I is low significantly decreases the number of required attempts to succeed. Recall that with the existence of intra-user variance in binary measurements, one may only need to guess a binary string variant of the template to be misrecognized as the genuine user. More specifically, the adversary would only need to modify $d_D = d_I - d_G$ bits to make a correct guess of the variant, thus decreasing the number of attempts required to succeed. Hence, apart from low d_I by small inter-user variance, high d_G by large intra-user variance would similarly incur less number of bits necessary to be corrected, thus reducing adversarial effort in making a correct guess.

Based on this ECA, the entropy of the event in which an adversary is misrecognized as the genuine user can be computed. Suppose that given a value of d_I and d_G where $d_I \geq d_G$, an adversary attempts to modify $d_D = d_I - d_G$ bits from the total k bits of the random binary template $\mathbf{b}_I$. Note that among the $\binom{k}{d_I - d_G}$ modification possibilities, there are only $\binom{d_I}{d_I - d_G}$ choices that would result in a right guess. Similar quantification can be obtained for the case of

$d_I \leq d_G$. Hence, the probability of a successful modification with a given value of d_I and d_G can be given by

$$Pm(d_G, d_I) = \begin{cases} \dfrac{\binom{d_I}{d_I - d_G}}{\binom{d_I - d_G}{k}} & \text{iff} \quad 0 \leq d_G \leq d_I \\ \dfrac{\binom{d_G - d_I}{k}}{\binom{d_G - d_I}{d_I}} & \text{iff} \quad 0 \leq d_I \leq d_G \end{cases} \tag{4}$$

Since d_I and d_G are selected from the estimated distributions from the local dataset, the probability of having both values d_I and d_G being selected is $P_G(d_G)P_I(d_I)$. With this, the overall probability of success can be quantified by

$$Ps(d_G, d_I) = P_G(d_G)P_I(d_I)Pm(d_G, d_I) \tag{5}$$

and the corresponding information is

$$Hs(d_G, d_I) = \begin{cases} -\log_2(Ps(d_G, d_I)) & \text{iff} \quad Ps(d_G, d_I) \neq 0 \\ 0 & \text{otherwise} \end{cases} \tag{6}$$

Considering all possible combinations of d_G and d_I, the average information or the distance entropy of a binary biometric representation can be obtained by

$$H_m = \sum_{d_G = -\infty}^{\infty} \sum_{d_I = -\infty}^{\infty} P_G(d_G)P_I(d_I)Hs(d_G, d_I) \tag{7}$$

3   Experimental Results

Our distance-entropy entropy estimation algorithm has been implemented on several binarization algorithms. Two popular face databases, namely CMU PIE [23] and FRGC [24] are employed in our experiments. In the CMU PIE database there are 68 individuals and 105 samples per individual. In the FRGC database, 350 individuals with 40 samples per individual are randomly chosen. Fisherface [4] is used to extract the original real-valued face template. The mean of the real-valued face templates from the same individual is used as the representative real-valued face template. A reference binary template is generated from the representative real-valued face template of each individual upon binarization. The binarization schemes chosen for our experiments are the biohashing [20] scheme, the multi-stage biohashing [21] scheme (stolen-token scenario), the minutiae descriptor binarization [16] scheme, the discriminability preserving [10] scheme, and the binary discriminant analysis [9] scheme.

The DOF proposed by Daugman [8] for measuring the Shannon entropy, the estimated average difference (m_d) between d_I and d_G, and the distance entropy of the binary representation generated by different binarization algorithms are shown in Table 1 and 2. It is generally observed that large m_d does not necessarily imply large distance entropy. For instance, the DP algorithm has a high value of m_d but a low distance entropy. This can be explained by that the genuine

Table 1. Information Content of The Binary Templates in CMU PIE Database

Algorithm	BH	MBH	FB	DP	BDA
k	50	150	204	50	511
DOF	58.72	142.59	187.76	52.33	505.88
m_d	12.27	22.37	27.92	39.11	164.60
Distance Entropy	22.38	62.22	77.58	9.95	125.69

Table 2. Information Content of The Binary Templates in FRGC Database

Algorithm	BH	MBH	FB	DP	BDA
k	200	600	1050	200	511
DOF	205.38	363.06	504.27	197.93	514.39
m_d	23.96	29.52	51.77	122.67	68.49
Distance Entropy	49.59	144.07	239.77	17.69	161.67

distribution of DP algorithm spans almost over the whole range of possible Hamming distances, causing ECA to succeed at a very high probability. Apart form that, the distance entropy is noticed to be much smaller than the dimension k and the DOF. This particularly justifies that by making use of the estimated genuine and imposter distributions to perform a guessing attack, the adversary can succeed at a much higher probability than guessing by brute force.

4   Conclusion

In this paper, a new measure called distance entropy has been proposed for appropriately quantifying information in binary biometric representation. Distance entropy measures the average information in binary biometric representation with respect to the discrimination power of the binary representation. Different from Shannon entropy which only corresponds to naive guessing by brute force, this measure is more appropriate for use when the adversary has the ability to estimate the population distribution and carry out an error-correcting attack to guess the binary string variant of a target user. Our experimental results shown that the distance entropy can be much lower than the Shannon entropy when an error-correcting attack is carried out. Hence, we advocate that the actual information of binary biometric representation extracted by future proposals of biometric binarization techniques should be estimated using the distance entropy, instead of the conventional Shannon entropy.

Acknowledgments. This project was partially supported by the Science Faculty Research Grant of Hong Kong Baptist University, National Natural Science Foundation of China Research Grants 61128009 and 61172136.

References

1. Alder, A.: Towards a Measure of Biometric Information. In: Canadian Conference on Electrical and Computer Engineering, pp. 210–213 (2006)
2. Adler, A., Youmaran, R., Loyka, S.: Information content of biometric features. In: Biometrics Consortium Conference, pp. 19–21 (2005)
3. Adler, A., Youmaran, R., Loyka, S.: Towards a Measure of Biometric Feature Information. Pattern Analysis and Applications 12(3), 261–270 (2009)
4. Belhumeur, P.N., Hespanha, J.P., Kriegman, D.J.: Eigenfaces vs. fisherfaces: Recognition using class specific linear projection. IEEE Trans. on PAMI 19(7), 711–720 (1997)
5. Chen, C., Veldhuis, R.: Extracting Biometric Binary Strings with Minimal Area Under the FRR Curve for the Hamming Distance Classifier. In: 17th European Signal Processing Conference (EUSIPCO 2009), pp. 50–54 (2009)
6. Chen, C., Veldhuis, R.: Binary Biometric Representation through Pairwise Adaptive Phase Quantization. EURASIP Journal on Information Security (2011)
7. Cover, T., Thomas, J.: Entropy, relative entropy and mutual information. In: Elements of Information Theory, pp. 12–49. Wiley, New York (1991)
8. Daugman, J.: The importance of being random: Statistical principles of iris recognition. Pattern Recognition 36(2), 279–291 (2003)
9. Feng, Y.C., Yuen, P.C.: Binary Discriminant Analysis for Generating Binary Face Template. IEEE Transactions on Information Forensics and Security 7(2), 613–624 (2012)
10. Feng, Y.C., Yuen, P.C., Jain, A.K.: A Hybrid Approach for Generating Secure and Discriminating Face Template. IEEE Transactions on Information Forensics and Security 5(1), 103–117 (2010)
11. Kullback, S., Leibler, R.: On information and sufficiency. Annals of Mathematical Statistics 22(1), 79–86 (1951)
12. Lim, M.-H., Teoh, A.B.J.: An Effective Biometric Discretization Approach to Extract Highly Discriminative, Informative and Privacy-Protective Binary Representation. EURASIP Journal on Advances in Signal Processing (107) (2011)
13. Lim, M.-H., Teoh, A.B.J.: Discriminative and Non-user Specific Binary Biometric Representation via Linearly-Separable Subcode Encoding-based Discretization. KSII Trans. on Internet and Information Systems 5(2), 374–3890 (2011)
14. Lim, M.-H., Teoh, A.B.J., Toh, K.A.: An Analysis on Linearly Separable SubCode-based Equal Width Discretization and its Performance Resemblances. EURASIP Journal on Advances in Signal Processing (82) (2011)
15. Lim, M.-H., Teoh, A.B.J., Toh, K.A.: An efficient dynamic reliability-dependent bit allocation for biometric discretization. Pattern Recognition 45(5), 1960–1971 (2012)
16. Nagar, A., Nandakumar, K., Jain, A.K.: A Hybrid Biometric Cryptosystem for Securing Fingerprint Minutiae Templates. Pattern Recognition Letters (2009)
17. Nanni, L., Brahnam, S., Lumini, A.: Biohashing applied to orientation-based minutia descriptor for secure fingerprint authentication system. Electronics Letters 47(15), 851–853 (2011)
18. Shannon, C.: A mathematical theory of communication. Bell System Technical Journal 27(3), 379–423 (1948)
19. Sutcu, Y., Sencar, H., Memon, N.: How to Measure Biometric Information. In: International Conference on Pattern Recognition (2010)

20. Teoh, A.B.J., Goh, A., Ngo, D.C.L.: Random Multispace Quantization as an Analytic Mechanism for BioHashing of Biometric and Random Identity Inputs. IEEE Transactions on Pattern Analysis and Machine Intelligence 28(12), 1892–1901 (2006)
21. Teoh, A.B.J., Yip, W.K., Lee, S.: Cancelable biometrics and annotations on BioHash. Pattern Recognition 41(6), 2034–2044 (2008)
22. Yue, F., Zuo, W., Zhang, D., Wang, K.: Orientation selection using modified FCM for competitive code-based palmprint recognition. Pattern Recognition 4(11), 2841–2849 (2009)
23. http://vasc.ri.cmu.edu/idb/html/face/index.html
24. http://www.frvt.org/FRGC/

Kernel Sparse Locality Preserving Canonical Correlation Analysis for Multi-modal Feature Extraction

Haifeng Hu

School of Information Science and Technology, Sun Yat-sen University, Guangzhou, 510275,
P.R. China
huhaif@mail.sysu.edu.cn

Abstract. In this paper, a kernel based sparse locality preserving canonical correlation analysis (KSLPCCA) method is presented for high dimensional feature extraction. Unlike many existing techniques such as DCCA and 2D CCA, SLPCCA aims to preserve the sparse reconstructive relationship of the data, which is achieved by minimizing a regularization-related objective function. The obtained projections contain natural discriminating information even if no class labels are provided. As SLPCCA is a linear method, nonlinear extension is further proposed which can map the input space to a high-dimensional feature space. Experimental results demonstrate the efficiency of the proposed method.

Keywords: Multi-Modal Feature Extraction, Kernel Sparse Locality Preserving Canonical Correlation Analysis (KSLPCCA), Dimensionality Reduction.

1 Introduction

Appearance-based methods have been widely used in many visual recognition applications. Most traditional algorithms, such as principal component analysis (PCA) [1] and linear discriminant analysis (LDA) [2], are unimodal and their performance in real applications may unpredictably deteriorate under noisy conditions. Thus multimodal recognition emerges and has been gained more and more attentions.

For multimodal recognition, it is a critical issue to effectively utilize the information stemming from different sources to improve the recognition performance. An effective solution to this problem is canonical correlation analysis (CCA) [3], which can fuse information from diverse sources to improve overall understanding of the recognition of an object. Wu et al. [4] proposed an incremental learning scheme to update the discriminant matrix for the analysis of canonical correlations (IDCC). Sun et al. [5] proposed the discriminative CCA (DCCA) which incorporates the class information into the framework of CCA for combined feature extraction. In [6], Sun et al. proposed a locality preserving canonical correlation analysis (LPCCA) method to uncover the potential nonlinear intrinsics of two image sets, which can outperform conventional CCA for data visualization and pose estimation. However, LPCCA adopts k-nearest-neighbor model for graph construction, which is very sensitive to data noises. Furthermore, the optimum of k is datum-dependent, and one single global parameter may result in unreasonable neighborhood structure for certain datum.

W.-S. Zheng et al. (Eds.): CCBR 2012, LNCS 7701, pp. 340–347, 2012.
© Springer-Verlag Berlin Heidelberg 2012

In this paper, we propose a ℓ^1-Graph based CCA method, called sparse locality preserving canonical correlation analysis (SLPCCA). In our algorithm, the projections of SLPCCA are sought such that the sparse reconstructive weights can be best preserved. As SLPCCA is a linear method, we present its nonlinear scenarios by applying the kernel trick methods.

The remainder of this paper is organized as follows. Section 2 describes the details of the proposed SLPCCA method and its nonlinear extension by using 'kernel' trick. Section 3 presents experimental results, and Section 4 concludes the paper.

2   Sparse Locality Preserving Canonical Correlation Analysis

2.1   Review of LPCCA

Given two sets of multivariate data, $\{x_i \in \mathbb{R}^m, i = 1, \cdots, N\}$ and $\{y_i \in \mathbb{R}^n, i = 1, \cdots, N\}$, LPCCA aims to seek a pair of projection vectors, $\mathbf{w}_x$ and $\mathbf{w}_y$, such that the correlation between $\mathbf{w}_x^T x$ and $y = \mathbf{w}^T y_i$, $i = 1, \cdots, N$ in a local field, is maximized [6]:

$$\arg\max_{\mathbf{w}_x, \mathbf{w}_y} \left(\mathbf{w}_x^T \sum_{i=1}^{N} \sum_{j=1}^{N} \mathbf{A}_x(i,j)(\mathbf{x}_i - \mathbf{x}_j) \mathbf{A}_y(i,j)(\mathbf{y}_i - \mathbf{y}_j)^T \mathbf{w}_y \right)$$

$$\text{s.t.} \quad \mathbf{w}_x^T \sum_{i=1}^{N} \sum_{j=1}^{N} \mathbf{A}_x^2(i,j)(\mathbf{x}_i - \mathbf{x}_j)(\mathbf{x}_i - \mathbf{x}_j)^T \mathbf{w}_x = 1 \tag{1}$$

$$\mathbf{w}_y^T \sum_{i=1}^{N} \sum_{j=1}^{N} \mathbf{A}_y^2(i,j)(\mathbf{y}_i - \mathbf{y}_j)(\mathbf{y}_i - \mathbf{y}_j)^T \mathbf{w}_y = 1$$

where $\mathbf{A}_x$ and $\mathbf{A}_y$ are weight matrices. A popular way of defining them is applying k-nearest-neighbor, as shown in [6]. However, k-nearest-neighbor method is very sensitive to data noises. Moreover, when the data are not evenly distributed, the k nearest neighbors of a datum may involve faraway inhomogeneous data if the k is set too large [7]. An effective solution to the problem is

2.2   Sparse Reconstructive Weights

In the past few years, sparse representation has been successfully applied to solve many practical problems in signal processing, statistics and pattern recognition [7]. In this section, we will construct the affinity matrix $\mathbf{A}_x$ and $\mathbf{A}_y$ based on a modified sparse representation framework.

Let $\mathbf{X} = [\mathbf{x}_1 \ \mathbf{x}_2 \cdots \mathbf{x}_N] \in \mathbb{R}^{m \times N}$ be the data matrix including all the training samples in its columns. Each sample $\mathbf{x}_i$ can be constructed by a sparse reconstructive weight vector $\mathbf{s}_i$ through the following modified ℓ^1 minimization problem [7]:

$$\min_{\mathbf{s}_i} \|\mathbf{s}_i\|_1, \quad \text{s.t.} \quad \|\mathbf{x}_i - \mathbf{X}\mathbf{s}_i\|_2^2 \leq \varepsilon \tag{2}$$

where $\mathbf{s}_i = \left[s_{i1}, s_{i2}, \cdots, s_{i,i-1}, 0, s_{i,i+1}, \cdots, s_{iN} \right]^T$ is an N-dimensional vector in which the i-th element is equal to zero, and the elements $s_{ij}, j \neq i$ denote the contribution of each $\mathbf{x}_j$ to reconstructing $\mathbf{x}_i$. $\mathbf{S}_x = \left[\mathbf{s}_1 \, \mathbf{s}_2 \cdots \mathbf{s}_n \right]^T$ is the sparse reconstructive weight matrix.

Eq. (2) is equivalent to the so-called LASSO problem [8]:

$$\min_{\mathbf{s}_i} \left\| \mathbf{x}_i - \mathbf{X}\mathbf{s}_i \right\|_2^2, \quad \text{s.t.} \quad \left\| \mathbf{s}_i \right\|_1 \leq \sigma \tag{3}$$

The above equation is essentially a sparsity-constrained least square estimation problem. When the residual $e = \mathbf{x}_i - \mathbf{X}\mathbf{s}_i$ follows the Gaussian distribution, the least square solution is the MLE solution. In practice, however, the distribution of residual e may be far from Gaussian or Laplacian distribution, especially when there are occlusions, corruptions and/or other variations. Hence, a modified model is adopted to find an MLE solution of the coding coefficients, which is defined as [8]

$$\min_{\mathbf{s}_i} \left\| \mathbf{W}^{1/2} \left(\mathbf{x}_i - \mathbf{X}\mathbf{s}_i \right) \right\|_2^2, \quad \text{s.t.} \quad \left\| \mathbf{s}_i \right\|_1 \leq \sigma \tag{4}$$

where $\mathbf{W}$ is a diagonal matrix defined as

$$\mathbf{W}(k,k) = \varpi_\theta(e_k) = \frac{\exp\left(\mu\delta - \mu e_k^2\right)}{1 + \exp\left(\mu\delta - \mu e_k^2\right)} \tag{5}$$

where μ and δ are positive scalars. μ controls the decreasing rate from 1 to 0, and δ controls the location of demarcation point. e_k is the coding residual.

Following [9], we employ the active set based subgradient descent algorithm to solve Eq. (4),

$$\mathbf{s}_{i,t+1} = \mathbf{s}_{i,t} - \beta_t \left. \frac{\partial G(\mathbf{s})}{\partial \mathbf{s}} \right|_{\mathbf{s}=\mathbf{s}_t} \tag{6}$$

where $G(\mathbf{s}_i) = \frac{1}{2}\left\| \mathbf{x}_i - \mathbf{X}\mathbf{s}_i \right\|_2^2 + \eta\left\| \mathbf{s}_i \right\|$, $R(\mathbf{s}_i) = \frac{1}{2}\left\| \mathbf{x}_i - \mathbf{X}\mathbf{s}_i \right\|_2^2$, $\partial G/\partial \mathbf{s}$ is the updating direction and β_t is the step size determined by a standard line search method [9].

By the above design, we can obtain the sparse weight matrix $\mathbf{S}_x$ and $\mathbf{S}_y$ which can reflect intrinsic geometric properties of the data. Thus, we can rewrite Eq. (1) as

$$
\begin{aligned}
& \mathbf{w}_x^T \sum_{i=1}^N \sum_{j=1}^N \mathbf{S}_x(i,j)\left(\mathbf{x}_i - \mathbf{x}_j\right)\mathbf{S}_y(i,j)\left(\mathbf{y}_i - \mathbf{y}_j\right)^T \mathbf{w}_y \\
& = \mathbf{w}_x^T \left(\sum_{i=1}^N \left(\sum_{j=1}^N \mathbf{S}_x(i,j)\mathbf{S}_y(i,j)\right)\mathbf{x}_i\mathbf{y}_i^T \right)\mathbf{w}_y + \mathbf{w}_x^T \left(\sum_{j=1}^N \left(\sum_{i=1}^N \mathbf{S}_x(i,j)\mathbf{S}_y(i,j)\right)\mathbf{x}_j\mathbf{y}_j^T \right)\mathbf{w}_y \\
& - \mathbf{w}_x^T \left(\sum_{i=1}^N \sum_{j=1}^N \mathbf{S}_x(i,j)\mathbf{S}_y(i,j)\left(\mathbf{x}_i\mathbf{y}_j^T + \mathbf{x}_j\mathbf{y}_i^T\right) \right)\mathbf{w}_y \\
& = \mathbf{w}_x^T \mathbf{X}\left(\mathbf{D}_{xy1} + \mathbf{D}_{xy2} - \mathbf{S}_{xy} - \mathbf{S}_{xy}^T \right)\mathbf{Y}^T \mathbf{w}_y = \mathbf{w}_x^T \mathbf{X}\mathbf{L}_{xy}\mathbf{Y}^T \mathbf{w}_y
\end{aligned}
\tag{7}
$$

where $\mathbf{D}_{xy1}(i,i) = \sum_{j=1}^N \mathbf{S}_x(i,j)\mathbf{S}_y(i,j), \mathbf{D}_{xy2}(i,i) = \sum_{i=1}^N \mathbf{S}_x(i,j)\mathbf{S}_y(i,j), \mathbf{S}_{xy}(i,j) = \mathbf{S}_x(i,j)\mathbf{S}_y(i,j)$.

In the similar way, we have

$$
\begin{cases}
\mathbf{w}_x^T \sum_{i=1}^{N} \sum_{j=1}^{N} \mathbf{S}_x(i,j)(\mathbf{x}_i - \mathbf{x}_j) \mathbf{S}_x(i,j)(\mathbf{x}_i - \mathbf{x}_j)^T \mathbf{w}_x = \mathbf{w}_x^T \mathbf{X} \mathbf{L}_{xx} \mathbf{X}^T \mathbf{w}_x \\
\mathbf{w}_y^T \sum_{i=1}^{N} \sum_{j=1}^{N} \mathbf{S}_y(i,j)(\mathbf{y}_i - \mathbf{y}_j) \mathbf{S}_y(i,j)(\mathbf{y}_i - \mathbf{y}_j)^T \mathbf{w}_y = \mathbf{w}_y^T \mathbf{Y} \mathbf{L}_{yy} \mathbf{Y}^T \mathbf{w}_y
\end{cases}
\tag{8}
$$

where $\mathbf{D}_{xx1}, \mathbf{D}_{xx2}, \mathbf{S}_{xx}, \mathbf{D}_{yy1}, \mathbf{D}_{yy2}, \mathbf{S}_{yy}$ are defined in the similar way with those of $\mathbf{D}_{xy1}, \mathbf{D}_{xy2}, \mathbf{S}_{xy}$ in respective.

Combing (7)-(8), we can obtain the projections $\mathbf{w}_x$ and $\mathbf{w}_y$ by solving the following generalized eigenvalue problem

$$
\begin{bmatrix} 0 & \mathbf{X} \mathbf{L}_{xy} \mathbf{Y}^T \\ \mathbf{Y} \mathbf{L}_{xy}^T \mathbf{X}^T & 0 \end{bmatrix} \begin{bmatrix} \mathbf{w}_x \\ \mathbf{w}_y \end{bmatrix} = \lambda \begin{bmatrix} \mathbf{X} \mathbf{L}_{xx} \mathbf{X}^T & 0 \\ 0 & \mathbf{Y} \mathbf{L}_{yy} \mathbf{Y}^T \end{bmatrix} \begin{bmatrix} \mathbf{w}_x \\ \mathbf{w}_y \end{bmatrix}
\tag{9}
$$

2.3   Kernel SLPCCA

As SLPCCA is a linear method, it may fail when the data are highly nonlinear distributed. In this section, we will extend SLPCCA to the nonlinear case.

For the given nonlinear mappings $\boldsymbol{\Phi}$ and $\boldsymbol{\psi}$, the input data space $\mathbf{x} \in \mathbb{R}^m$ and $\mathbf{y} \in \mathbb{R}^n$ y can be mapped into a potentially much higher dimensional feature space $\mathcal{F} : \boldsymbol{\Phi} : \mathbb{R}^m \to \mathcal{F}, \mathbf{x} \to \boldsymbol{\Phi}(\mathbf{x})$ and $\boldsymbol{\psi} : \mathbb{R}^n \to \mathcal{F}, \mathbf{y} \to \boldsymbol{\psi}(\mathbf{y})$. With the proper chosen $\boldsymbol{\Phi}$ and $\boldsymbol{\psi}$, an inner product $\langle \cdot, \cdot \rangle$ can be defined which makes for a so-called reproducing kernel Hilbert space [10]. More specifically, we have $\langle \boldsymbol{\Phi}(\mathbf{x}_i), \boldsymbol{\Phi}(\mathbf{x}_j) \rangle = k(\mathbf{x}_i, \mathbf{x}_j)$ and $\langle \boldsymbol{\psi}(\mathbf{y}_i), \boldsymbol{\psi}(\mathbf{y}_j) \rangle = k(\mathbf{y}_i, \mathbf{y}_j)$ hold where $k(\cdot, \cdot)$ is a positive semi-definite kernel function.

Let Υ_x and Υ_x be the projective function of $\mathbf{x}$ and $\mathbf{y}$ in the feature space and maximizing kernel based SLPCCA in $\mathcal{F}$ is converted to

$$
(\Upsilon_x, \Upsilon_y) = \arg\max \Upsilon_x^T \boldsymbol{\Phi}(\mathbf{X}) \mathbf{L}_{xy} \boldsymbol{\psi}^T(\mathbf{Y}) \Upsilon_y
$$
$$
\text{s.t.} \quad \Upsilon_x^T \boldsymbol{\Phi}(\mathbf{X}) \mathbf{L}_{xx} \boldsymbol{\Phi}^T(\mathbf{X}) \Upsilon_x = 1
\tag{10}
$$
$$
\Upsilon_y^T \boldsymbol{\psi}(\mathbf{Y}) \mathbf{L}_{yy} \boldsymbol{\psi}^T(\mathbf{Y}) \Upsilon_y = 1
$$

From the theory of reproducing kernels [10], Υ_x and Υ_x must lie in the span of all the training samples in the feature space. That is, $\Upsilon_x = \sum_{i=1}^{N} \alpha_i \boldsymbol{\Phi}(\mathbf{x}_i)$ and $\Upsilon_y = \sum_{i=1}^{N} \beta_i \boldsymbol{\psi}(\mathbf{y}_i)$.

Define two $N \times N$ Gram matrices $\mathbf{G}_x$ and $\mathbf{G}_y$ whose elements are determined by virtue of the kernel function, i.e.

$$\mathbf{G}_x(i,j) = \mathbf{\Phi}(\mathbf{x}_i)^T \mathbf{\Phi}(\mathbf{x}_j) = \langle \mathbf{\Phi}(\mathbf{x}_i), \mathbf{\Phi}(\mathbf{x}_j) \rangle = k(\mathbf{x}_i, \mathbf{x}_j)$$

$$\mathbf{G}_y(i,j) = \mathbf{\psi}(\mathbf{y}_i)^T \mathbf{\psi}(\mathbf{y}_j) = \langle \mathbf{\psi}(\mathbf{y}_i), \mathbf{\psi}(\mathbf{y}_j) \rangle = k(\mathbf{y}_i, \mathbf{y}_j)$$

Thus, optimizing (10) is equivalent to:

$$(\mathbf{\alpha}, \mathbf{\beta})_{opt} = \arg\max \mathbf{\alpha}^T \mathbf{G}_x \mathbf{L}_{xy} \mathbf{G}_y \mathbf{\beta}$$

$$\text{s.t.} \quad \mathbf{\alpha}^T \mathbf{G}_x \mathbf{L}_{xx} \mathbf{G}_x \mathbf{\alpha} = 1 \tag{11}$$

$$\mathbf{\beta}^T \mathbf{G}_y \mathbf{L}_{yy} \mathbf{G}_y \mathbf{\beta} = 1$$

and the corresponding eigen-problem is

$$\begin{bmatrix} 0 & \mathbf{G}_x \mathbf{L}_{xy} \mathbf{G}_y^T \\ \mathbf{G}_x \mathbf{L}_{xy}^T \mathbf{G}_y^T & 0 \end{bmatrix} \begin{bmatrix} \mathbf{\alpha} \\ \mathbf{\beta} \end{bmatrix} = \lambda \begin{bmatrix} \mathbf{G}_x \mathbf{L}_{xx} \mathbf{G}_x^T & 0 \\ 0 & \mathbf{G}_y \mathbf{L}_{yy} \mathbf{G}_y^T \end{bmatrix} \begin{bmatrix} \mathbf{\alpha} \\ \mathbf{\beta} \end{bmatrix} \tag{12}$$

where $\mathbf{\alpha} = [\alpha_1 \ \alpha_2 \ \cdots \ \alpha_N]^T$ and $\mathbf{\beta} = [\beta_1 \ \beta_2 \ \cdots \ \beta_N]^T$ respectively give the projective functions Υ_x and Υ_y in the high-dimensional feature space.

3   Experimental Results

In this section, we will investigate the performance of the proposed Kernel based SLPCCA algorithm for classification.

3.1   Datasets

Two datasets are used in our study, including face and handwritten digit databases. The important statistics of these datasets are summarized below

- The FacE REcognition Technology (**FERET**) facial database [11] displays diversity across gender, ethnicity, and age. The images are acquired different illumination condition, facial expressions, and the size of the face. We used a subset of FERET face DB that consists of 1800 face images of 600 people. For each person, there are three images associated with three different poses, including front (F), left (L), and right (R). We partition the dataset into two groups where one is a set of face images with frontal view and the other is a set of face images with non-frontal but the same pose.
- **Multiple Features** database consists of features of handwritten numerals ('0'-'9', total 10 classes) extracted from a collection of Dutch utility maps. 200 patterns per class have been digitized in binary images of size 30×48. Digits are represented in terms of Fourier coefficients (76 dimensions, referred to as FOU, 76), profile correlations (FAC, 216), Karhunen-Love coefficients (KAR, 64), pixel averages (PIX, 240), Zernike moments (ZER, 47) and morphological features (MOR, 6), respectively. In our experiments, FOU, MOR, PIX and ZER datasets are picked out to construct the X and Y set. For each combination, 100 pairs of feature vectors per class are randomly selected for training, the remaining 1000 pairs for test.

3.2   Performance Comparison Design

Five algorithms have been compared in our experiments, which include: Locality Preserving Canonical Correlation Analysis (LPCCA) [6], Sparse Locality Preserving Canonical Correlation Analysis (SLPCCA), Kernel based Direct Discriminant Analysis (KDDA) [12], Kernel Fisher Analysis (KFA) [10], and Kernel Sparse Locality Preserving Canonical Correlation Analysis (KSLPCCA).

The above algorithms are evaluated in an identification scenario and results are characterized in terms of rank-1 recognition rate. As for the kernel methods, fractional power polynomial model [10] is adopted and the power is set at 0.8. For the KDDA method, the regularization parameter is set at 0.01.

3.3   Results

In this section, we compare the performance of different feature extraction methods with using the FERET and Multiple Features databases in respective. The correct classification rates for each method on the three data sets are reported on the Tables 1-2. Note that we average the results over 20 random splits and report the mean as well as the standard deviation. From the results, we can obtain the following conclusions:

- KSLPCCA outperforms KFA and KDDA for all the cases. This indicates our method shows more power for extracting the discriminatory information from high dimensional data space. The success of KEMMC may lies on the fact that it makes use of the complementary information to emphasize the discriminative information for the problem.

Table 1. CCRs (%) obtained by different methods on the FERET database.

	Front-Left	Front-Right
LPCCA	62.62±1.14	64.19±0.97
SLPCCA	67.12±0.93	66.86±0.62
KFA	71.05±0.92	72.50±0.79
KDDA	72.22±1.27	71.14±0.81
KSLPCCA	**74.52±0.74**	**75.88±0.90**

Table 2. CCRs (%) obtained by different methods on the Multiple Features database

	FOU-MOR	FOU-ZER	MOR-PIX	MOR-ZER
LPCCA	82.26±1.09	86.92±0.84	88.27±0.66	82.79±0.73
SLPCCA	86.13±0.83	87.05±0.71	92.90±0.92	84.42±0.65
KFA	85.35±1.04	88.09±0.79	93.42±0.86	82.08±0.95
KDDA	87.04±0.89	88.62±0.94	93.94±0.83	83.61±0.74
KSLPCCA	**87.26±0.95**	**89.50±0.89**	**94.72±0.64**	**86.15±0.77**

- SLPCCA always shows better performance than LPCCA. The reason is, in our method, the sparse weight matrix reflects some intrinsic geometric properties of the data. Furthermore, the proposed method can naturally preserve the discriminant information, even if no class-labels are provided. Thus, it may convey greater discriminating power compared with the unsupervised LPCCA.

4   Conclusions

In this paper, we have presented a sparse locality preserving CCA (SLPCCA) method for high-dimensional feature extraction. SLPCCA aims to preserve the sparse reconstructive relationship of the data, which is achieved by minimizing a ℓ^1 regularization-related objective function. The obtained projections contain natural discriminating information even if no class labels are provided. Moreover, SLPCCA chooses its neighborhood automatically and hence can be more conveniently used in practice compared to LPCCA. As SLPCCA is a linear method, nonlinear extension is further proposed which can map the input space to a high-dimensional feature space. Experimental results have demonstrated the efficacy of the proposed method.

Acknowledgement. This work is supported by NSFC under Grant 60802069 and Grant 61273270, by the Fundamental Research Funds for the Central Universities of China, and by the Key Projects in the National Science & Technology Pillar Program during the 12th Five-Year Plan Period under Contract 2012BAK16B06.

References

1. Turk, M., Pentland, A.: Eigenfaces for recognition. J. Cogn. Neurosci. 3, 71–86 (1991)
2. Cooke, T.: Two Variations on Fisher's Linear Discriminant for Pattern Recognition. IEEE Trans. Pattern Anal. Mach. Intell. 24(2), 268–273 (2002)
3. Hardoon, D.R., Szedmak, S., John, S.T.: Canonical correlation analysis: An overview with application to learning methods. Neural Computation 16, 2639–2664 (2004)
4. Wu, X., Jia, Y., Liang, W.: Incremental discriminant analysis of canonical correlations for action recognition. Pattern Recognition 43, 4190–4197 (2010)
5. Sun, T., Chen, S., Yang, J., Shi, P.: A Novel Method of Combined Feature Extraction for Recognition. In: Eighth IEEE International Conference on Data Mining, pp. 1043–1048. IEEE Press, New York (2008)
6. Sun, T., Chen, S.: Locality preserving CCA with applications to data visualization and pose estimation. Image and Vision Computing 25, 531–543 (2007)
7. Cheng, B., Yang, J., Yan, S., Fu, Y., Huang, T.S.: Learning With ℓ^1-Graph for Image Analysis. IEEE Trans. on Image Processing 19(4), 858–866 (2010)
8. Yang, M., Zhang, L., Yang, J., Zhang, D.: Robust Sparse Coding for Face Recognition. In: IEEE Conference on Computer Vision and Pattern Recognition, pp. 625–632. IEEE Press, New York (2011)
9. Lee, H., Battle, A., Raina, R., Ng, A.Y.: Efficient sparse coding algorithms. In: Intl. Conf. on Neural Information Processing Systems, pp. 801–808. MIT Press (2006)

10. Liu, C.: Capitalize on dimensionality increasing techniques for improving face recognition grand challenge performance. IEEE Trans. Pattern Anal. Mach. Intell. 28(5), 725–737 (2006)
11. Phillips, P.J., Wechsler, H., Huang, J., Rauss, P.: The FERET Database and Evaluation Procedure for Face-Recognition Algorithms. Image and Vision Computing 16, 295–306 (1998)
12. Lu, J., Plataniotis, K.N., Venetsanopoulos, A.N.: Face Recognition Using Kernel Direct Discriminant Analysis Algorithms. IEEE Trans. on Neural Networks 14(1), 117–126 (2003)

Kernel Based Enhanced Maximum Margin Criterion for Feature Extraction

Haifeng Hu

School of Information Science and Technology, Sun Yat-sen University, Guangzhou, 510275, P.R. China
huhaif@mail.sysu.edu.cn

Abstract. A new kernel discriminant analysis algorithm, called Kernel-based Enhanced Maximum Margin Criterion (KEMMC), is presented for extracting features from high-dimensional data space. In this paper, the EMMC is firstly proposed which attempts to maximize the average margin between classes after dimensionality reduction transformation. In our method, a weighted matrix is introduced and the local property is taken into account so that the data points of neighboring classes can be mapped far away. Moreover, the regularized technique is employed to deal with small sample size problem. As EMMC is a linear method, it is extended to a nonlinear form by mapping the input space to a high-dimensional feature space which can make the mapped features linearly separable. Extensive experiments on handwritten digit image and face image data demonstrate the effectiveness of the proposed algorithm.

Keywords: Feature Extraction, Kernel based Enhanced Maximum Margin Criterion (KEMMC), Maximum Margin Criterion, Small Sample Size Problem.

1   Introduction

Linear Discriminant Analysis (LDA) [1] has been successfully used as a dimensionality reduction technique to many classification problems, such as speech recognition, face recognition, and multimedia information retrieval. The objective is to seek a linear transformation that maximizes the between-class scatter $\mathbf{S}_B$ and minimizes the within-class scatter $\mathbf{S}_W$. However, this method needs the inverse of $\mathbf{S}_W$. This is problematic because the dimensionality of the input data space is usually very high and, hence, $\mathbf{S}_W$ is often singular. Numerous methods have been proposed to solve this problem. A popular approach, called PCA+LDA method [1], applies PCA first for dimensionality reduction so as to make the $\mathbf{S}_W$ nonsingular before the application of LDA. However, applying PCA for dimensionality reduction may result in the loss of discriminative information. Zhuang et al. developed an inverse Fisher discriminant analysis (IFDA) method [2]. They modified the procedure of PCA and derived the regular and irregular information from the within-class scatter by inverse Fisher discriminant criterion.

W.-S. Zheng et al. (Eds.): CCBR 2012, LNCS 7701, pp. 348–355, 2012.

In [3], the Maximum Margin Criterion (MMC) is proposed to find the projection vectors. The advantage of MMC is that no requirement for computing the inverse of S_W, and thus the singularity problem can be avoided. However, as the estimation for the interclass distance measure is often extremely ill-posed in small sample size (SSS) situation, the performance of MMC may deteriorate rapidly when the SSS problem becomes severe. Liu et al. [4] improved MMC by regularization. Lu et al. [5] proposed a new discriminant locality preserving projections based on maximum margin criterion (DLPP/MMC), which seeks to maximize the difference between the locality preserving between-class scatter and locality preserving within-class scatter.

In this paper, a new dimensionality reduction approach, called enhanced maximum margin criterion (EMMC), is proposed for large scale discriminant analysis. EMMC can find projections that maximize the average margin between different classes. Moreover, the local information between classes and regularization information of the data points within a same class are incorporated. As EMMC is linear method, kernel based EMMC (KEMMC) is presented which can map nonlinearly the input space to a high-dimensional feature space.

The paper is organized as follows. Section 2 gives the details of the proposed KEMMC method. Section 3 provides the experimental results. The conclusions are given in Section 4.

2   The Proposed Method

2.1   Maximum Margin Criterion

Let $\mathbf{x}_i \in \mathbb{R}^N (i = 1, 2, \cdots, n)$ be N-dimensional samples and $y_i \in \{1, 2, \cdots, c\}$ be associated class labels, where n and c are the number of samples and classes respectively. Let n_ℓ be the number of samples in class ℓ. It is easy to verify that $\sum_{\ell=1}^{c} n_\ell = n$.

The maximum margin criterion (MMC) is given by [3]

$$J = \frac{1}{2} \sum_{i=1}^{c} \sum_{j=1}^{c} p_i p_j d(i, j) \tag{1}$$

where p_i is a priori probability of class i. $d(i, j)$ is the interclass distance between class i and class j, which is defined as

$$d(i, j) = d\left(\mathbf{m}^{(i)}, \mathbf{m}^{(j)}\right) - s(i) - s(j) \tag{2}$$

where $\mathbf{m}^{(i)}$ and $\mathbf{m}^{(j)}$ are the mean vectors of class i and class j respectively. $s(i)$ is the measure of the scatter of class i and it can be estimated by overall variance $\text{tr}(\mathbf{S}_i)$.

There are still two problems when applying MMC for feature extraction. Firstly, each sample class covariance matrix $\mathbf{S}_\ell$ may be biased and unreliable due to insufficient training samples. Secondly, MMC aims to preserve the global structure. However, in many real world applications, the local structure is more important, which motivates us to consider manifold based techniques for dimensionality reduction.

2.2   Regularized Individual Covariance Matrix

As the individual within-class scatter matrix $\mathbf{S}_\ell$ is highly ill-posed in SSS situation, a general solution is to introduce a regularization term as [6]

$$\tilde{\mathbf{S}}_\ell(\alpha) = \mathbf{S}_\ell + \gamma \cdot c \cdot \mathbf{S}_W \tag{3}$$

where $\mathbf{S}_W$ is the averaged within-class scatter matrix

2.3   New Distance Measure between Different Classes

Motivated by the utilization of graph as introduced in LPP [7], we redefine the distance measure between different classes with a weighted matrix as follows:

$$\tilde{d}\left(\mathbf{m}^{(i)}, \mathbf{m}^{(j)}\right) = \mathbf{A}_{i,j} \left\| \mathbf{m}^{(i)} - \mathbf{m}^{(j)} \right\|^2 \tag{4}$$

where $\|\cdot\|$ is the Euclidean norm in $\mathbb{R}^N$ and $\mathbf{A}_{ij}$ is an affinity matrix given by

$$\mathbf{A}_{ij} = \exp\left(-\left\| \mathbf{m}^{(i)} - \mathbf{m}^{(j)} \right\|^2 \big/ \tau\right) \tag{5}$$

where τ is a positive parameter.

2.4   Enhanced Maximum Margin Criterion

With (3) and (4), we have the enhanced maximum margin criterion (EMMC) as

$$\tilde{J} = \frac{1}{2} \sum_{i=1}^{c} \sum_{j=1}^{c} p_i p_j \left(\tilde{d}\left(\mathbf{m}^{(i)}, \mathbf{m}^{(j)}\right) - \operatorname{tr}\left(\tilde{\mathbf{S}}_i\right) - \operatorname{tr}\left(\tilde{\mathbf{S}}_j\right) \right)$$

$$= \frac{1}{2} \sum_{i=1}^{c} \sum_{j=1}^{c} p_i p_j \tilde{d}\left(\mathbf{m}^{(i)}, \mathbf{m}^{(j)}\right) - \frac{1}{2} \sum_{i=1}^{c} \sum_{j=1}^{c} p_i p_j \left(\operatorname{tr}\left(\tilde{\mathbf{S}}_i\right) + \operatorname{tr}\left(\tilde{\mathbf{S}}_j\right) \right) = \tilde{J}_1 - \tilde{J}_2 \tag{6}$$

where $\tilde{J}_1 = \frac{1}{2} \sum_{i=1}^{c} \sum_{j=1}^{c} p_i p_j \tilde{d}\left(\mathbf{m}^{(i)}, \mathbf{m}^{(j)}\right)$ and $\tilde{J}_2 = \frac{1}{2} \sum_{i=1}^{c} \sum_{j=1}^{c} p_i p_j \left(\operatorname{tr}\left(\tilde{\mathbf{S}}_i\right) + \operatorname{tr}\left(\tilde{\mathbf{S}}_j\right) \right)$.

With Eq. (4), $\tilde{J}_1$ can be written as

$$\tilde{J}_1 = \frac{1}{2} \sum_{i=1}^{c} \sum_{j=1}^{c} p_i p_j \left(\mathbf{m}^{(i)} - \mathbf{m}^{(j)}\right)^T \left(\mathbf{m}^{(i)} - \mathbf{m}^{(j)}\right) \mathbf{A}_{ij}$$

$$= \sum_{i=1}^{c} \sum_{j=1}^{c} \left(p_i \mathbf{m}_i\right)^T \mathbf{B}_{ij} \left(p_i \mathbf{m}_i\right) - \sum_{i=1}^{c} \sum_{j=1}^{c} \left(p_i \mathbf{m}_i\right)^T \mathbf{A}_{ij} \left(p_j \mathbf{m}_j\right) \tag{7}$$

$$= \frac{1}{n^2} \sum_{i=1}^{c} \sum_{j=1}^{c} \left(\mathbf{X}^{(i)} \mathbf{1}_{n_i}^T\right)^T \mathbf{F}_{ij} \left(\mathbf{X}^{(i)} \mathbf{1}_{n_i}^T\right) - \frac{1}{n^2} \sum_{i=1}^{c} \sum_{j=1}^{c} \left(\mathbf{X}^{(i)} \mathbf{1}_{n_i}^T\right)^T \mathbf{A}_{ij} \left(\mathbf{X}^{(j)} \mathbf{1}_{n_j}^T\right) = \frac{1}{n^2} \operatorname{tr}\left(\mathbf{X} \mathbf{L} \mathbf{Y} \mathbf{L}^T \mathbf{X}^T\right)$$

where $\mathbf{X}^{(\ell)} = \begin{bmatrix} \mathbf{x}_1^{(\ell)} & \mathbf{x}_2^{(\ell)} & \cdots & \mathbf{x}_{n_\ell}^{(\ell)} \end{bmatrix}$ and $\mathbf{X}^{(\ell)} = \begin{bmatrix} \mathbf{x}_1^{(\ell)} & \mathbf{x}_2^{(\ell)} & \cdots & \mathbf{x}_{n_\ell}^{(\ell)} \end{bmatrix}$. $\mathbf{x}_k^{(\ell)}$ is a sample from class ℓ and $\mathbf{1}_{n_\ell} = (1,1,\cdots,1) \in \mathbb{R}^{n_\ell}$. $\mathbf{B}$ is a matrix defined by $\mathbf{B}_{ij} - \mathbf{\Lambda}_{ij} \cdot p_j / p_i$. $\mathbf{F}$ is a $c \times c$ diagonal matrix whose diagonal element satisfies $\mathbf{F}_{ii} = \sum_{j=1}^{c} \mathbf{B}_{ij}$. $\Upsilon = \mathbf{P} - \mathbf{\Lambda}$ and

$$\mathbf{L} = \begin{pmatrix} \mathbf{1}_{n_1}^T & & \\ & \ddots & \\ & & \mathbf{1}_{n_c}^T \end{pmatrix} \in \mathbb{R}^{n \times n}$$

With Eq. (3), $\tilde{J}_2$ can be written as

$$\tilde{J}_2 = \frac{1}{2} \sum_{i=1}^{c} \sum_{j=1}^{c} p_i p_j \left(\text{tr}\left(\tilde{\mathbf{S}}_i\right) + \text{tr}\left(\tilde{\mathbf{S}}_j\right) \right) = \sum_{i=1}^{c} p_i \text{tr}(\mathbf{S}_i) + \gamma \cdot c \cdot \sum_{i=1}^{c} p_i \text{tr}(\mathbf{S}_w) = (1 + \gamma \cdot c) \text{tr}(\mathbf{S}_w) \quad (8)$$

From [7], we have $\mathbf{S}_w = \frac{1}{n} \mathbf{X} \mathbf{R} \mathbf{X}^T$ with $\mathbf{R} = \mathbf{I} - \mathbf{T} . \mathbf{T}$ is a $c \times c$ matrix defined by

$$\mathbf{T}_{ij} = \begin{cases} 1/n_\ell & \text{if } y_i = y_j \\ 0 & \text{otherwise} \end{cases}$$

Thus Eq. (8) can be expressed as

$$\tilde{J}_2 = \frac{1}{n}(1 + \gamma \cdot c) \cdot \text{tr}\left(\mathbf{X} \mathbf{R} \mathbf{X}^T\right) \quad (9)$$

Combing (7) and (9), we have

$$\tilde{J} = \frac{1}{n^2} \text{tr}\left(\mathbf{X} \mathbf{L} \Upsilon \mathbf{L}^T \mathbf{X}^T\right) - \frac{1}{n}(1 + \gamma \cdot c) \text{tr}\left(\mathbf{X} \mathbf{R} \mathbf{X}^T\right) = \text{tr}\left(\mathbf{X} \mathbf{H} \mathbf{X}^T\right) \quad (10)$$

where $\mathbf{H} = \frac{1}{n^2} \mathbf{L} \Upsilon \mathbf{L}^T - \frac{1}{n}(1 + \gamma \cdot c) \mathbf{R}$.

Now maximizing the EMMC is converted to solve:

$$\arg\max_{\mathbf{w}} \mathbf{w}^T \mathbf{X} \mathbf{H} \mathbf{X}^T \mathbf{w} \qquad \text{s.t.} \qquad \mathbf{w}^T \mathbf{w} = 1 \quad (11)$$

A Lagrangian can be introduced to solve the above optimization problem. That is

$$\mathbf{X} \mathbf{H} \mathbf{X}^T \mathbf{w} = \lambda \mathbf{w} \quad (12)$$

The above equation shows that the transformation vector $\mathbf{w}$ is given by the leading eigenvector of $\mathbf{X} \mathbf{H} \mathbf{X}^T$, associated with the largest eigenvalue. More generally, the transformation matrix $\mathbf{W}$ are the first r largest eigenvectors of $\mathbf{X} \mathbf{H} \mathbf{X}^T$. As $\mathbf{H}$ is a symmetric matrix, the matrix $\mathbf{W}$ obtained is an orthogonal transformation.

2.5   Kernel-Based EMMC

For a given nonlinear mapping $\mathbf{\Phi}$, the input data space $\mathbb{R}^N$ can be mapped into a potentially much higher dimensional feature space $\mathcal{F}$ [6]

$$\Phi: \mathbb{R}^N \to \mathcal{F},$$
$$\mathbf{x} \to \Phi(\mathbf{x}) \tag{13}$$

With a proper chosen Φ, an inner product $\langle \cdot, \cdot \rangle$ can be defined on $\mathcal{F}$ which makes for a reproducing kernel Hilbert space [6]. More specifically, $\langle \Phi(\mathbf{x}), \Phi(\mathbf{y}) \rangle = k(\mathbf{x}, \mathbf{y})$ holds where $k(\cdot, \cdot)$ is a positive semi-definite kernel function.

Let $\mathbf{v}$ be the projective function in the feature space and maximizing kernel based enhanced maximum margin criterion in $\mathcal{F}$ is converted to

$$\mathbf{v}_{opt} = \arg\max \mathbf{v}^T \Phi(\mathbf{X}) \mathbf{H} \Phi^T(\mathbf{X}) \mathbf{v} \tag{14}$$

From the theory of reproducing kernels, $\mathbf{v} \in \mathcal{F}$ must lie in the span of all the training samples in the feature space [6]

$$\mathbf{v} = \sum_{i=1}^{n} \theta_i \Phi(\mathbf{x}_i) \tag{15}$$

Let $\mathbf{G}$ be a $n \times n$ Gram matrix which is determined by

$$\mathbf{G}_{ij} = \Phi(\mathbf{x}_i)^T \Phi(\mathbf{x}_j) = \langle \Phi(\mathbf{x}_i), \Phi(\mathbf{x}_j) \rangle = k(\mathbf{x}_i, \mathbf{x}_j)$$

Thus, optimizing (14) is equivalent to:

$$\theta_{opt} = \arg\max \theta^T \mathbf{G} \mathbf{H} \mathbf{G} \theta \tag{16}$$

and the corresponding eigen-problem is

$$\mathbf{G} \mathbf{H} \mathbf{G} \theta = \lambda \theta \tag{17}$$

where $\theta = [\theta_1 \ \theta_2 \ \cdots \ \theta_n]^T$ gives a projective function $\mathbf{v}$ in the feature space.

3   Experimental Results

In this section, we will investigate the performance of the proposed Kernel based EMMC algorithm for classification.

3.1   Datasets

Two datasets are used in our study, including face and handwritten digit databases. The important statistics of these datasets are summarized below

The CMU PIE face database [8] contains 68 subjects with 41,368 face images as a whole. The face images were captured under varying pose, illumination and expression. We choose the five near frontal poses (C05, C07, C09, C27, C29) and use all the images under different illuminations and expressions. Thus we get 170 images for each individual. All the face images are manually aligned and cropped to 32×32 pixels. For each subject, $L(= 5, 10, 20, 30)$ images are randomly selected for training and the rest are used for testing.

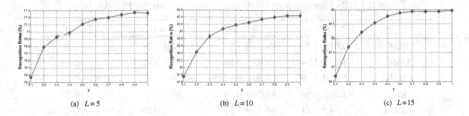

(a) $L=5$ (b) $L=10$ (c) $L=15$

Fig. 1. CRRs obtained by KEMMC versus different γ and L on the MNIST database

The MNIST handwritten digit database [9] has a training set of 60,000 samples (denoted as set A), and a testing set of 10,000 samples (denoted as set B). We take the first 2,000 samples from the set A as our training set and the first 2,000 samples from the set B as test set. A random subset with $L(= 10, 20, 50, 100)$ samples per digit from training set are selected for training.

3.2   Performance Comparison Design

Seven algorithms are compared in our experiments, which include: Regularized Discriminant Analysis (RDA) [6], Maximum Margin Criterion (MMC) [3], Enhanced Maximum Margin Criterion (EMMC), Kernel based Direct Discriminant Analysis (KDDA) [6], Kernel Fisher Analysis (KFA) [10], Kernel based Enhanced Maximum Margin Criterion (KEMMC).

The above algorithms are evaluated in an identification scenario and results are characterized in terms of rank-1 recognition rate. Moreover, the Euclidean distance measure is adopted. It should be noted that for the kernel methods, fractional power polynomial model [10] is adopted and the power is set at 0.8. And for the RDA and the KDDA methods, the regularization parameter is set at 0.01.

3.3   Results

3.3.1   Determination of Parameter γ

The first experiment is performed to determine the optimal value of γ with using the MNIST database. Fig. 1 shows the plots of the correct recognition rates obtained by KEMMC versus different γ and L. Note that the range of γ is set from 0.1 to 1 with the step 0.1. From the figure, we can find, the best performance is achieved when γ is set within [0.6, 1]. In the following test, γ is set at 0.7.

3.3.2   Performance Comparisons on Two Different Datasets

In this section, we compare the performance of different feature extraction methods using the CMU PIE and MNIST databases in respective. The correct classification rates for each method are reported in the Tables 1-2. Note that for each given L, we average the results over 20 random splits and report the mean as well as the standard deviation. From the results, we can obtain the following conclusions:

Table 1. CRRs (%) obtained by different methods on the PIE database

	$L=5$	$L=10$	$L=15$	$L=20$
RDA	70.61±1.30	79.47±1.76	85.14±0.87	92.32±0.43
MMC	68.20±1.04	76.93±0.88	82.61±0.92	91.56±0.55
EMMC	71.72±0.59	85.30±0.92	90.39±0.51	92.82±0.13
KFA	73.28±0.66	88.09±0.74	93.35±0.42	95.44±0.27
KDDA	70.44±1.11	86.48±1.05	93.13±0.36	95.38±0.27
KEMMC	**74.16±1.27**	**88.74±0.71**	**93.60±0.28**	**95.73±0.29**

Table 2. CRRs (%) obtained by different methods on the MNIST database

	$L=10$	$L=20$	$L=50$	$L=100$	$L=200$
RDA	72.97±1.22	77.40±1.15	80.33±0.80	81.99±0.49	82.40±0.38
MMC	73.85±1.52	76.33±1.77	81.20±1.16	82.01±0.99	82.55±0.94
EMMC	74.44±0.48	79.11±1.20	82.05±0.92	83.94±0.64	84.76±0.39
KFA	76.73±0.94	83.05±0.60	88.90±0.47	91.42±0.35	93.04±0.28
KDDA	76.31±1.12	82.09±0.68	88.42±0.66	91.08±0.30	92.96±0.30
KEMMC	**77.24±1.20**	**83.40±0.89**	**88.94±0.54**	**91.61±0.27**	**93.27±0.32**

(1) KEMMC outperforms KFA and KDDA for all the cases. This indicates our method shows more power for extracting the discriminatory information from high dimensional data space. The success of KEMMC may lies on the fact that it considers the local information between classes and regularization information of the data points within a same class, which make it more robust in finding the discriminative information from data space.

(2) EMMC always shows better performance than MMC. The reason is, in our method, the regularization technique is implemented for estimating the individual class covariance matrix S_i, which may be highly ill-posed in the SSS situation. Furthermore, compared with MMC, our method can get an optimal solution by adjusting the strength of the regularization, as shown in Fig. 1.

4   Conclusions

A new dimensionality reduction approach, called kernel based enhanced maximum margin criterion, is proposed for extracting features from high-dimensional data space. In this paper, EMMC is firstly presented which can maximize the average margin between different classes. In our method, the local information between classes and regularization information of the data points within a same class are incorporated, which make it more robust in finding the discriminative information. As EMMC is a linear method, nonlinear extension is further proposed which can map the input space to a high-dimensional feature space. We compare our method with some famous dimensionality reduction techniques with using the CMU PIE and MNIST databases. The results show our method can achieve high recognition performance for all the test conditions.

Acknowledgement. This work is supported by NSFC under Grant 60802069 and Grant 61273270, by the Fundamental Research Funds for the Central Universities of China, and by the Key Projects in the National Science & Technology Pillar Program during the 12th Five-Year Plan Period under Contract 2012BAK16B06.

References

1. Belhumeur, P.N., Hespanha, J.P., Kriegman, D.J.: Eigenfaces vs. fisherfaces: Recognition using class specific linear projection. IEEE Trans. Pattern Anal. Mach. Intell. 19(7), 711–720 (1997)
2. Zhuang, X.S., Dai, D.Q.: Improved discriminant analysis for high-dimensional data and its application to face recognition. Pattern Recognition 40(5), 1570–1578 (2007)
3. Li, H.F., Jiang, T., Zhang, K.: Efficient and robust feature extraction by maximum margin criterion. IEEE Trans. on Neural Networks 17(1), 157–165 (2006)
4. Liu, Q., Tang, X., Lu, H., Ma, S.: Face recognition using kernel scatter-difference-based discriminant analysis. IEEE Trans. Neural Networks 17(4), 1081–1085 (2006)
5. Lu, G.-F., Lin, Z., Jin, Z.: Face recognition using discriminant locality preserving projections based on maximum margin criterion. Pattern Recognition 43(10), 3572–3579 (2010)
6. Lu, J., Plataniotis, K.N., Venetsanopoulos, A.N.: Face Recognition Using Kernel Direct Discriminant Analysis Algorithms. IEEE Trans. on Neural Networks 14(1), 117–126 (2003)
7. He, X., Yan, S., Hu, Y., Niyogi, P., Zhang, H.: Face recognition using laplacianface. IEEE Trans. Pattern Anal. Mach. Intell. 27(3), 328–340 (2005)
8. Sim, T., Baker, S., Bsat, M.: The CMU pose, illumination, and expression database. IEEE Trans. Pattern Anal. Mach. Intell. 25(12), 1615–1618 (2003)
9. LeCun, Y., Bottou, L., Bengio, Y., Haffner, P.: Gradient-based learning applied to document recognition. Proceedings of the IEEE 86(11), 2278–2324 (1998)
10. Liu, C.: Capitalize on dimensionality increasing techniques for improving face recognition grand challenge performance. IEEE Trans. Pattern Anal. Mach. Intell. 28(5), 725–737 (2006)

A Novel Variance Minimization Segmentation Model

Bo Chen, Yan Li, Wen-Sheng Chen[*], and Jin-Lin Cai

College of Mathematics and Computational Science, Shenzhen University, Shenzhen 518060,
P.R. China
chenws@szu.edu.cn

Abstract. Chan-Vese (CV) model is a promising active contour model for image segmentation. However, CV model does not utilize local region information of images and thus CV model based segmentation methods cannot achieve good segmentation results for complex image with some in-homogeneity intensities. To overcome the limitation of CV model, this paper presents a new type of geometric active contour model using the strategy of variance minimization of image. The proposed model not only considers the first and second order moments of objective image statistical measurements, but also regularizes the level set function by incorporating the distance penalized energy function. Extensive experimental results demonstrate that the proposed approach is effective in image segmentation, especially for the image with in-homogeneity intensity.

Keywords: Image segmentation, active contour model, Chan-Vese model, variance minimization, level set.

1 Introduction

In the past years, geometric active contour models (GACMs) [1] have been widely applied to image segmentation, de-noising and object tracing tasks. It is known that GACMs, based on curve evolution and level set theories, can deal with topological change regions automatically in image segmentation. In general, GACMs can be roughly classified into two categories, namely the edge-based models [1] and the region-based models [2]. The edge-based models drive the curve to object boundary using image gradient information. As a result of avoiding the local minimization of optimization, edge-based models seriously depend on the initial curves. While for region-based models, they make use of region information to control the curve evaluation. Therefore, region-based models possess many advantages over the edge-based models. One of the most popular region-based models is the Chan-Vese model [2] derived from the Mumford–Shah segmentation techniques [3], which has been successfully applied to binary phase image segmentation. Additionally, Caselles [1] proposed the geodesic active contour model and Malladi [4] proposed the edge and gradient induced active contour models. Unfortunately, above mentioned three models all suffer the algorithm robust in the low-contrast regions with noise. Paragios *et al.* [5] replaced the vector field force with the well-known gradient vector flow

---

[*] Corresponding author.

W.-S. Zheng et al. (Eds.): CCBR 2012, LNCS 7701, pp. 356–363, 2012.

(GVF) introduced by Xu *et al.* [6] to increase the capture range. Compared with other GACMs, Chan-Vese model can detect the objects more accurately and it is more suitable for the images with noise and low contrast. However, since the convergence of the Chan-Vese model depends on the homogeneity of the segmented objects, Chan-Vese model cannot provide satisfactory segmentation results for in-homogeneity images such as carpal bones and knee bones images.

It is known that the variance information of statistical measurement of image represents the fluctuation magnitude of image intensities. This means that a charming segmentation can be obtained by minimizing the associated intensity variance of the image. So, by using the technique of variance minimization of images, this paper proposes a new type of geometric active contour model for accurately segmenting an image with in-homogeneity intensities. The idea of the proposed model is derived from the Chan-Vese model [2] and density distance model [7]. Especially, our proposed model fully considers the first and second order moments of objective image statistical measurements, and incorporates the distance penalized energy function to regularize the level set function. Experimental results demonstrate that the proposed approach is effective for medical image segmentation.

The rest of this paper is organized as follows: Section 2 introduces the related works and our proposed model. The experimental results are reported in Section 3. Finally, Section 4 draws the conclusions.

2   Description of the Proposed Model

2.1   Chan-Vese Model

Chan-Vese model derived from the two-value image segmentation, mean values divide the image into the targets and background. Chan-Vese model was formulated by minimizing the following energy functional:

$$E(C, c_1, c_2) = \mu Length(C)$$
$$+ \lambda_1 \int_{inside(C)} |u_0(x, y) - c_1|^2 dxdy \qquad (1)$$
$$+ \lambda_2 \int_{outside(C)} |u_0(x, y) - c_2|^2 dxdy$$

where C represents the moving contour, u_0 is the original image, $\mu \geq 0, \lambda_1, \lambda_2 > 0$ are the weights of each corresponding item, c_1 and c_2 are the mean of gray values inside and outside the moving contour. The first item is named the internal energy, which is used to regularize the geometric properties of the moving contour. The last two items are named the external energy, which are employed to drive the contour to the correct position.

c_1 and c_2 can be calculated by

$$c_1 = \frac{\int_\Omega u_0(x, y) H(\phi(x, y)) dxdy}{\int_\Omega H(\phi(x, y)) dxdy}, \quad c_2 = \frac{\int_\Omega u_0(x, y)(1 - H(\phi(x, y))) dxdy}{\int_\Omega (1 - H(\phi(x, y))) dxdy} \qquad (2)$$

where H is Heaviside functional [2, 8].

The corresponding variation level set formulation as follows,

$$\frac{\partial \phi}{\partial t} = \delta(\phi)\left[\mu div\left(\frac{\nabla \phi}{|\nabla \phi|}\right) - \lambda_1(u_0 - c_1)^2 + \lambda_2(u_0 - c_2)^2\right] \tag{3}$$

where $\delta(\phi)$ is Dirac functional.

2.2   The Density Distance Model

The density distance model [7] mainly tackle the problem that many model especially Chan-Vese model are not sufficient for a highly inhomogeneous object. In order to balance the difference between different regions, density functions are employed as an additional energy term into the Chan-Vese fitting term F(C). Bhattacharyya distance [9] is chosen in [7] for both its better performance in applications of signal selection and its simple analytical form.

The Bhattacharyya distance between the density functions inside and outside the curve C is defined as

$$D = -\log B(C)$$

where

$$B(C) = \int_{R^n} \sqrt{Pin(z)Pout(z)}, z \in R^n \tag{4}$$

and $Pin(z), Pout(z)$ are the density functions inside and outside the curve C.

$$Pin(z) = \frac{\int_{\Omega} \delta_0(z - u_0(x, y))H(\phi(x, y))dxdy}{\int_{\Omega} H(\phi(x, y))dxdy}$$

$$Pout(z) = \frac{\int_{\Omega} \delta_0(z - u_0(x, y))(1 - H(\phi(x, y)))dxdy}{\int_{\Omega} (1 - H(\phi(x, y)))dxdy} \tag{5}$$

The maximization of this distance is equivalent to the minimization of B(C). So the total energy functional is

$$E(C) = \mu Length(C) + \beta(F_1 + F_2) + (1 - \beta)B(C)$$

$$= \mu \int_{\Omega} \delta_\varepsilon(\phi)|\nabla \phi|dxdy + \beta(\int_{inside} |u_0(x, y) - c_1|^2 dxdy + \int_{outside} |u_0(x, y) - c_2|^2 dxdy) \tag{6}$$

$$+(1 - \beta)\int_{Z} \sqrt{Pin(z)Pout(z)}dz$$

where ϕ is the level set function, $u_0 : \Omega \to Z \subset R^n$ is a certain image feature such as gray values, C is the evolutional curve, μ, β are weight parameters. The first item is the length of the curve, the second item derives from Chan-Vese model, the last item is the density distance. Using Euler-Lagrange equation,

$$\frac{\partial B}{\partial \phi} = \frac{1}{2} \int_Z \left(\frac{\partial Pin(z)}{\partial \phi} \sqrt{\frac{Pout(z)}{Pin(z)}} + \frac{\partial Pout(z)}{\partial \phi} \sqrt{\frac{Pin(z)}{Pout(z)}} \right) dz \tag{7}$$

Then get

$$\frac{\partial B}{\partial \phi} = \frac{\delta_\varepsilon(\phi)}{2} \left(B\left(\frac{1}{Aout} - \frac{1}{Ain} \right) + \int_Z \delta_0(z - u_0(x,y)) \left(\frac{1}{Ain} \sqrt{\frac{Pout(z)}{Pin(z)}} - \frac{1}{Aout} \sqrt{\frac{Pin(z)}{Pout(z)}} \right) dz \right) \tag{8}$$

$$= \delta_\varepsilon(\phi) D$$

The final variational level set formulation of density distance model is as follows

$$\frac{\partial \phi}{\partial t} = \delta_\varepsilon(\phi) \left\{ \mu k + \beta \left[(u_0(x,y) - c_2)^2 - (u_0(x,y) - c_1)^2 \right] - (1-\beta)D \right\} \tag{9}$$

2.3   The New Variance Minimization Model

According to the definition of mean and variance, image segmentation can be regard as a variance minimization problem. Good segmental results can be obtained with small variance value. Therefore, we can improve the energy function of Chan-Vese model from the view of variance minimization.

Motivated by Chan-Vese model and the density distance model, energy function of the new variance minimization model is defined as,

$$E(\phi) = \mu \int_\Omega \delta_\varepsilon(\phi) |\nabla \phi| dxdy + p(\phi)$$

$$+ \lambda_1 \int_Z \frac{\int_\Omega \delta_0(z - u_0(x,y))(z - c_1)^2 Pin(z) H(\phi(x,y)) dxdy}{m_1} dz \tag{10}$$

$$+ \lambda_2 \int_Z \frac{\int_\Omega \delta_0(z - u_0(x,y))(z - c_2)^2 Pout(z)(1 - H(\phi(x,y))) dxdy}{m_2} dz$$

where $u_0 : \Omega \to Z \subset R^n$ as a certain image feature such as gray value, c_1 and c_2 are the mean of gray values inside and outside the moving contour, m_1, m_2 are the numbers of a certain gray value inside and outside the contour, they can be calculated as:

$$m_1 = \int_\Omega \delta_0(z - u_0(x,y)) H(\phi(x,y)) dxdy$$

$$m_2 = \int_\Omega \delta_0(z - u_0(x,y))(1 - H(\phi(x,y))) dxdy \tag{11}$$

where $Pin(z)$ and $Pout(z)$ in Eq (5) are the density functions inside and outside the curve.

An internal energy term $P(\phi)$ is used to regularize the level set function by penalizing the deviation of the level set function ϕ from a signed distance function. where

$$P(\phi) = \frac{1}{2} \int_{\Omega} \left(1 - |\nabla \phi|\right)^2 d\Omega \tag{12}$$

We can see from the following simple discrete example to understand concept of the variance of the image gray value.

Let us suppose that a digital image and its gray value distribution are:

$$u_0 : \begin{bmatrix} 1 & 2 & 3 & 4 \\ 1 & 1 & 2 & 3 \\ 2 & 2 & 1 & 2 \end{bmatrix},$$

X	1	2	3	4
P	$\frac{1}{3}$	$\frac{5}{12}$	$\frac{1}{6}$	$\frac{1}{12}$

The expectation and the variance are:

$$E = \sum XP = 1 \times \frac{1}{3} + 2 \times \frac{5}{12} + 3 \times \frac{1}{6} + 4 \times \frac{1}{12} = 2, \quad D = \sum (X - E)^2 p = \frac{5}{6}.$$

In Eq (10), we define

$$F_1 = \int_z \frac{\int_{\Omega} \delta_0 (z - u_0(x, y))(z - c_1)^2 \, Pin(z) H(\phi(x, y)) \, dx dx}{m_1} dz$$

$$F_2 = \int_z \frac{\int_{\Omega} \delta_0 (z - u_0(x, y))(z - c_2)^2 \, Pout(z)(1 - H(\phi(x, y))) \, dx dx}{m_2} dz \tag{13}$$

$$Ain = \int_{\Omega} H(\phi(x, y)) dx dy$$

$$Aout = \int_{\Omega} (1 - H(\phi(x, y))) dx dy \tag{14}$$

According to the definition of m_1, m_2 in Eq(11) and $Pin(z), Pout(z), Ain, Aout$ in Eq(5)(14),

$$Pin(z_0) = \frac{m_1(z_0)}{Ain}, \quad Pout(z_0) = \frac{m_2(z_0)}{Aout} \tag{15}$$

The final level set formulation of our model is as follows,

$$\frac{\partial \phi}{\partial t} = \eta \left(\Delta \phi - div \left(\frac{\nabla \phi}{|\nabla \phi|} \right) \right) + \delta_\varepsilon(\phi) \left\{ \mu div \left(\frac{\nabla \phi}{|\nabla \phi|} \right) \right.$$

$$- \lambda_1 \int_z \frac{1}{m_1(z)} \delta_0(z - u_0)(z - c_1)^2 \left(\frac{[\delta_0(z - u_0) - Pin(z)]}{Ain} H(\phi) + Pin(z) \right) dz \tag{16}$$

$$\left. - \lambda_2 \int_z \frac{1}{m_2(z)} \delta_0(z - u_0)(z - c_2)^2 \left(\frac{[Pout(z) - \delta_0(z - u_0)]}{Aout} (1 - H(\phi)) - Pout(z) \right) dz \right\}$$

2.4   Implementation of the New Model

The image segmentation algorithm based on variance model mainly includes three steps. The algorithm of the new model is as follows,

1. Initialize the level set function ϕ and choose the parameters $\lambda_1, \lambda_2, \mu$.
2. Compute the mean values of inside and outside the curve c_1 and c_2 by Eq(2).
3. Compute the area of inside and outside the curve $Ain, Aout$ by Eq(14).
4. Using covariance definition to compute $\dfrac{\partial \phi}{\partial t}$, and obtain ϕ^{k+1} by Eq(16).
5. Repeat steps 2 to 4 until convergence.

3   Experimental Results

In this section, we test the proposed model on various synthetic and real medical images in comparison with the conventional Chan-Vese model and the density distance model. The gray values of intensity images are employed in the paper. Our algorithm is implemented in Windows 7 Operating System, i3 Dual Core CPU 2.13 GHz, 2 GB RAM. The parameters are used as follows $\lambda_1 = \lambda_2 = 1$, $\mu = 0.1$, and other values are selected manually.

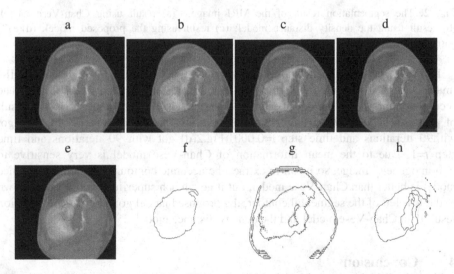

Fig. 1. The segmentation result of the CT image. (a)(e)original image and initialization with a single circle; (b) result using Chan-Vese model; (c) result using the density distance model; (d) result using the proposed model; (f)(g)(h) corresponding contour of (b)(c)(d).

Fig.1 shows the segmentation results of a CT bone image. The same initialization used a single circle, as show in Fig.1(e). The second column shows the segmentatal result of Chan-Vese model. The third column shows the result of density distance model. The fourth row shows the result of proposed model. Fig.1(f)(g)(h) are corresponding contours. Fig. 1(h) got with 55 iterations and time step $t=0.5$. Fig.1(g) got with 88 iterations and time step $t=0.00005$. Fig.1(f) got with 25 iterations and time step $t=0.1$. Seen from Fig.1, our method is better than Chan-Vese model and the density distance model in terms of   extraction the detail information of the CT image.

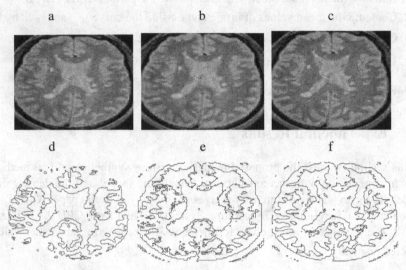

Fig. 2. The segmentation result of the MRI image.   (a) result using Chan-Vese model; (b) result using the density distance model; (c) result using the proposed model; (d)(e)(f) corresponding contour of (a)(b)(c).

In Fig.2, the experiment shows the segmentation results of a gray matter MRI image. The first column shows the segmentation results of Chan-Vese model. The second column shows the density distance model. The third column shows the result of proposed model. Fig. 2(f) got with 49 iterations and time step $t=1$. Fig.2(e) got with90 iterations and time step $t=0.0001$.Fig.2(d) got with 90 iterations and time step $t=1$. Due to the mean information of Chan-Vese model is very sensitive to in-homogeneity image, so it fail to extract the accurate contour. The density distance model is better than Chan-Vese model, but it gets much superfluous object. As shown in the low left of the segmental contour, the proposed model got a better segmentation result than Chan-Vese model and the density distance model.

4   Conclusions

Inspired by the idea of Chan-Vese model and density distance model, we proposed a new model which utilizes effectual statistical information especially the variance for image segmentation. For the in-homogeneity image, e.g., the medical image, the segmentation results are better than Chan-Vese model and the density distance model. Moreover, the proposed model is less sensitive to the initial contour. The experiment of medical image segmentation demonstrates the effectiveness of the proposed approach.

Acknowledgements. This paper is partially supported by NSFC (61272252, 61070087, 61105130), Natural Science Foundation of Guangdong Province (S2011040000433, S2011040004017), Science & Technology Planning Project of Shenzhen City (JC201105130447A, JC201105130461A) and the Opening Project of Guangdong Province Key Laboratory of Computational Science at the Sun Yat-sen University (201206001) and NSF of Guangdong province (S2012040007098).

References

1. Caselles, V., Kimmel, R., Sapiro, G.: Geodesic active contours. International Journal of Computer Vision 22(1), 61–79 (1997)
2. Chan, T., Vese, L.: Active contours without edges. IEEE Transactions on Image Processing 10(2), 266–277 (2001)
3. Mumford, D., Shah, J.: Optimal approximation by piecewise smooth function and associated variational problems. Communication on Pure and Applied Mathematics 42(5), 577–685 (1989)
4. Malladi, R., Sethian, J.A., Vemuri, B.C.: Shape modeling with front propagation a level set approach. IEEE Transactions on Pattern Analysis and Machine Intelligence 175, 158–175 (1995)
5. Paragios, N., Mellina-Gottardo, O., Ramesh, V.: Gradient vector flow fast geometric active contours. IEEE Transactions on Pattern Analysis and Machine Intelligence 26(3), 402–407 (2004)
6. Xu, C., Prince, J.: Snakes, shapes, and gradient vector flow. IEEE Transactions on Image Processing 7(3), 359–369 (1998)
7. Truc, P.T., Kim, T.-S., Lee, S., Lee, Y.-K.: Homogeneity and density distance-driven active contours for medical image segmentation. Computers in Biology and Medicine 41(5), 292–301 (2011)
8. Zhao, H.K., Chan, T., Merriman, B., Osher, S.: A variational level set approach to multiphase motion. Journal of Computational Physics 127, 179–195 (1996)
9. Kailath, T.: The divergence and Bhattacharyya distance measure in signal selection. IEEE Transactions on Communication Technology 15(1), 52–60 (1967)

Robust Integrated Locally Linear Embedding

Li-li Zhang, Ying Xie, Bin Luo, Chris Ding, and Jin Tang

Key Lab of Industrial Image Processing & Analysis of Anhui Province,
Hefei 230039, China
School of Computer Science and Technology, Anhui University, Hefei 230601, China
CSE Department, University of Texas at Arlington, Arlington, TX 76019, America
{zhanglilianhui,xieying.ahu,ahhftang}@gmail.com,
luobinahu@yahoo.com.cn, chqding@uta.edu

Abstract. Many real life applications often bring much high-dimensional and noise-contaminated data from different sources. In this paper, we consider de-noising as well as dimensionality reduction by proposing a novel method named Robust Integrated Locally Linear Embedding. The method combines the two steps in LLE into a single framework and deals with de-noising by solving a $l_{2,1}$-l_2 mixed norm based optimization problem. We also derive an efficient algorithm to build the proposed model. Extensive experiments demonstrate that the proposed method is more suitable to exhibit relationship among data points, and has visible improvement in de-noising, embedding and clustering tasks.

Keywords: Local Linear Embedding, dimensionality reduction, de-noising, embedding, clustering.

1 Introduction

In scientific data analysis and system engineering, dimensionality reduction is an important problem because data with high dimension is difficult to deal with. From the viewpoint of vector data embedding, there are two categories of embedding methods: Principal Component Analysis(PCA) for unsupervised data and Linear Discriminate Analysis(LDA) for supervised data[1, 2]. And Laplacian Embedding(LE)[3, 4] is a classical method for graph data embedding. Local Linear Embedding(LLE)[5] is a method of manifold learning, preserving distances from each point to its nearest neighbors. LLE goes beyond density modeling techniques such as local PCA or mixtures of factor analyzer which don't provide a consistent set of global coordinates by embedding observations across the entire manifold. Some other methods of manifold learning include Isomap[6], Local Tangent Space Alignment (LTSA)[7], Locality Preserving Projections(LPP)[8], etc. Besides, data is often noisy as well as high-dimensional. So many de-noising approaches are introduced, such as Generalized Principal Component Analysis (GPCA)[9], Low-Rank Representation(LRR)[10] and so on.

The nonnegative matrix factorization(NMF)[11] has been proved to be efficient in machine learning and data mining fields. Various extensions and variations of NMF have been proposed [12, 13]. NMF has the potential to revert

W.-S. Zheng et al. (Eds.): CCBR 2012, LNCS 7701, pp. 364–371, 2012.

the projection step by identifying the additive basis as well as the features, and some by-products decomposed can be used for data analysis directly[14].

Motivated by these recent work, we develop LLE into a robust similarity learning named Robust Integrated Locally Linear Embedding (RILLE) in this paper: (1) With $l_{2,1}$ norm, we aim to find a robust similarity matrix; (2) Combine the two steps in LLE into a single framework; (3) Learn a symmetric kernel to represent data relationship. Besides, the nonnegative embedding, a by-product of our model, can present the cluster structure directly. In the experiment section, we demonstrate the relative effects of de-noising, embedding, clustering in both visual effects and numerical values.

2   LLE and Reformulation

2.1   Formulation of LLE

The formulation of Locally Linear Embedding(LLE) is similar to Eq.(1)[5]. More precisely, each data point x_i is represented by a weighted sum of its k nearest neighbors (kNN), which is the ith column of the weight matrix W. Here W represents the connection/similarity between data points.

$$W = \arg\min_{W} \sum_{i=1}^{n} \|x_i - \sum_j w_{ij}x_j\|, \tag{1}$$

$$Y = \arg\min_{Y} \sum_{i=1}^{n} \|y_i - \sum_j w_{ij}y_j\|, \tag{2}$$

Let $X = (x_1, \cdots, x_n) \in \Re^{p \times n}$, $Y = (y_1, \cdots, y_n) \in \Re^{k \times n}$ and the constraints $\sum_j w_{ij} = 1$ and $YY^T = I$. Eq.(1) and Eq.(2) are equivalent to the following formulation:

$$W = \arg\min_{W} \|X - XW^T\|_F^2, \tag{3}$$

$$Y = \arg\min_{Y} \|\widetilde{W} - Y^T Y\|_F, \tag{4}$$

where $\widetilde{W} = (W + W^T - W^T W)/2$.

2.2   Reformulation

While data brought by model applications is often noisy, effectiveness of LLE in dimensionality reduction may be weakened. In this paper, we further develop the above LLE formulation into a robust embedding and similarity function learning framework.

First, we work on the robust version of Eq.(3):

$$W = \arg\min_{W} \|X - XW^T\|_{2,1}, \tag{5}$$

where the $l_{2,1}$ norm of a matrix $A \in \Re^{p \times n}$ is defined as $\|A\|_{2,1} = \sum_{i=1}^{n} \left(\sum_{d=1}^{p} A_{di}^2\right)^{1/2}$.

Second, we combine the two steps in LLE into a single framework

$$\min_{W,Y} \ \left\|X - XW^T\right\|_{2,1} + \alpha\left\|W - YY^T\right\|_F^2 \tag{6}$$

Third, we learn a symmetric kernel W:

$$\min_{W,Y} \ \left\|X - XW\right\|_{2,1} + \alpha\left\|W - YY^T\right\|_F^2 \tag{7}$$

$$s.t. \quad W = W^T, \ W \geq 0, \ Y \geq 0. \tag{8}$$

In summary, given the input dataset, our model learns a new similarity function W which is (M1) low-rank, (M2) semi-positive definition, (M3) nonnegative, (M4) symmetric. We call our model Robust Integrated Locally Linear Embedding(RILLE). Besides, a by-product of our model is the nonnegative embedding Y. Due to the nonnegativity, the cluster structure can be read off from Y directly.

3 Computational Algorithm

In this section, we present the computational algorithm of our model. The problem is dealt with by solving for Y and W alternately in a block coordinate descent fashion.

3.1 Solving for W While Fixing Y

When Y is fixed, Eq.(7) is a convex function, because both $l_{2,1}$ norm and l_2 norm are convex functions. The feasibility domain $W \geq 0, W = W^T$ is a convex set. Thus this optimization is a convex optimization. There is a unique global solution. We present an efficient algorithm to compute the solution.

We start from an existing W_0, precompute $\mathcal{K} = X^T X$ and store it. Suppose we have W_t, then we compute W_{t+1} using Eq.(9) which is gained by setting the derivative of Eq.(7) while fixing Y equal to zero.

$$W_{ij} \leftarrow W_{ij} \frac{(\mathcal{K}D + D\mathcal{K} + 4\alpha YY^T)_{ij}}{(\mathcal{K}WD + DW\mathcal{K} + 4\alpha W)_{ij}}, \tag{9}$$

where D is a diagonal matrix whose elements are

$$D_{jj} = \sqrt{1/\left[(I - W)\mathcal{K}(I - W)\right]_{jj}}. \tag{10}$$

3.2 Solving for Y While Fixing W

We solve Y while fixing W. The problem becomes the following

$$\min_{Y \geq 0} \|W - YY^T\|^2 \tag{11}$$

Algorithm 1. Robust Integrated Locally Linear Embedding
___
Input: dataset X, rank r of the similarity matrix W, model parameter α
Initialization:
Initialize W as explained in §3.1
Initialize Y as explained in §3.2
repeat
    Update W using Eq.(9)
    Update Y using Eq.(12)
until converged
Output: W,Y
___

We start from an existing Y_0, and iteratively update it using the following algorithm

$$Y_{ij} \leftarrow Y_{ij} \left(\frac{(WY)_{ij}}{(YY^TY)_{ij}} \right)^{1/4} \tag{12}$$

This algorithm is guaranteed to converge to a local optimal solution. For initialization, we follow the usual procedure in NMF by doing a K-means clustering on Kernel PCA feature space. This gives cluster indicators G: $G_{ik} = 1$ if x_i belongs to cluster k, otherwise, $G_{ik} = 0$. We set $Y_0 = G + 0.2$ to be a smoothed indicator matrix. The convergenceness of this algorithm has been studied in [15].

Above all, the algorithm is summarized in Algorithm 1. Let J_t denote the value of objective function(i.e., Eq.(7)) in tth iteration, the objective function converges when $(J_t - J_{t-1})/J_{t-1}$ is deemed sufficiently small($< 10^{-5}$).

4 Experiments

To validate the convergenceness of the proposed algorithm and effectiveness of RILLE, we experiment on 4 widely used datasets: AT&T, MNIST, USPS, and Coil20. To verify the robustness, we also experiment on these datasets with random 10% - 20% corruption to simulate noise in the real world. To show the de-noising performance of RILLE on the real dataset, we also experiment on the YaleB face dataset. Firstly, we provide a brief description of these datasets used in our experiments.

4.1 Datasets Description

The five datasets used in our experiments are summarized as the following.

AT&T Face Dataset contains ten different images of each 40 distinct persons and the size of each image is 92×112 pixels, with 256 grey levels per pixel. In the clustering task, each face image is resized into 30×30 and reshaped into a vector of 900 dimension.

MNIST Hand-Written Digit Dataset is consisted of 8-bit gray-scale images of digits from "0" to "9", about 6000 examples of each class(digit). Each image is centered on a 28×28 grid. Here, we randomly choose 50 images from each digit and convert them into vectors of 784 dimension.

USPS Dataset has normalized handwritten digits, automatically scanned from envelopes by the U.S. Postal Service. The original scanned digits are binary and of different sizes and orientations. The images here have been size-normalized, resulting in 16×16 grayscale images. 50 images are choosen from each digit and each is converted into vectors of 256 dimension.

Coil20 Dataset contains 20 objects. Each image of the same object is taken 5 degrees apart as the object is rotated on a turntable and each object has 72 images. The size of each image is 32×32 pixels, with 256 grey labels per pixel. Each image is represented by a 1024 dimensional vector.

YaleB Face Dataset contains 2414 cropped frontal face images of 38 individuals. Each image is sized 192×168. We only use the first 10 persons and each has 64 images varying illumination conditions.

4.2   Algorithm Convergence

Convergence line of the proposed algorithm for the AT&T dataset is shown in Fig. 1. We can find out the objective function converges in a few iterations. This proves the convergenceness of the proposed algorithm.

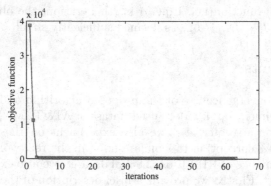

Fig. 1. Convergence line of the proposed algorithm. The object function has a sharp decline in the first two iterations and decreases slowly afterward.

4.3   Performance of De-noising

We compare the de-noising performance of RILLE with LLE on the YaleB dataset, as shown in Fig. 2. In LLE, the number of neighbors chosen is set to be 5 empirically, and the dimension of the embedding is set to be 3. From Fig. 2, it is easy to find that the images with low-level illumination are compensated by LLE and RILLE. However, as for the reconstructed images from images with low-level illumination, results of LLE have more wrong reconstructed images than those of RILLE. In addition, reconstructed images from LLE only remove

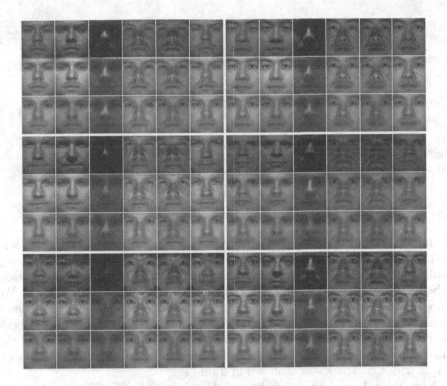

Fig. 2. Denoising results on the YaleB dataset. The figure is composed of six parts, and each part denotes a person. In each part, the first line are the original face images, the second line are the reconstructed face images from LLE, and the third line from RILLE.

part shadow, and don't compensate the difference within distinct persons like eyes-closed(like the first person), compared with the original images. While reconstructed images from RILLE remove some details, leaving images of the same person more similar and images of different persons more different.

4.4 Performance of Embedding

Both LLE and RILLE can get low-dimensional embedding, so three kinds of face images are chosen from the AT&T dataset with random 10% corrupted as our experiment dataset to compare their embedding result. Embeddings from LLE and RILLE are shown in Fig. 3, in which different colors and shapes represent different kinds of faces. From Fig. 3, we find out that one image of Face1 is far apart from the others, and may be confused into the other two kinds of faces. Compared with LLE's result, embedding of RILLE has apparent cluster structure and the three kinds of face images are all classified correct obviously.

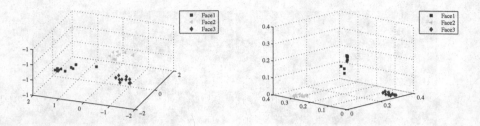

Fig. 3. Comparison of embedding. The left sub figure denotes embedding from LLE , and embedding from RILLE for the right sub figure.

4.5   Clustering Experiments

In this section, we perform the clustering task on different datasets: AT&T, MNIST, USPS, COIL20 and the corrupted version. We compare our clustering results with the other three methods including k-means[16] on original dataset, embedding from LLE, and embedding from Laplacian Embedding(LE)[3]. We run k-means 20 times and compare average clustering accuracy and the clustering accuracy when the objective function of k-means is optimal. In the experiment, the number of neighbors chosen in LLE is set to be 5 empirically, and the dimension of the embedding is set to be the number of categories of the dataset, so it is with LE. The result is shown in Table 1.

From Table 1, we can conclude that (1) there is much difference between average clustering accuracy and the optimal clustering accuracy with regard to the other three methods which demonstrates the instability of low-dimensional representation. (2) Clustering results of RILLE on datasets occluded are much better than that of LLE for its de-noising effect. (3) LLE performs better than k-means on original dataset and worse than the results of Laplacian Embedding and RILLE. This demonstrates that non-linear relationship among data is more suitable for real datasets on one hand, and RILLE can improve the clustering results more than Laplacian Embedding on the other hand. (4) RILLE performs better than the other three methods consistently.

Table 1. Clustering results on different datasets

Dataset	K-means	LLE	LE	RILLE
AT&T	0.662/0.705	0.684/0.708	0.697/0.743	0.714
USPS	0.637/0.702	0.636/0.668	0.710/0.768	0.726
MNIST	0.530/0.492	0.550/0.524	0.573/0.580	0.596
Coil20	0.606/0.676	0.609/0.704	0.616/0.644	0.659
AT&T OCC	0.646/0.665	0.659/0.695	0.658/0.733	0.677
USPS OCC	0.639/0.696	0.624/0.604	0.710/0.766	0.722
MNIST OCC	0.530/0.526	0.557/0.522	0.570/0.580	0.577
Coil20 OCC	0.561/0.622	0.606/0.604	0.606/0.698	0.641

5   Conclusion

This paper proposes a novel method for de-noising and dimensionality reduction named Robust Integrated Locally Linear Embedding(RILLE), which gains embedding of data by learning a robust similarity function that is low-rank, semi-positive definite, nonnegative and symmetric. Moreover, an efficient algorithm is built to solve the proposed model. Extensive experiments demonstrate that the proposed method is more suitable to exhibit relationship among data points,and has visible improvement in de-noising, embedding and clustering tasks.

Acknowledgments. The research of Li-li Zhang, Ying Xie, Bin Luo and Jin Tang are supported by the NSFC 61073116, 61003131. Chris Ding is supported by NSF-CCF-0830780, NSF-DMS-0915228, NSFCCF-0917274.

References

1. Duda, R.O., Hart, P.E., Stork, D.G.: Pattern Recognition, 2nd edn. Wiley Interscience, New York (2001)
2. Wang, H., Ding, C., Huang, H.: Multi-label Linear Discriminant Analysis. In: Daniilidis, K., Maragos, P., Paragios, N. (eds.) ECCV 2010, Part VI. LNCS, vol. 6316, pp. 126–139. Springer, Heidelberg (2010)
3. Mikhail, B., Partha, N.: Laplacian eigemaps for dimensionality reduction and data representation. Neural Computation 15(6), 1373–1396 (2003)
4. Luo, D.J., Chris, D., Huang, H., Li, T.: Non-negative laplacian embedding. In: NIPS, pp. 337–346 (2009)
5. Roweis, S.T., Saul, L.K.: Nonlinear dimensionality reduction by locally linear embedding. Science 290(22), 2323–2326 (2000)
6. Tenenbaum, J.B., Silva, V.D., Langford, J.C.: A global geometric framework for nonlinear dimensionality. Science 290(22), 2319–2323 (2000)
7. Zhang, Z.Y., Zha, H.Y.: Principal manifolds and nonlinear dimensionality reduction via tangent space alignment. Scientific Computing 26, 313–338 (2004)
8. He, X.F., Niyogi, P.: Locality preserving projections. In: Proc. Conf. Advances in Neural Information Processing Systems (2003)
9. Vidal, R.: Yi Ma, Sastry, S.: Generalized principal component analysis. In: CVPR, vol. 1, pp. 621–628 (2003)
10. Liu, G.C., Lin, Z.C., Yu, Y.: Robust Subspace Segmentation by Low-Rank Representation. In: ICML (2010)
11. Lee, D.D., Seung, H.S.: Algorithms for non-negative matrix factorization. In: Proceedings of the 2000 Conference, pp. 556–562. MIT Press (2001)
12. Wang, H., Huang, H., Cing, D.: Image annotation using multi-label correlated greens function. In: ICCV, pp. 2029–2034 (2009)
13. Mithun, D.G., Jing, X.: Non-negative matrix factorization as a feature selection tool for maximum margin classifiers. In: CVPR, pp. 2841–2848 (2011)
14. Chris, D., Tao, L., Michael, I.J.: Convex and Semi-Nonnegative Matrix Factorizations. IEEE Trans. Pattern Anal. Mach. Intell. 32(1), 45–55 (2010)
15. Feng, W., Tao, L., Xin, W., Zhu, S.H., Chris, D.: Community discovery using nonnegative matrix factorization. Data Min. Knowl. Discov. 22(3), 493–521 (2011)
16. Kenungo, T., Mount, D.M., Netanyahu, N.S., Piatko, C.D., Silverman, R., Wu, A.Y.: An efficient k-means clustering algorithm:Analysis and implementation. IEEE Trans. Pattern Anal. Mach. Intell. 24, 881–892 (2002)

Estimating the Total Variability Space Using Sparse Probabilistic Principal Component Analysis

Zhenchun Lei and Jihua Ye

School of Computer and Information Engineering, Jiangxi Normal University,
Nanchang, China
zhenchun.lei@hotmail.com, yjhwcl@163.com

Abstract. In this paper, we introduce a new method to estimate the total variability space using sparse probabilistic Principal Component Analysis (PCA) with the Baum-Welch statistics for speaker verification. In conventional method, probabilistic PCA is used, which is a probabilistic formulation for PCA. Recently some methods improve interpretability by sparse representation through adding an L1 regularizer. We introduce a Laplacian prior to each element in the transformation matrix, since Laplacian prior is equivalent to L1 regularization. Variational inference is used and we can drive the EM algorithm formulas for estimating the space with the statistics. After WCCN, the cosine similarity scoring is used for decision. The experiments have been run on the NIST SRE 2008 data, and the results show that the performance can be improved 10.2% for female and is comparable for male.

Keywords: speaker verification, i-vector model, sparse probabilistic principal component analysis.

1 Introduction

Joint Factor Analysis (JFA) [1, 2] has achieved the state of the art for text-independent speaker recognition in recent years, which find two subspaces representing the speaker and channel-variabilities respectively. Dehak [3] proposed a single space that models the two variabilities and named it the total variability space, which is a low-dimension space of the Gaussian Mixture Model (GMM) [4] supervector space. The vectors in the low-dimensional space are called i-vectors, which are smaller in size and can get recognition performance similar to that obtained by JFA.

In conventional method, the total variability matrix is processed by following a similar process to that of learning the eigenvoice matrix of JFA [1], in which a variant of the Probabilistic Principal Component Analysis (PPCA) [5,6] approach is introduced for estimating the parameters. The main difference between JFA and i-vector model is that in training the eigenvoice of JFA, all recordings of a given speaker are considered to belong to the same person, where in train the total variability matrix, each instance of a given speaker's set of utterances is regarded as having been produced by a different speaker.

W.-S. Zheng et al. (Eds.): CCBR 2012, LNCS 7701, pp. 372–379, 2012.

Principal component analysis (PCA) [7] is a widely used technique for data analysis and dimensionality reduction. PCA captures the largest information in the first few principal components, guarantees minimal information loss and minimal reconstruction error in a least squares sense. But the PCs are difficult to interpret and explain. Guan [8] and Bishop [9] introduce the Sparse Probabilistic PCA (SPPCA) by adding an L1 norm regularizer, which serves as a tractable estimate to L0 and leads to sparse solutions. The probabilistic model permits many extensions including extensions to mixture models and Bayesian methods for model selection. Ming Li [10] use sparse representation to model the i-vectors in the low-dimensional space after performing the WCCN [11] and LDA [12] channel compensation.

In this paper, we estimate the total variability space using SPPCA and the Baum-Welch statistics. We introduce a Laplacian prior to each element in the transformation matrix, since Laplacian prior are equivalent to L1 regularization. Variational inference is used and we can drive the EM algorithm formulas for estimating the space with the statistics.

This paper is organized as follows: We review the SPPCA model in section 2. We present our method for estimating the total variability space in section 3. Section 4 provides the results of our experiments. Finally, section 5 is devoted to the main conclusions and our future work.

2   Sparse Probabilistic Principal Component Analysis

PCA seeks a q-dimensional (q<d) linear projection that best represents the data in a least-squares sense. PCA can be reformulated as a maximum likelihood solution to a latent variable model. This probabilistic reformulation of PCA permits many extensions including a principled formulation of mixtures of principal component analyzers. Let x be a q-dimensional latent variable, the observed variable t is then defined as a linear transformation of x with additional noise :

$$t = Wx + m + \varepsilon \tag{1}$$

where W is a $d \times q$ linear transformation matrix, m is a d-dimensional vector that allow t to have a non-zero mean. Both the latent variable x and noise ε are assumed to be isotropic Gaussian:

$$p(x) \sim N(0, I_q) \tag{2}$$

$$p(\varepsilon) \sim N(0, \sigma^2 I_d) \tag{3}$$

therefore, the conditional distribution of t given x is:

$$p(t \mid x) \sim N(Wx + m, \sigma^2 I_d) \tag{4}$$

Sparsity is achieved in SPCA by adding an L1 regularizer, and Yue Guan propose the Sparse Principal Component Analysis by introducing a Laplacian prior to each element of the matrix W, since Laplacian priors are equivalent to L1 regularization. The Laplacian density has the following form:

$$p(W_{ij} \mid \lambda) = \frac{1}{2}\sqrt{\frac{2}{\lambda}}\exp(-\sqrt{\frac{2}{\lambda}}|W_{ij}|) \tag{5}$$

where $|\bullet|$is the absolute value operator. Assuming that the elements W_{ii} are independent, the prior probability for W is:

$$p(W \mid \lambda) = \prod_{i=1}^{d}\prod_{j=1}^{q} p(W_{ij} \mid \lambda) \tag{6}$$

The log joint distribution $\log(p(t,W,x,m,\sigma^2))$ includes two parts: the log-likelihood for probabilistic PCA and the Laplacian prior, result in a L1 regularization on W.

The variational inference is used to evaluate the marginal likelihood:

$$p(D) = \int p(D,\theta)d\theta \tag{7}$$

where $\theta = \{\theta_i\}$ denotes the set of all parameters and latent variables in the model.

Variational methods involve the introduction of a distribution $Q(\theta)$ which provides an approximation to the true posterior distribution.

$$\ln P(D) = \ln \int P(D,\theta)d\theta = \ln \int Q(\theta)\frac{P(D,\theta)}{Q(\theta)}d\theta \tag{8}$$

$$\geq \int Q(\theta)\ln\frac{P(D,\theta)}{Q(\theta)}d\theta = L(Q(\theta))$$

where Jensen's inequality is applied. The function $L(Q)$ forms a rigorous lower bound on the true log marginal likelihood.

3   Total Variability Space

3.1   I-Vector Model

Given speaker- and channel-dependent GMM supervector M can be modeled as follows:

$$M = M_0 + Tw \tag{9}$$

where M_0 is a speaker- and channel-independent supervector, usually UBM supervector is a good choice. T is a low rank matrix, which represents a basis of the reduced total variability space and w is a normal distributed vector which are referred to as i-vector. The M is assumed to be normally distributed with mean vector M_0 and covariance matrix $T \cdot T^T$. This model can be viewed like a principal component analysis of the larger supervector space that allows projecting the speech utterances in the total variability space.

A variant of the PPCA approach is used in training the total variability matrix T. The feature vector associated with a given recording is the MAP estimation of w, and the matrix T is estimated using the EM algorithm described in Kenny's paper [1]. The likelihood function as the estimation criterion is:

$$\prod_s \max\; p(X(s)\mid M_0 + Tw(s), \Sigma) \tag{10}$$

where s ranges over the recordings in the training set, X(s) is the recording data and Σ is the covariance matrix of GMM.

3.2   Estimating the Total Variability Space

Conventional total variability space maximizes the likelihood of the speaker's training data. Now we add an L1 regularizer by introducing a Laplacian prior to T_{ij} in total variability space:

$$p(T_{ij}\mid\lambda) = \frac{1}{2}\sqrt{\frac{2}{\lambda}}\exp(-\sqrt{\frac{2}{\lambda}}|T_{ij}|) \tag{11}$$

Assuming that the element Tij are independent:

$$p(T\mid\lambda) = \prod_{i=1}^{d}\prod_{j=1}^{q} p(T_{ij}\mid\lambda) \tag{12}$$

Like Guan and Bishop's methods, a two-level hierarchical decomposition of the Laplacian distribution is utilized. The first level assumes a Gaussian prior, and the second level is an exponential distribution:

$$p(T\mid\lambda) = \prod_{i=1}^{d}\prod_{j=1}^{q} p(T_{ij}\mid\lambda) \tag{13}$$

$$p(z_{ij}) = \frac{1}{\lambda}\exp(-\frac{z_{ij}}{\lambda}),\; z_{ij}\geq 0 \tag{14}$$

The joint distribution of the data D and parameters θ for out model is:

$$p(D,\theta) = \prod_s p(X(s)\mid w(s),T,z)p(w(s))$$
$$p(T\mid z)p(z) \tag{15}$$

We denote by $X(s)$ the entire collection of labeled frames for the recording. For each mixture component $c = 1,...,C$, let $N_c(s)$ be the number of frames in the training data for recording s which are accounted for by the given mixture component and set:

$$S_{X,c}(s) = \sum_t (X_t - \mu_c) \tag{16}$$

$$S_{XX^T,c}(s) = \sum_t (X_t - \mu_c)(X_t - \mu_c)^T \tag{17}$$

where the sums extend over all frames X_t for recording s that are aligned with the mixture component c and μ_c is the speaker independent mean vector. Let $N(s)$ be the $CF\times CF$ block diagonal matrix whose diagonal blocks are $N_1(s)I,...,N_C(s)I$

where I denotes the $F \times F$ identity matrix. Let $S_X(s)$ be the $CF \times 1$ vector obtained by concatenating $S_{X,1}(s), ..., S_{X,C}(s)$. Let $l(s)$ be the $R \times R$ matrix defined by

$$l(s) = I + T^T \Sigma^{-1} N(s) T \qquad (18)$$

After variational inference, we can derive the re-estimation formulas:

$$w(s) = l^{-1}(s) T^T \Sigma^{-1} S_X(s) \qquad (19)$$

$$T^i = (\sum_s S_X^i(s) E[w(s)^T]) \cdot (\Sigma_i^{-1} \cdot diag(\alpha_i) + \sum_s N^i(s) E[w(s) \cdot w(s)^T])^{-1} \qquad (20)$$

$$E[w(s) \cdot w(s)^T] = E[w(s)] E[w(s)^T] + l^{-1}(s) \qquad (21)$$

$$\alpha_{i,j} = \frac{2}{\lambda + \sqrt{2\lambda} |T_{i,j}|} \qquad (22)$$

where T^i denote the ith row of matrix T, and $diag(\alpha_i)$ denotes a diagonal matrix whose diagonal element are $\alpha_{i,i}$.

Like the conventional method, we estimate the model parameters using the EM algorithm with the Baum-Welch statistics. We don't update M_0 and Σ in the UBM for simplification, and the optimization proceeds by iterating the following two steps:

- The E-step: For each training recording s, use the estimate of T and equation (19) to find the i-vector w(s).
- The M-step: Estimate a new total variability space T given the old space and the new i-vectors over all recordings in the training set using equation (20).

4   Experiments

4.1   Experiment Set-Up

The features were derived from the waveforms using 19 mel-frequency cepstral coefficients on a 20 millisecond frame every 10 milliseconds. Delta and delta-delta coefficients were computed making up a thirty nine dimensional feature vector. And the band limiting was performed by retaining only the filter bank outputs form the frequency range 300-3400 Hz. Mean removal, preemphasis and a hamming window were applied, and energy-based end pointing eliminated nonspeech frames.

Our experiments were performed on the 2008 NIST SRE dataset. NIST SRE2004 1side training corpus was used to train two gender-dependent UBMs with 512 Gaussian components. The rank of the total variability matrix T was chosen to be 400. NIST SRE2004, SRE 2005, and SRE 2006 telephone datasets were used for estimating the total variability space and the projection matrix in WCCN [11] for inter-session compensation. There were 11656 female utterances and 8615 male utterances in the training datasets. The cosine similarity scoring [13, 14] was used for the decision, and the zt-norm score normalization [15] is applied. For measuring the performance, we used equal error rate (EER) and the minimum decision cost function (DCF).

4.2   Results on Phonecall Condition

The first experiment was run on the 1conv-1conv 2008 SRE core phonecall condition. In our experiment, the total variability space generated by SPPCA is obviously better than that by PPCA for female, and the performance is improved 10.2%. But for male, the space generated by SPPCA is a little worse than that by PPCA.

Table 1. Comparison results between the total variability spaces generated by PPCA and SPPCA. The results are on the 1conv-1conv 2008 SRE core telephone condition

method	gender	EER(%)	DCF
PPCA	female	8.98	0.045
SPPCA	female	8.06	0.043
PPCA	male	5.73	0.031
SPPCA	male	5.97	0.031

4.3   Results on Cross-Channel Condition

The second experiment was run on the 1conv-1conv 2008 SRE core cross-channel condition. Training the total variability space and the projection matrix in WCCN were still on the NIST 2004, 2005, 2006 telephone datasets.

Table 2 shows the results of experiments on female part of the 2008 SER data. The performance of the total variability space generated by SPPCA is better than that by PPCA on cross-channel condition. Table 3 shows the result of experiments on male data, and the performance in these two spaces is comparable.

Table 2. Comparison results between the total variability spaces generated by PPCA and SPPCA on the female portion of the 1conv-1conv 2008 SRE core cross-channel condition

method	training	testing	EER(%)	DCF
PPCA	phonecall	phonecall	8.98	0.045
	phonecall	interview	10.57	0.047
	interview	phonecall	12.28	0.051
	interview	interview	17.32	0.068
	all	all	13.94	0.068
SPPCA	phonecall	phonecall	8.06	0.043
	phonecall	interview	9.76	0.045
	interview	phonecall	11.14	0.048
	interview	interview	16.91	0.066
	all	all	13.36	0.069

Table 3. Comparison results between the total variability spaces generated by PPCA and SPPCA on the male portion of the 1conv-1conv 2008 SRE cross-channel condition

method	training	testing	EER(%)	DCF
PPCA	phonecall	phonecall	5.73	0.031
	phonecall	interview	7.02	0.030
	interview	phonecall	8.63	0.032
	interview	interview	12.40	0.051
	all	all	10.42	0.053
SPPCA	phonecall	phonecall	5.97	0.031
	phonecall	interview	7.52	0.030
	interview	phonecall	8.86	0.032
	interview	interview	12.31	0.051
	all	all	10.42	0.053

5   Conclusions

We propose a method to estimate the total variability space using sparse probabilistic principal component analysis. In conventional method the PPCA is used with the Baum-Welch statistics of utterances. We introduce a Laplacian prior to each element in the transformation matrix, since Laplacian prior are equivalent to L1 regularization. Variational inference is used and we can drive the EM algorithm formulas for estimating the space with the statistics. Finally, the WCCN is used for inter-session compensation and the cosine similarity scoring is used for decision. Our experiments were run on NIST SRE dataset. The results show that the performance of our method is obviously better for female and comparable for male.

JFA has been reinterpreted as signal coding using overcomplete dictionaries in Danile's paper [16], and the i-vecor model can also be reinterpreted in the same way. Some theories and algorithms in overcomplete dictionaries have been developed rapidly in recent years. We will also do more research on the basis of the total variability space.

Acknowledgements. This work is supported by Educational Commission of Jiangxi Province of P.R.China (GJJ12198).

References

1. Kenny, P., Gilles, B., Pierre, D.: Eigenvoice Modeling With Sparse Training Data. Proc. IEEE Trans. Speech and Audio 13(3), 345–354 (2005)
2. Kenny, P., et al.: Joint Factor Analysis Versus Eigenchannels in Speaker Recognition. Proc. IEEE Trans. Speech and Language 15(4), 1435–1447 (2007)
3. Dehak, N., et al.: Support vector machines versus fast scorring in the low-dimensional total variability space for speaker verification. In: Interspeech, Brighton, UK (2009)
4. Reynolds, D.A., Quatieri, T., Dunn, R.: Speaker verification using adapted Gaussian mixture models. Digital Signal Processing 10(1-3) (2000)

5. Tipping, M., Bishop, C.: Mixtures of probabilistic principal component analyzers. Neural Computation 11, 435–474 (1999)
6. Roweis, S.: EM Algorithms for PCA and SPCA. In: Advances in Neural Information Processing Systems (1998)
7. Jolliffe, I.T.: Principal Component analysis. Springer, New York.(1986)
8. Guan, Y., Dy, J.G.: Sparse Probabilistic Principal Component Analysis. In: Proceedings of the 12th International Conference on Artificial Intelligence and Statistics, Clearwater Beach, Florida, USA, vol. 5 (2009)
9. Bishop, C.M.: Variational Principal Components. In: Proceedings Ninth International Conference on Artificial Neural Network, vol. 1, pp. 509–514
10. Li, M., et al.: Speaker Verification using Sparse Representations on Total Variability I-Vector. In: Interspeech, Florence, Italy (2011)
11. Hatch, A., Kajarekar, S., Stolcke, A.: Withinclass covariance normalization for svm-based speaker recognition. In: Interspeech – 9th International Conference on Spoken Language Processing-ICSLP, vol. 3, pp. 1471–1474 (2006)
12. Martinez, A.M., Kak, A.C.: PCA versus LDA. IEEE Transactions on Pattern Analysis and Machine Intelligence 23(2), 228–233 (2004)
13. Shum, S., et al.: Unsupervised Speaker Adaptation based on the Cosine Similarity for Text-Independent Speaker Verification, Odyssey. In: The Speaker and Language Recognition Workshop (2010)
14. Dehak, N., et al.: Cosine Similarity Scoring without Score Normalization Techniques, Odyssey. In: The Speaker and Language Recognition Workshop (2010)
15. Auckenthaler, R., Carey, M., Thomas, H.L.: Score Normalization for Text-Independent Speaker Verification Systems. Digital Signal Processing 10, 42–54 (2000)
16. Daniel, G.R., Carol, Y.E.W.: Joint Factor Analysis for Speaker Recognition reinterpreted as Signal Coding using Overcomplete dictionaries, Odyssey. In: The Speaker and Language Recognition Workshop (2010)

A Competitive Model for Semi-supervised Discriminant Analysis*

Weifu Chen[1], Guocan Feng[1], Xiaolin Zou[2], and Zhiyong Liu[1,3]

[1] School of Math. and Comput. Science, Sun Yat-sen University, Guangzhou, China
[2] School of Math. and Inform. Science, Zhaoqing University, Zhaoqing, China
[3] Industry Center, ShenZhen Polytechnic, Shenzhen, China

Abstract. This paper presents a general linear framework and a competitive model for discriminant analysis with partially labeled data. Our method first utilizes the competitive model to find the reliable training samples. Two indices are given to measure the reliability. In the second stage, discriminant vectors are computed by the proposed framework. We show that under different graph models some popular discriminant analysis algorithms are special cases of the proposed framework. Experimental results suggest that our algorithm is effective and can significantly improve the recognition accuracy.

Keywords: discriminability index, competitive index, discriminant analysis, semi-supervised learning.

1 Introduction

In pattern recognition, many applications suffer from the so-called small sample size (SSS) problem. In general, we should have sufficient labeled samples to discover the underlying data structure. However, labeling work is both time consuming and costly. Conversely, abundant unlabeled data are quite easy to get. Since the performance of supervised methods heavily depends on the number of labeled training samples, quite a few graph-based semi-supervised algorithms [1], [2], [3], [4], [5], [6] have been developed for learning all data information.

This work first introduces a semi-supervised linear embedding framework called *semi-supervised flexible liner embedding (SSFLE)*. Analysis shows that using the trick introduced in [7], semi-supervised versions of some popular LDA-based algorithms such as Regularized Discriminant Analysis (RDA) [8], Discriminative Common Vectors (DCV) [9] and Maximum Margin Criterion (MMC) [10] (denoted by SSRDA, SSDCV, and SSMMC respectively) are special cases of SSFLE. Secondly, a competitive model is introduced for selecting the reliable training samples based on two measurements, namely discriminability index (DI) and competitive index (CI). DI is proposed to measure how far a labeled sample is from the class boundary. We define DI in a way introduced by Zou and Yuen

---

* This work is partially supported by National Science Foundation of China under grant No. 60975083 and U0835005.

[11] except that we use the Gaussian kernel function as the similarity function for the Parzen window. A labeled sample is reliable if it is with a high DI. CI is presented to reflect how far an unlabeled sample is away from a reliable labeled sample. The higher CI, the more reliable it can be used for soft-label assignment.

2 Semi-Supervised Flexible Linear Embedding (SSFLE)

Suppose that the column vectors of $X = [x_1, \cdots, x_n, x_{n+1}, \cdots, x_m]$ $(x_i \in \mathcal{R}^p)$ are training samples, where $X_L = [x_1, \cdots, x_n]$ are labeled training samples with labels $\{l_1, \cdots, l_n\}$ and $X_U = [x_{n+1}, \cdots, x_m]$ are unlabeled training samples. Our purpose is to find a matrix $Y = [y_1, \cdots, y_m] \in \mathcal{R}^{q \times m}$ $(y_i \in \mathcal{R}^q$, usually $q \ll p)$ whose column vectors are low dimensional representations of $x_1, \cdots, x_m$. Without loss of generality, assume that $\frac{1}{m} \sum_{i=1}^m x_i = 0$. Let $G(X, E, S)$ represent a weighted undirected graph with nodes $\{x_1, \cdots, x_m\}$, edges E and symmetric *affinity matrix* $S = (s_{ij})$, where s_{ij} is the similarity of x_i and x_j. Define the degree of x_i as $d_i = \sum_{j=1}^m s_{ij}$, the *degree matrix* as $D = Diag(d_1, d_2, \cdots, d_m)$ and, the unnormalized and the normalized Laplacian matrices as $L = D - S$ and $L_{sym} = I - D^{-1/2} S D^{-1/2}$, where I is an identity matrix.

Belkin et al. [4] presented a manifold regularization framework for semi-supervised learning, employing two regularization terms:

$$\frac{1}{n} \sum_{i=1}^n v(x_i, l_i, f) + \lambda_A \|f\|_{\mathcal{F}}^2 + \lambda_I \|f\|_I^2, \tag{1}$$

where $\|f\|_{\mathcal{F}}$ controls the complexity of f and $\|f\|_I$ preserves the local data structure.

Inspired by Belkin's work, when considering the problem of dimensionality reduction, we regularize the process of minimizing the reconstruction error using these two norms. As we know, for a finite linear transformation f, it can be represented by a matrix W (in our case, $W \in \mathcal{R}^{p \times q}$). For easy reconstruction, we usually assume that W is column-orthonormal. Then $\|f\|_{\mathcal{F}}^2 \triangleq tr(W^T W) = q$ which is constant if q is pre-fixed, and f^{-1} can be approximated by W, i.e., $f^{-1}(y) = Wy$. Finally, SSFLE is designed to minimize the regularized reconstruction error

$$\frac{1}{n} \sum_{i=1}^n h(x_i, f^{-1}(y_i)) + \frac{\lambda_L}{n^2} \sum_{i,j=1}^n s_{ij}^L \left(\frac{f(x_i)}{\sqrt{d_i}} - \frac{f(x_j)}{\sqrt{d_j}}\right)^2 + \frac{\lambda_I}{m^2} \sum_{i,j=1}^m s_{ij}(f(x_i) - f(x_j))^2,$$

$$\tag{2}$$

If set $h(.,.)$ to be the squared loss function and define $\gamma_L = \frac{2\lambda_L}{n}$, $\gamma_I = \frac{2\lambda_I}{m}$, SSFLE can be simplified as

$$\max_{W^T W = I} tr[W^T (X_L X_L^T - \gamma_L X_L L_{sym}^L X_L^T - \gamma_I X L X^T) W], \tag{3}$$

where $X_L L_{sym}^L X_L^T$ and $X L X^T$ are two Laplacian regularized terms for labeled training samples and all training samples respectively.

As it is well known, when the dimension of the data is much higher than the number of the training samples, LDA cannot avoid suffering from the SSS problem. MMC, DCV and RDA are some popular LDA-based variants proposed to deal with the SSS problem. Proposition 1 shows that the connections of SSFLE to SSMMC, SSDCV and SSRDA [7].

Proposition 1. *Let n_k be the number of labeled samples in the k-th class. Define $s_{ij}^L = \frac{1}{n_k}$ if x_i and x_j belong to the kth class; 0 otherwise. Then*
(1) when $\gamma_L > 1$, SSMMC can be deduced from the SSFLE framework;
(2) when γ_L approaches to $+\infty$, SSFLE obtains the same discriminative vectors as SSDCV.

Liu et al. [12] showed that DCV attains the same projection subspace as RDA when the ridge regularized coefficient of RDA tends to zero. Hence, according to Proposition 1, SSRDA can be deduced from SSFLE when the ridge regularized coefficient in RDA tends to zero and γ_L in (3) approaches to $+\infty$.

3   A Competitive Model for Semi-Supervised Learning

Since the quality of the training samples partially determines the performance of a method, we will introduce the DI and CI for finding the reliable labeled and unlabeled training samples.

3.1   Discriminability Index (DI)

We illustrate the DI using a two-class problem as shown in Fig. 1(a). Suppose that ω_1 and ω_2 are two classes, and x_1 and x_2 are two reference samples belonging to the same class ω_1. Since the distributions of ω_1 and ω_2 are overlapped, some

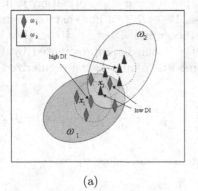
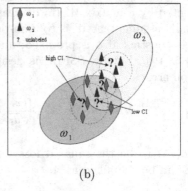

(a)   (b)

Fig. 1. Illustration of DI and CI. (a) Six samples are selected from ω_1 and ω_2 respectively. x_1 and x_2 belong to ω_1. x_1 has high DI, while x_2 has low DI. (b) Four unlabeled samples are randomly distributed on the sample space. Two of them have high CI, and the others have low CI.

of the training samples are far from the class boundaries (such as x_1), and some are lying on the boundaries (such as x_2). How to measure the discriminability? By Bayes decision rule [13], if $P(\omega_1|x) > P(\omega_2|x)$, we decide x belongs to ω_1; otherwise x belongs to ω_2. Following the Bayes formula $P(\omega_i|x) = \frac{p(x|\omega_i)P(\omega_i)}{p(x)}$, if there is no information about the prior probabilities, we usually assume that $P(\omega_1) = P(\omega_2)$. Since the evidence factor $p(x)$ is unimportant as far as making a decision is concerned, the decision rule is set as

Decide ω_1 if $p(x|\omega_1) > p(x|\omega_2)$; otherwise decide ω_2.

Then the DI of $x \in \omega_{i_0}$ can be defined as

$$DI(x) = p(x|\omega_{i_0}) - \max_{i \neq i_0} p(x|\omega_i). \tag{4}$$

Now the problem becomes to estimate $p(x|\omega_i)$, which will be estimated by the Parzen window method [13] in this work. First, define the window width t_i for the ith class as

$$t_i = \frac{1}{n_i} \sum_{j=1}^{n_i} \|x_j - \hat{\mu}_i\|_2, \tag{5}$$

where $\hat{\mu}_i = \frac{1}{n_i} \sum_{j \in \omega_i} x_j$. Second, for every $x_i \in \omega_{i_0}$, find its k nearest neighbors (denoted by $x_{i1}, x_{i2}, \cdots, x_{ik}$) in the labeled sample set, and define the window function $\varphi(x_i, x_{ij})$ as

$$\varphi(x_i, x_{ij}) = exp\{-\frac{\|x_i - x_{ij}\|_2}{t_{i_0}}\}. \tag{6}$$

Finally, if we denote n_{j_k} as the number of samples among $x_{i1}, x_{i2}, \cdots, x_{ik}$ belonging to the jth class, we can estimate the likelihood by

$$p(x|\omega_j) = \begin{cases} \frac{1}{n_{j_k}} \sum_{x_{ij} \in \omega_j} \varphi(x_i, x_{ij}) & \text{if } n_{j_k} \neq 0 \\ 0 & \text{otherwise} \end{cases}. \tag{7}$$

We demonstrate this procedure in Fig. 1(a) setting $k = 3$. Once we have computed the DI for every labeled training sample, we give our criterion to select the reliable labeled training samples:

Given a labeled sample x, x is a reliable labeled sample, if $DI(x) > \varepsilon$, where $\varepsilon > 0$ is a threshold; otherwise, x is unreliable.

3.2 Competitive Index (CI)

In practice, though labeled data are scarce, unlabeled data are easy to get. Existing semi-supervised learning algorithms usually weighed them the same importance. However, if unlabeled samples are in the overlapping area, error will be introduced. We know that matching quality reflects the relationship between the labeled training samples and the unlabeled training samples. For example, suppose that x_i and x_j are labeled samples, and x_k is an unlabeled sample. If $\phi(x_i, x_k) > \phi(x_j, x_k)$, there is a high probability that x_i and x_k share the same label than that of x_j and x_k, where $\phi(x, y)$ is a function measuring the similarity between x and y. We generalize this idea. Assume that we have got r reliable labeled samples $RLS = \{z_1, \cdots, z_r\}$. First, we define the similarity function between the labeled samples and the unlabeled samples:

$$\phi(x, y) = exp\{-\frac{\|x - y\|_2}{t_i}\}, \tag{8}$$

where $x \in \omega_i$ is a labeled sample, y is an unlabeled sample, and t_i is defined by (5). Second, for $z_i \in RLS$ (suppose that $z_i \in \omega_{i_0}$), find its l nearest neighbors (denoted by $z_{i1}, \cdots, z_{il}$) in X_U, and for every z_{ij} $(1 \leq j \leq l)$ compute

$$x_0 = \arg \max_{x \in X_L} \phi(x, z_{ij}). \tag{9}$$

Let $l(x)$ represent the label of x and define the CI of z_{ij} with respect to z_i as

$$CI(z_{ij}, z_i) = \begin{cases} \phi(z_i, z_{ij}) + \phi(x_0, z_{ij}) \text{ if } l(z_i) = l(x_0) \\ \phi(z_i, z_{ij}) - \phi(x_0, z_{ij}) \text{ otherwise} \end{cases}. \tag{10}$$

Then the criterion to select reliable unlabeled samples is

z_{ij} is a reliable unlabeled sample w.r.t z_i, if $CI(z_i, z_{ij}) > \epsilon$, where $\epsilon > 0$ is a threshold; otherwise, z_{ij} is unreliable w.r.t z_i.

z_i is called a winner of z_{ij} if they are with the highest CI. Fig. 1(b) shows the unlabeled samples with high CI and the other unlabeled samples with low CI.

3.3   Semi-supervised Discriminant Analysis

Denote the reliable unlabeled sample set as $RUS = \{u_1, \cdots, u_t\}$, and the corresponding winner set $WS = \{w_1, \cdots, w_t\}$. Assign u_i the soft label as $sl(u_i) = l(w_i)$. Note that $sl(u_i)$ may differ from the true label of u_i and it is not the final assignment label neither. For convenience, assume that the training samples are in following order: the first n samples are labeled, the following t samples are reliable unlabeled samples with soft labels, and the final $m-n-t$ samples are the others. Denote $\tilde{X}_L = X_L \cup RUS$. Then SSFLE for semi-supervised discriminant analysis (3) with DI and CI can be rewritten as

$$W^* = \arg \max_{W^T W = I} tr[W^T(\tilde{X}_L \tilde{X}_L^T - \gamma_L \tilde{X}_L \tilde{L}_{sym}^L \tilde{X}_L - \gamma_I X \tilde{L} X^T)W], \tag{11}$$

where $\tilde{L}_{sym}^L$ and $\tilde{L}$ are the revised Laplacian matrices for the enlarged "labeled" training samples and all the training samples respectively. And the corresponding affinity matrices $\tilde{S}^L$ and $\tilde{S}$ are defined in the following way. For $1 \leq i, j \leq n+t$,

$$\tilde{s}_{ij}^L = \begin{cases} 1 & \text{if } l(x_i) = l(x_j) \\ \phi(x_i, x_j) & \text{if } l(x_i) = sl(x_j) \text{ or } sl(x_i) = l(x_j) \\ \phi(x_i, w(x_i)) \cdot \phi(x_j, w(x_j)) & \text{if } sl(x_i) = sl(x_j) \\ 0 & \text{otherwise} \end{cases}, \tag{12}$$

To compute $\tilde{S}$ is a little more complicated, since we have to deal with the labeled and unlabeled, the reliable and unreliable relationships. Fig. 2 demonstrates the relationships. Obviously, $\tilde{S}_1$ could be substituted by $\tilde{S}^L$ directly. Since $\tilde{S}_2$ and $\tilde{S}_3$ are the relationships between unreliable unlabeled data and generalized "labeled" data, we compute them as follows

step1: For each x_i ($n + t < i \leq m$), find its k nearest neighbors in X. If x_j is among the k nearest neighbors, put an edge between x_i and x_j.

step2: For $n + t < i \leq m$ and $1 \leq j \leq m$, compute $\tilde{s}_{ij} = e^{\frac{-\|x_i - x_j\|_2}{t}}$ if node i and j are connected; 0 otherwise, where t is a heat kernel parameter.

Algorithm 1 summarizes SSFLE for semi-supervised learning with DI and CI .

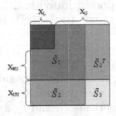

Fig. 2. Illustration of the relationships between X_L and X_U, between reliable unlabeled data (X_{RU}) and unreliable unlabeled data (X_{UU}) in the modified affinity matrix $\tilde{S}$.

Algorithm 1. SSFLE for Semi-supervised learning with DI and CI

Input: Data $X = X_L \bigcup X_U$ ($x_i \in \mathcal{R}^p$); regularized coefficients γ_L and γ_I; numbers of near neighbors k and l; heat kernel parameter t; thresholds ε and ϵ

Output: The transformation matrix W;

1: Data pre-processing: $x_i \leftarrow x_i - \bar{x}$, where $\bar{x}$ is the sample mean.
2: Compute the reliable labeled training set RLS following the procedure in Subsection 3.1.
3: Compute the reliable unlabeled training set RUS following the procedure in Subsection 3.2.
4: Define $\tilde{X}_L = X_L \cup RUS$, and compute $\tilde{L}^L_{sym}$ and $\tilde{L}$ following the procedure stated in Subsection 3.3.
5: Let $M \triangleq \tilde{X}_L \tilde{X}^T_L - \gamma_L \tilde{X}_L \tilde{L}^L_{sym} \tilde{X}_L - \gamma_I X \tilde{L} X^T$, and calculate the top $c - 1$ largest eigenvalues $\lambda_1, \lambda_2, \cdots, \lambda_{c-1}$ and the corresponding eigenvectors $w_1, w_2, \cdots, w_{c-1}$ of M. Then $W = [w_1, w_2 \cdots, w_{c-1}]$ is the projection matrix.
6: **return** W;

---

4   Experiments

Nie et al. [6] showed that GFHF [1], LGC [2] and LapRLS/L [3] are special cases of FME. Hence, face recognition results are given to compare our method with SDA [5] and FME [6]. We apply the nearest-neighbor classifier for its simplicity and employ the Euclidean distance for classification.

The benchmarks used in our experiments include: **Yale** database contains 165 images of 15 individuals (11 images per person). Extended **YALEB** database contains 2414 images including 38 individuals and around 64 near frontal images under different illuminations per subject. **ORL** database contains ten different images of each of 40 distinct subjects. **PIE** database contains 41,368 images of 68 individuals. We randomly choose a subset with 80 near frontal images per person, varying illuminations and expressions. All the images in those databases are resized to 32×32 pixels.

For each database, we randomly select 50% data as the training set and use the remaining 50% data as the testing set. Among the training set, we randomly label n_0 samples per class and treat the others as unlabeled data where n_0 is set as 2 and 3, respectively. Recognition accuracy for the unlabeled training samples and the testing set are reported individually. For fair comparison, we set each parameter to $\{10^{-9}, 10^{-6}, 10^{-3}, 10^{-2}, 10^{-1}, 10^{0}, 10, 10^{2}, 10^{3}, 10^{6}, 10^{9}\}$, and

Table 1. Top-1 recognition performance (mean recognition accuracy ± standard deviation %) of SDA, FME and SSFLE over 10 random splits on five datasets. The optimal parameters are also shown in parentheses (α and β in SDA, μ and γ in FME, γ_L and γ_I in SSFLE).

dataset	method	2 labeled samples		3 labeled samples	
		Unlabeled (%)	Test (%)	Unlabeled (%)	Test (%)
Yale	SDA	54.6 (± 7.34) $(10^{-9},10^{-9})$	54.5 (± 6.52) $(10^{-9},10^{-9})$	61.3 (± 6.13) $(10^{-9},10^{-9})$	63.2 (± 5.59) $(10^{-9},10^{-9})$
	FME	57.0 (± 6.13) $(10^{-9},10^{-6})$	**58.0 (± 6.26)** $(10^{-9},10^{-6})$	**65.1 (± 5.84)** $(10^{-9},10^{-3})$	**66.8 (± 4.42)** $(10^{-9},10^{-3})$
	SSFLE	**58.3(± 7.16)** $(10^{2},10^{-9})$	56.8 (± 8.17) $(10^{2},10^{-9})$	62.2 (± 7.70) $(10^{1},10^{-3})$	66.4 (± 5.88) $(10^{1},10^{-3})$
YaleB	SDA	42.1 (± 1.53) $(10^{-9},10^{-9})$	41.6 (± 2.87) $(10^{-9},10^{-9})$	57.0 (± 3.04) $(10^{-9},10^{-9})$	57.5 (± 2.58) $(10^{-9},10^{-9})$
	FME	49.0 (± 1.54) $(10^{3},10^{-3})$	48.2 (± 2.01) $(10^{-9},10^{-3})$	55.9 (± 3.06) $(10^{3},10^{-3})$	56.2 (± 1.88) $(10^{3},10^{-3})$
	SSFLE	**50.7(± 2.66)** $(10^{6},10^{-1})$	**50.7 (± 2.67)** $(10^{6},10^{-1})$	**64.0 (± 2.80)** $(10^{3},10^{-1})$	**64.6 (± 2.80)** $(10^{3},10^{-1})$
ORL	SDA	75.2 (± 3.66) $(10^{-9},10^{-9})$	77.1 (± 2.84) $(10^{-9},10^{-9})$	87.6 (± 2.79) $(10^{-1},10^{-9})$	86.7 (± 1.62) $(10^{-1},10^{-9})$
	FME	**82.4 (± 3.63)** $(10^{-9},10^{-6})$	82.9 (± 1.10) $(10^{-9},10^{-6})$	90.0 (± 3.17) $(10^{-9},10^{-6})$	89.1 (± 1.49) $(10^{6},10^{-6})$
	SSFLE	82.3(± 3.57) $(10^{2},10^{-9})$	**83.2 (± 1.88)** $(10^{2},10^{-9})$	**90.1(± 3.35)** $(10^{1},10^{-9})$	**90.6(± 1.83)** $(10^{1},10^{-9})$
PIE	SDA	38.1 (± 2.32) $(10^{-9},10^{-9})$	37.5 (± 1.69) $(10^{-9},10^{-9})$	50.8 (± 1.86) $(10^{-1},10^{-9})$	50.7 (± 1.16) $(10^{-1},10^{-9})$
	FME	40.6 (± 2.70) $(10^{3},10^{-3})$	40.3 (± 1.86) $(10^{-9},10^{-6})$	48.6 (± 0.58) $(10^{-9},10^{-6})$	48.6 (± 0.95) $(10^{-9},10^{-6})$
	SSFLE	**45.3(± 3.44)** $(10^{2},10^{-2})$	**45.0(± 3.58)** $(10^{2},10^{-2})$	**57.9(± 2.63)** $(10^{1},10^{-9})$	**58.1(± 2.51)** $(10^{1},10^{-9})$

report the top-1 recognition accuracy from the best parameter configuration as demonstrated in Table 1. We can observe that as the number of the labeled data increasing, the performance of the algorithms are improving, which confirms that labeled data are essential for classification. We can also see that our method SSFLE outperforms SDA and FME in most of the cases in terms of mean recognition accuracy. All the methods produce relatively poor results on PIE database, partially due to extreme lighting conditions.

5   Conclusion

This work first introduced a linear embedding framework for discriminant analysis Then a competitive model based on two indices was introduced for the selection of reliable training samples. We found that while labeled data are scarce and unlabeled data are abundant, our method could reliably assign more importance to those samples lying far away from the separating boundaries, which can be treated as a novel way to deal with SSS problem.Experiments on several benchmarks show the effectiveness of the proposed model.

References

1. Zhu, X., Ghahramni, Z., Lafferty, J.: Semi-supervised learning using Gaussian fields and harmonic functions. In: ICML, pp. 912–919 (2003)
2. Zhou, D., Bousquet, O., Lal, T., Weston, J., Schölkopf, B.: Learning with local and global consistency. In: NIPS, pp. 321–328 (2004)
3. Sindhwani, V., Niyogi, P., Belkin, M., Keerthi, S.: Linear manifold regularization for large scale semi-supervised learning. In: ICML (2005)
4. Belkin, M., Niyogi, P., Sindhwani, V.: Manifold regularization: a geometric framework for learning from labeled and unlabeled examples. JMLR 7, 2399–2434 (2006)
5. Cai, D., He, X., Han, J.: Semi-supervised discriminant analysis. In: ICCV (2007)
6. Nie, F., Xu, D., Tsang, I., Zhang, C.: Flexible manifold embedding: A framework for semi-supervised and unsupervised dimension reduction. IEEE TIP 19(7), 1921–1932 (2010)
7. Song, Y., Nie, F., Zhang, C., Xiang, S.: A unified framework for semi-supervised dimensionality reduction. Pattern Recognition 41, 2789–2799 (2008)
8. Friedman, J.H.: Regularized discriminant analysis. JASA 84(405), 165–175 (1989)
9. Cevikalp, H., Neamtu, M., Vilkes, M., Barkana, A.: Discriminative common vectors for face recognition. IEEE TPAMI 27(1), 4–13 (2005)
10. Li, H., Jiang, T., Zhang, K.: Efficient and robust feature extraction by maximum margin criterion. IEEE TNN 17(1), 157–165 (2006)
11. Zou, W., Yuen, P.C.: Discriminability and reliability indices: Two new measures to enhance multi-image face recognition. Pattern Recognition 43, 3483–3493 (2010)
12. Liu, J., Chen, S., Tan, X.: A study on three linear discriminant analysis based methods in small sample size problem. Pattern Recognition 41, 102–116 (2008)
13. Duda, R.O., Hart, P.E., Stork, D.G.: Pattern Classification, 2nd edn. Wiley (2000)

Author Index